T0336638

RSF: The Russell Sage Foundation Journal of the Social Sciences

Changing Job Quality: Causes, Consequences, and Challenges

VOLUME 5, NUMBER 4, SEPTEMBER 2019

RSF: The Russell Sage Foundation Journal of the Social Sciences   ISSN 2377-8261

The Russell Sage Foundation

The Russell Sage Foundation, one of the oldest of America's general purpose foundations, was established in 1907 by Mrs. Margaret Olivia Sage for "the improvement of social and living conditions in the United States." The foundation seeks to fulfill this mandate by fostering the development and dissemination of knowledge about the country's political, social, and economic problems. While the foundation endeavors to assure the accuracy and objectivity of each book it publishes, the conclusions and interpretations in Russell Sage Foundation publications are those of the authors and not of the foundation, its trustees, or its staff. Publication by Russell Sage, therefore, does not imply foundation endorsement.

Mission Statement

RSF: The Russell Sage Foundation Journal of the Social Sciences is a peer-reviewed, open-access journal of original empirical research articles by both established and emerging scholars. It is designed to promote cross-disciplinary collaborations on timely issues of interest to academics, policymakers, and the public at large. Each issue is thematic in nature and focuses on a specific research question or area of interest. The introduction to each issue will include an accessible, broad, and synthetic overview of the research question under consideration and the current thinking from the various social sciences.

Opinions expressed in this journal are not necessarily those of the editors, editorial board, trustees, the Russell Sage Foundation, or the W.K. Kellogg Foundation.

We invite scholars to submit proposals for potential issues to journal@rsage.org. Submissions should be addressed to Suzanne Nichols, Director of Publications.

To view the complete text and additional features online please go to **www.rsfjournal.org**.

Russell Sage Foundation
112 East 64th Street
New York, NY 10065

ISSN (print):	**2377-8253**
ISSN (electronic):	**2377-8261**
ISBN:	**978-0-87154-984-6**

The W.K. Kellogg Foundation (WKKF), founded in 1930 as an independent, private foundation by breakfast cereal innovator and entrepreneur Will Keith Kellogg, is among the largest philanthropic foundations in the United States. Guided by the belief that all children should have an equal opportunity to thrive, WKKF works with communities to create conditions for vulnerable children so they can realize their full potential in school, work, and life.

The Kellogg Foundation is based in Battle Creek, Michigan, and works throughout the United States and internationally, as well as with sovereign tribes. Special emphasis is paid to priority places where there are high concentrations of poverty and where children face significant barriers to success. WKKF priority places in the United States are in Michigan, Mississippi, New Mexico, and New Orleans; and internationally, are in Mexico and Haiti. To learn more, visit wkkf.org or follow WKKF on Twitter at @wk_kellogg_fdn.

*RSF: The Russell Sage Foundation
Journal of the Social Sciences*

VOLUME 5, NUMBER 4,
SEPTEMBER 2019

Changing Job Quality: Causes, Consequences, and Challenges

ISSUE EDITORS
David R. Howell, the New School
Arne L. Kalleberg, University of North
Carolina at Chapel Hill

CONTENTS

Declining Job Quality in the United States: Explanations and Evidence

DAVID R. HOWELL AND ARNE L. KALLEBERG

The declining quality of jobs has emerged as a key challenge for researchers and policymakers in the twenty-first century. The growing realization that the quality of jobs is central to addressing a myriad of social and economic problems—such as economic development, family formation and social integration, poverty and inequality, and individual well-being—has put this age-old topic on the front burner for social scientists in the United States and around the world. This essay offers our perspective on the job quality problem and debate. We document changes in American job quality since the late 1970s, survey leading explanations, and review the recent evidence.

After briefly reviewing the meaning of job quality, we describe American job quality, focusing on three dimensions of the post-1979 low-wage crisis: stagnation or decline in real (inflation-adjusted) income and wage levels, sharply rising overall wage inequality, and a high and rising incidence of low pay. In contrast to the egalitarian tendency during the first three postwar decades, post-1979 incomes have either worsened or stagnated across most of the wage distribution, generating a growing polarization between top 10 percent incomes and the bottom 90 percent, and even more dramatically, between the top 1 percent and the bottom 50 percent (Piketty, Saez, and Zucman 2018; Acemoglu and Autor 2011; see also Sullivan, Warren, and Westbrook 2001; Atkinson and Brandolini 2011). Market incomes (before taxes and benefits) for the average working-age American adult actually fell between 1980 and 2014, reversing the strong upward trend of previous decades. The incidence of low-wage and very low-wage jobs (which we term *poverty-wage*) grew, spectacularly so for young workers (age eighteen through thirty-four) with less

David R. Howell is professor of economics and public policy at the Milano School of Policy, Management, and Environment, the New School. Arne L. Kalleberg is Kenan Distinguished Professor of Sociology at the University of North Carolina at Chapel Hill.

© 2019 Russell Sage Foundation. Howell, David R., and Arne L. Kalleberg. 2019. "Declining Job Quality in the United States: Explanations and Evidence." *RSF: The Russell Sage Foundation Journal of the Social Sciences* 5(4): 1–53. DOI: 10.7758/RSF.2019.5.4.01. We thank the participants of the conference on Changing Job Quality held at the Russell Sage Foundation in June 2018 for their helpful input on this paper as well as the valuable feedback we received from three external reviewers. We especially appreciate the comments on earlier drafts that we received from Eileen Appelbaum, Alison Campion, Peter Cappelli, Maury Gittleman, Sabrina Howell, Jennifer Hunt, Lane Kenworthy, Jeffrey Madrick, and John Schmitt. Howell thanks the Washington Center for Equitable Growth for the support that helped make possible some of the empirical results that appear in the paper. Direct correspondence to: David R. Howell at howell@newschool.edu, 72 5th Ave., #702, New York, NY 10011; and Arne L. Kalleberg at arnekal@email.unc.edu, CB #3210 Hamilton Hall, University of North Carolina, Chapel Hill, NC 27599.

than a college degree. The poverty-wage share even increased for workers with a college degree. Young workers also experienced sizable declines in their median wage (males after 1979, women after around 2000).

Declines in nonwage benefits such as employer-paid health insurance and pensions have also been greater for lower-wage workers, another source of rising absolute and relative inequality in job quality. The expansion of low-wage jobs has often been linked to concerns about the growth of nonstandard jobs—for example, temporary help agency workers, on-call workers, contract workers, and (especially) independent contractors or freelancers—and though the question of the extent of the increase in the share of nonstandard jobs remains controversial, evidence (and perception) is considerable that many dimensions of job quality have worsened for both standard and nonstandard workers. In short, as measured by these and other indicators of job quality, the last four decades have been characterized by unshared—even extractive—economic growth.[1]

We consider leading explanations for these striking changes in job quality and labor market inequality by grouping them into three perspectives concerning how labor markets work. At one end of the theoretical spectrum is the mainstream economist's competitive market model, which explains the wage distribution strictly in terms of the interaction of the supply and demand for worker skills in highly competitive external labor markets (for example, Goldin and Katz 2007; Acemoglu and Autor 2011, 2012; Autor and Dorn 2013). In this view, protective labor institutions, like labor unions, are inefficient interventions, but skill-biased production technologies are reducing their importance, making the perfect competition model an increasingly good approximation for how labor markets work. The result is the law of one wage, in which workers in the same skill group are paid the same wage in similar jobs no matter where they work. The low-wage problem is explained by the failure of worker skills (college degrees) to keep pace with increases in

employer demands for them as computerization (and perhaps offshoring) transform the workplace, eliminating the need for humans to do routine tasks.

In contested market models, wage-setting takes place in firms that operate in imperfect markets, and under these conditions employers typically have substantial bargaining (monopsony) power and make use of strategic wage policies to elicit optimal effort, leading to the existence of good and bad jobs for similarly skilled workers (for example, respectively, Manning 2011; Lazear and Shaw 2007). This is a neoclassical view in which market failures are seen as essential features of product and labor markets, and as a result, corrective institutions can improve efficiency and well-being. The low-wage problem reflects rising monopsony power and, reflecting this power, the growing use of human resource practices that push wages below competitive market levels.

Social-institutional approaches share the contested market vision of the centrality of bargaining power within the firm, but broaden the relevant terrain by underscoring the importance of social, political, and structural forces; the effectiveness of protective labor institutions; and workplace culture and conflict (for example, Kaufman 1988, 2004; Osterman 2011). This is a political economy vision in which the power wielded by different key stakeholders generates the institutional configuration and organizational diversity that in turn helps determine key outcomes, including not just wages and nonwage job quality but also the nature and use of available production technologies. The low-wage problem is rooted in deregulation and technological advances that have increased employer power, manifested in firm restructuring and adversarial labor practices aimed at cutting labor costs as the countervailing power of labor institutions collapsed. In this view, the decline in post-1979 job quality can be explained by a declining *willingness to pay* decent wages by lead firms with considerable market power and a declining *ability to pay* decent wages by their suppliers and other firms

---

1. By extractive growth, we mean unshared growth in which increasing inequality is characterized not just by a growing gap between top and bottom parts of the wage-income distribution, but by absolute declines in inflation-adjusted wages or incomes at the bottom.

confronted with increasingly competitive product markets (Appelbaum 2017).

These three perspectives assign different roles for markets, institutions, and conflict. In contested market and social-institutional approaches, large shifts in labor demand and supply can be important sources of wage and other job quality outcomes. For example, a surplus pool of workers vying for jobs can be expected to undermine their bargaining power, as Adam Smith argued centuries ago (discussed further later). But the same is not the case for the role of protective institutions (formal and informal) in the textbook competitive market explanation. Here the wage is set in the external labor market by supply and demand, and wage inequality reflects the "race" between education and technology. This model excludes by its construction surplus (rents, or excess profits), much less bargaining over it. Rather than acting as countervailing sources of bargaining power that can offset inefficiencies generated by market power, protective labor institutions alter distributional outcomes only at the cost of economic efficiency, resulting in lower overall output and employment.

We next consider the recent evidence. Guided by the competitive market model, researchers have sought evidence showing computer-related shifts in labor demand (measured by changes in the occupational distribution of employment) and shifts in the supply of skills (often measured by the share of college graduates). This demand-supply explanation has become increasingly controversial and we consider a number of questions that have been raised about the measurement, interpretation, and implications of occupational employment polarization and the college-wage premium. In addition to the challenges posed by these questions, the competitive market explanation has no ready answer for recent evidence that strongly supports the long-standing view among early postwar labor economists that wage differentials are substantial, and perhaps growing, for similar workers employed in similar jobs but working in different establishments, firms, and industries (Freeman 1988; Kaufman 1988, 2004). Another challenge is the difficulty of explaining vastly different wage and inequality trends across similarly rich

countries that face similar technological advances and globalization pressures.

Researchers who see the labor market through the lenses of the two bargaining power approaches have focused on evidence of rising monopsony power, increases in employment restructuring to reduce labor costs through outsourcing nonessential tasks formerly done in house, and the eroding power of countervailing labor institutions (such as laws governing the labor process, collective bargaining protections, and minimum wage legislation). In addition, social-institutional scholarship has pointed to the effects of changes in national and local public policies that affect human resource practices (such as labor laws and tax policy), the state of labor supply (such as policies that affect unemployment levels, trade, and immigration), and declines in the social wage (non–employment-related social provision for working-age families).

Building on the industrial relations economists of the early postwar period, researchers have recently explored newly available linked data sets for individuals and the firms in which they work, which have revolutionized the ability to address questions about firm versus individual effects on wages. The evidence strongly suggests that substantial wage differentials exist for similar workers in similar jobs but employed in different establishments and firms, and that this is a central feature of the American labor market. This evidence is consistent with the view that a shift in bargaining power toward employers has been an important part of the post-1979 collapse in job quality—at least as indicated by wage stagnation, rising wage inequality, and the increasing incidence of low-wage jobs.

Finally, we consider the implications of these alternative views of the labor market for public policies related to job quality. Nearly all researchers concerned with the quality of jobs agree that improving education and training are important for economic growth, employment opportunities, and individual wage outcomes. The question is whether strong upward movement in worker educational achievement, which has characterized the last four decades, can substantially increase overall real wage growth, reduce overall wage inequality, and lower the incidence of low- and poverty-wage jobs. For those wedded to the competitive market view, the answer is an unequivocal yes. In this view, institutional labor protections designed to increase shared growth through higher real wages and reduced wage inequality will only slow growth and diminish employment. Those who see shifts in bargaining power at the root of wage stagnation and the explosion in wage inequality focus more attention on the potential benefits of national regulatory policy (ranging from antitrust and anticollusion regulations), labor laws that guard individual workers and collective bargaining rights, and protective institutions and policies such as the minimum wage and social wage policies. They point to evidence that an increasing challenge for similarly skilled workers is to find and keep a good job, and that institutional change and policy intervention is needed to change the mix of good and bad jobs. In this view, it is not the level and distribution of worker skills, and certainly of educational attainment, but instead differences in institutional regimes that explain the vast gap in the incidence of low pay between the United States (25 percent) and, say, Australia (15.3 percent) or Belgium (3.4 percent).[2]

Given the centrality of work to human welfare and the functioning of organizations and societies, enhancing the quality of jobs is a pressing issue for public policy. In our view, all these policy directions should be pursued as long as they promote a return to shared growth. As precision machinist Daniel Wasik wrote in a letter to the editor of the *New York Times*, "We must find a more equitable balance between wages, productivity and profits. A rise in productivity should trigger a rise in salary, and when profits soar, the working people instrumental in that success should share in its bounty" (January 21, 2019).

JOB QUALITY: CONCEPTS AND MEASURES

Jobs consist of the specific tasks that people do to earn a living. Jobs represent bundles of re-

wards and the multidimensionality of these rewards is reflected in common definitions of job quality, such as those used by the International Labor Organization (ILO) and the European Union. The ILO's conceptualization of *decent work* includes nearly a dozen components (each comprising numerous indicators), including opportunities for productive work, adequate earnings, decent hours, stability and security of work, arrangements to combine work and family life, fair treatment in employment, a safe work environment, social protections, social dialogue and workplace relations, and characteristics of the economic and social context of work (for example, Ghai 2003). The European Commission's related concept similarly includes ten components, such as intrinsic job quality, skills, gender equality, health and safety at work, flexibility and security, and work-life balance (2001; see also Green 2006). The core dimensions of job quality certainly include economic compensation such as earnings and (especially in the United States), benefits such as health insurance and pensions, as well as the degree of job security and opportunities for advancement to better jobs, the extent to which people are able to exercise control over their work activities and to experience their jobs as interesting and meaningful, and whether people are able to exercise control over their work schedules so as to permit them to spend time with their families or engage in other, nonwork activities they enjoy. Although a number of definitions, measures, and even indexes of job quality exist, no consensus has been established about what constitutes an adequate summary empirical indicator of job quality (Findlay, Kalleberg, and Warhurst 2013).

Defining whether a job is good for a person depends in part on individuals' motivations for taking one (for example, whether mainly for the money, to make contributions to society or particular groups, or to obtain intrinsic meaning and accomplishment). In general, a good job is likely to be harder to define than a bad one: what we consider to be a good job depends not only on economic benefits—wages and non-

---

2. These figures come from the OECD (Employment Outlook 2017, Statistical Annex, table O) for 2015. For comparison, Finland, Denmark, France, and the Netherlands had low-pay incidence rates of 7.8, 8.2, 9.1, and 14 percent respectively. Rates for Germany, the UK, and Canada were 15.3, 20.0, and 22.2 percent,

wage benefits such as health and pension coverage—but also on having control over one's schedule and autonomy over the content of work (Kalleberg 2011, 2016). Some good jobs can also be considered better than others, and so we distinguish good from merely decent jobs. By contrast, it is easier to define certain types of jobs as bad if they have extremely low levels of earnings and benefits that are not enough for full-time workers to achieve a minimal standard of living and allow workers little control over the scheduling and conditions of their work.

Types of work arrangements and job quality are related empirically but are distinct concepts. Nonstandard work arrangements depart from the standard employment relations as normative forms of good jobs, but nonstandard jobs are not necessarily bad jobs and might be quite good. Country differences in labor market and social welfare protection institutions are crucial for evaluating the quality of jobs associated with these arrangements. Temporary jobs are not inherently undesirable, for example, because some people would prefer to work on a temporary basis provided that they could still obtain needed economic rewards such as enough earnings and benefits such as health and pensions. This is the case in countries such as Denmark, where such benefits are provided to all citizens regardless of their work status (Kalleberg 2018).

In the discussion that follows, we operationalize job quality mainly as economic compensation such as wages or earnings. This is the most widely used indicator of job quality for which data are available for long periods. We will also consider other dimensions, however, including economic benefits such as health insurance and retirement assistance, as well as non-economic benefits such as control over work schedule and working conditions. These dimensions of job quality are, in general, positively related, and so we can speak of the overall goodness or badness of jobs.

POST-1979 AMERICAN JOB QUALITY: A STATISTICAL PORTRAIT

This overview of important dimensions of post-1979 American job quality begins with national evidence of a striking shift between the broadly shared and moderately egalitarian growth of the three decades between the late 1940s and mid-1970s and the unshared inegalitarian growth of the post-1979 period. We then turn to what has happened to real wages; wage inequality; the incidence of poverty-, low-, and decent-wage jobs; and a variety of nonwage dimensions of jobs quality. We conclude with an overview of the evidence on nonstandard jobs.

The Economic Context: Four Decades of Unshared Growth

It is now well established that the proceeds of American economic growth since the late 1970s have been almost entirely appropriated by those at the very top of the income ladder, reversing the more egalitarian outcomes of the earlier postwar decades (1946–1980). Thomas Piketty, Emmanuel Saez, and Gabriel Zucman report that in the thirty-four years before 1980, real (inflation-adjusted) pre-tax incomes for the bottom 50 percent and the middle 40 percent (the 50th through 90th percentiles) of adults (ages twenty and older) rose substantially, by 102 and 105 percent respectively, which was more than twice the increase of the top 1 percent (47 percent) (2018, table II). In striking contrast, in the thirty-four years since 1980, bottom-50th and middle-40th percentile adults increased by just 1 percent and 42 percent, whereas top-1 incomes rose by 205 percent. The same pattern holds for post-tax incomes (2018, appendix tables II-B7, II-B8, and II-B10).

Because our concern in this issue is with job quality, a better indicator of shared growth via the labor market is the market income (pre-tax) for working-age adults (twenty to sixty-four), displayed in figure 1.

This figure shows not just the stagnation of the bottom-50 and the increasing growth of incomes as you move up the income ladder, but also the suddenness of the shift between shared and unshared growth regimes around 1980. Top-1 incomes rose at rates broadly similar to per capita gross domestic product (GDP) and top-10, middle-40, and bottom-50 incomes between 1962 and 1980, but show a striking upward decoupling of the top-1 in the aftermath of the 1980 and 1982 recessions, early in the first term of President Ronald Reagan. Although the economy grew by 77 percent between 1980 and

Figure 1. Growth of GDP and Market Incomes of Working-Age Adults, 1962–2014

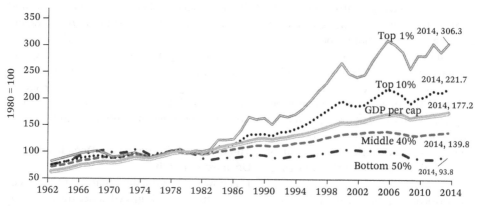

Source: Authors' compilation.

Note: GDP per head in constant dollars from OECD.stat (extracted April 3, 2018); market incomes for working-age (twenty to sixty-four) individuals from Piketty, Saez, and Zucman 2018 (appendix II, update November 2017, tables II: B7, B8, B10).

2014, the average market income for the bottom-50 actually fell by 6.2 percent (as noted), reflecting a decrease in income of almost $2,000 from $18,049 to $16,136—below the 1966 level of $16,388.

A sharp divergence around 1980 can also be seen in real weekly wages at the 90th, 50th, and 10th wage deciles for all full-time workers and male and female workers separately (Acemoglu and Autor 2011, figures 7a–7c). The trends at the bottom of the distribution show wage stagnation; male workers' real weekly earnings were lower in the mid-2000s than in 1970, and female earnings rose modestly only after 1994. But outcomes are even worse when the pay indicator is hourly wages and all (including part time) workers: "downward movements at the 10th percentile are far more pronounced in the hourly wage distribution than in the full-time weekly data" (Acemoglu and Autor 2011, 1065).

Another way to depict the post-1979 decou-

pling of worker incomes from economic growth is with the Economic Policy Institute's by now iconic figure,[3] which sets the growth in labor productivity against the growth in the average hourly compensation of production and non-supervisory workers, who account for about 80 percent of total payroll employment. Between 1947 and 2017, productivity rose by 246 percent, but average worker compensation increased by less than half that, 115 percent. This gap was almost entirely attributable to the post-1979 decades. Although labor productivity and labor compensation increased together between 1948 and 1973 (97 percent and 91 percent), the gap grew to more than 60 percentage points between 1973 and 2016, reflecting an increase of 73.7 percent for productivity and just 12.3 percent for the typical worker.[4]

A way to better understand what post-1979 unshared growth has meant for workers at the bottom of the wage distribution is to compare

---

3. Not shown; see EPI 2018.

4. The typical worker is often identified in the data as either the median worker, or in this case, as the average for the subset of production and nonsupervisory workers. About 80 percent of this gap is attributable to the weakening of labor's position, a combination of rising wage inequality and the decline in labor's share of total income. The remainder (20 percent) is accounted for by differences in the change in the deflators—one for labor compensation, the other for output—used to adjust for inflation (see Mishel and Bivens 2017). A recent paper by Anna Stansbury and Larry Summers argues that, while there is still a relationship between labor productivity and worker compensation, "other forces" have "pushed the other way." They do not challenge the growing gap shown in figure 1 (2017).

Table 1. Wages at the 20th Percentile and Wage Inequality, 1979–2017

	Wages			Wage Inequality	
	Total	Male	Female	Total	Total
				50:10	95:50
1979	$10.79	$13.06	$9.69	1.76	2.36
1999	10.92	11.90	10.17	1.97	2.74
2017	11.40	12.05	10.88	1.85	3.28

Source: Authors' compilation based on Economic Policy Institute (EPI 2017, "Wages by Percentile," accessed March 1, 2019, http://www.epi.org/data/#/?subject=wage-percentiles&g=*).

hourly pay to what it would take a full-time worker to generate a minimally decent standard of living for herself, much less a family. As table 1 shows, even at the 20th percentile of the overall wage distribution, average hourly pay was just $11.40 in 2017, far below a 2016 basic-needs budget for a single adult in cities like Bakersfield ($14.64), Phoenix ($14.10) and Colorado Springs ($13.45), as calculated by the Economic Policy Institute (EPI) (see Tung, Lathrop, and Sonn 2015, table 3.1, projected for 2016 from EPI's Family Budget Calculator). This wage was just sixty-one cents higher than thirty-eight years earlier—an average increase of about 1.5 cents per year. The table shows that 20th percentile male workers experienced a decline of $1.01 between 1979 and 2017, and that the average 20th percentile female worker wage rose by $1.19 over these four decades (from a much lower base), to a wage of $10.88.

The columns on the right of table 1 report two measures of wage inequality, the ratio of the 50th to the 10th percentile worker (bottom-end inequality), and the 95th to the 50th percentile worker (top-end inequality). Like figure 1, the 95:50 ratio shows the top dramatically pulling away from the typical (median) worker, from a ratio of 2.36 in 1979 to 3.28 in 2017. In contrast to the strong and persistent rise in top income inequality, the 50:10 ratio shows fairly stable bottom-end inequality, rising modestly from 1.76 in 1979 to 1.97 in 1999, and then declining to 1.85 in 2017. This stability in the bottom half of the wage distribution will be important for our discussion about the way changes in the incidence of low-wage and decent-wage jobs should be measured.

Wage Contours and the Incidence of Jobs by Wage Quality

A key assumption of the Organization for Economic Cooperation and Development's recent work on cross-country patterns of job quality has been that *earnings quality*, arguably by far the most important job-quality dimension for most workers, should be understood as a reflection of both pay levels and pay inequality: a given wage is better the higher the standard of living it can purchase *and* the higher it is relative to, say, the median wage of a relevant reference group of wage earners (OECD 2014, chapter 3). If this is the case, jobs in a more compressed wage distribution will be, all else equal, better jobs.

The changing wage quality of jobs can be measured in a variety of ways. John Schmitt and Janelle Jones, for example, define the earnings threshold for a good job as one that pays the same in inflation-adjusted terms as the median wage of men in 1979 ($18.50 in 2010) and find a rising incidence of good-wage jobs between 1979 and 2010, from 40.6 to 47.2 percent of employment. This improvement is driven by wage increases for women, which more than offsets the decline in the incidence of good-wage jobs for men from 57.4 to 54.6 percent (Schmitt and Jones 2012, 3–4).[5] Jennifer Hunt and Ryan Nunn define their "wage bins" (groups ranked by their average wages) similarly, with 1979 wage thresholds defining each bin, and find an increase in the share of workers in the top wage bin but no evidence of a "declining middle" (2019). These results hold whether the wage distribution is organized into four, five, or ten bins. This is a quasi-absolute wage approach

5. An earlier version was published in *Challenge* (Schmitt 2008).

that fixes the definition of a good job in terms of the median wage in a 1979 economy, with no adjustment for any sharing in productivity growth. The problem with this approach—if the purpose is to identify good-wage jobs—is that it takes no account of productivity growth, which is normally assumed to be shared to some degree with the workforce. The real, inflation-adjusted wage that qualifies as "good" should be defined not relative to a 1979 (or 1959) wage threshold but to a current one.

Harry Holzer and his colleagues define a good job as one that pays a wage premium above the "market value of the portable component of an individual's skills and attitudes" (2011, 21).[6] This approach is consistent with a competitive market perspective—wages are good if they pay more than the market-clearing level, which should be the worker's marginal product. Reviewing data for twelve states for a single decade, from 1992 to 2003, the authors conclude that "good jobs remain quite plentiful in the United States—but they are becoming harder for workers with limited skills and education to obtain" (19).

The far more conventional approach to the measurement of changes in the wage quality of jobs is to define a wage in each period (year or quarter) as the benchmark, typically some fraction of the overall median wage, and calculate the incidence of employment above it (the good- or decent-wage share) or below it (the low-wage or poverty-wage share). The Russell Sage Foundation's low-wage project, for example, defined the incidence of low pay as jobs paying less than two-thirds of the median wage. Using this definition, they find that low pay "was already high in the 1970s and has changed little since then" (Mason and Salverda 2010, 36). The Organization for Economic Cooperation and Development (OECD) defines low pay similarly but restricts the benchmark wage to the median for full-time workers. Because full-time workers are generally paid higher wages for the same work and the full-time to part-time wage gap has in-

creased in the United States, the OECD's approach yields both a somewhat higher level and a moderately growing incidence of low pay for the United States (OECD 2014, table Y).

In sum, the message of the literature on the incidence of low-wage and good-wage jobs has varied with the definitions but, broadly, asserts rough *stability* or slight improvement since the 1970s—a period of (as we have seen) stagnant or declining real wages, a dramatically widening compensation-productivity gap, and exploding inequality. One explanation for this apparent anomaly is that a low-wage job is conventionally defined relative to the median wage, so it measures changes in wage inequality in the bottom half of the distribution. Table 1 showed that bottom-half inequality (as measured by the conventional 50:10 ratio) has changed little since the late 1980s, which translates into stable low-pay incidence, even though the standing of the entire bottom half of wage earners declined relative to the top half, increasingly so with each percentile from the 60th to the 95th.

There is no substantive reason why the benchmark for measuring the incidence of low pay should be the median, however, any more than the fraction of the median should be set at two-thirds (instead of, say three-fifths or one-half). At the same time, reliance on the median instead of the mean can result in perverse effects, such as a declining incidence of low wages (presumably a positive outcome) as real wages fall across the entire bottom of the wage distribution but most rapidly at the median (clearly a negative outcome).[7] It also explicitly rules out the view that increases above the 50th percentile of the wage distribution have, or should have, an influence on what is understood as a low wage. The usual critique of replacing the median with the mean is that the incidence of low pay should not be determined by what is happening at the very top of the income ladder. But this is actually a moot point, because the conventional measurement of incidence rates has always relied on survey or

6. For example, building cleaners who are paid $10 in a local labor market in which pay for similar skills is just $9 would have a good job.

7. This is not necessarily hypothetical; the polarization literature has argued that just this sort of twist in the bottom of the wage distribution helps explain overall wage inequality since the late 1980s (Autor and Dorn 2013).

census data, which excludes as much as the top 5 percentiles of the wage distribution (to ensure individual anonymity), and these few percentiles account for the vast bulk of the rise in top-end inequality since the early 1980s.

Figure 2 presents the incidence of low pay with two approaches, one defined by the median, the other by the mean.[8] Panel A reports low-pay incidence with the conventional low-wage definition: jobs that pay less than two-thirds of the median wage for full-time wage and salary workers, which was $13.33 in 2017. Based on evidence from basic-needs budgets, this is a wage that, even on a full-time basis, would make it extremely difficult to support a minimally adequate standard of living for even a single adult anywhere in the country. This wage threshold ($13.33) is just above the wage cutoff for food stamps ($12.40) and Medicaid ($12.80) for a full-time worker (thirty-five hours per week, fifty weeks per year) with a child; full-year work at thirty hours per week would make a family of two eligible for the food stamps with a wage as high as $14.46 and as high as $14.94 for Medicaid.[9] For this reason, we refer to this as the poverty-wage threshold.

Panel A shows that, consistent with evidence from the OECD for low-wage incidence, which uses the same definition, the poverty-wage share was fairly stable for all workers (eighteen through sixty-four) over the last four decades, ranging from 26 to 31 percent (see OECD 2017, statistical annex, table O). This stability was driven by outcomes for prime-age workers (thirty-five to fifty-nine), which fluctuate moderately around 20 percent in the bottom line in panel A. This stability also reflects averaging the results for men (which shows a rising incidence of poverty-wage jobs) and females (falling or stable poverty-wage rates until the late 1990s, and rising since). In sharp contrast, panel A shows that the incidence of poverty-wage jobs has exploded for young workers, rising from 31.5 percent in 1979 to a peak of around 48 percent in 2013 before falling to 42.8 percent in 2017.

Panel B defines a low wage as less than two-thirds of the mean for full-time prime-age workers, with low-wage jobs falling below the decent-wage threshold of $17.50 in 2017. This wage is well above the wage that would make a full-time (or near-full-time) worker eligible for food stamps and several dollars above the basic-needs budget for a single adult in most American cities, but is conservative in that the basic-needs budget for a single adult with one child ranges from $22 to $30 (Howell 2019). The decent-wage threshold, which uses the mean as the benchmark, increases the incidence of low pay (compare with panel A), but also has implications for changes over time in a period of rising relative pay of those between the 50th and 95th percentiles. Panel B shows that the low-wage share (those with wages below the decent-wage threshold) for all workers (age eighteen through sixty-four) rose from 39.1 percent in 1979 to 42.6 percent in 2001 and continued to increase to 45.2 percent at the end of

8. The hourly wage is taken from the Outgoing Rotation Groups of the Current Population Survey, and the version used here was accessed from the Center for Economic and Policy Research (CEPR). The sample was limited to wage and salary workers with reported gross (pre-tax) hourly wages between $0.50 and $200 in 1989 dollars. For salaried workers, the hourly wage was calculated by dividing gross pay by usual weekly hours. To adjust for cost-of-living changes, the CPI-U-RS is used as the deflator, which is the standard for wages (for example, see Autor 2010; for a detailed description and assessment of alternative deflators, see Moulton 2018).

9. The gross monthly eligibility income for food stamps for a household of two persons (such as a mother and child) was $1,736 in 2017 (Saving to Invest, "2016–2017 Food Stamp (SNAP) Income Eligibility Levels, Deductions and Benefit Allotment Payments," accessed March 1, 2019, http://www.savingtoinvest.com/food-stamp -snap-income-eligibility-levels-deductions-and-benefit-allotment-payments). Working thirty-five hours a week (140 hours per month), a worker could have been paid as much as $12.40 and still be eligible for food stamps; at thirty hours, eligibility would have extended up to $14.46. Medicaid eligibility in 2017 for a family of two was $22,411 (PeopleKeep, "2017 Federal Poverty Level Guidelines," Febuary 7, 2017, accessed March 1, 2019, https:// www.peoplekeep.com/blog/2017-federal-poverty-level-guidelines), which is $12.80 per hour for a full-time worker, defined as 1,750 hours. At 1,500 hours (thirty hours per week, fifty weeks a year), the Medicaid eligible wage would be $14.94. Full-time employment in many other rich countries is around 1,500 hours per year.

Figure 2. Incidence of Low Pay in the United States, 1979–2017: Two Perspectives

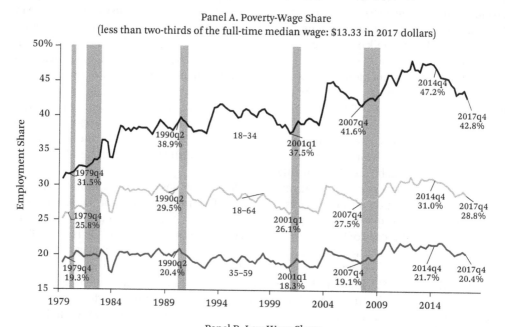

Panel A. Poverty-Wage Share
(less than two-thirds of the full-time median wage: $13.33 in 2017 dollars)

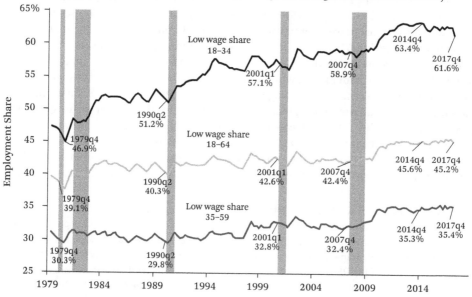

Panel B. Low-Wage Share
(less than two-thirds of the full-time prime-age mean wage: $17.50 in 2017 dollars)

Source: Howell 2019.

Note: The poverty-wage threshold is the conventional low-wage cutoff: two-thirds of the median wage for full-time workers. The decent-wage threshold is defined as two-thirds of the mean wage for full-time prime-age workers. Lower tier decent wage jobs are those that pay up to 50 percent above the decent job threshold. Employment shares report the share of employed workers (eighteen to sixty-four) with wages within each contour or segment wage range. The data are from the merged outgoing rotation groups (MORGs) from the Current Population Surveys (CPS) for 1979 to 2017, accessed from the Center for Economic Policy Research (CEPR).

Figure 3. Structure of American Wage Quality Circa 2017

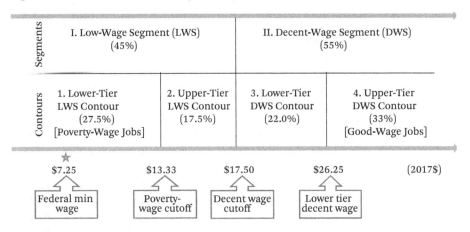

Source: Authors' compilation.
Note: The poverty-wage threshold is the conventional low-wage cutoff: two-thirds of the median wage for full-time workers. The decent-wage threshold is defined as two-thirds of the mean wage for full-time prime-age workers. Lower-tier decent-wage jobs are those that pay up to 50 percent above the decent-job threshold. Employment shares report the share of employed workers (eighteen to sixty-four) with wages within each contour or segment wage range. The data are from the merged outgoing rotation groups (MORGs) from the Current Population Surveys (CPS) for 1979 to 2017, accessed from the Center for Economic Policy Research (CEPR).

2017. The low-wage incidence for prime-age workers was stable through the mid-1990s at around 30 percent, rose to 32 to 33 percent until the 2008 financial crisis, and has hovered around 35 percent since. In contrast to this moderate worsening for prime-age workers, the low-wage employment share for young workers exploded from 46.9 percent in 1979 to a peak of 63.4 percent in 2014 and was slightly lower at the end of 2017 (61.6 percent).

These two wage threshold formulas are used to generate the two-segment, four-contour wage structure shown in figure 3 (Howell 2019). The decent-wage threshold distinguishes the decent-wage from the low-wage segment. Poverty-wage jobs make up the bottom tier (contour) of the low-wage segment. The decent-wage segment can also be divided into wage contours, with the highest—good jobs—defined as those with wages above 150 percent of the decent-wage threshold, which was $26.25 in 2017. By these definitions, 45 percent of wage and salary workers were in the low-wage segment in 2017, with 27.5 percent in the bottom, poverty-wage contour; 55 percent were in the two decent-wage segments, with one-third

of all workers in the upper good-wage job contour.

Although grounded in evidence from basic-needs budgets and Supplemental Nutrition Assistance Program (food stamp) and Medicaid eligibility, the specific contour and segment boundaries are arbitrary—as all such schema must be. But changes by a dollar or two one way or another does not change the employment shares of each contour segment much, and even less the trends over time. This conception of the wage structure also corresponds closely to both the older labor market segmentation (LMS) and the more recent polarization literatures. The poverty-wage contour consists mainly of low-wage service and blue-collar jobs that characterize the secondary segment in the LMS literature (Gordon, Edwards, and Reich 1982; Gittleman and Howell 1995) as well as the nonroutine manual task jobs in the polarization literature (Autor, Katz, and Kearney 2005, 2008; Autor and Dorn 2013). The two middle contours—the upper-tier low-wage contour and lower-tier decent-wage contour ($13.33 to $26.25 in 2017)—overlap closely with the LMS's subordinate primary segment's routine white-collar

Table 2. Employment Shares for Wage Segments and Contours, 1979–2017 (percentages)*

Age Group	Segments or Contours	1979q4	2000q4	2014q4	2017q4
Eighteen to sixty-four	I. decent-wage job segment	61.5	57.9	55.9	55.0
	1. upper-tier dw contour	34.5	33.4	33.9	33.0
	2. lower-tier dw contour	27.0	24.5	22.0	22.0
	II. low-wage job segment	38.5	42.1	44.1	45.0
	3. upper-tier lw contour	12.8	16.4	12.9	17.5
	4. lower-tier lw contour	25.6	25.8	31.2	27.5
Eighteen to thirty-four < col	I. decent-wage job segment	48.2	31.8	24.9	23.4
	1. upper-tier dw contour	20.4	10.6	8.7	7.4
	2. lower-tier dw contour	27.7	21.2	16.2	16.0
	II. low-wage job segment	51.8	68.2	75.1	76.6
	3. upper-tier lw contour	16.1	22.4	15.3	23.1
	4. lower-tier lw contour	35.7	45.8	59.8	53.5
Eighteen to thirty-four >= col	I. decent-wage job segment	78.0	79.7	70.3	68.1
	1. upper-tier dw contour	44.9	49.7	43.5	40.3
	2. lower-tier dw contour	33.0	30.1	26.9	27.8
	II. low-wage job segment	22.0	20.3	29.7	31.9
	3. upper-tier lw contour	9.6	11.7	13.7	17.3
	4. lower-tier lw contour	12.4	8.6	16.0	14.6

Source: Authors' compilation.

Note: The poverty-wage threshold is the conventional low-wage cutoff: two-thirds of the median wage for full-time workers. The decent-wage threshold is defined as two-thirds of the mean wage for full-time prime-age workers. Lower-tier decent-wage jobs are those that pay up to 50 percent above the decent job threshold. Employment shares report the share of employed workers (eighteen to sixty-four) with wages within each contour or segment wage range. The data are from the merged outgoing rotation groups (MORGs) from the Current Population Surveys (CPS) for 1979 to 2017, accessed from the Center for Economic Policy Research (CEPR).

and high-wage blue-collar job contours (Gittleman and Howell 1995) as well as the polarization literature's routine manual job group. Finally, the overall mix of jobs in the upper-tier decent-wage contour is broadly similar to the LMS literature's independent primary segment and to the polarization literature's nonroutine high cognitive skill jobs.

Table 2 presents employment shares for each of these contour segments for three demographic groups defined by age and education for 1979, 2000, 2014, and 2017. The top panel reports that the share of all employed wage and salary workers (ages eighteen through sixty-four) in the decent-wage segment fell from 61.5 percent to 57.9 percent between 1979 and 2000, and then fell further to 55 percent by the end of 2017; its mirror image, the low-wage job segment, grew steadily from 38.5 percent to 45.0 percent in 2017. Declining job shares character-

ized each of the two decent-wage contours between 1979 and 2017 (from 34.5 percent to 33 percent for the upper-tier decent-wage contour, and from 27.0 percent to 22 percent for lower-tier decent jobs). In contrast, the employment shares of both low-wage contours increased (from 12.8 percent to 17.5 percent in the low-wage upper tier and from 25.6 to 27.5 percent for the lower, poverty-wage job tier).

The middle and bottom panels of table 2 report changes in employment shares across the four job-quality contours for young workers (ages eighteen through thirty-four) by education level. For young workers with less than a college degree, the middle panel shows that the share employed in the decent-wage segment fell from 48.2 to 23.4 percent between 1979 and 2017, and grew spectacularly in the poverty-wage contour, from 35.7 to 53.5 percent. The bottom panel shows that this pattern even held for

Figure 4. Decent Job Rates, Median Wages, and Employment Rates for Young Workers Without a College Degree, 1979–2017

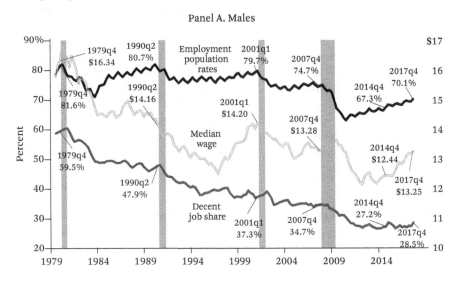

Panel A. Males

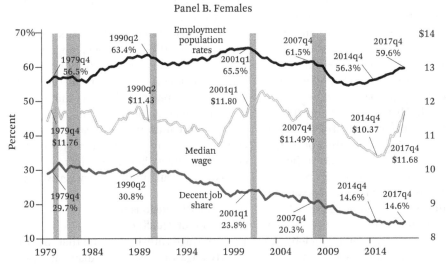

Panel B. Females

Source: Howell 2019.

Note: Young is ages eighteen to thirty-four. Amounts in 2017 dollars.

young workers with a college degree: the employment share of young college-degree holders in the decent-wage segment fell from 78.0 to 68.1 percent. As a result, the share of workers with college degrees employed in the low-wage segment grew from 22.0 to 31.9 percent.

Figure 4 presents time series trends for two indicators of job quality for young workers without a college degree—the decent-wage share and the overall median wage—with male

workers shown in panel A and female workers in panel B. These figures also show the employment rate for each of these demographic groups (for details, see Howell 2019). Panel A of figure 4 reports that among young male workers with less than a college degree, the incidence of decent jobs has fallen steadily and colossally between 1979 (59.5 percent) and 2017 (28.5 percent). This was also true for non–college-degree prime-age workers (ages thirty-five through fifty-nine, not shown), whose incidence of decent jobs fell from 82.5 to 59.3 percent. Panel B shows that the decent-wage share for young non–college-degree female workers was roughly stable at about 30 percent through the early 1990s and has fallen steadily since, reaching just 14.6 percent in 2014 (and 2017). The decent-wage share for prime-age non–college-degree women rose from 42.1 to 47.3 percent between 1979 and 1990 and then fell to 39.3 percent by the end of 2017 (much of the decline took place between 2007 and 2010).

It is not just the share of decent jobs that has declined sharply for these workers. The quality of jobs, as measured by the median wage, has dropped off sharply as well. Panel A of figure 4 shows that the overall median wage for young less-educated men fell from $16.34 (less than the decent-wage cutoff) to just $13.25 in 2017 (below the poverty-wage cutoff). Although the general trend was downward, changes in the tightness of the labor market clearly mattered a great deal: panel A reports a large and steep increase in the second half of the 1990s and an equally sharp decline between the end of 2009 and 2012. For similarly defined female workers, overall job quality as measured by the median was roughly stable between 1979 and 2000 (a median wage in the neighborhood of $11.50) but after peaking in 2003 at $11.80, the noncollege young female wage fell to just $10.37 at the end of 2014. Although it subsequently increased to $11.68 in the fourth quarter of 2017, this was still $1.65 below the $13.33 poverty-wage threshold.

Such large declines in job quality, as measured by both opportunities for decent jobs and the median wage, are likely to affect people's labor supply decisions. Figure 4 shows that employment rates for young workers with less than a college degree have ratcheted downward since around 2000. For young male workers without a college degree (panel A), employment rates fell dramatically, from 79.7 percent in the first quarter of 2001 to 67.3 percent at the end of 2014, before rising to 70.1 percent in the fourth quarter of 2017. Panel B shows that employment rates for young less-educated female workers increased from 56.5 percent in 1979 to 65.5 percent in 2001, fell back to 56.3 percent in 2014, and then recovered to 59.6 percent in 2017.

The rise in low-wage jobs we have docu-

mented here makes it important to know how this and other labor market changes have affected mobility out of low-wage work over time. In this issue, Michael Schultz uses data from the U.S. Panel Study of Income Dynamics from 1968 to 2014 to examine the changing patterns of mobility out of low-wage jobs in the United States (2019). His analysis shows that over the whole period about 42 percent of workers entering low-wage jobs below our "poverty threshold" between the ages of twenty-five and fifty-four were able to move to higher wages within two years, and that about 63 percent do so within six years. A key finding is that after controlling for a wide variety of demographic and educational characteristics, mobility rates out of low-wage work have fallen since the late 1990s and worsened further since the Great Recession. Women and nonwhites are less likely to move out of low wages and only minimal progress has been made in closing these gaps since the late 1960s.

Tom VanHeuvelen and Katherine Copas (in this issue) show that since 2000, geographic differences have mattered much more for high-wage than low-wage workers in the United States. Geographical differences among high-wage labor markets are great, but places are becoming more uniform for those in low-paying and insecure work (2019). They also find evidence that affluent households increasingly depend on the availability of low-wage workers.

Nonwage Dimensions of American Job Quality

The two wage thresholds, one that identifies poverty-wage jobs (using a median wage threshold) and the other that defines decent-wage jobs (relative to a mean wage threshold), provide alternative approaches to the measurement of long-run changes in wage quality. Changes in the incidence of poverty-wage and decent-wage jobs can be viewed as measures of changes in job quality if other important dimensions of employment valued by workers— such as health, pension and days-off benefits, and important working conditions—are closely associated with wage levels, and the (positive) relationships between pay and these other job-quality dimensions have not substantially weakened much over time.

Nonwage job-quality characteristics are notoriously difficult to reliably measure over extended periods.[10] But available evidence on one important category of nonwage job-quality characteristics—nonwage benefits—shows no meaningful compensating increases that could be said to offset the stagnation in real pay and rise in the incidence of low-wage jobs just documented. Nonwage compensation grew by 10.1 percent between 1979 and 2016, only slightly higher than the 9.2 percent increase in the median wage (Schmitt, Gould, and Bivens 2018).

At the same time, the share of workers receiving employer-paid health and pension benefits has declined sharply. The Economic Policy Institute reports that the share of workers receiving at least partially paid health insurance from their employers in 2016 ranged from 24.3 percent in the bottom fifth of the wage distribution to 73.1 percent in the top fifth. Not only were low-wage workers much less likely to have this benefit, but the share with paid health benefits has declined much more for lower- than for higher-wage workers: the bottom fifth experienced twice the percentage drop as the top fifth between 1979 and 2016, a decline of 35.9 percent (down from 37.9 percent in 1979) relative to 18.3 percent for the top fifth (down from 89.5 percent); between these, the middle fifth experienced a decline that was also in the middle: a fall in the share with health insurance of 23.6 percent (from 74.7 percent in 1979 to 57.1 percent in 2016).[11] A better indicator would take into account changes in the level of employer subsidy, which has likely also fallen faster for lower- than for higher-wage workers.

The decline in the share of workers with employer provided pension coverage was similar across the wage distribution in percentage terms: from 18.4 percent to 11.3 percent for the bottom quintile (–38.6 percent), from 52.3 percent to 34 percent for the middle quintile (–35 percent), and from 78.5 percent to 49.6 percent for the top quintile (–6.8 percent).[12] It should also be recognized that, with the decline of defined benefit pensions, retirement income risk has shifted sharply from employers to workers.

Although we do not have time series data on days-off benefits and on-the-job working conditions, the 2015 Rand Survey of American Working Conditions provides a variety of indicators that can be associated with pay for a single year. The survey included responses from 2,066 persons between the ages of eighteen and seventy-one who were working for pay at the time of the survey (Maestas et al. 2017, 4). Table 3 tabulates some key results of the Rand survey by wage contour. The distribution of employed survey respondents is similar to that of the Current Population Surveys (CPS)—it is smallest in the second contour (14.7 percent versus 17.5 percent in the CPS), second largest in the bottom (poverty-wage) job contour (21.5 percent versus 27.5 percent), and largest in the top, good-wage contour (43 percent versus 33 percent).

Rows 3 through 5 of table 3 show that the share of workers in firms that offer health, pension, and disability benefits are far higher in the two decent-wage contours (columns 3 and 4) than in the bottom poverty-wage contour (column 1), and the gaps are strikingly similar across benefit types. The two decent-wage contours show worker shares with health insurance offered (but not necessarily paid) by the employer at 81.5 percent and 73.4 percent in 2015, relative to 40.6 percent in the poverty-wage contour.[13] Whereas 42.6 percent of bottom contour workers work for firms that offer disability benefits, the other three contours range from 69.4 to 71.9 percent.

Six indicators of paid time off are shown in rows 6 through 11. For each, benefits are better

---

10. Schmitt and Jones point to the difficulties involved in generating a consistent series of the value to workers of employer contributions to health and pension benefits over the post-1979 decades (2012).

11. Authors' calculations based on Economic Policy Institute figures ((EPI 2017, "Health Insurance Coverage," accessed March 1, 2019, https://www.epi.org/data/#?subject=healthcov&d=*).

12. Authors' calculations based on Economic Policy Institute figures (EPI 2017, "Pension Coverage," accessed March 1, 2019, https://www.epi.org/data/#/?subject=pensioncov&d=*).

13. The good-wage job contour (4) had a substantially lower share than the lower-tier decent jobs contour (3). The same pattern holds for employer offered pension benefits.

Table 3. Working Conditions and Employment-Related Benefits by Wage Contour, 2015

	Contour 1	Contour 2	Contour 3	Contour 4
1. Wage range, 2015$	<= $12.67	$12.68–$16.41	$16.42–$24.62	>= $24.63
2. Survey respondents (share of total)	434 (21.5%)	297 (14.7%)	422 (20.1%)	870 (43.0%)
Health-pension benefits				
3. Employer offered health insurance (% yes)[a]	40.6	71.5	81.5	73.4
4. Employer offered pension (% yes)[a]	37.0	68.0	80.9	75.6
5. Employer offered disability insurance (% yes)	42.6	70.0	69.4	71.9
Paid time off				
6. Paid sick time offered (% yes)	35.0	66.9	79.4	76.8
7. Paid sick days per year (three)	9.7	10.3	12.2	15.2
8. Paid holidays (% yes)	41.4	64.4	72.1	72.2
9. Paid vacation time (% yes)	40.3	66.6	84.3	75.9
10. Paid vacation days given (#)	12.4	16.1	22.2	22.8
11. Paid vacation days taken (#)	11.6	12.0	13.7	16.3
Hours and schedule				
12. Good fit of working hours with family and social commitments (% well–very well)	18.4	12.6	20.1	39.6
13. Regular and steady work throughout year (% yes)	17.6	13.4	21.9	40.4
Indirect job quality indicators				
14. Looking for a job (% yes)	39.0	29.9	32.5	22.2
15. Union member (% yes)	6.5	12.6	16.6	22.7

Source: Authors' calculations based on Survey of American Working Conditions (Rand 2015).
Note: Contour 1 = lower tier of low-wage segment; contour 2 = upper tier of low-wage segment; contour 3 = lower tier of decent-wage segment; contour 4 = upper tier of decent wage segment. For wage contour definitions, the poverty-wage threshold is the conventional low-wage cutoff: two-thirds of the median wage for full-time workers. The decent-wage threshold is defined as two-thirds of the mean wage for full-time prime-age workers. Lower tier decent wage jobs are those that pay up to 50 percent above the decent job threshold. Employment shares report the share of employed workers (eighteen to sixty-four) with wages within each contour or segment wage range. The data are from the merged outgoing rotation groups (MORGs) from the Current Population Surveys (CPS) for 1979 to 2017, accessed from the Center for Economic Policy Research (CEPR).
[a]The question asks whether the respondent's employer offers health insurance, pension-retirement benefits, or disability benefits. This appears to leave open how much, if anything, is contributed by the employer to the costs of these benefits.

the higher the wage contour. For example, the share of workers with paid sick time (row 6) is almost twice as high for contour 2 (66.9 percent) as for contour 1 (35 percent), and the share is higher still in the decent-wage contours (79.4 percent and 76.8 percent). Row 7 shows that the number of paid sick days increases systematically across the wage contours, from 9.7 to 10.3, 12.2, and 15.2. The same pattern holds for paid holidays, paid vacation time, and paid vacation days that are both given and taken.

Rows 12 and 13 report two hours and work

schedule indicators. Workers in good-wage jobs (contour 4) are much more likely than workers in poverty-wage jobs (contour 1) to agree that their job offers both "a good fit of working hours with family and social commitments" (39.6 percent versus 18.4 percent) and that the job offers "regular and steady work" (40.4 percent versus 17.6 percent). At the same time, a smaller share of workers in the upper tier of the low-wage segment, contour 2, say they have regular and steady work than those in poverty-wage jobs (13.4 percent to 17.6 percent). Although workers in the highest wage contour (4) are by far the most advantaged on these hours and scheduling criteria, far fewer than half report that their work schedules offer a good fit (39.6 percent) or regular and steady work (40.4 percent).

We included two additional indicators because they are likely to be highly associated with job quality as indicated by wages, benefits, satisfactory hours and work schedule, and job conditions: the share looking for a different job (row 14, a likely consequence of job quality) and the share reporting union membership (row 15, a likely cause of job quality). Active job search is much higher for workers in poverty-wage jobs (39 percent) than the middle two wage contours (29.9 percent and 32.5 percent), which in turn is far above the search rate for workers in the good-wage jobs (22.2 percent). Similarly, union membership increases from 6.5 percent in contour 1 to 22.7 percent in contour 4.

These data strongly support the view that, at least at the highly aggregated level of four wage contours, nonwage benefits and working conditions vary systematically with wage quality, from worst in the poverty-wage contour (1) to best in the good-wage contour (4). This suggests that wages are a good approximation for overall job quality.

Nonstandard Work Arrangements and Job Quality

Changes in job quality are often linked to transformations in work arrangements from the post–World War II norm of standard employment relations to the current emphasis on nonstandard work arrangements. Our analysis in the previous section focused mainly (though not completely) on workers who had standard employment relations: wage and salaried workers, including part-timers but not the self-employed. Here, we examine how nonstandard work arrangements are related to job quality.

Trends in Nonstandard Work Arrangements
A prominent theme in recent research on job quality is the rise of nonstandard work arrangements that depart from the previously widely accepted norm of standard employment relations involving permanent, full-time work directed by an employer at the employer's place of business and with regular pay and benefits. They include temporary work (hired both through agencies and directly), part-time work (which is more nonstandard in some countries than others), contract work, irregular and casual work, and some types of self-employment and independent contracting. In general, nonstandard forms of work are uncertain and insecure and (especially in the United States) often lack the social and statutory protections that have come to be associated with regular, standard employment relations in the early post–World War II period (see, for example, Vosko 2010; Kalleberg 2011; Weil 2014).

Unfortunately, interest in and theories of nonstandard work arrangements have outrun empirical evidence based on representative data and using consistent definitions and adequate measures. Systematic data are in short supply about trends in the various types of nonstandard work arrangements that span a relatively long period; until recently, only relatively poor information on the extent of nonstandard work arrangements and how this has changed during the past several decades has been available. In the United States, nationally representative data on nonstandard work (such as temporary work or independent contractors) were not collected systematically until the mid-1990s with the Contingent Work Supplements (CWS) to the February Current Population Surveys conducted in 1995, 1997, 1999, 2001, 2005, and in May 2017. These provide the most extensive estimates of nonstandard work arrangements in the United States.

Figure 5 presents estimates (from the 1995, 2005, and 2017 CWS) of the percentage of the U.S. labor force working in four kinds of nonstandard work arrangements: employees of contract companies, employees of temporary

Figure 5. Nonstandard Work Arrangements in the United States

Source: Authors' compilation based on analyses of 1995, 2005, and 2017 Current Population Surveys' Contingent Work Supplements.

help agencies, on-call workers (who are called to work by employers on an as-needed basis, such as substitute teachers), and independent contractors (which include freelancers and workers who are self-employed but have no employees).

The percentage of workers in nonstandard work arrangements has increased only slightly since 1995: from 9.8 percent of the labor force in 1995 to 10.1 percent in 2017. About 1 percent of the labor force was employed by temporary help agencies and about 0.5 percent worked for contract companies, and the sizes of these groups were similar between the original survey in 1995 and 2017. The percentage of on-call workers was 1.7 percent in 2017, slightly greater than in 1995. The percentage of independent contractors, the largest category of nonstandard work, was 6.9 percent in 2017, slightly more than in 1995 and a decline from 7.4 percent in 2005 (see also Appelbaum, Kalleberg, and Rho 2019).

These relatively flat trends in the CWS estimates of nonstandard work arrangements undoubtedly underestimate both the size and the growth of the nonstandard labor force. The CWS is a household survey of workers that asks about the worker's main job (in a particular week) and thus does not count second or third jobs (Mishel, Bernstein, and Allegretto 2007, 239). By contrast, estimates of independent contractors based on administrative data such as tax records register independent contracting at any point in the year and on supplementary as well as main jobs; these estimates show much higher (and increasing) rates of independent contracting (Abraham et al. 2017). The 2017 BLS CWS result differs from Lawrence Katz and Alan Krueger's finding of an increase in the percent of independent contractors from in 7.4 percent in 2005 to 8.4 percent in 2015 (2016). The authors also report an increase in all four categories of nonstandard work from 10.7 percent in 2005 to 15.8 percent in 2015. More recently, they note that their estimates of nonstandard work arrangement were too high, as they were skewed by spotty data and the recession of a decade ago (2019).

Estimating the number of workers employed by contract companies is especially problematic. The low percentages of contract company workers as identified by the CWS does not square with the case study evidence about the rise of outsourcing and organizational *fissuring* in recent years (see, for example, Weil 2014, 2017; Bernhardt et al. 2015; Appelbaum and Batt 2017). Many workers do not know whether their company is a contract company; transformations in how business organizes work are also "invisible to most of us as consumers" (Weil 2014, 3).

Moreover, we need to keep in mind that the recent rise of nonstandard work arrangements in the United States began in the mid-1970s (Kalleberg 2011), and the lack of information on these types of work from these earlier periods makes it difficult to assess long-term trends (for a discussion of this problem, see Green 2006). The incidence of nonstandard work arrangements is also greater in some countries than in the United States (see ILO 2016; Kalleberg 2018). In Japan, slightly more than one-third of Japanese workers in 2010 were in nonstandard work arrangements (Osawa, Kim, and Kingston 2013). In countries where employment protections are strong, such as France and Spain, numbers of temporary workers are high because employers are reluctant to hire permanent workers they will have difficulty shedding. By contrast, employers in liberal market economies such as the United States and United Kingdom have fewer incentives to offer fixed-term, temporary contracts because employment protections for permanent workers are weak. In the United States, the vast majority of workers are employees "at will," except for the small number of union members (especially in the private sector) and some well-paid professionals with individual employment contracts.

A relatively large proportion of jobs that have been created in recent years have been in nonstandard work arrangements: a recent OECD study of twenty-six European countries showed that about half of the jobs created between 1995 and 2013, and about 60 percent of those created between 2007 and 2013, were in nonstandard jobs (OECD 2015). This suggests a substantial shift in the nature of work in these countries, and one that grows more pronounced over time. Further, in 2013, about one-third of all jobs in these countries were in nonstandard work arrangements, divided about equally among temporary jobs, permanent part-time jobs, and self-employment.[14]

Nonstandard Work Arrangements and Job Quality

Low-wage and nonstandard jobs are interconnected in significant ways. Some nonstandard jobs may be good ones, such as well-paid consultants who have a great deal of control over the terms and conditions of work. Independent contractors and other forms of self-employment may provide higher wages than regular full-time workers in standard jobs, though workers in these nonstandard arrangements are less apt to receive fringe benefits. Moreover, independent contractors are likely to prefer to work in them (see Kalleberg et al. 1997; Kalleberg, Reskin, and Hudson 2000).

However, many nonstandard jobs are characterized by low pay, low security, poor working conditions, high anxiety, and result in poor mental and physical health. Some nonstandard work, such as temporary help agency employees, on-call workers and day laborers, and part-time workers are consistently more likely than regular full-time workers to have low pay and to lack health insurance and pension benefits (see, for example, Tilly 1996; Kalleberg 2000; Stancanelli 2002). They also often lack statutory protections in the form of labor laws. Moreover, workers in low-wage and nonstandard jobs often tend to be the most vulnerable members of the labor force such as racial and ethnic minorities, women, immigrants, and undocumented workers.

Contract company workers, moreover, are likely to have jobs that are of lower quality than comparable jobs in which production is not outsourced. As Eileen Appelbaum and Rosemary Batt summarize the literature on this topic, "Most empirical research in both the USA and Europe suggests that the rise of the networked firm and outsourcing of production has led to a deterioration in the jobs and pay of workers and to a growth in wage inequality" (2017, 77). Outsourcing work to contract companies relieves large firms from having to maintain internal equity pay norms. Contractors are also likely to be subject to greater cost pres-

14. The extent to which regular part-time work can be considered to be precarious differs among countries: in some, part-time work can be fairly stable and associated with social and statutory protections akin to those enjoyed by regular, full-time workers and so are less likely to be precarious than are short-term and irregular jobs, for example.

sures, leading them to lower wages and make wage theft more likely. Nevertheless, the difficulties in measuring contract work underscore the need for additional research on the quality of such jobs (see, for example, Bernhardt et al. 2015).

The quality of nonstandard jobs should be judged in relation to the job quality of standard employment relations. All nonstandard work arrangements are associated with insecurity and uncertainty, and this is generally true also for all workers, in both high- as well as low-skill jobs. Although nonstandard jobs often pay low wages, then, low-wage jobs are also increasingly found in standard employment relations: the shifting of risks from employers to workers has reduced protections for standard workers as well, leading to a stagnation or deterioration of wages for many who are employed on a permanent basis (Bernhardt 2014). Even among workers who continue to work full time with their employers on standard employment contracts, the greater incidence of downsizing and related human resource practices shifts risks of work from employers (and the government) to workers and is illustrated by trends such as the growth of defined-contribution relative to defined-benefit pension plans and the increasing proportion of health insurance premiums paid by employees rather than their employers. This risk shifting occurs with temporary or contract jobs, but also characterizes the decline of social protections associated with standard employment relations.

Linking nonstandard work arrangements to job quality raises a number of important issues related to work and workers. Several articles in this issue address some of these correlates of nonstandard work, such as their demographic composition, the consequences of working in nonstandard jobs for health, and how labor market dynamics are reflected in the search process for standard and nonstandard jobs. These studies help bolster our understanding of this underdeveloped area of research on labor markets and inequality.

Cathy Liu and Luísa Nazareno use data from the CWS and show that workers in nonstandard employment receive increasingly lower earnings and work fewer hours than comparable workers in traditional arrangements (2019). However, the penalties for working in nonstandard jobs differ for subgroups of workers: for example, high-skill workers in nonstandard jobs are more disadvantaged relative to those in standard jobs than are low-skill workers. Trevor Peckham and his colleagues demonstrate that those who had nonstandard and dead-end jobs had lower general and mental health as well as more occupational injuries than those who had standard employment relations (2019). Susan Lambert, Julia Henly, and Jaeseung Kim find that nonstandard and precarious work schedules are both widespread in the U.S. labor market but also introduce instability as well as unpredictability into workers' lives (2019). In particular, they find that the relationship between schedule volatility and financial insecurity is greater for salaried than for hourly workers, suggesting that variability in hours does not translate directly into perceived earnings instability. Finally, David Pedulla and Katariina Mueller-Gastell document differences in the job search process between nonstandard workers, whom they define as part-time and temporary workers, in the United States (2019). They find that young workers and those with less education are more likely to apply for nonstandard jobs.

EXPLAINING JOB QUALITY: THEORETICAL PERSPECTIVES

The current focus on job quality is motivated by the widespread recognition and concern that American economic growth since the late 1970s has been unshared with the workforce, resulting in a four-decade long increase in wage, income, and wealth inequality. What explains how the proceeds of economic growth are shared with workers across the wage distribution? And what explains the sharp U-turn in shared growth around 1980? Because the wage is a critical indicator of job quality for most workers, the wage-setting process must be at the center of any answer to these questions. But even narrowed to wage setting, the terrain is far too large and complex to do more here than provide a bird's-eye perspective through the particular lenses we bring to the question.

Explanations for the post-1979 low-wage crisis—wage stagnation or decline, rising wage inequality, and increases in the incidence of poverty and low wages—derived from alternative visions of how the labor market works. Systematic efforts to explain wage outcomes date back to the beginning of the industrial revolution, and in particular, to Adam Smith's *Wealth of Nations*. Because the essential features of the contemporary debate can be found in Smith, we begin by briefly summarizing Smith's views. We then argue that current perspectives about how the labor market works are widely interpreted to reflect either a *market* (supply and demand) or an *institutional* (bargaining power) vision. This terminology can be misleading, given that the market is an institution and could not function—even the special case of the economist's textbook (neoclassical) perfect competition model—without a variety of other formal institutions (for example, those that establish property rights and enforcement) and informal ones (for example, social norms that establish trust). It also fails to recognize the recent development of a market-optimization vision in which bargaining power is central, which can be referred to as contested market models.

We view differences in the dynamics, evolution, and performance of the labor market—and consequently changes in job quality—to be rooted in alternative perspectives on institutions and their effects on economic outcomes. Institutions are typically understood as the formal and informal rules of the game, often manifested in regulations and in public and private organizational policies, that evolve over time and that reflect collective and political choices governing interactions between individuals as well as groups of individuals (including organizations, communities, and governments). They provide the framework within which decisions and actions take place, help motivate individual behavior, and define the structure and operation of groups. Inherently political constructs, institutions reflect "socio-political compromises established in historically-specific conditions" (Amable 2016, 79).

In mainstream labor economics, the conception of institutions is narrower but not necessarily inconsistent with this understanding.

For example, according to a leading textbook, "A labor market institution is a system of laws, norms, or conventions resulting from a collective choice and providing constraints or incentives that alter individual choices over labor and pay" (Boeri and van Ours 2013, 8). In this view, institutions form a "wedge between the value of the job for a firm and the reservation wage of the individual," and hence are, relative to the economist's perfect labor market, inherently inefficient (8). Alternatively, if labor markets are imperfect in important ways, institutions can be corrective and improve efficiency. This is the position of contested market (monopsony search and personnel economics) models. In social-institutional approaches, the employment relation is inherently socially embedded because the labor that is exchanged for pay cannot be separated from the worker (unlike a material commodity). Institutions, even protective labor institutions, are not presumed to be inherently inefficient, nor do they merely serve to correct market failures. Instead, by defining the nature of the employment relation and helping to allocate power to key parties with conflicting interests, they are essential features of the labor market and central to the determination of labor outcomes.

Markets, Institutions, and Bargaining Power: Smith's Vision

To understand how labor markets in capitalist economies work, and specifically how wages are set, it is useful to start with Adam Smith, whose "invisible hand" theorem about the benefits of market competition has long been the keystone of mainstream economics (1937 [1776]). But whereas Smith is widely seen as the father of free market economics, *The Wealth of Nations* makes it clear that institutions, social norms, and market pressures are all central to the balance of bargaining power between "masters" and "workmen." Smith's chapter 8 ("of the Wages of Labor") highlights the ways in which "monopsony power" (the ability to set wages through the "collusion" of masters), social norms (subsistence consistent with "common humanity"), institutions (the use of state power to ensure low wages), and the swings in the market between "scarcity of hands" and "scarcity of employment" all matter a great deal. Smith begins with wage setting as the outcome of self-interested bargaining: "What are the common wages of labour, depends everywhere upon the contract usually made between those two parties, whose interests are by no means the same. The workmen desire to get as much, the masters to give as little, as possible. The former are disposed to combine in order to raise, the latter in order to lower, the wages of labour. It is not, however, difficult to foresee which of the two parties must, upon all ordinary occasions, have the advantage in the dispute, and force the other into a compliance with their terms" (1937 [1776], 66).

Employers have a number of structural advantages in the wage dispute. First, they can hold out much longer than workers. Although masters "could generally live a year or two upon the stock which they have already acquired. Many workmen could not subsist a week." Second, employers easily collude with one another to keep wages low: "being fewer in number, they can combine much more easily. . . . Masters are always and everywhere in a sort of tacit, but constant and uniform combination, not to raise the wages of labour above their actual rate." And, third, employers are politically more powerful and can rely on the police powers of the state: "the law, besides, authorizes, or at least does not prohibit their combinations, while it prohibits those of the workmen. . . . [the masters] never cease to call aloud for the assistance of the civil magistrate, and the rigorous execution of those laws which have been enacted with so much severity against the combinations of servants, labourers, and journeymen" (Smith 1937 [1776], 66).

Despite these overwhelming employer advantages, wages tend not to fall below socially acceptable subsistence levels for working families, due both to social norms that keep the

wage above "the lowest which is consistent with common humanity" (Smith 1937 [1776], 68) and to employers' self-interest in reproducing a healthy and productive workforce.[15] At the same time, market forces matter: in good years of strong economic growth, "The scarcity of hands occasions a competition among masters, who bid against one another, in order to get workmen, and thus voluntarily break through the natural combination of masters not to raise wages" (68). But in lean years, in a "scarcity of employment," workers compete with one another and drive the wage back down to the rate just consistent with "common humanity." Workers who must invest to learn their trade will get a compensating wage premium (now termed the return to "human capital"), but Smith does not explain wage differentials as a simple reflection of differences in worker productivity; instead, wages are sometimes set above the market-clearing level to spur worker morale, reduce turnover, and increase productivity (now known as an efficiency wage).[16]

In sum, we can find important roles in Smith for *market forces* (the relative jobs scarcity of jobs and workers), monopsony *bargaining power* (employer collusion), *social norms* (the social subsistence wage as the lower wage threshold), *formal institutions* (the advantages to employers of prevailing legal rules), and *wage-driven productivity growth* (not just productivity-driven wage growth). Together, these can help explain substantial persistent cross-firm (and industry) differences in wages and nonwage job quality for similar workers that have been observed by researchers since 1776.

The Contemporary Debate

As in Smith's vision of the mid-eighteenth-century English labor market, three key dimensions—market forces, institutions, and social

---

15. "Thus far at least seems certain, that, in order to bring up a family, the labour of the husband and wife together must, even in the lowest species of common labour, be able to earn something more than what is precisely necessary for their own maintenance" (Smith 1937 [1776], 68).

16. "The liberal reward of labour, as it encourages the propagation, so it increases the industry of the common people. The wages of labour are the encouragement of industry, which, like every other human quality, improves in proportion to the encouragement it receives. . . . Where wages are high, accordingly, we shall always find the workmen more active, diligent, and expeditious, than where they are low" (Smith 1937 [1776], 81).

forces or structures—are inextricably linked in contemporary real-world wage setting. As Richard Freeman notes, "All countries rely on a mixture of the market interaction of supply and demand and labor institutions to determine employment, wages, and conditions of work" (2013, 15). But most efforts to explain labor market outcomes have been seen as falling into one of two broad categories, either institutional (stressing all sources of bargaining power) or market competition (the overwhelming dominance of the forces of supply and demand for skills). For example, in the late 1950s, written in the context of the recent high-profile debate on the merits of the competitive model (marginal productivity theory) as a useful guide to actual real-world wage setting, Melvin Reder's survey of wage theory framed it this way: "There are two general approaches to the theory of wage structure. One is the market theory, or the competitive hypothesis, the other is what we might roughly term institutional. Each has its place and, under pressure, most students of the labor market will concede this" (quoted in Kaufman 2004, 31).[17]

Although the competitive market model has continued to dominate textbook economic presentations and economists' professional work, the post-1979 wage problem has triggered a new interest in the effects of institutions and policies on the balance of bargaining power. As in the 1940s and 1950s, these bargaining power approaches are increasingly challenging the mainstream competitive market model, whose advocates have risen to the defense. For example, Gregory Mankiw unfavorably contrasts Joseph Stiglitz's view that rising wage inequality and stagnant wages reflect large-scale rent-seeking behavior in an economy increasingly rigged to benefit the employers and the rich with Claudia Goldin and Katz's technology-driven supply and demand explanation for rising wage inequality (Mankiw 2013, 23). Similarly, Steven Kaplan and Joshua Rauh argue that the evidence on the determination of sharply rising CEO pay, and top incomes more generally, favors "theories that

root inequality in economic factors, especially skill-biased technological change, greater scale, and their interaction" as opposed to "those who suggest that the increase in pay at the top is driven by a recent removal of social norms regarding pay inequality" (2013, 15; see also Gabaix, Landier, and Sauvagnat 2014).

On the other side, arguing that the erosion of institutional protections is central to the wage crisis, sociologists Bruce Western and Jake Rosenfeld write that "Union decline forms part of an institutional account of rising inequality that is often contrasted with a market explanation" (2011, 513). Similarly, the economist Henry Farber and his colleagues motivate their path-breaking study on union wage effects on the grounds that "These new data sources allow us to revisit the role of unions in shaping the income distribution and contribute to the long-running 'institutions versus market forces' debate" (2018, 2).

At the international level, Florence Jaumotte and Carolina Osorio Buitron of the IMF note that "Explanations for the rise of inequality in the developed world either focus on market-driven forces or institutional changes" (2015, 7). Similarly, in reviewing the literature on the importance of cognitive skills in explaining international differences in wage inequality, a recent OECD study explains that "what was really at stake was the role of the market (demand and supply) as an explanation for differences in the returns to skill versus an alternative explanation that attributes skill prices to differences in institutional setups, like the minimum wage and unionization. This mirrors a wider debate in the economic literature that has pitched the market (including the role of technological change and international trade) against institutions in explaining wage dispersion" (Broecke, Quintini, and Vandeweyer 2019, 251–52).

Three Views of the Labor Market
Despite this long history of framing explanations of the way the labor market works in terms of markets versus institutions, in recent

---

17. The leading figures in the debate were Richard Lester for the critique and Fritz Machlup for the defense (see Kerr 1994; Kaufman 1988).

decades the literature seems better described by three fundamental visions. The mainstream neoclassical approach, characterized by putting market forces and individual optimization at the center of the analysis, includes both those convinced that perfectly competitive markets are a good approximation of the way labor markets work and those who see asymmetric information and transaction costs as pervasive and fundamental, leading to the need for models of imperfect competition in bargaining over rents (above competitive market returns). The yawning gap that has developed in recent decades between these competitive and contested market approaches is nicely summarized by Alan Krueger:

> Although economists' go-to model of the labor market is often one with perfect competition—where bargaining power is irrelevant because supply and demand determine the wage, and there is nothing firms can do about it—in many applications I think it is more appropriate to model the labor market as imperfectly competitive, subject to monopsony-like effects, collusive behavior by firms, search frictions, and surpluses that are bargained over. As a result of these labor market features, firms should be viewed as wage-setters or wage-negotiators, rather than wage-takers. (2018,1)

Two very different traditions share this vision in which bargaining power is central. While the imperfect competition (or "contested market") view shares with the political economy (or "social-institutional") perspective a focus on collusive behavior and bargaining over rents, the later places much greater emphasis on non-optimizing behavior and conflict between groups of stakeholders within firms and the structuring of this conflict by workplace cultures and worker identities, internal labor markets, external labor institutions, and public policies. This section considers each of these perspectives in turn.

The Competitive Labor Market Model

In the competitive textbook model, "Earnings are made dependent on the amounts invested in human capital, and the latter are assumed to be determined by a rational comparison of benefits and costs" (Becker 1975, 133).[18] In this view, without the interference of protective institutions, the labor market will clear and price adjustments ensure no excess labor supply or demand, a single price (wage) will prevail for a given level of worker skill, and that wage will be the worker's marginal product—the extra value the worker contributes. In their labor economics textbook, *The Economics of Imperfect Labor Markets,* Tito Boeri and Jan van Ours explain that the analysis of imperfect labor markets must begin with the baseline of a perfectly competitive labor market, in which "the market is transparent, workers and firms are perfectly informed about wages and labor services offered by other firms, and there are no frictions or costs (e.g., no time related to job search and no transportation costs when going to job interviews) involved in the matching of workers and vacancies, that is, of labor supply and demand" (2013, 7). Although this is recognized as a highly simplified model with strong assumptions, it

---

18. The textbook neoclassical model consists of two key elements that combine to generate an equilibrium that is Pareto-optimal, that is, one that maximizes efficiency such that any deviation from it will reduce overall economic welfare. One is the assumption of a particular market structure, perfect market competition, in which all agents are price-takers (wage-takers), there is no bargaining power, and workers are paid their marginal products. The other is the behavioral assumption of constrained maximization, in which all agents (workers and employers) are rational, which is understood as self-interested maximizing behavior (Becker 1975; Kaufman 2004). An example of a much broader, less rigorous conception is Dani Rodrik's: "At the core of neoclassical economics lies the following methodological predisposition: social phenomena can best be understood by considering there to be an aggregation of purposeful behavior by individuals . . . interacting with each other and acting under the constraints that their environment imposes" (2007, 3). We find Rodrik's definition much too broad to be helpful in understanding important cleavages in the literature; it is hard to imagine any leading social scientists who would not agree that individual behavior can be viewed as at least attempting to be broadly purposeful.

is also accepted by many mainstream economists as capturing the essential features of contemporary labor markets.

Seen through the lens of the competitive market model, wage outcomes (and job quality more generally) are best explained by shifts in the supply and demand for skills. On the demand side, computerization of the workplace has increased the demand for skills, but the supply of college-degree workers has not kept pace. Because computer technologies most easily substitute for workers doing routine noncognitive tasks, employment becomes polarized, with faster job growth at the bottom and top of the skill distribution than in the middle. David Autor and Katz offer a good summary of this view: "Two forces are rapidly shifting the quality of jobs, reshaping the earnings distribution, altering economic mobility, and redefining gender roles in OECD economies. These forces are, one, employment polarization (a demand-side force) and, two, a reversal of the gender gap in higher education (a supply-side force), reflecting women's rising educational attainment and men's stagnating educational attainment. The result has been a labor market that greatly rewards workers with college and graduate degrees but is unfavorable to the less-educated, particularly less-educated males" (2010, 1).

Similarly, Daron Acemoglu and Autor's chapter on wage inequality in the most recent *Handbook of Labor Economics* aims "to account for recent changes in the earnings and employment distribution in the United States" and

does so with a perfectly competitive demand-supply model (2011, 1157).[19] They extend the canonical demand and supply model (which is also referred to as the textbook model) with "a tractable task-based model," but the theoretical foundation is the same, one that "crucially depends on competitive labor markets, where each worker is paid the value of his or her marginal product" (2011, 1159; see also Autor, Katz, and Kearney 2006, 2008; Goldin and Katz 2007, 2008; Autor and Dorn 2013).[20] Nancy Folbre terms this a "just desserts" vision of the labor market in which factors of production (such as workers) get what they contribute (2016).[21]

This marginal productivity framing rules out a meaningful role for institutional effects on wage setting and the possibility of important (and growing) within- and between-firm wage differentials for similarly skilled workers doing similar job tasks. This helps explain why protective labor institutions and within-firm bargaining power are all but unmentioned in this literature (see, for example, Autor, Katz, and Kearney 2006, 2008; Goldin and Katz 2007, 2008; Autor and Katz 2010; Acemoglu and Autor 2011, 2012; Autor and Dorn 2013). As Goldin and Katz put it, "Stripped to essentials, the ebb and flow of wage inequality is all about education and technology" (2009, 1).

Contested Market Competition
Whether the canonical competitive market model and its variants can adequately explain recent rises in the college-wage premium and employment and wage polarization is contro-

19. The handbook, edited by Ashenfelter and Card (2011), can be viewed as the definitive statement of the current state-of-the-art in mainstream labor economics; it comprises twenty chapters in two volumes (1,827 pages).

20. "Even though workers of the same skill level perform different tasks, in equilibrium they will receive the same wage—a simple 'law of one price' that has to hold in any competitive equilibrium. . . . In any equilibrium, all tasks employing low skill workers must pay them the same wage, W_L, since otherwise, given the competitive market assumption, no worker would supply their labor to tasks paying lower wages. Similarly, all tasks employing medium skill workers must pay a wage W_M, and all tasks employing high skill workers must pay a wage W_H. As a consequence, the values of the marginal product of all workers in a skill group must be the same in all the tasks that they are performing" (Acemoglu and Autor, 2011, 1122–23).

21. The marginal productivity vision of wage setting is taught in every standard economics (and labor economics) textbook and appears in professional and popular articles whose purpose is to weigh in on the sources of contemporary wage inequality. As Mankiw puts it, "In the standard competitive labor market, a person's earnings equal the value of his or her marginal productivity. . . . The key issue is the extent to which the high incomes of the top 1 percent reflect high productivity rather than some market imperfection" (2013, 30).

versial (see the following section). However, as Alan Manning points out, the competitive model has a hard time accounting for many other labor outcomes: "Many empirical observations (e.g., equilibrium wage dispersion, the gender pay gap, the effect of minimum wages on employment, employers paying for general training, costs of job loss for workers with no specific skills to list only a few) that are puzzles if one thinks the labor market is perfectly competitive are simply what one might expect if one thinks the labor market is characterized by pervasive imperfect competition" (2011, 1031).[22]

In the early 1930s, Joan Robinson, a prominent Cambridge University economist, recognized that just as firms could have monopoly power in product markets, they could also have substantial monopsony power in buyer's (input) markets. The presence of monopoly power in the product market can generate monopsony power in the labor market, as can any frictions that cause workers not to know about other job opportunities (such as imperfect information about contract terms or the working conditions on the new job) or that make it difficult to take a new job or switch jobs (commuting costs, family obligations). These sources of employer bargaining power can cause wages to be set below the worker's marginal product.[23] "The very fact that we turn up to the same employer day after day strongly suggests there are some rents from that relationship" (Manning 2011, 977).

Another dimension of monopsony power, which may be particularly important to understanding the post-1979 wage crisis, is between lead firms and their suppliers. Spurred by technological advances, deregulation, and the shift from the managerial to the financial model of the firm, large firms have restructured by outsourcing specialized and peripheral functions to contractor firms. This has led to increasing competitive pressures in supplier firms, and predictable consequences for wages in the contractor firms (Weil 2014, 2017; Appelbaum 2017; Handwerker 2018; Wilmers 2018). We mention restructuring and fissuring here because of the tie to monopsony power, but it is consistent with, and most developed by researchers associated with, the social-institutional view.

In this contested market view, because wage bargaining takes place over a range of possible wages given by the worker's marginal product (the upper limit) and the workers' reservation wage (the lower limit), a firm with monopsony power may pay wages that are too low and employ too few workers, resulting in inefficient and inequitable outcomes. Policy responses to monopsony power that could promote both efficiency (employment) and equity (higher wages) include the establishment of wage floors via minimum wage regulation or effective collective bargaining. In short, because markets are no longer perfect, efficiency may require the establishment of protective labor institutions. As Manning explains, "One's views of the likely effects of labor market regulation should be substantially altered once one recognizes the existence of imperfect competition" (2011, 1031). At the same time, despite the central role of market imperfections, rents, and bargaining powers for understanding wage outcomes, imperfect competition models retain the demand-supply framing, grounded in maximizing behavior of self-interested agents.

A complementary new personnel economics (NPE) literature is concerned with a fundamental problem of modern capitalism: the organization of a firm's production process that maximizes productivity and minimizes unit costs. This is a problem ruled out in the canonical textbook model, under which either perfect contracting is assumed or a firm or a fictitious social planner organizes the production pro-

22. Manning defines imperfect competition as the operation of markets in which an "employer or employee or both get some rents from an existing employment relationship" (2011, 974). Such rents violate the fundamental assumptions of the perfect competition model.

23. Imperfect competition models share with the competitive market view the centrality of a demand-supply framework in which the demand curve is given by the worker's marginal product. But unlike the competitive model, in the monopsony model firms can pay workers less than their marginal product (for an institutionalist critique of labor demand as the worker's marginal product, see Kaufman 2007).

cess.[24] The NPE literature is neoclassical in the sense that it "assumes that both the worker and the firm are rational maximizing agents, seeking utility and profits" but, like the imperfect competition literature, it "allows for constraints or imperfections, such as imperfect information and transaction costs, and permits an individual's utility to be influenced by a variety of factors such as personal identity, competition, and peer pressure" (Lazear and Shaw 2007, 91–92). The goal is to understand and model optimal management practices on promotions, raises, the compensation structure (pay-for-performance), the balance between wages and benefits, and the use of teams. More generally, NPE can be seen as the study of ways to organize production and allocate rents optimally, defined from the perspective of the employer's goal of profit maximization. Less attention has been focused on how conflict between groups of stakeholders is resolved, given workplace cultures, power dynamics, and the influence of outside institutions and public policies (Osterman 2011).[25]

Social-Institutional Bargaining Power Approaches

As Bruce Kaufman argues, the social-institutional vision "starts with an imperfect world with humans as they are. . . . Because all contracts are incomplete, people must solve their coordination, allocation, and pricing and output decisions through an evolutionary process of institution-building and a mix of markets, formal organizations, and social institutions" (2004, 34). A long tradition in the social sciences has viewed the economy as "socially embedded" (Granovetter 2005). Robert Solow, one of the giants of postwar economics, points out what might seem obvious: "Wage rates and jobs are not exactly like other prices and quantities" and "Once you admit to yourself that wage rates and employment are profoundly en-

twined with social status and self-esteem you have already left the textbook treatment of the labor market behind" (1990, 23, 10). The employment relationship is contested, as Adam Smith underscored, with management required to make the organization and payment of the "factors of production" profitable for the firm, a central insight of both the new personnel economics and Marxian economics (albeit from very different perspectives).

Building on Adam Smith, prevailing academic and political debates, and their own extensive experience in the workshops and slums of late-nineteenth-century London, Beatrice Webb and Sidney Webb argued more than a century ago that the two parties in the wage negotiation come to the table with vastly unequal capacities to bargain, from financial resources (ability to hold out) and political connections (access to state power) (1897). Further, they maintained that the perfect market assumption was a scholastic fiction, and—importantly—that many of the "imperfections" (more appropriately understood as natural and fundamental features of nearly all real-world labor markets) served to enhance the already dominant bargaining power advantage of employers. As a result, market forces tend to determine at best only the upper and lower boundaries of the wage, a view developed by Richard Lester a half century later in his article "A Range Theory of Wage Differentials" (1952). The wage would normally gravitate to the bottom of the range because the imperfections systematically favored the employer, as Smith argued. For example, "asymmetric information favors employers since they have superior information about market conditions" (Kaufman 2004, 20).

Another central dimension of the institutional approach is exemplified by the work of the early postwar American labor economists

24. "Since there are no distortions, the equilibrium allocation can be characterized by solving the social planner's problem. In each time period, the planner chooses the level of capital K(t), and the allocation of labor Lm(t) to manual tasks in the service sector that maximize aggregate utility" (Autor and Dorn 2013, 1563).

25. Michael Reich and James Devine write that the conflict between workers and employers (labor and capital) "is not resolved by the operation of markets. Conflict is inherent in the employment relation because the employer does not purchase a specified quantity of labor, but rather control over the worker's capacity to work over a given time period, and because the worker's goals differ from that of the employer" (1981, 27).

and industrial relations scholars, such as Sumner Slichter, Clark Kerr, John Dunlop, Richard Lester. and Lloyd Reynolds, who drew attention to what Dunlop referred to as "persistent and pervasive" wage differentials that cannot be accounted for by worker skills. Rather than reflecting the balance of supply and demand for skill, wage levels and differentials were best explained by relative bargaining power, rooted in the structure of production and product markets, and only partly explained by collective bargaining outcomes. According to Dunlop, "The differentials are related to product market groupings of firms and within a given product grouping, to the size of the establishment, or in some circumstances to the size of the enterprise. Different competitive conditions in product markets are related to different compensation levels for the job classification in the local labor market" (1985, 31). In most cases, wages are set for jobs in internal labor markets, not for individuals in external markets. "The internal labor market is the unit within which relative wage rates are also determined among job classifications, not among individuals, with the aid of job evaluation or incentive systems or by decisions exercised by management or through collective bargaining" (31).

In this tradition, non–skill-related wage differences are explained in large part by the ability and willingness of firms to pay wages higher than the minimum market-clearing wage, which translates into interindustry and interfirm wage differentials for workers with similar skills (Howell 1989; Howell and Wolff 1991). Important determinants of the *ability to pay* are monopoly rents, reflecting dominant product market positions that make possible price markups and therefore high and rising value productivity that can be shared with workers (or not). Because the demand for labor is derived from product demand, employers are able to pay more (and hence workers will have more bargaining power, all else equal) the less responsive product demand is to labor costs. This ability to pay will also vary with the labor share of costs (production technology). In addition, employers will also differ in their *willingness to pay* (or incentive to pay) "efficiency wages" that promote higher morale and higher productivity

(as noted by Adam Smith) that reduce the threat of unionization and that lower the cost associated with "shirking, sabotage, striking, and quitting" (Howell 1989, 35; see also Lester 1952; Howell and Wolff 1991; Kristal and Cohen 2014).

It is this focus on the many dimensions of the employment relationship that has been the domain of industrial relations scholarship, the social-institutional counterpart to modern human resource management and personnel economics. The sheer complexity of the dynamics that produce the wide range of wage rates for similarly skilled workers, the variation in employment contracts governing nonwage dimensions of the job, and more generally the management practices that govern the workplace that vary widely even across plants and establishments of the same company (Bloom et al. 2017), cannot be explained by competitive market pressures (which should produce convergence). Instead, as Richard Freeman argues in his assessment of the contributions of the early postwar industrial relations economists, understanding these labor outcomes requires "the reliance on informed priors, based on personal observation and common economic sense" coupled with a central focus on firm behavior, industry structures, worker resistance, and social norms in understanding both individual wage setting and collective bargaining outcomes (1988, 206; for examples of more recent scholarship in the industrial relations tradition field, see Doeringer and Piore 1971; Kochan, Katz, and McKersee 1994; Locke, Kochan, and Piore 1995; Weil 2014).

Within a given institutional context (laws, regulations, and social norms) and the state of worker resistance, "The proposition of industrial relations is that interactive variation in the external environment of firms, their internal structure and organizational characteristics and their organizational goals and strategies lead the owners/executives to craft a finite number of distinct ES (employment system) configurations or 'HRM [human resource management] architectures'" (Kaufman 2010, 95). Changes in these within-firm configurations and architectures are important to the understanding of wage outcomes since the 1970s.

Other important social-institutional perspectives on employment relations, wages, and job quality have emerged from sociology and political science. For example, power resources theory emphasizes how the differential power resources of workers through political parties and unions help determine the institutions governing the labor market as well as the inclusiveness of welfare provisions by the state, which in turn has major consequences for worker bargaining power (see, for example, Korpi 1985; Esping-Andersen 1990). A related perspective, the varieties of capitalism approach, emphasizes how economic activity is coordinated between workers and firms, and how coherent sets of institutions have evolved differently across capitalist countries to manage employment and wages and their connections to educational and skill formation institutions (Hall and Soskice 2001; Amable 2016).

These approaches have in common the view that economic activity and processes are socially embedded in "social networks, culture, politics and religion" (Granovetter 2005, 35). A good example is the treatment of roles social networks play, which are important to economic outcomes for three reasons: they "affect the flow and the quality of information"; they "are an important source of reward and punishment"; and trust "emerges, if it does, in the context of a social network" (33). As recognized in contested market models (the economics of imperfect competition), an essential feature of a well-functioning labor market is efficiently matching workers to jobs. But the socially embedded approach is different: "Economic models typically assume that workers and jobs are matched through a search whose costs and benefits are equalized at the margin. But in most real labor markets, social networks play a key role. Prospective employers and employees prefer to learn about one another from personal sources whose information they trust" (Granovetter 2005, 37).[26]

As a result, the institutional vision regards job matching and the fundamental nature of the employment relationship as inherently social and governed by social structures and relations, economic institutions, and public policies. Job search, job matching, and rent sharing in the employment relationship takes place "only in the context of, and mediated by, social relations that require them to behave in line with rules that are social rather than economic" (Streeck 2005, 255).

If these considerations are important, well-designed institutions and social policies, along with effective human resource policies, can increase both the equity and efficiency of wage and employment outcomes (Agell 1999; Howell and Huebler, 2005; Freeman 2007). In this view, extensive state regulation is necessary for a well-functioning labor market and workplace.[27]

Labor Market Regulation and Performance: Three Perspectives

Each of the three labor market perspectives has generated extensive research designed to help explain the stagnation in wages and the rise in wage inequality since the late 1970s. We conclude this section with the implications of each view of how the labor market works for the relationship between labor market regulation and labor market performance. The ability of protective labor market institutions and policies to raise job quality for some workers, at least for some time, is not in question. But can these collective, social actions serve to improve labor market outcomes for all—or at least most—workers over the long term?

We organize the discussion around figure 6,

---

26. An important dynamic effect is lost in the static costs-benefits model: "when mobility results from network connections, it changes network structure that then feeds back into future mobility patterns. Thus, network structure can be partially endogenized in labor market analysis" (Granovetter 2005, 37).

27. As David Brady and Benjamin Sosnaud write, "States do not simply follow what markets have initiated; states enable and allow markets to happen" (2010, 535). In this light, institutional economics, in Kaufman's words, is inevitably "political economy, because it focuses on the nexus between law and economics, the central role of the state in forming and enforcing the legal regime, and how the politically determined rules of the game affect economic behavior and performance (and vice versa)" (2007, 16).

which presents a stylized picture of how each of the three labor market perspectives imagines the trade-off and complementarity between protective labor regulation and performance, understood as the quality of outcomes for workers.

Labor market performance can be thought of as measured by a combination of productivity growth, real wage growth, and low unemployment. Our preferred interpretation is to privilege outcomes for the bottom half of the wage distribution. The higher on the vertical scale, the better off these workers are because they have greater opportunities for employment at higher wages. The horizontal axis shows the degree of labor market regulation, or alternatively, contracting freedom between workers and employers in the labor market. This runs from unregulated contracting on the far right (at A) to perfectly regulated, or administered, at the far left: labor institutions and social policies designed to increase worker wages, reduce wage inequality, and provide more security, get stronger and more effective moving left from point A. These protections might include the coverage and power workers have in collective bargaining and job security, the degree of strictness of employment protection laws, and the greater the generosity of minimum wages, unemployment benefits, and the social wage (income available to those of working age with little or no employment income).

In the competitive market model, the analysis begins with the state of perfect labor market liberty, at A. At this competitive equilibrium, the value of the job to the employer is equal to the reservation wage of the worker, and because no institutions (regulations, policies, social norms) stand in the way of perfectly informed voluntary employer-worker contracting, the market clears at maximum output and full employment. As protective constraints increase, labor market performance declines. This prediction is consistent with the conventional economist's view of an inherent trade-off between equality and efficiency as well as with Albert Hirschman's "perversity thesis" in which policies and institutions (such as the minimum wage, collective bargaining, and work hour restrictions) end up harming the intended beneficiaries (1991).

In the contested market, imperfect competition vision, market failures—imperfect information, transaction costs and monopsony power—create rents that must be bargained over by employers and workers. Because no labor market can function without some social norms that govern the job-matching process and constrain employer power in the employment relationship, the starting point for the imperfect competition vision is shown as point B, just to the left of the perfect market freedom of point A. As Manning puts it, "If labor markets are imperfectly competitive there is no such presumption that the market is efficient and there is at least the potential for some regulation to improve efficiency" (2011, 1024). Although the sharply different predictions of the effects of minimum wage regulations in imperfectly competitive markets relative to those of the canonical competitive model have received the most attention, others are numerous.[28] In addition, as the NPE literature stresses, management practices must be optimized to maximize firm competitiveness and profitability, which may require human resource practices that promote fairness or, alternatively, undermine solidarity through divide-and-rule management.

For these reasons, the figure shows increasing labor protections (and human resource practices) generating improved labor market performance, reaching the optimal point at C, after which additional constraints will tend to reduce performance, resulting in lower real wage growth, employment, or both. The goal of regulation (and management) in this view is to get the market back to the competitive ideal by compensating for market imperfections in the hiring and promotion process.

Social-institutional perspectives imagine no such competitive ideal. Piece-work production processes are the exception and team work is typical; transaction costs are pervasive; information and markets are profoundly imperfect; and thus the worker's marginal product cannot

---

28. "For example, one can show that regulation to restrict aspects of labor contracts like hours or holidays can improve employment" (Manning 2011, 1026).

Figure 6. Markets, Institutions, and Bargaining Power: Three Visions of Labor Market Regulation and Performance

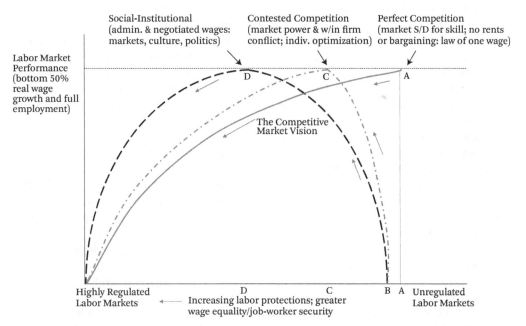

Source: Authors' adaptation of Robert Boyer's diagram (Boyer 2006, figure 1).

be a meaningful concept for real-world wage determination, and well-functioning protective labor institutions are a prerequisite for labor market efficiency. Understanding the labor market as "a social institution," as Solow puts it, the social-institutional perspective on regulation and performance is depicted as an inverted U: optimal economic performance requires a substantial set of protective labor institutions and social policies. Internal labor markets must be designed with respect to within-workplace group interests and cultures. Moving from right to left on the regulatory freedom axis, as the strength and effectiveness of protective labor institutions and policies increase, economic efficiency also increases, reflecting the complementarity between protective regulation and efficiency. But this occurs only up to a point, identified in the figure as D, beyond which the workplace enters a zone of trade-offs because regulatory intervention threatens productivity and employment.

These three labor market perspectives offer a wide range of predictions about the relationship between labor market regulation and performance, from a strict trade-off (the competitive model), to modest opportunities for complementarity followed by competitive model–like trade-offs (contested market models), to substantial complementarity (social-institutional models). These alternative views have important implications for policy priorities, which we consider after reviewing the evidence.

CHANGES IN AMERICAN JOB QUALITY: EXPLANATIONS AND EVIDENCE

The descriptive evidence presented earlier showed that, by many conventional indicators, post-1979 job quality has either declined or failed to improve for most workers—in sharp contrast to the three previous postwar decades (the late 1940s through the late 1970s). Average market incomes for working-age adults in the bottom half of the income distribution actually fell; wage and benefit compensation for production and nonsupervisory workers, some 80 percent of payroll workers, grew little and far slower than labor productivity; and the incidence of low-wage jobs rose—and the share of decent-wage jobs fell—and did so most dramatically for young workers.

A useful way to understand these changes in labor outcomes is by reference to three distinctive perspectives on how the labor market works. Here, we describe and assess some important recent research aligned with these theoretical perspectives. The empirical literature framed by the competitive market explanation has focused on wages by skill group (for example, as measured by the college-wage premium) and on the pattern of occupational employment growth by level of worker skill (typically indicated by the wage).[29] In contrast, perspectives that focus on imperfect labor markets, generated by firm concentration and frictions (and transaction costs) in the employment relationship, have focused their research efforts on the monopsony power of firms, resulting in wages that for similar workers vary substantially across establishments and firms. Research framed by the social-institutional tradition extends this focus on firm-level bargaining power but puts particular emphasis on the sources of bargaining power within the firm, firm restructuring and workplace fissuring, and the erosion of countervailing protective labor market institutions, such as labor laws, collective bargaining, and the legal minimum wage.

The Canonical Market Model and the Evidence

Through the lens of the "canonical supply-demand model" (Autor 2017, 1), the post-1979 stagnation in wages and the rise in wage inequality are explained by the failure of the supply of worker skills (usually measured by the college-educated share of the workforce) to keep up with accelerating computer-driven increases in the demand for skills by employers.[30]

In this view, the worsening of the wage problem—wage stagnation at the bottom, rising top-half wage inequality, and a high and rising incidence of low-wage work—is mainly the consequence of a long-term mismatch between the supply and demand for skills. For empirical support, this literature has focused mainly on evidence of, first, a close correspondence between occupation skill levels (usually measured by the average wage) and occupation employment growth, and, second, a rising college-wage premium. Both have been interpreted to suggest that skill-biased demand shifts have been outpacing increases in the supply of skills.

Empirical research in the competitive market paradigm has explored these predictions in two iterations. The first, now referred to as the canonical skill-biased technological change model, asserted a close monotone relationship between occupational employment growth and the skill-wage level of the occupation: as the workplace computerized, the skill-biased effects of technological change on the demand for worker skills accelerated, leading to higher employment growth for workers with higher cognitive skills (Katz and Murphy 1992; Autor, Katz, and Krueger 1998). But, as early as the mid-1990s, critics called attention to the failure of the canonical SBTC explanation to explain several basic facts of the timing and pattern of wage changes. In particular, skill upgrading had been taking place for decades before the introduction of computers and evidence was scant that the rate of SBTC had accelerated over the course of the 1980s in ways that could explain the growth in inequality, well before most workplaces were transformed by computer-based production technologies (Mishel and Bernstein 1994, 1998; Howell and Wieler 1998; Howell 2002; Card and DiNardo 2002). Another problem was the breakdown in the monotone

---

29. The college-wage premium is defined as the ratio of the wage of workers with at least a college degree to those with just a high school degree.

30. "Under the Tinbergian assumption that technology is skill-biased, technological progress will necessarily widen inequality among skill groups unless it is countered by increases in the supply of human capital. The steady accumulation of human capital has thus been the main equalizer in the U.S. labor market" (Acemoglu and Autor 2012, 427). In the contested market and especially in the social-institutional view, the technology chosen and how it is implemented is a strategic choice reflecting a variety of factors that determine how skill-biased it is, and if it is upwardly skill-biased, effects on inequality can be offset not just by supply shifts, but by countervailing labor institutions.

relationship between skill levels and employment growth: the 50:10 wage ratio (bottom-end inequality) stopped increasing around 1987, reflecting a flattening of growth in the middle of the wage distribution. It was recognized that the middle of the occupational employment distribution was growing more slowly than both high-skill and low-skill occupations, which became known as job polarization (Autor, Levy, and Murnane 2003; Autor Katz, and Kearney 2006; Goos and Manning 2007).

These empirical facts led to the development of a more compelling second-generation version of the canonical market account, known as the tasks framework, which highlights the differential effects of computers on the demand for routine tasks (downward) and nonroutine tasks (upward); the canonical SBTC model now took a *routine-biased* form (RBTC) (Acemoglu and Autor 2011, 2012). But the basic model remained the same—the demand and supply of skills in a setting or workplace computerization—but now, rather than a simple linear relationship between computerization and the demand for skills, the relationship becomes U-shaped, caused by declining demand for routine-task jobs in the middle of the wage-skill distribution relative to rising demand at the top (because high-skill nonroutine-task jobs are complementary with computerization) and at the bottom (because demands for nonroutine manual and people-skill task jobs increase—for example, in the case of low-wage service occupations). If labor demand shifts toward the top and bottom, the supply of high cognitive skill workers is inadequate, and some middle-wage routine-task workers are redundant, the result should be rising *wage* polarization.[31]

This RBTC research has in turn generated a number of critical questions about the measurement, interpretation, and implications of the college-wage premium and occupational employment and wage polarization. For example, what is the significance of the fact that most of the rise in the college-wage premium has been driven by workers with advanced degrees? Do changes in the college-wage premium reflect mainly shifts in the demand and supply of skills, as presumed in this literature, or increased sorting of highly educated workers to high-wage firms, or changes in the bargaining power of workers with an advanced degree (professionals, financiers, executives), many of whom are protected from pay competition by credential and licensing requirements? What explains the apparent slowdown in the demand for cognitive skills and the college-wage premium after the late 1990s? Is this slowdown consistent with the computer-driven demand shift explanation? How much of the observed occupational polarization can be accounted for by the long-standing shift away from manufacturing toward services, a development that predates computerization by several decades? How well does occupational employment polarization translate into occupational wage polarization, and how does the latter correspond to individual wage outcomes, especially for production and nonsupervisory workers (about 80 percent of the workforce)?

Job Polarization

It has become widely accepted that employment polarization is one of the defining features of the post-1970s labor market, both in the United States and across the rich world (Autor, Katz, and Kearney 2008; Acemoglu and Autor 2011; OECD 2017). From the vantage point of the early 2000s, the evidence suggested that workplace technologies had led to an important shift from monotone growth in the 1980s across occupations (slowest at the bottom to highest at the top) to polarized employment growth (with slowest growth in the middle) in the 1990s. But when examining the data by census decade, the 2000s has failed to support continued polarization (Mishel, Schmitt, and Shierholz 2013; Autor 2015), which requires explanation: Why would computerization generate occupational employment polarization in the 1990s but not since?

Lawrence Mishel, John Schmitt, and Heidi Shierholz argue that "the declining middle" has

---

31. The explanation for rising employment shares at the bottom and the translation of this into rising average wage relative to the middle is less developed in this literature (but see Autor and Dorn 2013; for critiques, see Mishel, Schmitt, and Shierholz 2013; Hunt and Nunn 2019).

been taking place since the 1950s (2013). Similarly, Zsófia Bárány and Christian Siegel show that occupation-level polarization in the United States can be traced back to the 1950s, decades before the use of computers in the workplace, and argue that it has been generated mainly by sector shifts away from manufacturing and toward high- and low-skill services—the hollowing out of the middle from deindustrialization (2018). The long-run perspectives of both Mishel and his colleagues and Bárány and Siegel support the deindustrialization perspective of Barry Bluestone and Bennett Harrison and others as early as the 1980s (Bluestone and Harrison 1982; Harrison and Bluestone 1988).

Mishel and his colleagues show that, while occupation-based employment polarization can be observed in the decade of the 1990s, even for that decade "the lines traced out fit the data very poorly" (2013, 5). They conclude that "changes within occupations greatly dominate changes across occupations so that the much-focused-on occupational trends, by themselves, provide few insights" (5). This assessment contrasts with Dwyer and Wright's results (this issue), which show strong evidence of polarization between the early 1990s and 2009 to 2017 (2019) at the level of jobs (occupation-industry cells).

Using a highly aggregated occupation scheme, the OECD portrays the more recent period, from 1995 to 2015, as characterized by dramatic and pervasive polarization across the rich world, but offers ambiguous assessments of the role of skill-biased computerization (2017, figure 3.1). This research allocates eight of the nine large standard (ISCO-88) occupation groups to high-, middle-, and low-skill groups. The OECD evidence shows striking differences between the sharply declining employment growth of the three middle-skill groups (clerks, craft and related trades workers, and plant and machine operators and assemblers), the moderate growth of the two low-skill occupations (service workers and shop and market sales workers, elementary occupations), and the rapid growth of the three high-skill occupations (legislators, senior officials, and managers; professionals; technicians and associate professionals). The OECD authors find that 29 percent of the observed polarization can be ex-plained by the decline in manufacturing; the rest is associated with the increase in the use of information and communication technologies (ICT). But, crucially, they find no statistical effects for ICT on employment polarization outside of manufacturing and no support for their measure of globalization in either manufacturing or nonmanufacturing sectors (OECD 2017, tables 3.2, 3.3). This evidence suggests a strong but largely unexplained pattern of occupation-based polarization.

The overall lesson from this evidence seems to be that both manufacturing and service sectors have strong tendencies to polarize: manufacturing because of productivity growth (and offshoring), and service sectors because of the inherent nature of the demand for both high- and low-skill services (given that computerization has contributed to the decline in routine clerical work).

In addition to the mixed evidence on occupational employment polarization and the difficulty of attributing the hollowing out of the middle to computerization, the existence of a strong link between occupational employment and occupational wage polarization is controversial (Mishel, Schmitt and Shierholz 2013).

Equally important, recent evidence shows that any hollowing out of the middle of the occupational wage distribution (declining relative wage growth in middle-wage occupations) explains little of the growth in overall individual wage inequality. Hunt and Nunn show, for example, that most individual workers in the occupations assigned to the fourth occupation decile do not have wages in the fourth decile of the overall individual wage distribution (2019, figure 10). "One therefore cannot think of the middle occupation-based percentiles as mapping to middle-wage workers." The same problem holds at the bottom of the wage distribution: "Many workers in the bottom two occupation-based percentiles are not low-paid workers" (10). They conclude that "When using workers' wages to indicate job quality we find no employment polarization for men or women in any period of time covered by the Current Population Survey (1973–2017), a finding that is robust to adjustment for age and education" (2).

The wage contour results presented earlier

are consistent with the Hunt and Nunn findings (2019). The two-segment, four-contour wage quality structure (see table 2 and figure 3) can be transformed into a tripartite one by combining the middle two wage contours (2 and 3). For all workers (ages eighteen to sixty-four), this wage structure shows substantial employment stability: between 1979 and 2017, the top contour's employment share fell from 34.5 to 33 percent; the middle two contours remained about the same; and the bottom (poverty-wage) contour's employment share rose from 25.6 to 27.5 percent.

The College-Wage Premium
In addition to evidence of job polarization, empirical support for the competitive model has been centered on the rise in the college-wage premium. According to Autor, "A key implication of the rising college/high school wage premium is that a central causal factor behind rising inequality in the United States has been the slowdown in the accumulation of skills by young adults almost 30 years ago" (2014, 847). Autor also speculates that "Had the supply of college graduates risen as rapidly in the decades after 1980 as it did in the decades immediately before, it is quite plausible that there would have been no sustained rise in the skill premium in the U.S. labor market" (847).

Following Autor and his colleagues, Goldin and Katz, and others, Acemoglu and Autor present empirical evidence that the relative wages of college graduate workers to high school graduates has shown a tendency to increase over multiple decades despite the large secular increase in the relative supply of college-educated workers (2011, 1044; see also Autor et al. 2008; Goldin and Katz 2007, 2008). But it is notable that the college-wage premium as measured in this literature has been rising since 1973, mainly because of both large increases in pay for advanced degree workers and the flat or slightly falling wages for those with a high school degree or less (Mishel, Bivens, and Gould 2012, table 4.12).

This raises a fundamental question about the direction of causation, one that is not adequately addressed in this literature. The rise in the college premium may not be exclusively, or even mainly, an outcome of the demand and supply of skill, but rather a reflection of the sharp rise in top incomes generated by increasing bargaining power of professional, managerial, and technical workers (protected by credential and licensing constraints and located disproportionately in high-rent firms, especially in the finance sector) and the decline in protective labor institutions and changes in employer practices that have undermined the bargaining power of production and nonsupervisory workers. In support of this alternative social-institutional explanation, Niklas Engbom and Christian Moser find that "where you work mediates a substantial share of returns to education at the bachelor's and master's level, and to a lesser extent among doctorates" (2017, 374). Other important recent studies using linked employee-employer data sets have found substantial sorting of highly educated workers into higher paying firms (Card, Cardoso, Heining and Kline 2016; Song et al. 2019). At the same time, firms have restructured, concentrating lower educated workers into low-wage contractor firms (Weil 2014; Handwerker, 2018; Wilmers 2018). These findings are consistent with increasing firm concentration (monopoly power) and the ability to mark up product prices, and therefore in monopsony power (Barth et al. 2016; De Loecker, Eeckhout, and Unger 2018; Benmelech et al. 2018). This research strongly suggests that "where you work" matters a great deal for what you get paid, and this is likely to explain a substantial part of the rise in the college wage premium.

An important question for a competitive market explanation of the wage problem that relies on evidence of increases in the college-wage premium concerns the adequacy of educational attainment as an indicator of cognitive skills. Much of this literature is characterized by a conflation of skills, education, and wages. Samuel Bowles, Herbert Gintis, and Melissa Osborne's 2001 review of the relevant literature concludes that after controlling for cognitive skills (such as test scores), a large return to schooling remains, which is unexplained in most standard statistical tests. Their review of the evidence suggests that this unexplained return to schooling can be attributed to noncognitive, skill-related behavioral characteristics and social skills (for more recent evidence, see also Deming 2017). College degrees not only signal levels of cognitive skills, but also provide employers with a screening device for workers with desired behavioral and personal characteristics (Cappelli 2015, 270).

This evidence of the importance of education as a screening device for behavioral characteristics that may have little connection to workplace productivity raises the question of the ability of cognitive skills (whether measured by test scores or educational attainment) to explain the wage distribution. A key motivation for the development of search theory was to explain persistent large differences in wages paid to similar workers. As Dale Mortensen puts it, "Observable worker characteristics that are supposed to account for productivity differences typically explain no more than 30 percent of the variation in compensation across workers in these studies" (2005, 1). Mortensen's explanation is that worker wages reflect productivity differences across firms. "If the same worker is more productive in one firm than in another, then the more productive firm finds it more profitable to compete by offering a higher wage." It is precisely this non–skill-related wage dispersion that much recent empirical work in the contested market and social-institutional traditions has attempted to explain by extending the argument from the distribution of employer productivity (Mortensen) to the distribution of employer power and the strategic use of it (Manning 2011; Krueger 2018). As Appelbaum argues, the evidence linking high wages to productive firms measures the latter as revenue productivity, which may reflect more market power than efficiency, or as she puts it, the "greater ability that strong firms have to lay claim to rents and to jointly profit relative to weaker firms" (2017, 15).

Another question concerns the fact that the rise in the 90:50 wage differential has continued into the 2000s, despite a flattening of the college wage premium for both males and females after 2000, even when workers with advanced degrees are included (Autor 2014, figure 1). This corresponds in timing to what appears to be a substantial decline after 2000 in the growth in demand for cognitive skills (Beaudry, Green, and Sand 2013). If computerization drives the demand for jobs with high cognitive skills,

there is no obvious reason for the break in the trend that takes place around 2000. David Deming shows that in fact it is not jobs with the highest cognitive (measured as math) skill requirements that have grown fastest, but those with the highest social skills (2017).

Paul Beaudry, David Green, and Benjamin Sand suggest that the supply of college-educated workers may have outstripped demand for them—reversing the logic of the canonical SBTC-RBTC models: as the share of college-educated workers has continued to grow "they have moved down the occupational ladder and have begun to perform jobs traditionally performed by lower-skilled workers" and these lower-skilled workers do the same to workers beneath them (2013, 2). This over-education cascading dynamic of college graduates pushing down the wages of less-educated workers is consistent with the recent literature on skill mismatch (for a summary, see Cappelli 2015). It could also help explain the rising incidence of low-wage and poverty-wage jobs and the decline in decent jobs, especially for young American workers with less than a college degree. At a minimum, these considerations complicate the computer-driven shift in demand toward high cognitive skills as a compelling explanation for wage stagnation and rising wage inequality.

Bargaining Power Explanations and the Evidence

From the vantage point of the contested market and social-institutional perspectives, the employment relationship is characterized by imperfect information and transaction costs. For this reason, labor markets are necessarily imperfect and most workers are therefore employed in firms and organizations that have some wage-setting power. Following Sanford Jacoby (2005), Adam Cobb argues that "systems of corporate employment can be categorized broadly into two ideal types: organizational or market oriented" (2016, 12). But a market orientation does not mean that firms are "price-takers," with wages and working conditions set in the external labor market. Even most small firms operating in highly competitive markets rely on human resource management functions, internal or contracted out. For organizationally oriented firms, the demand and supply for skills are most relevant at "ports of entry" to the firm (Dunlop 1985; Osterman 1994). In this setting, the ability, willingness, and incentives to pay a higher wage than the minimum set by a worker's reservation wage (that is, the wage it takes for a worker to supply their work effort to the firm) sets a range for wages both at ports of entry to the firm and for mobility among jobs within the firm. This approach calls for a research agenda that begins with the premise that labor outcomes will vary substantially across establishments, firms, and industries for similar workers doing similar sets of tasks, which in turn suggests that some jobs are better than others depending on where you work (Barth et al. 2016). As Krueger puts it, these features of the labor market are better understood not as "imperfections" but as "the way the labor market works," which helps explain many well-documented labor market outcomes "such as the high variability in pay for workers with identical skills in different industries or firms, the lack of evidence that minimum wage increases reduce employment, and the reluctance of firms to raise wages when vacancies are hard to fill" (2018, 1).

From the social-institutional perspective, job-quality outcomes documented earlier can best be explained by a large-scale post-1979 shift in bargaining power away from production and nonsupervisory workers toward executives, top professionals, and financiers. These shifts mainly reflect political choices rooted in the dominance of ideas about the merits of free markets, most notably regarding the benefits of deregulation, tax cuts, small government, and financialization. This regime shift took place in the context of macro-structural changes such as the shift to a service economy and technological advances in production,

communications, and transportation technologies that have facilitated the outsourcing and offshoring of work. A central factor in the shift to unshared growth was the ascendancy of the financial sector and the role of finance in non-financial corporations' decision making, featuring the maximization of shareholder value as the fundamental corporate objective.[32] Central to this redirection were concerted attacks on unions and the collective bargaining system, the real value of the minimum wage, and protective laws and regulations governing the employment relationship, resulting in a decline in the effectiveness of these protective labor market institutions. This, in turn, facilitated the restructuring of employment systems to achieve greater flexibility and lower labor costs through domestic outsourcing and production offshoring (moving parts of the production process abroad). The result was a fissured workplace in which workers formerly employed in lead firms now worked for outside suppliers (Weil 2014; Appelbaum 2017; Handwerker 2018).[33]

We have organized our review of recent empirical work framed by the contested market and social-institutional traditions under three headings, employer wage-setting power, the decline of protective labor institutions, and the restructuring of the employment relationship.

Employer Wage-Setting Power
Employer wage-setting power can be expected to increase with both concentration in product markets (monopoly power) and labor markets (conventional monopsony power) as well as with labor market frictions and related transaction costs (dynamic monopsony power). In conditions of conventional monopsony, because fewer firms control a particular product market, workers in particular types of jobs

32. In what seems striking testimony to the importance of the interplay between ideas and interests, following the publication of a paper by Jensen and Meckling in 1976 that applied principal-agent theory to the theory of the firm, companies began "to adopt the financial model of the firm . . . in which managers—the agents—are charged with single-mindedly serving the interests of the principals—the firm's shareholders—by maximizing shareholder returns . . . (and in so doing) altered the logic of value creation" (Appelbaum 2017, 6). This contributed to gigantic increases in top management pay, the rise of leveraged buyouts by private equity firms, and the fissured workplace—all of which increased income inequality and reduced nonsupervisory worker wages.

33. For evidence from Germany on the effects of contracting-out on wages (downward) and wage inequality (upward), see Goldschmidt and Schmieder 2017.

have few if any alternative employment options, which increases employer bargaining power. More generally, however, any impediment to job mobility that raises transaction costs for workers (for example, transportation costs or social amenities that develop from time spent on the job in a particular workplace) will also increase employer bargaining power (Manning 2003, 2011; Krueger 2018). At the same time, lead firms have increased their monopsony power over their suppliers, which has cascading consequences for wages in contract firms.

A considerable literature has developed in recent years on the growing concentration of firms in narrowly defined economic sectors and geographic areas, demonstrating that higher concentration is associated with lower wages. To the extent that firms differ in market power, this could be a source of growing wage inequality (see Furman and Orszag 2015; CEA 2016; Bivens et al. 2018). The rise in corporations' product market power has stemmed in part from political choices to reduce antitrust enforcement against mergers and collusion and to strengthen patent protections, but also as a consequence of new products and technologies characterized by scale and network economies (CEA 2016; Appelbaum 2017). Perhaps the strongest evidence on rising firm concentration is at the sector level, in retail and wholesale, finance, transportation, agriculture, and hospitals (CEA 2016, 4). But the long-term increase in profitability offers additional compelling evidence. For example, the 90th percentile firm had twice the returns on capital as the median firm in 1990; by 2014, returns had increased to five times the median firm (CEA 2016, 5). Jose Azar, Ioana Marinescu, and Marshall Steinbaum find a close relationship between local labor market concentration (the dominance of a small number of employers for an occupation in a commuting zone) and worker wages: "In a nutshell, we find that labor market concentration in the average market is high, and higher concentration is associated with significantly lower posted wages" (2017, 1). John Abowd and his colleagues (2012, 2017) and David Card and his colleagues (2016) find strong support for Mortensen's proposition (consistent with the postwar industrial relations economists such as John Dunlop and Sumner Slichter) that high productivity firms pay more. Abowd and his colleagues conclude that workers benefit from working at a top-paying firm in two ways: they earn more at a point in time and they have a higher probability of moving to a higher wage the following year (2017, 3). But as noted earlier, productivity is measured in value terms, so high productivity may reflect as much the capture of rents as much as production efficiency.

Recent work on price markups (the increase product prices above marginal costs) finds that markups were "relatively constant between 1950 and 1980 at around 20 percent above marginal costs" (De Loecker, Eeckhout, and Unger 2018, 31; see also Barkai 2016). From 1980 onward, change in this pattern has been clear: markups steadily increased from an average of 18 percent to nearly 67 percent in 2014, a three-and-a-half-fold increase. This is associated with rising profitability, falling labor share of income, falling low-skill wages, and rising wage inequality. In another recent study, Efraim Bemelech, Nittai Bergman, and Hyunseob Kim focus more directly on the concentration-wage relationship and find a powerful correspondence between them (2018).[34] Similarly, Nathan Wilmers shows a clear increase in the power of

34. "We use manufacturing plant-level data from the U.S. Census Bureau from 1977 to 2009 to provide evidence that wages are significantly lower in local labor markets in which employers are more concentrated. . . . We argue that the results are consistent with firms exploiting workers in the form of lower wages (than a competitive market level) in monopsonistic labor markets, particularly when labor bargaining power is weak and worker mobility is limited. We suggest that the decline in U.S. unionization and labor mobility during the 1980s and 1990s is important in explaining stagnation in wages. In addition, we show how higher employer concentration impairs the transmission of productivity growth into wage increases. Finally, we document an indirect China effect in which competition with Chinese exporters leads to a higher concentration of employers, resulting in even lower worker wages" (Bemelech, Bergman, and Kim 2018, 23–24).

larger "buying" firms over smaller "supplying" firms, as well as sizable downward effects on worker wages in the latter: "Suppliers that are more profitable or have a larger market share face increased negative waged effects when they become dependent on dominant buyers" (2018, 231). He estimates that "rising buyer power could explain around 10 percent of wage stagnation among nonfinancial firms since the 1970s" (231). In this issue, Wilmers shows that institutional and organizational constraints such as multi-employer collective and pattern bargaining, or employer collusion operated to lower inequality in the United States from 1968 to 1977 (2019). Moreover, unionization, establishment size, and pension provision reduced inequality not only among co-workers within workplaces, but also across workplaces.

The Decline in Countervailing Labor Institutions
Historically, collective bargaining and protective public policies, such as minimum wage legislation, have helped promote shared growth. Combined with the effects of declining employment in formerly union-intensive goods-producing sectors, anti-union government and corporate actions have led to precipitous declines in membership and coverage. For example, the union member share of employment for young (eighteen to thirty-four) male workers with less than a college degree fell from 24 percent in 1983 to 11.1 percent in 2001 and even further to 8.8 percent in 2014; for similar female workers, the decline was from 12.9 percent to 6.7 percent in 2001 and to 5.2 percent in 2014. By 2014, young male and female college graduates had much higher union membership rates

than those with less than a college degree (13.1 percent versus 8.8 percent for males; 9.8 percent versus 5.2 percent for females) (Howell 2019).[35]

Some have argued that the decline in union power has played little or no role in the rise in wage inequality,[36] but a long history of post–World War II research documents substantial union effects on both wage levels and wage inequality (Freeman and Medoff 1984; DiNardo, Fortin, and Lemieux 1996; Card 2001; Western and Rosenfeld 2011). In an important new study, Farber and his colleagues take advantage of new data that extend the record back to the 1930s and find large union effects on inequality (2018, 2–3).[37]

As the unionized share of the workforce has declined, the direct effects of unions on wage inequality has fallen (Goldin and Katz 2009, 5), but the lesson is not that unions are not an important part of the post-1979 decline in wage inequality. It is the reverse. The ebbing strength of unions has mattered a great deal for non-union workers as well as union members. Studying evidence dating to the 1940s, James Mosher finds that "when unionization was a credible threat in the U.S., nonunion firms paid a premium to workers to remain nonunion" (2007, 227), an effect that appears to be highly relevant to contemporary wage setting, as suggested by the wage policies of Amazon and other large retailers (see also Cardiff-Hicks, Lafontaine, and Shaw 2014). Mosher also makes the case that swings in union power have played an important role in explaining changes in the college-wage premium. Similarly, David Jacobs and Lindsey Meyers conclude that "politically inspired reductions in union membership, and

35. Young workers with a college degree experienced a similarly drastic decline in membership in the 1980s (from 22.4 percent to 14.8 percent for male workers, and from 16.7 percent to 10.9 percent for female workers between 1983 and 1990). It then remained roughly stable between 1990 and 2010. By 2014, 13.1 percent of young employed male college graduates and 9.8 percent of comparable female graduates were union members.

36. "Most economists, however, discount the role of unions in the increase in inequality" (Acemoglu, Aghion, and Violante 2001, 2, quoted in Farber et al. 2018, 1).

37. "We show that the income advantage accruing to union households relative to non-union households with the same demographics and skill proxies is roughly constant (between fifteen and twenty log points) over our eighty-year period, despite the huge swings in union density and composition." The authors argue that unions confer "a substantial advantage to what would otherwise have been low-income households, thus compressing the income distribution" (Farber et al. 2018, 3).

labor's diminished political opportunities during and after Reagan's presidency, meant unions no longer could slow the growth in U.S. inequality" (2014, 1; see also Schmitt and Mitukiewicz 2011).

An important source of the weakening of collective bargaining has been the increasing frequency of anti-union tactics by employers, which Kate Bronfenbrenner documents for 1986 through 2003 (2009). "The overwhelming majority of employers, either under the direction of an outside management consultant or their own in-house counsel, are running aggressive campaigns of threats, interrogation, surveillance, harassment, coercion, and retaliation" (Bronfenbrenner, quoted in Stelzner 2017, 233). Mark Stelzner documents the substantial changes in laws and norms after the early 1980s that facilitated these aggressive and effective actions. Three developments were particularly important: a reinterpretation of the National Labor Relations Act (NLRA) that produced a sharp shift from favorable to unfavorable adjudications; extensive delays in processing times in cases brought against employers for violations of the NLRA, mainly concerning certification of bargaining units and union election outcomes; and the sudden shift in management norms after President Reagan fired 11,400 air traffic controllers in 1981 that led to the increasing use of permanent replacement workers in strikes. "Employers suddenly became much more willing to use or threaten to use permanent replacements when workers went on strike" (Stelzner 2017, 240). The result was a dramatic decline in total case intake at the National Labor Relations Board and a collapse in the number of work stoppages per year (Stelzner 2017, figures 1 and 2).

The erosion of the value of the federal minimum wage is also pointed to as contributing substantially to the payment of low wages. Recent evidence overwhelmingly supports the existence of large positive wage effects of increasing minimum wages with little or no harmful consequences for employment or even hours worked (see, for example, Card and Krueger 1994; Schmitt 2013; Howell, Fiedler, and Luce 2016). In an important new study, Doruk Cengiz and his colleagues use new methods and data

to "infer the total change in jobs due to the policy by comparing the number of missing jobs below the new minimum wage to the excess number of jobs paying at (and above) the new minimum wage" (2018, 2). They find that for forty-six substantial minimum wage increases, after five years, "average wages of the affected earners increase significantly by 10.8 percent. We also find employment is little changed with a statistically insignificant increase of 0.2 percent" (2). Similarly, in a study of the effects of local minimum wages on food service wages and employment in six cities, Sylvia Allegretto and her colleagues find "statistically positive effects on earnings" but cannot "detect negative significant employment effects in any of the individual cities, or when pooling them together" (2018, 39). It is increasingly accepted that the decline in the real value of the legal minimum wage has played an important role in the post-1979 wage problem for workers at the bottom of the distribution.

Employment Restructuring Within the Firm
According to Weil's fissured workplace hypothesis, an important driver of the growth in wage inequality "over the last three decades has been an evolution of business organization that has fundamentally altered the employment relationship and, in turn, the way that wages are set for workers in a growing range of industries" (2017, 210). The same workers doing exactly the same tasks in the same jobs get lower wages after their tasks have been shifted to outside contractors (224). Examples include janitors, security guards, and cleaning service and food service workers. Considering the post-1979 increase in outsourcing to low-wage contractor firms, Appelbaum's research points to a "new labor market segmentation between lead firms and contractor firms. . . . The position of the worker's employer in the production network directly affects the worker's pay and working conditions. Thus, worker' wages depend not only on their own productivity characteristics, but on the relative power of their employer vis-à-vis other organizations in the network" (2017, 14).

Elizabeth Handwerker and James Spletzer provide strong supporting evidence of the growth in employment outsourcing and its effect on wages by measuring changes in occupation concentration, defined as the variety of occupations in particular establishments (2015). Driven by downward pressure on low-wage workers, "as much as 52 percent of overall wage inequality growth (63 percent of wage inequality growth between employers)" can be explained by their measures of occupational concentration (2). In updated work, Handwerker confirms these earlier findings, and concludes that "workers in establishments that are more concentrated in occupations overall earn lower wages" and that "changes in the distribution of occupational concentration are related to the growth in private-sector wage inequality" over this period (2018, 3). This restructuring and fissuring of the workplace helps explain recent evidence of substantial between-firm and between-establishment wage differentials for similarly skilled workers (see, for example, Abowd et al. 2012; Barth et al. 2016; Song et al. 2019).

In addition to the fissuring caused by domestic outsourcing, the offshoring of production and the rise in trade competition, especially with China, have put downward pressure on wages. But the effects of these developments on production and nonsupervisory workers are concentrated in manufacturing sectors. While these are often vitally consequential for local communities, some have argued that these are not at the root of the wage inequality problem. According to Lemieux, "On balance, there is at best some weak evidence that offshoring has contributed to the growth in wage inequality in the United States over the last few decades" (2011, 18).

Although wage setting in the United States takes place almost exclusively within the firm, large and persistent non–skill-based wage differentials have been shown at the industry level in many studies that extend back to at least the 1940s. As Furman and Orszag point out, much recent research is consistent "with the notion that firms are wage setters rather than wage takers in a less than perfectly competitive market-place" (2015, 1). One example is the recent work of Tali Kristal and Yinon Cohen, who have explored the relative importance of technology-driven demand for skills, the supply of skills, and institutional factors. They conclude that "Contrary to that [SBTC] view, we find that the decline of pay-setting institutions is almost twice as important as technology-driven demand for skilled labor in explaining rising inequality within US industries" (2014, 207).

Institutions and Job Quality:
How the United States Compares
One way to explore the importance of the institutional setting for job quality—and for who gets good jobs—is with comparisons across similarly developed countries confronted by similar technological, deindustrializing, and globalization pressures. Interpreting the evidence on wage and wage inequality trends as broadly similar across rich countries, John Van Reenen concludes that similar market forces, rather than institutional differences, must be the main explanation because he sees inequality trends as quite similar across countries: "in terms of these major long-term trends (in inequality), many of the similarities across countries suggests to me that country-specific institutions are unlikely to be the fundamental causes of such changes, as institutions differ so much between nations" (2011, 731). By contrast, Acemoglu and Autor, citing nine studies, argue that "changes in the earnings distribution have been quite different in different countries" (2011, 1160). But in their (competitive market) view, regulations and other institutional "constraints" contribute to differences in wage outcomes across countries not directly, through their effects on bargaining power, but because they determine which technologies are adopted.[38]

We share Acemoglu and Autor's view of the cross-country variation in wage levels and wage inequality but suggest a much simpler and far more plausible explanation: that institutions, policies, and employer practices play central roles in determining differences in the strength

---

38. See also Acemoglu and Autor, who mention *institution* just once, and the reference is to educational institutions (2012).

and character of worker bargaining power across countries. This conclusion is supported by a number of recent cross-country studies. For example, the Russell Sage Foundation's low-wage project concluded that "the most important influence on the observed differences in low-wage work is the 'inclusiveness' of a country's labor market institutions" (Gautié and Schmitt 2010, 7). Similarly, a recent study by IMF researchers Florence Jaumotte and Carolina Buitron explores the causes of rising inequality in the rich world (2015). According to the authors, although "high-income countries have been affected in broadly similar ways by SBTC and globalization, they have seen inequality rise at different speeds" and for this reason they focus "on the role played by labor market institutions in 20 advanced countries during 1980–2010" (5). "We find evidence that the decline in union density—the fraction of union members in the workforce—is strongly associated with the rise of top income shares. . . . Our empirical results also indicate that unions can affect income redistribution through their influence on public policy. We further find that reductions in the minimum wage relative to the median wage are related to significant increases in inequality" (6).

Senior researchers at the OECD have also attempted to explain rising inequality across rich countries with empirical data that allow them to explore the importance of cognitive skills and institutions (Broeke et al. 2019). They interpret recent cross-country research as finding that differences in the "net supply of skills" (the quantity supplied versus demanded) have explained only a small part of the variation in wages across countries, citing Blau and Kahn (1996, 2005) and Devroye and Freeman (2001). While Edwin Leuven, Hessel Oosterbeek, and Hans van Ophem claim "that around one-third of the variation in relative wages between skill groups across countries could be explained by differences in the net supply of skills" (2004, cited in Broecke, Quintini, and Vandeweyer 2019, 251), more recently, and with the use of a

far superior measure of cognitive skills, the OECD's Survey of Adult Skills (PIAAC), studies by Anita Pena (2014) and Marco Paccagnella (2015) "also find that skills contribute very little to international differences in wage inequality, and that skill prices play a far more important role" and conclude that "differences in inequality must be driven primarily by differences in institutions—a view echoed by another recent paper" (cited in Jovicic 2015, 252).[39]

Challenging these conclusions on the relatively minor role played by cognitive skills in explaining cross-country wage inequality, Stijn Broecke, Glenda Quintini, and Marieke Vandeweyer argue that these studies may have failed to fully account for the effects of "skills supply and demand" on variations in wage inequality (2019). To test this possibility, they use the same PIAAC data with a "demand and supply model to study the relationship between the net supply of skills . . . and wage inequality" and find that "market forces do indeed matter" but only for the top half of the distribution (the 90:50 wage ratio), accounting for less than one-third (29 percent) of the gap between the United States and other rich countries (253). Their measure of the net supply of skills "explains little of the higher wage inequality at the bottom of the wage distribution" (253).

This failure of skills to explain any of the far higher American wage inequality in the bottom half would seem to be the headline finding. Another seemingly important but unnoted result is the strong statistical links between institutions and cross-country differences in "bottom-end" job quality: although cognitive skills show no effect on the 50:10 wage ratio in any of their tests, when controlling for the net supply of skills, a number of institutional variables (the minimum wage, collective bargaining coverage, the size of the public sector) are found to be highly significant predictors (table 7.5, panel c).

In sum, a large and empirically sophisticated recent literature has shown that the demand and supply of cognitive skill cannot ex-

---

39. Institutional effects on cross-country differences in bottom-end wage inequality are best shown in separate regression tests because, as the authors point out, "there is a high degree of collinearity between the institutional variables" (Broecke, Quintini, and Vandeweyer 2019, 274).

plain trends in cross-country wage inequality. Thomas Lemieux has concluded that "the routinization hypothesis, just like SBTC, cannot really explain why inequality expanded in some countries but not in others" (2011, 17).

ENHANCING JOB QUALITY: POLICIES

Many of the severe labor market problems that American workers experience today, and will experience in the coming decade, are rooted not in the shortage of jobs, or in the quality of workers themselves, but in the quality of jobs employers offer. The most devastating effects of declining job quality, especially for workers with less than advanced degrees, has been stagnant or declining real (inflation-adjusted) wages and compensation, growing wage inequality, and the increasing incidence of low- and poverty-wage jobs—especially pronounced for young workers (ages eighteen to thirty-four). In addition, many have asserted a rapid expansion in job insecurity in standard, full-time jobs, and in the various forms of nonstandard jobs. The increasing severity of the low-wage problem, rising job insecurity, and the likely growth in nonstandard work arrangements has been linked to a large number of social and economic problems, such as family fragmentation, poverty and inequality, and poor individual well-being. Our discussion of the problem of low job-quality points to the need for new labor and social policies to shift the American economy from the extractive growth path of the post-1979 period to a new shared-growth path.

The different explanations for recent trends in job quality we have summarized have sharply different policy implications. In the competitive market vision, the forces of supply and demand external to the firm drive wage growth and wage inequality (and more broadly job quality). If the main source of rising earnings inequality is a rising demand for highly educated workers from computer-driven technological change unmatched by increases in the supply of college graduates (Autor 2010, 35), then raising worker skills must be the main policy solution. Indeed, in his overview of the RBTC-polarization account of earnings inequality for the Hamilton Project, Autor offers four policy recommendations, three of which are skills related: increase the supply of college graduates, improve K–12 education, and expand training programs (2010, 35). The fourth is to increase investment in research and development and infrastructure. The need to rebalance bargaining power between employers and workers is not mentioned.

By contrast, the contested market (imperfect competition) and social-institutional perspectives see wage and labor market outcomes as mainly a function of bargaining power, which in turn is driven by prevailing institutions and social policies in addition to market forces and the strategic goals of firms (such as the reduction of labor costs via workplace fissuring). The extent to which technology, education, and other workplace-relevant skills matter for long-term changes in the distribution of wages and income is also determined by prevailing institutions and policies. If bargaining power is central to job-quality outcomes, it is necessary to implement both product market regulations designed to increase competitive market forces by reducing employer monopoly and monopsony power over suppliers and workers, and protective labor regulations that can provide workers with countervailing power.

These differences across labor market perspectives are not mutually exclusive because each emphasizes indispensable components of a comprehensive set of policies needed to enhance job quality. It is essential to upgrade worker skills because high-quality jobs of the future will require workers with high levels of various kinds of skills. Access to educational opportunities needs to be extended to all, just as alternatives to colleges and universities to train future workers need to be nurtured. Policies that enhance education and skills as well as social capital are necessary to enable people to navigate relatively insecure labor market conditions; the rapidity of technological change means that people need to refresh their skills periodically. Policies that increase the demand for good jobs, such as public investments in needed infrastructure, are also necessary to maintain full employment and create well-paying jobs that engage the skills that result from education and training. The list of pressing needs is long; it includes rebuilding our nation's decaying infrastructure of roads, bridges, schools, airports, trains, and mass transit.

Nevertheless, in our view, a serious attack on unshared growth—one that can make a big difference in the next decade or so—requires major institutional and policy changes designed to alter bargaining power over rents (above-market returns) in the labor market between employers and workers. Institutions can make a big difference in enhancing the quality of jobs, as Françoise Carré and Chris Tilly demonstrate vividly in their study of differences in job quality of retail jobs in different companies and countries (2017). This is consistent with cross-country evidence that strongly suggests that institutional or policy arrangements are possible that can generate far more equitable and efficient outcomes than are often observed in the United States.

Thus, policies to increase good jobs and make bad jobs better need to focus on institutional changes as well as on supply and demand. The Economic Policy Institute's agenda of enhancing the quality of jobs for working Americans offers a variety of suggestions for needed institutional changes (Bivens et al. 2014, 2018; see also Osterman 2008; Krueger 2018). These include policies supporting good jobs such as increasing the federal minimum wage and making labor law friendlier to both collective bargaining (such as ending forced arbitration in employment contracts) and individual bargaining (such as restricting the use by firms of noncompete clauses that keep workers from moving to other employers, and the closely related no-poaching clauses in franchise contracts).

It is also essential to decouple economic security from market work as much as possible. In this issue, Dwyer and Wright propose the use of state subsidies and policies to facilitate the "social and solidarity" economy such as the provision of eldercare and childcare in Quebec (2019). Moreover, as discussed, concerns about nonstandard work arrangements such as temporary work stem from the fact that workers in these arrangements often do not have access to health insurance benefits. The Affordable Care Act is an important step in this direction,

though it has yet to be fully implemented, and much more support is needed for childcare and paid sick and family leaves. Later in this issue, Lambert, Henly, and Kim point to the importance of laws regarding fair and predictable scheduling for mitigating some of the negative effects of precarious work (2019).

Realizing these needed policy changes depends on the ability of workers to push the government to adopt protective labor market and welfare institutions and to encourage collaborative efforts between managers and workers. The decline of unions is a major reason for the shift in power relations from the more balanced situation during the thirty years after World War II to the greater power exercised by employers in the United States since the 1980s. A key question here concerns the kind of worker power best suited to meet the challenges created by the changing nature of employment relations, whether these be traditional unions or forms such as occupational groups or other worker associations.

The necessary policy changes must also recognize the growing diversity of the labor force especially in terms of age, race-ethnicity, immigration status, and gender that has resulted in different people having distinct needs. Elsewhere in this issue, Liu and Nazareno show that low-skill workers (especially minority and immigrant workers) are more likely to be in nonstandard jobs, underscoring the overrepresentation of the more vulnerable groups in the population in nonstandard jobs (2019). Family structures have become more diverse and include growing numbers of dual-earner and single-parent families that need help to reconcile demands of work and family life through better provision of childcare, parental leave policies, flextime, and other forms of flexible scheduling.

The obstacles to implementing policies to enhance job quality that would require a tougher stance on monopoly (price setting) and monopsony (wage setting) power, stronger protective labor institutions and policies, shifts in human resource policies and norms about shared within-firm productivity growth are enormous. Nevertheless, because low-wage and insecure jobs are key factors behind the concerns and resentments that have fueled social and political transformations of recent years, enhancing job quality remains a pressing concern. Although policies to address these problems require public policy actions at both national and local levels, progress in the short term is most likely to occur at the local level because states and localities have taken the lead in minimum wage laws, flexible scheduling, and other ways of enhancing job quality.

REFERENCES

Abowd, John M., Francis Kramarz, Paul Lengermann, Kevin L. McKinney, and Sebastien Roux. 2012. "Persistent Inter-Industry Wage Differences: Rent Sharing and Opportunity Costs." *IZA Journal of Labor Economics* 1(1): 7. Accessed February 28, 2019. https://izajole.springeropen.com/articles/10.1186/2193-8997-1-7.

Abowd, John M., Kevin L. McKinney, and Nellie L. Zhao. 2017. "Earnings Inequality and Mobility Trends in the United States: Nationally Representative Estimates from Longitudinally Linked Employer-Employee Data." *NBER* working paper no. 23224. Cambridge, Mass.: National Bureau of Economic Research.

Abraham, Katherine G., John C. Haltiwanger, Kristin Sandusky, and James R. Spletzer. 2017. "Measuring the Gig Economy: Current Knowledge and Open Issues." Paper presented at Measuring and Accounting for Innovation in the 21st Century, Cambridge, Mass. (March 10–11, 2017).

Acemoglu, Daron, Philippe Aghion, and Giovanni L. Violante. 2001. "Deunionization, Technical Change and Inequality." In *Carnegie-Rochester Conference Series on Public Policy*, vol. 55, edited by Marvin Goodfriend and Stanley E. Zin. New York: Elsevier.

Acemoglu, Daron, and David Autor. 2011. "Skills, Tasks and Technologies: Implications for Employment and Earnings." *Handbook of Labor Economics*, vol. 4B, edited by Orley Ashenfelter and David Card. San Diego, Calif.: Elsevier.

——. 2012. "What Does Human Capital Do? A Review of Goldin and Katz's *The Race Between Education and Technology*." *Journal of Economic Literature* 50(2): 426–63.

Agell, Jonas. 1999. "On the Benefits from Rigid Labour Markets: Norms, Market Failures, and Social Insurance." *Economic Journal* 109(453): 143–64.

Allegretto, Sylvia, Anna Godoey, Carl Nadler, and Michael Reich. 2018. "The New Wave of Local Minimum Wage Policies: Evidence from Six Cities." Berkeley: University of California, Institute for Research on Labor and Employment, Center on Wage and Employment Dynamics.

Amable, Bruno. 2016. "Institutional Complementarities in the Dynamic Comparative Analysis of Capitalism." *Journal of Institutional Economics* 12(1): 79–103.

Appelbaum, Eileen. 2017. "What's Behind the Increase in Inequality?" Washington, D.C.: Center for Economic and Policy Research (September).

Appelbaum, Eileen, and Rosemary Batt. 2017. "The Networked Organization: Implications for Jobs and Inequality." In *Making Work More Equal: A New Labour Market Segmentation Approach*, edited by Damian Grimshaw, Colette Fagan, Gail Hebson, and Isabel Tavora. Manchester, UK: Manchester University Press.

Appelbaum, Eileen, Arne Kalleberg, and Hye Jin Rho. 2019. "Nonstandard Work Arrangements and Older Americans, 2005–2017." Washington, D.C.: Center for Economic and Policy Research and Economic Policy Institute.

Ashenfelter, Orley, and David Card, eds. 2011. *Handbook of Labor Economics*, vol. 4B. Amsterdam: Elsevier-North Holland.

Atkinson, Anthony B., and Andrea Brandolini. 2011. "On the Identification of the Middle Class." *ECINEQ* working paper no. 2011-217. Rome: Society for the Study of Economic Inequality.

Autor, David H. 2010. *The Polarization of Job Opportunities in the U.S. Labor Market: Implications for Employment and Earnings*. Washington, D.C.: Center for American Progress and The Hamilton Project.

——. 2014. "Skills, Education, and the Rise of Earnings Inequality Among the 'Other 99 Percent'." *Science* 344(6186): 843–50.

——. 2015. "Why Are There Still So Many Jobs? The History and Future of Workplace Automation." *Journal of Economic Perspectives* 29(3): 3–30.

——. 2017. "How Long Has This Been Going On? A Discussion of 'Recent Flattening in the Higher / Education Wage Premium: Polarization, Skill Downgrading, or Both?' By Robert G. Valletta."

Paper presented at the NBER Conference on Research and Income in Wealth "Measuring and Accounting for Innovation in the 21st Century," Washington, D.C. (March 10–11, 2017).

Autor, David H., and David Dorn. 2013. "The Growth of Low-Skill Service Jobs and the Polarization of the U.S. Labor Market." *American Economic Review* 103(5): 1553–97.

Autor, David H., and Lawrence Katz. 2010. "Grand Challenges in the Study of Employment and Technological Change." Paper submitted to the National Science Foundation. Arlington, Va. (September 27, 2010).

Autor, David H., Lawrence F. Katz, and Melissa S. Kearney. 2005. "Rising Wage Inequality: The Role of Composition and Prices." *NBER* working paper no. 11628. Cambridge, Mass.: National Bureau of Economic Research.

———. 2006. "The Polarization of the U.S. Labor Market." *American Economic Review* 96(2): 189–194.

———. 2008. "Trends in U.S. Wage Inequality: Revising the Revisionists." *Review of Economics and Statistics* 90(2): 300–23.

Autor, David H., Lawrence F. Katz, and Alan Krueger. 1998. "Computing Inequality: Have Computers Changed the Labor Market?" *Quarterly Review of Economics* 113(4): 1169–214.

Autor, David H., Frank Levy, and Richard J. Murnane. 2003. "The Skill Content of Recent Technological Change: An Empirical Exploration." *Quarterly Journal of Economics* 116(4): 1279–333.

Azar, Jose, Ioana Marinescu, and Marshall I. Steinbaum. 2017. "Labor Market Concentration." *NBER* working paper no. 24147. Cambridge, Mass.: National Bureau of Economic Research.

Bárány, Zsófia L., and Christian Siegel. 2018. "Job Polarization and Structural Change." *American Economic Journal: Macroeconomics* 10(1): 57–89.

Barkai, Simcha. 2016. "Declining Labor and Capital Shares." Chicago: The University of Chicago Booth School of Business. Accessed March 26, 2019. http://home.uchicago.edu/~barkai/doc/BarkaiDecliningLaborCapital.pdf.

Barth, Erling, Alex Bryson, James C. Davis, and Richard Freeman. 2016. "It's Where You Work: Increases in Earnings Dispersion across Establishments and Individuals in the United States." *Journal of Labor Economics* 34(S2): S67–S97.

Beaudry, Paul, David A. Green, and Benjamin M. Sand. 2013. "The Great Reversal in the Demand for Skill and Cognitive Tasks." *NBER* working paper no. 18901. Cambridge, Mass.: National Bureau of Economic Research.

Becker, Gary S. 1975. *Human Capital*. Cambridge, Mass.: National Bureau of Economic Research.

Benmelech, Efraim, Nittai Bergman, and Hyunseob Kim. 2018. "Strong Employers and Weak Employees: How Does Employer Concentration Affect Wages?" *NBER* working paper no. 24307. Cambridge, Mass.: National Bureau of Economic Research.

Bernhardt, Annette. 2014. "Labor Standards and the Reorganization of Work: Gaps in Data and Research." *IRLE* working paper no. 100–14. Berkeley, Calif.: University of California, Institute for Research on Labor and Employment.

Bernhardt, Annette, Rosemary Batt, Susan Houseman, and Eileen Appelbaum. 2015. "Domestic Outsourcing in the U.S.: A Research Agenda to Assess Trends and Effects on Job Quality." Paper prepared for the Future of Work Symposium, U.S. Department of Labor, Washington (December 2015).

Bivens, Josh, Elise Gould, Lawrence Mishel, and Heidi Shierholz. 2014. "Raising America's Pay: Why It's Our Central Economic Policy Challenge." Briefing Paper no. 378. Washington, D.C.: Economic Policy Institute.

Bivens, Josh, Lawrence Mishel, and John Schmitt. 2018. "It's Not Just Monopoly and Monopsony: How Market Power Has Affected American Wages." Washington, D.C.: Economic Policy Institute.

Blau, Francine D., and Lawrence M. Kahn. 1996. "International Differences in Male Wage Inequality: Institution Versus Market Forces." *Journal of Political Economy* 104(4): 791–837.

———. 2005. "Do Cognitive Test Scores Explain Higher U.S. Wage Inequality?" *Review of Economics and Statistics* 87(1): 184–93.

Bloom, Nicholas, Erik Brynjolfsson, Lucia Foster, Ron S. Jarmin, Megha Patnaik, Itay Saporta-Eksten, and John Van Reenen. 2017. "What Drives Differences in Management?" *NBER* working paper no. 23300. Cambridge, Mass.: National Bureau of Economic Research.

Bluestone, Barry, and Bennett Harrison. 1982. *The Deindustrialization of America*. New York: Basic Books.

Boeri, Tito, and Jan van Ours. 2013. *The Economics of Imperfect Labour Markets*, 2nd ed. Princeton, N.J.: Princeton University Press.

Bowles, Samuel, Herbert Gintis, and Melissa Osborne. 2001. "The Determinants of Earnings: A Behavioral Approach." *Journal of Economic Literature* 39(4): 1137–76.

Boyer, Robert. 2006. "Employment and Decent Work in the Era of 'Flexicurity.'" *DESA* Working Paper no. 32. New York: United Nations.

Brady, David, and Benjamin Sosnaud. 2010. "The Politics of Economic Inequality." In *Handbook of Politics: State and Society in Global Perspective*, edited by Kevin Leicht and Craig Jenkins. New York: Springer.

Broecke, Stijn, Glenda Quintini, and Marieke Vandeweyer. 2019. "Wage Inequality and Cognitive Skills: Reopening the Debate." In *Education, Skills, and Technical Change: Implications for Future US GDP Growth*, edited by Charles R. Hulten and Valerie A. Ramey. NBER Studies in Income and Wealth, vol. 77. Chicago: University of Chicago Press.

Bronfenbrenner, Kate. 2009. "No Hold Barred: The Intensification of Employer Opposition to Organizing." Briefing paper no. 235. Washington, D.C.: Economic Policy Institute.

Cappelli, Peter H. 2015. "Skill Gaps, Skill Shortages, and Skill Mismatches: Evidence and Arguments for the United States." *ILR Review* 68(2): 251–90.

Card, David. 2001. "The Effect of Unions on Wage Inequality in the US Labor Market." *ILR Review* 54(2): 296–315.

Card, David, Ana Rute Cardoso, Jorg Heining, and Patrick Kline. 2016. "Firms and Labor Market Inequality: Evidence and Some Theory." *NBER* working paper no. 22850. Cambridge, Mass.: National Bureau of Economic Research.

Card, David, and John E. DiNardo. 2002. "Skill-Biased Technological Change and Rising Wage Inequality: Some Problems and Puzzles." *Journal of Labor Economics* 20(4): 733–83.

Card, David, and Alan B. Krueger. 1994. "Minimum Wages and Employment: A Case Study of the Fast-Food Industry in New Jersey and Pennsylvania." *American Economic Review* 84(4): 772–93.

Cardiff-Hicks, Briana, Francine Lafontaine, and Kathryn Shaw. 2014. "Do Large Modern Retailers Pay Premium Wages?" *NBER* working paper no. 20313. Cambridge, Mass.: National Bureau of Economic Research.

Carré, Françoise, and Chris Tilly. 2017. *Where Bad Jobs Are Better: Retail Jobs Across Countries and Companies*. New York: Russell Sage Foundation.

CEA. 2016. "Labor Market Monopsony: Trends, Consequences, and Policy Responses." Washington: White House Council of Economic Advisors.

Cengiz, Doruk, Arindrajit Dube, Attila Lindner, and Ben Zipperer. 2018. "The Effect of Minimum Wages on Low-Wage Jobs: Evidence from the United States Using a Bunching Estimator." *CEP* discussion paper no. 1531. London: London School of Economics and Political Science, Centre for Economic Performance.

Cobb, Adam. 2016. "How Firms Shape Income Inequality: Stakeholder Power, Executive Decision Making, and the Structuring of Employment Relationships." *Academy of Management Review* 41(2): 324–48.

De Loecker, Jan, Jan Eeckhout, and Gabriel Unger. 2018. "The Rise of Market Power and the Macroeconomic Implications." Unpublished manuscript, Department of Economics, Katholieke Universiteit Leuven. Accessed February 28, 2019. http://www.janeeckhout.com/wp-content/uploads/RMP.pdf.

Deming, David J. 2017. "The Growing Importance of Social Skills in the Labor Market." *Quarterly Journal of Economics* 132(4): 1593–640.

Devroye, Dan, and Richard Freeman. 2001. "Does Inequality in Skills Explain Inequality of Earnings Across Advanced Countries?" *NBER* working paper no. 8140. Cambridge, Mass.: National Bureau of Economic Research.

DiNardo, John, Nichole M. Fortin, and Thomas Lemieux. 1996. "Labor Market Institutions and the Distribution of Wages, 1973–1992: A Semiparametric Approach." *Econometrica* 64(5): 1000–1046.

Doeringer, Peter B., and Michael J. Piore. 1971. *Internal Labor Markets and Manpower Analysis*. Lexington, Mass: D. C. Heath.

Dunlop, John. 1985. "Needed: An Interdisciplinary Approach to Labor Markets and Wage Differentials." *Monthly Labor Review* 108(7): 30–32.

Dwyer, Rachel E., and Erik Olin Wright. 2019. "Low-Wage Job Growth, Polarization, and the Limits and Opportunities of the Service Economy." *RSF: The Russell Sage Foundation Journal of the Social*

Sciences 5(4): 56–76. DOI: 10.7758/RSF.2019 .5.4.02.

Economic Policy Institute (EPI). 2017. *State of Working America Data Library*. Updated February 13, 2017. Accessed March 1, 2019. https://www .epi.org/data.

———. 2018. "The Productivity-Pay Gap." Accessed March 1, 2019. https://www.epi.org/productivity -pay-gap.

Engbom, Niklas, and Christian Moser. 2017. "Earnings Inequality and the Minimum Wage: Evidence from Brazil." *CESifo* working paper series no. 6393. Munich: Center for Economic Studies.

Esping-Andersen, Gøsta. 1990. *The Three Worlds of Welfare Capitalism*. Princeton, N.J.: Princeton University Press.

European Commission. 2001. *Employment in Europe 2001: Recent Trends and Prospects*. London: European Commission, Employment & Social Affairs.

Farber, Henry, Daniel Herbst, Ilyana Kuziemko, and Suresh Naidu. 2018. "Unions and Inequality Over the Twentieth Century: New Evidence from Survey Data." Sante Fe, N.M.: Santa Fe Institute. Accessed February 28, 2019. http://tuvalu.santafe .edu/~snaidu/papers/union_sub3.pdf.

Findlay, Patricia, Arne L. Kalleberg, and Chris Warhurst, eds. 2013. "The Challenge of Job Quality." *Human Relations* 66(4): 441–51.

Folbre, Nancy. 2016. "Just Deserts? Earnings Inequality and Bargaining Power in the U.S. Economy." Working paper. Washington, D.C.: Washington Center for Equitable Growth.

Freeman, Richard B. 1988. "Does the New Generation of Labor Economists Know More Than the Old Generation?" In *How Labor Markets Work: Reflections on Theory and Practice by John Dunlop, Clark Kerr, Richard Lester and Lloyd Reynolds*, edited by Bruce Kaufman. Lanham, Md.: Lexington Books.

———. 2007. "Labor Market Institutions Around the World." *NBER* working paper no. 13242. Cambridge, Mass.: National Bureau of Economic Research.

———. 2013. "Failing the Test? The Flexible U.S. Job Market in the Great Recession." *NBER* working paper no. 19587. Cambridge, Mass.: National Bureau of Economic Research.

Freeman, Richard B., and James L. Medoff. 1984. *What Do Unions Do?* New York: Basic Books.

Furman, Jason, and Peter Orszag. 2015. "A Firm-Level Perspective on the Role of Rents in the Rise in Inequality." Presentation at *A Just Society* Centennial Event in Honor of Joseph Stiglitz, Columbia University, New York City (October 16, 2015).

Gabaix, Xavier, Augustin Landier, and Julien Sauvagnat. 2014. "CEO Pay and Firm Size: An Update After the Crisis." *The Economic Journal* 124(574) (February): F40–F59.

Gautié, Jérôme, and John Schmitt, eds. 2010. *Low-Wage Work in the Wealthy World*. New York: Russell Sage Foundation.

Ghai, Dharam. 2003. "Decent Work: Concept and Indicators." *International Labour Review* 142(2): 113–45.

Gittleman, Maury, and David R. Howell. 1995. "Changes in the Structure and Quality of Jobs in the United States: Effects by Race and Gender, 1973–1990." *Industrial and Labour Relations Review* 48(3): 420–40.

Goldin, Claudia, and Lawrence F. Katz. 2007. "Long-Run Changes in the Wage Structure: Narrowing, Widening, Polarizing." *Brookings Papers on Economic Activity* no. 2. Washington, D.C.: Brookings Institute. Accessed February 28, 2019. https:// www.brookings.edu/bpea-articles/long-run -changes-in-the-wage-structure-narrowing -widening-polarizing.

———. 2008. *The Race Between Education and Technology*. Cambridge, Mass.: Harvard University Press.

———. 2009. "The Future of Inequality: The Other Reason Education Matters so Much." In *Improving "No Child Left Behind": Linking World-Class Standards to America's Economic Recovery*. Washington, D.C.: Aspen Institute.

Goldschmidt, Deborah, and Johannes F. Schmieder. 2017. "The Rise of Domestic Outsourcing and the Evolution of the German Wage Structure." *Quarterly Review of Economics* 132(3): 1165–217.

Goos, Maarten, and Alan Manning. 2007. "Lovely and Lousy Jobs: The Rising Polarization of Work in Britain." *Review of Economics and Statistics* 89(1): 118–33.

Gordon, David M., Richard Edwards, and Michael Reich. 1982. *Segmented Work, Divided Workers*. New York: Cambridge University Press.

Granovetter, Mark. 2005. "The Impact of Social Structure on Economic Outcomes." *Journal of Economic Perspectives* 19(1): 33–50.

Green, Francis. 2006. *Demanding Work: The Paradox of Job Quality in the Affluent Economy*. Princeton, N.J.: Princeton University Press.

Hall, Peter A., and David Soskice. 2001. "Introduction to Varieties of Capitalism." In *Varieties of Capitalism: The Institutional Foundations of Comparative Advantage*, edited by Peter A. Hall and David Soskice. Oxford: Oxford University Press.

Handwerker, Elizabeth Weber. 2018. "Increased Concentration of Occupations, Outsourcing, and Growing Wage Inequality in the United States." Unpublished manuscript, U.S. Bureau of Labor Statistics.

Handwerker, Elizabeth Weber, and James R. Spletzer. 2015. "The Role of Establishments and the Concentration of Occupations in Wage Inequality." *IZA* discussion paper no. 9294. Bonn: Institute for the Study of Labor.

Harrison, Bennett, and Barry Bluestone. 1988. *The Great U-Turn: Corporate Restructuring and the Polarizing of America*. New York: Basic Books.

Hirschman, Albert O. 1991. *The Rhetoric of Reaction: Perversity, Futility, Jeopardy*. Cambridge, Mass.: Harvard University Press.

Holzer, Harry J., Julia I. Lane, David B. Rosenblum, and Fredrik Andersson. 2011. *Where Are All the Good Jobs Going?* New York: Russell Sage Foundation.

Howell, David R. 1989. "Production Technology and the Interindustry Wage Structure." *Industrial Relations* 28(1): 32–50.

———. 2002. "Increasing Earnings Inequality and Unemployment in Developed Countries: Markets, Institutions, and the 'Unified Theory.'" *Politics & Society* 30(2): 193–243.

———. 2019. "What Happened to Decent Jobs? The Decline in American Job Quality, 1979–2014." Working Paper. Washington, D.C.: Washington Center for Equitable Growth.

Howell, David R., Kea Fiedler, and Stephanie Luce. 2016. "What's the Right Minimum Wage? Reframing the Debate from 'No Job Loss' to a 'Minimum Living Wage.'" Washington, D.C.: Washington Center for Equitable Growth.

Howell, David R., and Friedrich Huebler. 2005. "Wage Compression and the Unemployment Crisis: Labor market Institutions, Skills, and Inequality-Unemployment Tradeoffs." In *Fighting Unemployment: The Limits of Free Market Orthodoxy*, edited by David R. Howell. Oxford: Oxford University Press.

Howell, David R., and Susan S. Wieler. 1998. "Skill-Biased Demand Shifts and the Wage Collapse in the United States: A Critical Perspective." *Eastern Economic Journal* 24(3): 343–66.

Howell, David R., and Edward N. Wolff. 1991. "Skills, Bargaining Power and Rising Interindustry Wage Inequality Since 1970." *Review of Radical Political Economics* 23(1-2): 30–37.

Hunt, Jennifer, and Ryan Nunn. 2019. "Is Employment Polarization Informative About Wage Inequality and Is Employment Really Polarizing." Unpublished manuscript, Rutgers University.

International Labour Organization (ILO). 2016. *Key Indicators of the Labor Market*. Geneva: ILO.

Jacobs, David, and Lindsey Myers. 2014. "Union Strength, Neoliberalism, and Inequality: Contingent Political Analyses of U.S. Income Differences Since 1950." *American Sociological Review* 79(4): 1–23.

Jacoby, Sanford M. 2005. *The Embedded Corporation: Corporate Governance and Employment Relations in Japan and the United States*. Princeton, N.J.: Princeton University Press.

Jaumotte, Florence, and Carolina Osorio Buitron. 2015. "Inequality and Labor Market Institutions." *IMF* staff discussion note. Washington, D.C.: International Monetary Fund.

Jensen, Michael C., and William H. Meckling. 1976. "Theory of the Firm: Managerial Behavior, Agency Costs and Ownership Structure." *Journal of Financial Economics* 3(4): 305–60.

Jovicic, Sonja. 2015. "Wage Inequality, Skill Inequality, and Employment: Evidence from PIACC." *Schumpeter* discussion paper no. 2015-007. Wuppertal, Germany: University of Wuppertal.

Kalleberg, Arne L. 2000. "Nonstandard Employment Relations: Part-Time, Temporary, and Contract Work." *Annual Review of Sociology* 26(1): 341–65.

———. 2011. *Good Jobs, Bad Jobs: The Rise of Polarized and Precarious Employment Systems in the United States, 1970s to 2000s*. New York: Russell Sage Foundation.

———. 2016. "Good Jobs, Bad Jobs." In *The Sage Handbook of the Sociology of Work and Employment*, edited by Stephen Edgell, Heidi Gottfried, and Edward Granter. Thousand Oaks, Calif.: Sage Publications.

———. 2018. *Precarious Lives: Job Insecurity and Well-Being in Rich Democracies*. Cambridge: Polity Press.

Kalleberg, Arne L., Edith Rasell, Naomi Cassirer, Barbara F. Reskin, Ken Hudson, David Webster, and Eileen Appelbaum. 1997. *Nonstandard Work, Substandard Jobs: Flexible Work Arrangements in the U.S.* Washington, D.C.: Economic Policy Institute and Women's Research and Education Institute.

Kalleberg, Arne L., Barbara F. Reskin, and Ken Hudson. 2000. "Bad Jobs in America: Standard and Nonstandard Employment Relations and Job Quality in the United States." *American Sociological Review* 65(2): 256–78.

Kaplan, Steven N., and Joshua Rauh. 2013. "It's the Market: The Broad-Based Rise in the Return to Top Talent." *Journal of Economic Perspectives* 27(1): 35–56.

Katz, Lawrence F., and Alan B. Krueger. 2016. "The Rise and Nature of Alternative Work Arrangements in the United States, 1995–2015." *NBER* working paper no. 22667. Cambridge, Mass.: National Bureau of Economic Research.

———. 2019. "Understanding Trends in Alternative Work Arrangements in the United States." *NBER* working paper no. 25425. Cambridge, Mass.: National Bureau of Economic Research.

Katz, Lawrence F., and Kevin Murphy. 1992. "Changes in Relative Wages, 1963–1987: Supply and Demand Factors." *Quarterly Journal of Economics* 107 (February): 35–78.

Kaufman, Bruce E. 1988. "The Postwar View of Labor Markets and Wage Determination." In *How Labor Markets Work: Reflections on Theory and Practice by John Dunlop, Clark Kerr, Richard Lester, and Lloyd Reynolds*, edited by Bruce Kaufman. Lanham, Md.: Lexington Books.

———. 2004. "The Institutional and Neoclassical Schools in Labor Economics." In *The Institutionalist Tradition in Labor Economics*, edited by Dell P. Champlin and Janet T. Knoedle. Armonk, N.Y.: M. E. Sharpe.

———. 2007. "The Impossibility of a Perfectly Competitive Labour Market." *Cambridge Journal of Economics* 31 (April): 775–87.

———. 2010. "The Theoretical Foundation of Industrial Relations and Its Implications." *Industrial and Labor Relations Review* 64(1): 74–108.

Kerr, Clark. 1994. "The Social Economics Revisionists: The 'Real World' Study of Labor Markets and Institutions." In *Labor Economics and Industrial Relations: Markets and Institutions*, edited by Clark Kerr and Paul D. Staudohar. Cambridge, Mass.: Harvard University Press.

Kochan, Thomas A., Harry C. Katz, and Robert B. McKersie. 1994. *The Transformation of American Industrial Relations*. Ithaca, N.Y.: ILR Press.

Korpi, Walter. 1985. "Developments in the Theory of Power and Exchange." *Sociological Theory* 3(1): 31–45.

Kristal, Tali, and Yinon Cohen. 2014. "The Causes of Rising Wage Inequality: The Race Between Institutions and Technology." *Socio-Economic Review* 15(1): 187–212.

Krueger, Alan B. 2018. "Reflections on Dwindling Worker Bargaining Power and Monetary Policy." Economic Policy Symposium, Jackson Hole, Wyo. (August 24, 2018).

Lambert, Susan J., Julia R. Henly, and Jaeseung Kim. 2019. "Precarious Work Schedules as a Source of Economic Insecurity and Institutional Distrust." *RSF: The Russell Sage Foundation Journal of the Social Sciences* 5(4): 218–57. DOI: 10.7758/RSF.2019.5.4.08.

Lazear, Edward P., and Kathryn L. Shaw. 2007. "Personnel Economics: The Economist's View of Human Resources." *Journal of Economic Perspectives* 21(4): 91–114.

Lemieux, Thomas. 2011. "Wage Inequality: A Comparative Perspective." *Australian Bulletin of Labour* 37(1): 2–32.

Lester, Richard A. 1952. "A Range Theory of Wage Differentials." *Industrial and Labor Relations Review* 5 (July): 433–50.

Leuven, Edwin, Hessel Oosterbeek, and Hans van Ophem. 2004. "Explaining International Differences in Male Skill Wage Differentials by Differences in Demand and Supply of Skills." *Economic Journal* 114(495): 466–86.

Liu, Cathy Yang, and Luísa Nazareno. 2019. "The Changing Quality of Nonstandard Work Arrangements: Does Skill Matter?" *RSF: The Russell Sage Foundation Journal of the Social Sciences* 5(4): 104–28. DOI: 10.7758/RSF.2019.5.4.04.

Locke, Richard, Thomas Kochan, and Michael Piore. 1995. *Employment Relations in Changing World Economy*. Cambridge, Mass.: MIT Press.

Maestas, Nicole, Kathleen J. Mullen, David Powell, Till von Wachter, and Jeffrey B. Wenger. 2017. "The American Working Conditions Survey Data: Codebook and Data Description." Santa Monica,

Calif.: Rand Corporation. Accessed February 28, 2019. https://www.rand.org/pubs/tools/TL269.html.

Mankiw, N. Gregory 2013. "Defending the One Percent." *Journal of Economic Perspectives* 27(1): 21–34.

Manning, Alan. 2003. *Monopsony in Motion: Imperfect Competition in Labor Markets*. Princeton, N.J.: Princeton University Press.

———. 2011. "Imperfect Competition in the Labor Market." In *Handbook of Labor Economics*, vol. 4B, edited by Orley Ashenfelter and David Card. Amsterdam: Elsevier-North Holland.

Mason, Geoff, and Wiemer Salverda. 2010. "Low Pay, Working Conditions, and Living Standards." In *Low-Wage Work in the Wealthy World*, edited by Jérôme Gautié and John Schmitt. New York: Russell Sage Foundation.

Mishel, Lawrence R., and Jared Bernstein. 1994. *Is the Technology Black Box Empty?: An Empirical Examination of the Impact of Technology on Wage Inequality and the Employment Structure*. Washington, D.C.: Economic Policy Institute.

———. 1998. "Technology and the Wage Structure: Has Technology's Impact Accelerated Since the 1970s?" *Research in Labor Economics* 17: 305–55.

Mishel, Lawrence, Jared Bernstein, and Sylvia Allegretto. 2007. *The State of Working America 2006/2007*. Ithaca, N.Y.: Cornell University Press, ILR School.

Mishel, Lawrence R., and Josh Bivens. 2017. "New Paper on Pay-Productivity Link Does Not Overturn EPI Findings." *Working Economics Blog*, November 9, 2017. Accessed March 1, 2019. https://www.epi.org/blog/new-paper-on-pay-productivity-link-does-not-overturn-epi-findings.

Mishel, Lawrence R., Josh Bivens, and Elise Gould. 2012. *The State of Working America, 2012*. Washington, D.C.: Economic Policy Institute.

Mishel, Lawrence, John Schmitt, and Heidi Shierholz. 2013. "Don't Blame the Robots: Assessing the Job Polarization Explanation of Growing Wage Inequality." *EPI-CEPR* working paper. Washington, D.C.: Economic Policy Institute.

Mortensen, Dale T. 2005. *Wage Dispersion: Why Are Similar Workers Paid Differently?* Cambridge, Mass.: The MIT Press.

Mosher, James S. 2007. "U.S. Wage Inequality, Technological Change, and Decline in Union Power." *Politics & Society* 35(2): 225–64.

Moulton, Brent R. 2018. "The Measurement of Output, Prices, and Productivity: What's Changed Since the Boskin Commission?" Washington, D.C.: Brookings Institution.

OECD. 2014. "How Good Is Your Job? Measuring and Assessing Job Quality." In *The Employment Outlook 2014*. Paris: Organization for Economic Cooperation and Development.

———. 2015. *In It Together: Why Less Inequality Benefits All*. Paris: Organization for Economic Cooperation and Development.

———. 2017. "How Technology and Globalization Are Transforming the Labour Market." In *The Employment Outlook 2017*. Paris: Organization for Economic Cooperation and Development.

Osawa, Machiko, Myoung Jung Kim, and Jeff Kingston. 2013. "Precarious Work in Japan." *American Behavioral Scientist* 57(3): 309–34.

Osterman, Paul. 1994. "Internal Labor Markets: Theory and Change." In *Labor Economics and Industrial Relations: Markets and Institutions*, edited by Clark Kerr and Paul D. Staudohar. Cambridge, Mass.: Harvard University Press.

———. 2008. "Improving the Quality of Low-Wage Work: The Current American Experience." *International Labour Review* 147(2-3): 115–34.

———. 2011. "Institutional Labor Economics, the New Personnel Economics, and Internal Labor Markets: A Reconsideration." *Industrial and Labor Relations Review* 64(4): 637–53.

Paccagnella, Marco. 2015. "Skills and Wage Inequality: Evidence from PIAAC." *OECD Education* working paper no. 114. Paris: Organization for Economic Cooperation and Development.

Peckham, Trevor, Kaori Fujishiro, Anjum Hajat, Brian P. Flaherty, and Noah Seixas. 2019. "Evaluating Employment Quality as a Determinant of Health in a Changing Labor Market." *RSF: The Russell Sage Foundation Journal of the Social Sciences* 5(4): 258–81. DOI: 10.7758/RSF.2019.5.4.09.

Pedulla, David S., and Katariina Mueller-Gastell. 2019. "Nonstandard Work and the Job Search Process: Application Pools, Search Methods, and Perceived Job Quality." *RSF: The Russell Sage Foundation Journal of the Social Sciences* 5(4): 130–58. DOI: 10.7758/RSF.2019.5.4.05.

Pena, Anita A. 2014. "Revisiting the Effects of Skills on Economic Inequality: Within- and Cross-Coutry Comparisons Using PIAAC." Presentation at Taking the Next Step with PIAAC: A Research-to-Action Conference, Arlington, Va. (December 11–12, 2014).

Piketty, Thomas, Emmanuel Saez, and Gabriel Zucman. 2018. "Distributional National Accounts: Methods and Estimates for the United States." *Quarterly Journal of Economics* 133(2): 1–57.

Rand Education and Labor (Rand). 2015. "American Working Conditions Survey." Accessed March 1, 2019. https://www.rand.org/education-and-labor/projects/american-working-conditions.html.

Reich, Michael, and James Devine. 1981. "The Microeconomics of Conflict and Hierarchy in Capitalist Production." *Review of Radical Political Economics* 12(4): 27–45.

Rodrik, Dani. 2007. *One Economics—Many Recipes: Globalization, Institutions, and Economic Growth.* Princeton, N.J.: Princeton University Press.

Schmitt, John. 2008. "The Decline of Good Jobs: How Have Jobs with Adequate Pay and Benefits Challenge Done?" *Challenge* 51(1): 5–25.

———. 2013. "Why Does the Minimum Wage Have No Discernible Effect on Employment?" Washington, D.C.: Center for Economic and Policy Research.

Schmitt, John, Elise Gould, and Josh Bivens. 2018. "America's Slow-Motion Wage Crisis." Washington, D.C.: Economic Policy Institute.

Schmitt, John, and Janelle Jones. 2012. "Where Have All the Good Jobs Gone?" Washington, D.C.: Center for Economic and Policy Research. Accessed March 26, 2019. http://cepr.net/documents/publications/good-jobs-2012-07.pdf.

Schmitt, John, and Alexandra Mitukiewicz. 2011. "Politics Matter: Changes in Unionization Rates in Rich Countries, 1960–2010." Washington, D.C.: Center for Economic and Policy Research.

Schultz, Michael A. 2019. "The Wage Mobility of Low-Wage Workers in a Changing Economy, 1968 to 2014." *RSF: The Russell Sage Foundation Journal of the Social Sciences* 5(4): 159–89. DOI: 10.7758/RSF.2019.5.4.06.

Smith, Adam. 1937 (1776). *An Inquiry into the Nature and Causes of The Wealth of Nations*, Modern Library Edition. New York: Random House.

Solow, Robert. 1990. *The Labor Market as a Social Institution.* Cambridge: Basil Blackwell.

Song, Jae, David J. Price, Fatih Guvenen, Nicholas Bloom, and Till von Wachter. 2019. "Firming Up Inequality." *Quarterly Journal of Economics* 134(1): 1–50.

Stancanelli, Elena. 2002. "Do Temporary Jobs Pay? Wages and Career Perspectives of Temporary Workers." Working paper. Tilburg, Germany: Tilburg University.

Stansbury, Anna, and Larry Summers. 2017. "Productivity and Pay: Is the Link Broken?" *NBER* working paper no. 24165. Cambridge, Mass.: National Bureau of Economic Research.

Stelzner, Mark. 2017. "The New American Way—How Changes in Labour Law Are Increasing Inequality." *Industrial Relations Journal* 48(3): 231–55.

Streeck, Wolfgang. 2005. "The Sociology of Labor Markets and Trade Unions." In *The Handbook of Economic Sociology*, edited by Neil J. Smelser and Richard Swedberg. Princeton, N.J.: Princeton University Press.

Sullivan, Teresa A., Elizabeth Warren, and Jay Lawrence Westbrook. 2001. *The Fragile Middle Class: Americans in Debt.* Austin: University of Texas Press.

Tilly, Chris. 1996. *Half a Job: Bad and Good Part-Time Jobs in a Changing Labor Market.* Philadelphia, Pa.: Temple University Press.

Tung, Irene, Yanet Lathrop, and Paul Sonn. 2015. "The Growing Movement for $15." Washington, D.C.: National Employment Law Project.

Van Reenen, John. 2011. "Wage Inequality, Technology and Trade: 21st Century Evidence." *Labour Economics* 18(6): 730–41.

VanHeuvelen, Tom, and Katherine Copas. 2019. "The Geography of Polarization, 1950 to 2015." *RSF: The Russell Sage Foundation Journal of the Social Sciences* 5(4): 77–103. DOI: 10.7758/RSF.2019.5.4.03.

Vosko, Leah F. 2010. *Managing the Margins: Gender, Citizenship, and the International Regulation of Precarious Employment.* Oxford: Oxford University Press.

Webb, Sidney, and Beatrice Webb. 1897. *Industrial Democracy.* London: Longmans, Green, and Co.

Weil, David. 2014. *The Fissured Workplace.* Cambridge, Mass.: Harvard University Press.

———. 2017. "Income Inequality, Wage Determination, and the Fissured Workplace." In *After Piketty: The Agenda for Economics and Inequality*, edited by Heather Boushey, J. Bradford DeLong, and Marshall Steinbaum. Cambridge, Mass.: Harvard University Press.

Western, Bruce, and Jake Rosenfeld. 2011. "Unions,

Norms, and the Rise in U.S. Wage Inequality." *American Sociological Review* 76(4): 513–37.

Wilmers, Nathan. 2018. "Wage Stagnation and Buyer Power: How Buyer-Supplier Relations Affect U.S. Workers' Wages, 1978–2014." *American Sociological Review* 83(2): 213–42.

———. 2019. "Solidarity Within and Across Workplaces: How Cross-Workplace Coordination Affects Earnings Inequality." *RSF: The Russell Sage Foundation Journal of the Social Sciences* 5(4): 190–215. DOI: 10.7758/ RSF.2019.5.4.07.

PART I

The Transformation of American Job Quality— Perspectives and Dimensions

Low-Wage Job Growth, Polarization, and the Limits and Opportunities of the Service Economy

RACHEL E. DWYER AND ERIK OLIN WRIGHT

We analyze U.S. job growth from the 1980s to the 2010s. We define jobs as occupations within sectors to capture position in the production system as well as skill hierarchies. Low-wage jobs outgrew middle-wage jobs over much of this period, particularly for women and nonwhite workers. Service work drove most low-wage job growth, but even a small resurgence in manufacturing job growth in the 2010s was concentrated in low-wage jobs. Given the constraints of economic restructuring on the growth of decent jobs, we consider alternative logics for the creation of jobs in twenty-first-century economies. The prospects for job growth in the future, we argue, requires a robust defense of these alternative logics that can and do thrive alongside and within a capitalist market economy.

Keywords: jobs, inequality, polarization, low-wage work, labor policy

Does the American economy generate enough quality jobs to support prosperity and security for all? The answer to this question appeared far less promising at the end of the twentieth century than it had in earlier decades. Changes in industrial organization and employment relations after the 1970s made it harder for workers to achieve a decent standard of living in the United States. Declining unionization and weakening business regulation reduced worker power in negotiations with employers. The shift from a manufacturing to a service economy accelerated declining worker power as growth slowed in more-unionized sectors and

Rachel E. Dwyer is professor of sociology at Ohio State University. **Erik Olin Wright** was Vilas Distinguished Research Professor of Sociology and director of the A.E. Havens Center for Social Justice at the University of Wisconsin-Madison.

© 2019 Russell Sage Foundation. Dwyer, Rachel E., and Erik Olin Wright. 2019. "Low-Wage Job Growth, Polarization, and the Limits and Opportunities of the Service Economy." *RSF: The Russell Sage Foundation Journal of the Social Sciences* 5(4): 56–76. DOI: 10.7758/RSF.2019.5.4.02. Acknowledgment from Rachel E. Dwyer: Erik Olin Wright passed away on January 23, 2019, only ten months after being diagnosed with an aggressive strain of acute myeloid leukemia. It was one of the great privileges of my life to learn from and collaborate with him. We conducted a long-running collaboration on job structure in the United States, for which I am deeply grateful now, most of all because of the time I was so lucky to share with him while working on it. This project was coming to fruition in several articles when the Russell Sage Foundation journal call came out. Erik was delighted by its inclusion in this issue, in particular because the issue was coedited by Arne Kalleberg, his comrade in research on economic inequality. To learn more about Erik's extraordinary life and work, please see remembrances at: https://thelifeandworkoferikolinwright.wordpress.com/. Direct correspondence to: Rachel Dwyer at dwyer.46 @osu.edu, 238 Townshend Hall, 1885 Neil Avenue Mall, Columbus, OH 43085.

boomed in less-unionized ones, resulting in a more precarious economy that produced an abundance of low-wage jobs (Gautié and Schmitt 2009; Kalleberg 2011). These dynamics culminated in the emergence of job polarization in the 1990s when, at least according to several prominent analyses, employment growth became concentrated among the lowest-wage and highest-wage jobs and slumped among the middle-wage jobs that underwrote a more widely shared prosperity in the 1960s (Autor, Levy, and Murnane 2003; Wright and Dwyer 2003).

Economic restructuring continued into the first two decades of the 2000s but a number of disjunctures between trends in wages and employment in this period raised questions about the quality of jobs generated as well as the possibilities for stronger growth in the future. For one, employment trends followed a rather bumpy trajectory. Slow job growth in the early 2000s culminated in massive job losses during the Great Recession and a very slow recovery after, all of which significantly depressed labor market opportunities over an extended period for American workers after the turn of the new century (BLS 2019). The economic expansion after the Great Recession became more robust over time, however, offering some intimations of recovery in lower- to middle-wage jobs (BLS 2019). Employment trends also diverged more from wage trends in this period than in the preceding decades. There had been greater agreement that employment polarized in the 1990s (including in some countries in Europe) along with growing wage inequality, though the causes were debated (Wright and Dwyer 2003; Goos and Manning 2007; Oesch and Menés 2011; Autor, Katz, and Kearney 2006; Dwyer 2013; Liu and Grusky 2013; Fernández-Macías 2012). Debate has been more vigorous about the empirical trends in the 2000s, which show less evidence of wage polarization, slowing returns to higher education and growing challenges to the evidence of tight coupling between employment and wage trends even for the 1990s (Mishel, Schmitt, and Shierholz 2013; Beaudry, Green, and Sand 2016; Hunt and Nunn 2018). These divergences have led to greater efforts to analyze patterns of employment growth separate from trends in individual wage distribu-

tions, most studies so far focused on understanding the distinctive wage trends in the 2000s. We take the alternative tack of studying employment trends distinct from individual wage trends. We followed this approach in our earlier analysis of job polarization in the 1990s, arguing that the job structure is irreducible to the individual attributes of workers making up those positions (Wright and Dwyer 2003).

We study the American jobs structure because jobs are the site of economic interests that flow not just from the material resources of wages, but also from position in the organization of production. Jobs deliver wages and other benefits to individuals but do so in social organizational units that are the result of interest contestation, organizational dynamics, and the political regulation (and deregulation) of labor and capital (Wright 1997; Fernandez 2001; Weeden 2002; Mouw and Kalleberg 2010; Liu and Grusky 2013; Kristal 2013). Jobs thus bundle rights and responsibilities that shape the quality of work beyond the particular wages they provide. That social organization imposes constraints on what jobs are available to workers based on institutional rules, spatial distributions, and both discriminatory and conventional understandings of the types of worker suited to different jobs (Milkman and Dwyer 2002; Sassen 2001; England 2010). The relatively weak social safety net provided by the federal government makes the quality of jobs created in the American economy all the more important: jobs exert outsized influence on livelihoods in societies such as the United States where government benefits and insurance provide a low social wage. Indeed, the large number of low-wage jobs in the United States is understood to be in part a consequence of the low social wage, in that more Americans are forced to accept any employment compared to their counterparts in countries with higher social wages (Gautié and Schmitt 2009).

In this article, we study patterns of job growth and decline at the turn of the twenty-first century as indicators of change in the prospects for shared growth in the American economy. We focus on the trajectory of low-wage jobs in the transition from a manufacturing to a service economy because we are interested in the relative production of bad versus decent jobs in this period. The quantity of jobs created in a national economy is widely recognized as a valuable indicator of the health of an economy. The Organization for Economic Cooperation and Development metric of labor market performance, for example, includes measures of overall levels of employment as well as measures of job quality realized in compensation, job security, and the conditions of work (OECD 2014; Cazes, Falco, and Menyhért forthcoming). Our approach integrates job quantity and quality by evaluating employment growth and decline (job quantity) across the distribution of job median wages (job quality). The quantity of low-quality versus high-quality jobs is an indicator of the degree to which social groups all share in economic growth (Fernández-Macías, Storrie, and Hurley 2012). We focus especially on the growth of low-wage jobs relative to higher-wage jobs, and on understanding job growth in the early decades of the 2000s compared to the 1980s and 1990s. We also analyze gender and race-ethnic divides in low-wage job growth in order to understand the disparate impacts of economic restructuring on diverse socioeconomic groups.

We reflect on the prospects for more broadly shared economic growth in the American economy—any economy—that depends on capitalist production and consider sources of job growth that are particularly likely to support social equality and justice. We argue that more equally shared growth requires a reinvestment in public goods and a broader vision of a social economy, which produces livelihoods not only in the service of capitalist growth, but in support of human flourishing.

CHANGE IN THE AMERICAN JOBS STRUCTURE

Studies of job polarization in the 1990s brought increased attention to the American jobs structure (and to similar changes in other countries) but differed in the operationalization of jobs and in the extent to which they focused on job trends versus wage trends. Our approach is distinctive not only in focusing on jobs rather than individual wages (as discussed), but also in understanding jobs as occupations within sectors rather than as synonymous with occupations.

These alternative approaches provide different views of economic change; our approach is particularly valuable for understanding the low-wage labor market and possibilities for decent work to support livelihoods for all.

Prior analyses of the job structure often attempt to link wage and employment, with mixed results. Indeed, David Howell and his colleagues show that wages and employment were only weakly associated in the 1980s up to 1997, significant numbers of jobs experiencing high hours growth but little or no wage growth, and other jobs experiencing the reverse (2001). Later analyses of the full 1990s expansion by David Autor and his colleagues argue that wage inequality and job polarization were more strongly correlated (2003, 2006, 2008). This pattern supports skill-biased technological change explanations that computerization increased the demand for the highest-skill jobs but reduced it for the most routine middle-skill jobs that could be automated relative to the most manual low-skill jobs that still require human labor (Acemoglu and Autor 2011). Many studies question the canonical role of technological change, arguing that other factors, including changing labor market institutions and shifts in the social organization of services, also significantly increase inequality (Liu and Grusky 2013; Dwyer 2013). Some argue that significant discontinuities between wages and jobs undercut the skill-biased technological change (SBTC) conclusions (Mishel, Schmitt, and Shierholz 2013; Hunt and Nunn 2018). First, the 1980s saw a surge in wage inequality, but the strongest job polarization emerged in the 1990s (Mishel, Schmitt, and Shierholz 2013). Second, the evidence for the 1990s is based in part on the particular operationalization of jobs (more on this shortly). Third, even if the 1990s were a period of the strongest associations between wages and employment growth, the 2000s brought new challenges as trends in wage inequality and employment growth became even less aligned (Mishel, Schmitt, and Shierholz 2013; Hunt and Nunn 2018). Slow wage growth in the 2000s was associated with less wage polarization because most wage gains shifted to the very top of the distribution of workers (Piketty and Saez 2006; Hunt and Nunn 2018). High-skill jobs thus became less clearly linked to employment and wage growth and the returns to skill slowed into the 2000s (Beaudry, Green, and Sand 2016). Trends in wage inequality are thus likely best understood by focusing on individual wage distributions but not expecting that they will move tightly with employment trends. Job growth remains an important indicator, however, of labor market opportunity in the American economy.

Studies that link wages and employment typically define jobs as synonymous with occupations because they prioritize skill developments over other changes in the production system. Research in the SBTC tradition focuses on occupational polarization, embedding the priority of a skills-based approach into the analytic design (Autor, Levy, and Murnane 2003; Mishel, Schmitt, and Shierholz 2013; Liu and Grusky 2013). The extent and causes of occupational polarization are debated, however. Some studies argue that the evidence for wage polarization was strongest for occupations in the 1990s, but also susceptible to coding discontinuities in occupations (Mishel, Schmitt, and Shierholz 2013; Hunt and Nunn 2018). At the same time, substantial heterogeneity within occupations is part of the source of the decoupling of wage and occupational growth trends.

Industrial sectors are one of the key sources of wage variability within occupations as well as a key feature of the labor market structure that shapes opportunities for individual workers. Industrial sectors organize the work of the economy and more directly reflect policy decisions about economic investment and institutional responses to changes in technology, global competition, and the makeup of the American workforce than occupational groupings do (Tomaskovic-Devey and Skaggs 2002). Indeed, analyses of the labor market impacts of trade competition foreground sectoral exposures over occupational dynamics (Autor, Dorn, and Hanson 2016; Acemoglu et al. 2016; Goos, Manning, and Salomons 2014). Sectoral dynamics also significantly shape the opportunities for rent-seeking, worker bargaining power, and other factors that affect the quality of jobs for individual workers. For example, the finance sector provides higher wages across all occupations, and some occupations within that sector also have structural advantages in capturing rents (Tomaskovic-Devey and Lin 2011; Böhm, Metzger, and Strömberg 2018). The monopsony power of some employers and the structural power of different industries shape the bargaining contexts between capital and labor (Dickens and Katz 1987; Krueger and Summers 1988; Manning 2003; Tomaskovic-Devey 2017). Sectoral dynamics thus likely contribute to divergences between individual wage trends and occupational wage trends. Sectoral change also captures the large-scale economic restructuring that shapes the emergence of new opportunities and the decline of formerly valuable sources of livelihoods (Goos, Manning, and Salomons 2009, 2014). Occupational dynamics still matter because the demand for skill shapes which positions are growing and declining, but this demand occurs within the context of sectoral dynamics.

Our focus on the job structure also requires more careful attention to expansionary and recessionary periods than studies that focus on secular shifts in the demand for skill as a result of computerization. Indeed, evidence suggests that the patterning of job polarization is sensitive to measurement at different points of the business cycle (Wright and Dwyer 2003; Gaggl and Kaufmann 2015). Recessionary periods appear to shape the trajectory of job growth in crucial ways, especially in the wake of significant downturns such as the Great Recession (Gaggl and Kaufmann 2015). Sectoral dynamics may be particularly sensitive to the business cycle (Goos et al. forthcoming), consistent with our expectation that sectors shape the transformation of the job structure.

RESEARCH QUESTIONS: LOW-WAGE JOB GROWTH IN THE 2000S

We pursue several questions in order to understand change in the quality of jobs created in the American economy and identify the locations in the American economy that could provide more equally shared resources in the future. First, what was the trend in low-wage job growth in the 2000s relative to middle-wage and higher-wage jobs? We are interested in this question overall, but also for its implications for the sociodemographic groups most likely to hold low-wage jobs, and for the sectoral composition of low-wage job growth.

Second, has the distribution of low-wage job growth across women and men and between racial groups changed in the 2000s relative to earlier periods? Women and disadvantaged racial and ethnic populations have disproportionately held low-wage jobs; white workers have disproportionately held the highest-wage jobs (Applebaum, Bernhardt, and Murnane 2006). Polarization thus entailed disparities in livelihoods between socioeconomic groups as well as a division in the quality of growing jobs (Wright and Dwyer 2003; Dwyer 2013). Over time, women and racially disadvantaged groups continued to make gains in education that may have reduced disparities, while economic restructuring hit some disproportionately white communities particularly hard. Immigration slowed significantly during and after the Great Recession, resulting especially in shifting the balance of U.S.-born to Latino-immigrant workers (Kochar 2014). Has the American jobs structure become more integrated and inclusive by gender and race over time? These questions become intertwined with questions about economic restructuring given the differential position of gender and race groups in the U.S. labor market (Gittleman and Howell 1995).

Third, has job growth across manufacturing and service sectors continued to produce polarization in the 2000s and especially since the Great Recession? There are a number of reasons to expect change in job growth across sectors. Varied efforts to improve service jobs with unionization, efforts to increase wages, and a strengthening labor market after the Great Recession may have contributed to stronger growth in the middle (Applebaum, Bernhardt, and Murnane 2006). Manufacturing employment rebounded as well, leading to public interest in a revitalization of that sector as a source of improved job quality in the American economy. However, the same institutional constraints on worker power that contributed to polarization at the end of the twentieth century remained in force at the beginning of the twenty-first (Kalleberg 2011). The relative strength of job growth at the bottom versus the middle of the labor market is a crucial indicator of how broadly shared economic growth is and can be under the institutional conditions of twenty-first-century American labor markets.

DATA AND METHODS

We study more than thirty years of low-wage job growth in the United States using the Current Population Survey (CPS), the major source of data on the American job structure. The CPS is a nationally representative sample of U.S. households, conducted monthly since the 1940s, and includes an expanded set of employment information starting in 1979. The basic monthly survey includes core demographic and labor-force participation questions, which are used to track the U.S. unemployment rate. The CPS also provides supplements with more detailed employment data, which we used in our analyses of low-wage job growth over time. From the 1980s through 2017, we use the Outgoing Rotation Group Earner Study (NBER 2017). In all samples across years, we include all full- and part-time civilian workers age eighteen to sixty-five. We exclude self-employed workers because the related wage data are incompatible with that on employees.

Jobs Defined by Occupations Within Sectors

The CPS coding of occupation and industry follows the U.S. Census Bureau codes, which are revised after each decennial census. These coding changes reflect changes in the economy but also produce discontinuities in our data series. The coding schemes changed significantly after the 1980 Census, and thus we start our analyses in 1983 when the CPS implemented the new codes, and again in 2002 after a significant revision following the 2000 Census. The Census Bureau made more minor changes in the periods in between the bigger revisions.

Sector

We create a consistent set of twenty-three industrial sector codes over all periods of analysis. Starting in 1970, the CPS provides data on industry in several hundred three-digit codes. The coding of the more disaggregated industry changes over time and results in some shifting of jobs across our standard two-digit categories, but for the most part these categories remain fairly stable. We also aggregate the twenty-three sectors into eight categories to better analyze larger-scale sectoral trends: extractive and manufacturing; construction, transport, and repair; communications, utilities, and sanitary service; wholesale trade; retail trade, private and personal services, and entertainment and recreational service; business service, other professional service, and finance, insurance, and real estate; health services; and educational service, social services, and public administration. We also combine all services together and compare them with nonservice sectors.

Occupation

We create a consistent set of forty-five occupation codes that we use in all analyses. The underlying occupational coding scheme changes, reflecting shifts in the U.S. economy. CPS occupation codes changed significantly over the fifty years of our analysis. We use a consistent set of codes based on the 1990 scheme for all periods. The 1980 and 1990 schemes are relatively similar (after a larger reclassification after 1970). Changes to the census coding scheme for 2000 were significant but mainly entailed a reorganization of the code along with greater detail within categories. We use the crosswalk developed by the Bureau of Labor Statistics to make a consistent set of codes across the 1990s and 2000s (Meyer and Osborne 2005).

Jobs

We define jobs as cells in the occupation within sector matrix, making up almost one thousand individual jobs. A few small jobs drop out of the analysis when no workers are in a particular cell at the beginning or end of a period.

Job Wages

We index job types by one salient characteristic: the wages they typically generate. Wages are an imperfect but valuable proxy for other measures of job quality. This is particularly true in the U.S. context, where various benefits come along with jobs yielding different levels of pay because of the relatively low social wage. We calculate median hourly wages in every period in order to rank jobs by wage levels. We use the median rather than mean for each job because the CPS top-codes wages, which skews calculations of the average.[1] We convert salaries and other forms of nonhourly pay into hourly pay using usual weekly earnings and usual hours worked per week. We adjust all dollar amounts consistent 2017 dollars using the CPI-U adjustment. We follow Barry Hirsch and Edward Schumacher (2004) and exclude imputed wage data, which are calculated using very highly aggregated occupational categories and thus are likely particularly noisy for our purposes.

Our approach here captures relative pay between jobs rather than absolute wage trends as an indicator of trends in job quality (Applebaum, Bernhardt, and Murnane 2006). Thus our focus on the distribution of types of jobs as such is distinct from the question of growing wage inequality between the best and worst jobs, which would indicate growing distance between positions at the poles of the job-wage distribution.

Sociodemographic Groups

We analyze job growth for women relative to men and for several racial-ethnic groups. The CPS questions on race and ethnicity follow changes in the U.S. Census data collection on race, becoming more detailed over time and, in the latest years, allowing respondents to select multiple categories. We create a consistent set of categories over time, including non-Hispanic white, black, other race, and all Hispanic. We include all races other than black and white in one category because of limitations in the CPS sample and coding practices for creating more disaggregated groups. Other race, thus, is a highly heterogeneous category. We follow standard census practices in including all Hispanic workers in one category, and use the

---

1. Some scholars use the mean instead of median to rank jobs (usually defined as occupations). Lawrence Mishel, John Schmitt, and Heidi Shierholz draw the same conclusion we do that median job wages provide a more consistent data series in the CPS and also have the virtue of being less susceptible to skew as a result of a small number of top earners in a job (2013). The authors test the ranking of jobs (defined as occupations) using both approaches and find little difference in results.

term *Hispanic* because this is the language used in the questionnaire instrument even though *Latinx* better captures evolving race-ethnic categorizations in the United States. For the later years, we combine multiple race workers into single categories to construct a consistent coding series over time even though this oversimplifies racial identification. Sensitivity analyses with alternative definitions in the years that this is possible show the same pattern of results.

Analytic Strategy

First, we rank-order jobs from the lowest to the highest median hourly wage and then group them into three ordered categories each containing about one-third of the employment at the beginning of an economic expansion. The bottom tercile contains the roughly one-third of employment at the beginning of a job expansion that are in the jobs with the lowest median wages, the highest tercile contains the roughly one-third of the employment in jobs with the highest median weekly wages, and so on. These job-wage terciles capturing relative pay are the primary categories we use in assessing the quality of the expansion of jobs in the American economy. We focus on the bottom tercile as an approximation of low-wage jobs that has particular salience given the concentration of job growth in that range of job wages. We analyze the distribution of net changes in number of jobs within each tercile (especially the bottom tercile) during periods of job expansion and contraction. Our measure of net job change represents the outcome of processes of the creation of new jobs and the destruction of old jobs. Net job change is different from measures of job openings given that turnover and retirements may produce vacancies even in the absence of overall net growth.

In our main analysis, we study net job change over the four expansions and three recessions since the early 1980s. We organize our data into annual increments and thus our measures of expansionary and recessionary periods are not as precise as the National Bureau of Economic Research definitions, which define the beginning and end of these periods by month (NBER 2017), but provide us with the necessary sample sizes within jobs to produce reasonable esti-

mates of job median wages. This annual level of precision is sufficient for our purposes in capturing general patterns of job growth over time. We also have to make some accommodations to beginning and ending dates for periods depending on data availability and changes in the CPS coding.

We undertook a range of supplementary analyses to ensure that the main findings we report here are robust to alternative specifications of the jobs structure. In these analyses, we ranked jobs into more disaggregated categories of quintiles as well as defined jobs weighted by hours worked, and these approaches show similar patterns at the level we discuss here. Although each analytic approach yields insight, terciles are an effectively parsimonious strategy for presenting our findings relative to our questions in this article.

One final note of comparison to studies of job polarization that link shifts to wage inequality or the demand for skill. We explicitly bracket questions about what jobs are growing as a percentage share of the overall economy and whether evidence indicates that job growth clearly matches occupational or individual characteristics. Instead, we focus on the pattern and character of employment growth in itself. Which jobs in the job-wage distribution grow and how has this changed over time? Thus we focus on the opportunity structure of the American employment system as whole. Economic change is complex and proceeds along multiple, sometimes empirically conflicting, dimensions. We see our analyses of the job structure as complementary to studies of wages trends, including the wage contours analyzed in the introduction to this issue, and studies of occupational change, but as distinctively focused on trends in the labor market positions that so many depend on for their livelihoods (Howell and Kalleberg 2019).

LOW-WAGE WORK AND TRANSFORMATIONS OF THE U.S. JOB STRUCTURE

We start by analyzing the overall pattern of job growth across terciles in every expansion and recession from the 1980s to the 2000s. We then analyze gender and racial inequality in job growth over the same time period. Finally, we

Figure 1. Job Growth Across Job-Wage Terciles During Economic Expansions and Recessions

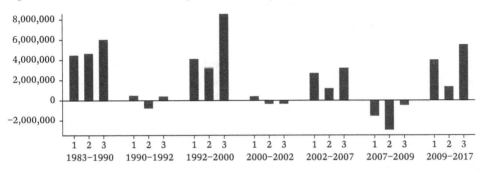

Source: Authors' analysis based on 1983–2017 data from the Current Population Survey (NBER 2019). *Note:* Jobs are defined by the cells in a matrix of detailed occupations by economic sectors. Job-wage terciles are defined by jobs ranked by median hourly wage: job cells are rank-ordered on the basis of median hourly wages, and these rank-ordered job-cells grouped into equal population terciles at the beginning of each period. The top (third) tercile thus represents the one-third of the employed labor force in the best-paying types of jobs and the bottom (first) tercile represents the one-third of the employed labor force in the worst-paying types of jobs. The number of categories varied for different periods because of occupation and sector coding changes in the CPS.

evaluate economic restructuring from manufacturing to service in the 2000s.

Low-Wage Job Growth and Polarization in the 2000s

We find significant job polarization in the 2000s for occupation by sector positions in the U.S. labor market. Figure 1 tracks the total job growth across wage-terciles of jobs in each expansion and recession from the 1980s to the 2010s. The terciles correspond to widely accepted understandings of the distribution of job quality as divided between bad, decent, and good jobs, the bottom tercile being entirely low-wage jobs (Kalleberg 2011; Howell and Kalleberg 2019). In the 2009 to 2017 expansion, for example, the median wage in the bottom tercile was $12.80 (2017 dollars), which for a full-time, full-year worker yields an annual income right at the U.S. poverty line for a family of four in 2017 dollars (U.S. Census Bureau 2018). The top boundary of the bottom tercile is $15.80, which

approximates commonly suggested minimums for a $15 an hour living wage (Desmond 2019).[2] Thus, tracking employment growth in the bottom tercile of job median wages captures the low-wage labor market yet is also somewhat more expansive than the poverty-wage market.

Every period of expansion had stronger growth in the top and bottom terciles than in the middle tercile, but the bottom became a larger share in the 2000s. Recessionary periods show much lower levels of net job change for the most part, the important exception being the Great Recession period, from 2007 to 2009, which ushered in more job loss than the other downturns in our time series did. Even recessionary periods show a polarized pattern in which job losses were worse in the middle tercile. Low-wage jobs stand out in maintaining even higher growth than the top during even the first two economic downturns in the early 1990s and 2000s. In contrast, the middle tercile not only showed decelerating levels of growth

2. The bottom tercile of jobs in an economy are not necessarily bad jobs just because they are the worst jobs in that economy. In economies governed by labor market institutions that accord more power to workers, the lowest-wage jobs can be quite decent (Gautié and Schmitt 2009). Our understanding of the bottom tercile as encompassing bad jobs is due both to evidence that these wage levels are below the level of a living wage and to evidence that low-wage jobs in the United States have low levels of autonomy, schedule control, and employment security (Kalleberg 2011).

Table 1. Shares of Job Growth, 1983–2017

	Relative Share by Tercile			Ratio of Terciles	
	1	2	3	T1/T2	T1/T3
1983–1990	30%	31%	40%	0.96	0.74
1992–2000	26	20	54	1.29	0.48
2002–2007	38	17	45	2.27	0.84
2009–2017	37	12	51	2.99	0.73

Source: Authors' analysis based on 1983–2017 data from the Current Population Survey (NBER 2019).

across economic expansions, but also shouldered the majority of the job losses during recessions. The 1980s and 1990s were more robust periods of expansion overall; job growth weakened in the 2000s, though with a more robust recovery in the 2009 to 2017 expansion.[3]

Over time, jobs in the bottom tercile of job median wages became a larger share of job growth in the bottom half of the wage distribution and maintained relatively robust levels of growth in contrast to the middle of the job structure. Table 1 reports the percentage share of growth by tercile in the left panel and the ratio of growth in the bottom relative to the middle and top in the right panel. The share of growth in the bottom tercile grew from 30 percent in the 1980s to 38 percent in the 2000s. The middle underperformed relative to the bottom and became a lower percentage over time, while the top outpaced growth in the bottom. The ratios in the right panel show that the share of employment growth at the bottom grew relative to the middle across every period. The ratio between the bottom and top shifted more because the top usually outgrew the bottom, but at different rates depending on how robust the expansion was. During the anemic expansion of 2002 to 2007, growth at the top and bottom came closest to even, but the top pulled ahead again as the 2009 to 2017 expansion picked up steam.

The analyses so far combine full-time and part-time jobs, consistent with our focus on the overall distribution of discrete jobs. Low-wage jobs are, however, both disproportionately part time and particularly susceptible to being downgraded in hours during contractions in the United States. The high degree of employer flexibility in U.S. labor markets makes hours reduction (including shifting positions from full-time to part-time status) a target for cost savings, and, given a weak safety net, workers have few options during economic downturns to leave positions that keep them underemployed. Figure 2 reports job growth stacked by full-time versus part-time job status. The balance between full- and part-time jobs was cyclical across the entire thirty-five year period, with part-time work more dominant in recessions than during expansions. Part-time jobs made up a greater share of bottom tercile growth in the two 2000s expansions than during the 1980s and 1990s, and in fact part-time work declined in the bottom tercile during the 1990s expansion. Essentially all job growth during recessions was for part-time jobs. The Great Recession saw a particularly large decline in full-time positions and growth in part-time jobs. The bottom tercile was most susceptible to the cyclical hours constriction, reflecting the flexibility of work hours in the U.S. economy, especially among low-wage jobs. Although workers may benefit from the availability of part-time work in slack times, the overall degree of volatility in work hours makes wages less certain, benefits more insecure, and family life more chaotic (Kalleberg 2011; Pugh 2015).

Our analysis brings to the forefront both continuity and change in low-wage job growth in the United States. Taking the evidence first of the strong continuities, low-wage job growth is a stubbornly persistent feature of the American labor market. Low-wage jobs grew steadily across distinct economic periods marked by different trends in wage inequality, returns to skill, technological innovations, and trade dy-

3. Most of the job growth in the post–Great Recession period occurred after 2012.

Figure 2. Job Growth Across Job-Wage Terciles Stacked by Full-Time and Part-Time Status

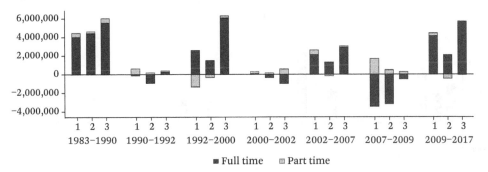

Source: Authors' analysis based on 1983–2017 data from the Current Population Survey (NBER 2019). *Note:* Jobs are defined by the cells in a matrix of detailed occupations by economic sectors. Job-wage terciles are defined by jobs ranked by median hourly wage: job cells are rank-ordered on the basis of median hourly wages, and these rank-ordered job-cells grouped into equal population terciles at the beginning of each period. The top (third) tercile thus represents the one-third of the employed labor force in the best-paying types of jobs and the bottom (first) tercile represents the one-third of the employed labor force in the worst-paying types of jobs. The number of categories varied for different periods because of occupation and sector coding changes in the CPS. Full time and part time defined as usual hours worked per week.

namics. They grew during robust expansions such as the tech-boom 1990s as well as during anemic recoveries such as the post-2001 war economy, and across periods distinguished by Democratic and Republican control of the executive branch. Other research suggests those jobs are worsening on a number of job-quality dimensions, even if at times the strong demand for low-wage jobs has produced some wage growth. The relative stability of low-wage job growth across expansions discussed here occurred alongside other changes that degraded low-wage work: lower job security, more varied work schedules, growing managerial discretion, and employment at will. The findings on full-time versus part-time work schedules illustrate the aggregate effects of this degradation. Given the typical focus of research on declining job quality on change in the conditions of work, the persistence of low-wage job growth can be overlooked. What has changed more significantly is the surrounding context of low-wage growth: in relative terms, low-wage jobs have become a greater share of job growth overall. The job-growth patterns in the middle and top tercile changed more than at the bottom, and indeed much of the theory about job polarization focuses on shifts in returns to skill in

middle-wage and high-wage jobs (Autor and Dorn 2013). The persistent growth of low-wage work raises as many questions about the overall project of relying on the labor market for livelihoods as about the quality of the labor market dynamics themselves, questions which we return to after considering gender and racial inequality in job growth.

Gender and Racial Inequality in Job Growth

Sociodemographic groups were affected differently by changes in the job structure. These differences highlight the disparate impact of economic restructuring given the labor market position of diverse populations, a key reason it is important to study the job structure in addition to individual wage distributions, which obscure some of these impacts. Gender and racial inequality in job growth also helps us understand economic restructuring itself because groups with different histories of labor market incorporation face different labor market opportunities given past entrenched inequalities.

Both women and men experienced increasingly polarized job growth over time, but polarization began earlier for women than for men and became more sharply divided over time. Figure 3 reports job growth across time sepa-

Figure 3. Job Growth Across Job-Wage Terciles, by Gender

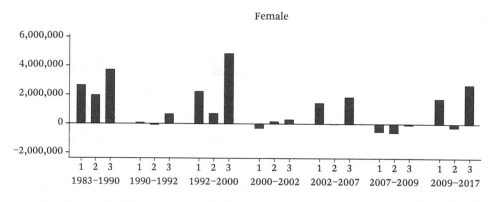

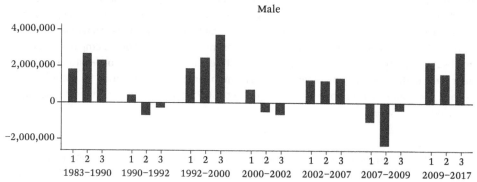

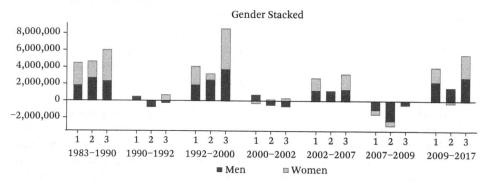

Source: Authors' analysis based on 1983–2017 data from the Current Population Survey (NBER 2019).

rately for women and men. The core gender difference is that men maintained stronger growth in the middle over time relative to women. Job growth for women was polarized by our measure even starting in the 1980s. For men, however, it became truly polarized only with the heavy job losses in the middle during the Great Recession and was followed by weaker growth in the middle in the 2009 to 2017 expansion. Men and women both see more similar patterns of growth at the bottom and top across

time. Women see somewhat higher absolute levels of growth in the earlier periods, reflecting the increasing labor-force participation among women. The more polarized pattern for women likely reflects underlying gender occupational segregation and lower pay for female-dominated positions, both of which are particularly severe across working-class jobs (England 2010). Women also entered the labor force in larger numbers after periods of highest unionization so that women are less likely to be in the unionized and more-protected positions in the middle. Further, the middle-wage jobs that women did hold in the past were primarily clerical and less likely to be unionized (Dwyer 2013; McCall 2011).

The overall continuity in low-wage job growth across economic periods masks significantly changes in the racial-ethnic composition of employment growth. Figure 4 shows job growth separated into panels for non-Hispanic white, non-Hispanic black, non-Hispanic other race, and all Hispanic workers. The panels reflect not only different labor market positions but also different levels of growth. White workers saw disproportionately strong growth at the top over all periods. However, job losses for white workers were significant at the middle and bottom in the 2000s, a factor that may be related to growing populism and discontent among white workers. Black and Hispanic workers were more heavily weighted to the bottom than their white counterparts but maintain somewhat more even growth over time. Job growth for non-Hispanic black and non-Hispanic other race workers became more polarized over time, however, and these groups made up a growing share of low-wage job growth in the 2000s. Hispanic workers remained heavily weighted to the bottom in all periods, though the low-wage share dropped somewhat over time. In supplemental analyses, we compare job growth for U.S.-born and immigrant Hispanic workers. We find that Hispanic job growth became increasingly dominated by U.S.-born Hispanics, who are more likely to gain higher-wage jobs than are immigrant workers, reflecting slowing immigration in the 2000s (Kochar 2014).[4] The finding that high levels of low-wage job growth persist even in times of lower immigration is consistent with comparative evidence that the size of the low-wage labor market has more to do with labor market institutions and the social wage

than with levels of immigration (Applebaum, Bernhardt, and Murnane 2006, 148).

In supplemental analyses of gender by race groups, we find that men and women within given racial groups experience patterns of job growth more similar to each other than to the patterns of job growth for same-gender groups. However, nonwhite women in particular often experience less growth in middle-wage jobs but higher growth in low-wage jobs than men of the same race or ethnic group. Thus job growth among nonwhite women drives the distinctive trajectory of women relative to men. The net effect of the changes reported in figure 4 result in job growth at every level becoming more diverse as the U.S. demography has become more diverse. The drop in the middle is in the aggregate driven by declines among white workers.

Stability and Change in the Sectoral Composition of Low-Wage Job Growth

The shift from an economy based on manufacturing and production to one based on services fueled the emergence and persistence of job polarization over time. The service sector has long been polarized between low-wage and high-wage jobs. As job growth in manufacturing and related sectors declined, the underlying polarization of services came to dominate job growth overall. Does any evidence indicate improvements in service jobs or a resurgence of manufacturing that could bring back more decent jobs? The persistence of job polarization in the 2000s is a worrying sign, but differences in sectoral trajectories may underlie the overall numbers.

We are interested in the sectoral composition of job growth at different levels rather than understanding the contributions relative to the overall size of the sectors. Figure 5 shows job change across job-wage terciles in service sectors, manufacturing sectors, and all other sectors.[5]

4. Results available on request. We do not report here because of complications in interpreting both changing job growth and changing immigration trends, which require a more detailed analysis (López, Bialik, and Radford 2018). Future research should return to this question with, possibly, additional data sources more effective in capturing the immigrant worker population including undocumented immigrants.

5. Service sectors include private and personal services; entertainment and recreational services; business services, other professional service, and finance, insurance and real estate; health services; and educational service, social services and public administration; and retail trade. Manufacturing sectors include durable and

Figure 4. Job Growth Across Job-Wage Terciles, by Race-Ethnicity

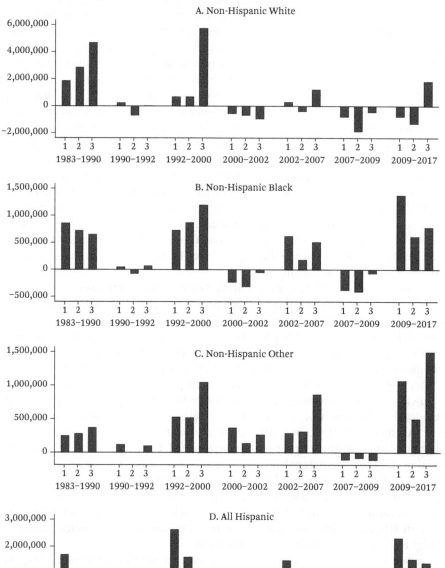

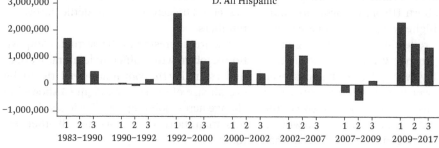

Source: Authors' analysis based on 1983–2017 data from the Current Population Survey (NBER 2019).
Note: Jobs are defined by the cells in a matrix of detailed occupations by economic sectors. Job-wage terciles are defined by jobs ranked by median hourly wage: job cells are rank-ordered on the basis of median hourly wages, and these rank-ordered job-cells grouped into equal population terciles at the beginning of each period. The top (third) tercile thus represents the one-third of the employed labor force in the best-paying types of jobs and the bottom (first) tercile represents the one-third of the employed labor force in the worst-paying types of jobs. The number of categories varied for different periods because of occupation and sector coding changes in the CPS.

Figure 5. Job Growth Across Job-Wage Terciles, by Sector

Source: Authors' analysis based on 1983–2017 data from the Current Population Survey (NBER 2019). *Note:* Jobs are defined by the cells in a matrix of detailed occupations by economic sectors. Job-wage terciles are defined by jobs ranked by median hourly wage: job cells are rank-ordered on the basis of median hourly wages, and these rank-ordered job-cells grouped into equal population terciles at the beginning of each period. The top (third) tercile thus represents the one-third of the employed labor force in the best-paying types of jobs and the bottom (first) tercile represents the one-third of the employed labor force in the worst-paying types of jobs. The number of categories varied for different periods because of occupation and sector coding changes in the CPS. Service sectors include private and personal services; entertainment and recreational services; business services, other professional service and finance, insurance and real estate; health services; and educational service, social services and public administration; and retail trade. Manufacturing includes durable and nondurable manufacturing as well as all extractive sectors. All other sectors include wholesale trade; construction, transport, and repair; communications, utilities, and sanitary.

The findings show significant continuity in the dominance of service-sector jobs at the top and the bottom as we expected, but more change in the pattern of job growth in manufacturing sector. Most employment growth over the entire period of study concentrated in services, and services themselves were even more polarized than jobs overall. Taking the long view of services in the U.S. economy reminds us that the decline of manufacturing and clerical jobs that have received so much attention in explanations of job polarization revealed a fundamental feature of the service economy rather than created it. Although the increasing polarization of the service sector over time likely was driven by factors that also influenced decline in middle-wage jobs, including both technological and institutional dynamics, polarization has been a long-standing feature of the service economy.

Job growth and decline in manufacturing changed more over time. Persistent decline in manufacturing brought the middle down, especially during recessions, but also during the expansions of the 1990s and early 2000s. Evidence also indicates greater growth in manufacturing in the 2009 to 2017 expansion in all terciles. The absolute growth of those sectors was still smaller than the decline was during the Great Recession; however, manufacturing declines in the recessions of the early 1990s and 2000s were followed by continuing declines in the expansions that came after. Manufacturing job growth was disproportionately in the bottom tercile relative to the middle and bottom, in contrast to the 1980s, when the small growth that occurred was in the middle and top. The growth at the bottom reflects evidence that the manufacturing jobs that are returning are less likely to be unionized and more likely to be out

nondurable manufacturing as well as all extractive sectors. Extractive sectors account for a fairly small share of job growth, but typically are understood to be significantly related to manufacturing in processes of economic restructuring. Remaining sectors include wholesale trade; construction, transport, and repair; and communications, utilities, and sanitary.

of the major central firms than when manufacturing jobs led the middle class (Rothstein forthcoming).

CAN BAD JOBS BECOME GOOD JOBS?

Our analysis of the long-running dominance of low-wage service jobs at the bottom of the U.S. labor market presents both challenges and opportunities for the chances of developing a greater share of decent jobs in the future. Low-wage service jobs have grown significantly and consistently over time, representing a reliable source of employment for many decades and suggesting they may provide some opportunity for better jobs in the future. Yet the persistence of service jobs at the bottom over decidedly different economic periods also demonstrates a stubborn stickiness of low wages for such jobs.

The decline in growth in the middle of the labor market as polarization took hold makes the improvement of these jobs appear even more remote. The same pressures that suppressed job growth in middle-wage jobs present obstacles for converting low-wage service jobs into better jobs and may be degrading low-wage jobs as well. Declining jobs in the middle may also result in fewer routes to mobility for workers hoping to improve their careers over their life course. The overall slumping of employment growth in the first expansion of the 2000s along with employment loss in the Great Recession is a concern even for those still unconvinced that job polarization is significant. The more robust growth in the 2009 to 2017 expansion has recovered some of those losses, though not all, and long-term effects persist for those who entered the labor market or were retiring during that downturn (Mishel, Schmitt, and Shierholz 2013; Krueger 2017). Worries about the spread of automation to low-wage jobs, including increasingly to service jobs, raise further concerns (Autor 2015).

Declining worker power also limits the possibilities of policies that focus on skill given that even highly skilled workers appear to be losing bargaining power. Indeed, the routes through which manufacturing and clerical jobs became better jobs earlier in the twentieth century, including especially unionization and bureaucratized internal labor markets, entailed strategies aimed at improving bargaining power rather than skill. The decline of worker power made it more difficult for workers in even growing jobs to demand better conditions unless they could demand rents through skills or access to the levers of power within organizations through managerial positions. In a context of declining worker power, managers and organizations have had relatively free rein to degrade middle-wage jobs or limit the emergence of new good jobs. Managerial strategies focused on efficiency and (perhaps) limiting solidarity may split a mixed skill job into two, dividing the skills into two jobs by concentrating the cognitive skills that demand educational credentials into a higher-wage job, and the manual or lower-credentialed skills into a lower-wage position. One example is the increasing divide in the work of nursing between highly skilled RNs and less-skilled LPNs and other health aides (Duffy 2011). The same process may also manifest in a shift in demand from similar jobs from middle- to lower-skill positions.

Given the importance of declining worker power to our current situation of an increase in low-wage jobs but stagnating or declining job quality, investing in institutions that build opportunities for low-skill workers to achieve decent, life-sustaining jobs should be a policy priority (Osterman and Shulman 2011). It is politically popular to argue for the return of manufacturing, and indeed our results show both persistent job growth and some evidence of resurgent growth in production and extractive sectors. This growth, however, came mainly at the bottom of the job-wage structure. Rather than restoring the growth of the past, this growth is simply another indication of the degrading quality of work. Proposals to rebuild the institutions that existed in the 1960s may face the same obstacles, potentially achieving only shadows of the earlier era. Furthermore, given contemporary conditions, some of those institutions may be less useful in providing quality jobs. Clerical work has followed a similar trajectory to manufacturing jobs in formerly providing middle-wage jobs but now seeing slowing growth or disappearing. Calls to restore clerical and related jobs are notably few and far between, perhaps because those jobs were important for women whereas male-dominated manufacturing jobs appeal more on the basis of out-of-date assumptions about whose work is most valuable. We also suspect the different conversation about manufacturing versus clerical work may also derive from wider recognition that high levels of clerical work simply belonged to different social conditions in a way that the powerful imagery of manufacturing resists. In any case, we need a new vision of quality job growth in the twenty-first century.

In general terms, if we wish to improve the quality of jobs available to most people in developed capitalist economies, we can either attempt to influence the kinds of jobs generated by capitalist firms—by changing their incentives or by imposing constraints on their strategies—or we can attempt to generate jobs outside the ordinary processes of capitalist markets. Many policy proposals focus on the first of these approaches, and we would endorse many of those proposals. We close, however, by reflecting on the potential opportunities associated with creating jobs outside of capitalist markets, and consider two major options with salience given the evidence we have presented about the types of jobs that are growing.

First, we could reinvest in public jobs programs. Even in the United States, the developed capitalist country that maintains among the lowest levels of public employment, roughly 15 percent of jobs are provided by federal, state, and local governments. After adding to this number jobs that are directly the result of state contracting to private firms, the figure is probably above 25 percent. Unlike in capitalist markets, the character of these jobs is not dictated by profit-maximizing criteria and market logics, but instead by political and normative considerations. When states decide to create jobs, they have considerable economic latitude in deciding the pay scales, requirements, working conditions, and other attributes that distinguish good jobs from bad jobs. Of course, the expansion of public-sector employment is constrained by market processes. This is one of the hallmarks of the state in a capitalist society: revenues to pay for state employment come from taxation of various forms of income generated mainly in the market economy. It is only a constraint, however, and does not determine

a strict level of employment, let alone the character of that employment. In these terms, the level of public-sector employment in the United States is clearly far below the carrying capacity of the country's capitalist economy given that taxation as a proportion of gross domestic product is so much lower in the United States than in nearly all comparable economies. Even in Europe, however, no hard economic limit restricts the relative size of public-sector employment relative to private-sector employment. The constraints are not primarily economic, but instead political and ideological (Wright 2019).

The second form of noncapitalist income-generating employment is less familiar to many people: the social and solidarity economy. This term is used in a variety of different ways to describe a range of economic activities that are organized neither by capitalist firms nor by states (Wright 2019). At the core of the social-solidarity economy are nonstate organizations producing goods and services directly to meet the needs of people—either of the members of the organization or the people they serve. Nonprofit organizations and nongovernmental organizations are often included in this category. Worker and consumer cooperatives are also often included to the extent that they are primarily oriented to meeting the needs of their members rather than maximizing profits. Sometimes what are called *social enterprises*—profit-making firms in which a social mission has priority over profits—are also included in the social economy. The social-solidarity economy may by facilitated by a range of state policies and subsidies, but the activities within the social-solidarity economy are not themselves run by the state. A particularly vibrant example of the social economy as a source of significant job creation exists in Quebec in the provision of eldercare and childcare services. As of early 2008, more than forty thousand people were employed in the Quebec childcare cooperatives and roughly eight thousand in eldercare cooperatives.

One virtue of investing in the social economy is that capitalist nations already have a thriving care economy, but one that often undersupplies care because of market failures (Folbre 2002; England, Budig, and Folbre 2002;

Figure 6. Job Growth Across Care Jobs, Stacked by Women and Men

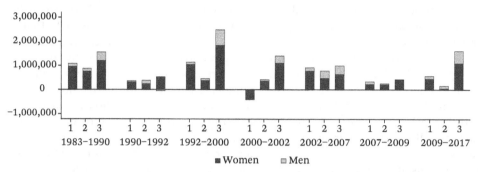

Source: Authors' analysis based on 1983–2017 data from the Current Population Survey (NBER 2019).
Note: Jobs are defined by the cells in a matrix of detailed occupations by economic sectors. Job-wage terciles are defined by jobs ranked by median hourly wage: job cells are rank-ordered on the basis of median hourly wages, and these rank-ordered job-cells grouped into equal population terciles at the beginning of each period. The top (third) tercile thus represents the one-third of the employed labor force in the best-paying types of jobs and the bottom (first) tercile represents the one-third of the employed labor force in the worst-paying types of jobs. The number of categories varied for different periods because of occupation and sector coding changes in the CPS. The care domain includes occupations and industries that contribute to the health and development of people. Occupations include nurses, doctors, allied health professionals and aides, teachers, childcare workers, professors, allied education professionals, social workers, and religious support workers. Industries include educational service, hospital service, other medical services, and social services. Alternative measures of care work include what is sometimes termed *reproductive labor,* including food preparation, house cleaning, and other related physical labors of care. We exclude here, but note that if we included those jobs, the bottom tercile would show higher levels of growth given the concentration of reproductive labor jobs at the bottom (Duffy 2011).

Duffy 2011). Figure 6 reports job growth in jobs (occupations and sectors) that contribute to the health and development of human beings, including education, health care, and social services. The figure shows that care-work jobs grew in every period, even during recessions, including the Great Recession. Job growth in care-work jobs was generally polarized, however, between the top and bottom terciles. The social-solidarity economy may provide a route to upgrading the lowest-wage care-work jobs and providing more robust middle-wage growth as is more common in jobs, such as construction, that support the physical infrastructure (Dwyer 2013). This is especially important for women given that these jobs are disproportionately held by women workers of all racial-ethnic groups, in contrast to the middle-wage jobs that have been disproportionately held by men.

Although investing in alternative arrangements such as the public and social economy to create jobs poses a number of political and economic challenges, our findings demonstrate an apparently significant demand for just the sorts of jobs typically created in such arrangements. Many of the services that have grown most robustly are those that in many times and places have been supported by public expenditures, including in the United States. The care domain involves the work that connects to public goods such as health, education, and the support of young children (Albelda et al. 2009; Antonopoulos et al. 2010). We have emphasized the strength of care and household services that are often provided in both the public sector and social-solidarity sector. Those represent investments in the human and social infrastructure. Demand is also considerable for investments in the physical infrastructure, which also demands jobs with lower levels of education, often in the bottom and middle terciles of the job-wage distribution, such as construction, carpentry, and transport. Investments in green technology that produce a more sustainable economic system in the future would also thrive under alternative economic arrangements.

The jobs created to remedy these challenges may be higher-quality jobs that provide more opportunities for fulfillment and flourishing than the good jobs of the past. Although manufacturing and clerical jobs provided better wages and benefits, and many provided fulfilling and interesting work, some were repetitive and provided little in the way of autonomy or creativity. If the future of the American jobs structure depends on investing in the human and physical infrastructure, positive externalities in the quality of life as well as the quality of jobs would be numerous. Evidence is significant that we suffer under both care deficits and infrastructure deficits that harm and limit the development of human potential. When we develop proposals for good jobs, we should focus on improving all aspects of job quality and broader societal goals rather than limiting our vision to a return to perhaps idealized jobs of the past. The prospects for more equally shared growth in the future requires grappling with the limits and opportunities of the service economy in the twenty-first century.

REFERENCES

Acemoglu, Daron, and David H. Autor. 2011. "Skills, Tasks and Technologies: Implications for Employment and Earnings." In *Handbook of Labor Economics*, vol. 4, part B, edited by David Card and Orley Ashenfelter. San Diego, Calif.: Elsevier.

Acemoglu, Daron, David H. Autor, David Dorn, Gordon H. Hanson, and Brendan Price. 2016. "Import Competition and the Great U.S. Employment Sag of the 2000s." *Journal of Labor Economics* 34 (S1): S141–98.

Albelda, Randy, Mignon Duffy, and Nancy Folbre. 2009. *Counting on Care Work: Human Infrastructure in Massachusetts*. Amherst: University of Massachusetts.

Antonopoulos, Rania, Kijong Kim, Thomas Masterson, and Ajit Zacharias. 2010. "Investing in Care: A Strategy for Effective and Equitable Job Creation." *Levy Economics Institute* working paper no. 610. Annandale-on-Hudson, N.Y.: Bard College.

Applebaum, Eileen, Annette Bernhardt, and Richard J. Murnane, eds. 2006. *Low Wage America: How Employers Are Reshaping Opportunity in the Workplace*. New York: Russell Sage Foundation.

Autor, David H. 2015. "Why Are There Still So Many Jobs? The History and Future of Workplace Automation." *Journal of Economic Perspectives* 29(3): 3–30.

Autor, David H., and David Dorn. 2013. "The Growth of Low-Skill Service Jobs and the Polarization of the US Labor Market." *American Economic Review* 103(5): 1553–97.

Autor, David H., David Dorn, and Gordon H. Hanson. 2016. "The China Shock: Learning from Labor Market Adjustment to Large Changes in Trade." *Annual Review of Economics* 8(1): 205–40.

Autor, David H., Lawrence F. Katz, and Melissa S. Kearney. 2006. "The Polarization of the U.S. Labor Market." *American Economic Review: Papers and Proceedings* 96(2): 189–94.

———. 2008. "Trends in U.S. Wage Inequality: Revising the Revisionists." *Review of Economics and Statistics* 90(2): 300–23.

Autor, David H., Frank Levy, and Richard J. Murnane. 2003. "The Skill Content of Recent Technological Change: An Empirical Exploration." *Quarterly Journal of Economics* 118(4): 1279–333.

Beaudry, Paul, David A. Green, and Benjamin M. Sand. 2016. "The Great Reversal in the Demand for Skill and Cognitive Tasks." *Journal of Labor Economics* 34(1): S199–247.

Bureau of Labor Statistics (BLS). 2019. "Labor Force Statistics." Accessed March 12, 2019. https://www.bls.gov/data/#employment.

Böhm, Michael J., and Daniel Metzger, and Per Strömberg. 2018. "'Since You're So Rich, You Must Be Really Smart': Talent and the Finance Wage Premium." *Riksbank* research paper series no. 137. Stockholm: Sveriges Riksbank.

Cazes, Sandrine, Paolo Falco, and Balint Menyhért. Forthcoming. "Job Quality in Emerging Economies Through the Lens of the OECD Job Quality Framework." In *The Oxford Handbook of Job Quality*, edited by Christopher Warhurst, Christopher Mathieu, and Rachel E. Dwyer. Oxford: Oxford University Press.

Desmond, Matthew. 2019. "Dollars on the Margins." *New York Times Magazine*, February 21. Accessed March 12, 2019. https://www.nytimes.com /interactive/2019/02/21/magazine/minimum -wage-saving-lives.html.

Dickens, William T., and Lawrence F. Katz. 1987. "Inter-Industry Wage Differences and Industry Characteristics." In *Unemployment and the Structure of Labor Markets*, edited by Kevin Lang and Jonathan S. Leonard. New York: Basil Blackwell.

Duffy, Mignon. 2011. *Making Care Count: A Century of Gender, Race, and Paid Care Work*. New Brunswick, N.J.: Rutgers University Press.

Dwyer, Rachel E. 2013. "The Care Economy? Gender, Economic Restructuring, and Job Polarization in the U.S. Labor Market." *American Sociological Review* 78(3): 390–416.

England, Paula. 2010. "The Gender Revolution: Uneven and Stalled." *Gender & Society* 24(2): 149–66.

England, Paula, Michelle Budig, and Nancy Folbre. 2002. "Wages of Virtue: The Relative Pay of Care Work." *Social Problems* 49(4): 455–73.

Fernandez, Robert. 2001. "Skill-Biased Technological Change and Wage Inequality: Evidence from a Plant Retooling." *American Journal of Sociology* 107(2): 273–320.

Fernández-Macías, Enrique. 2012. "Job Polarization in Europe? Changes in the Employment Structure and Job Quality, 1995–2007." *Work and Occupations* 39(2): 157–82.

Fernández-Macías, Enrique, Donald Storrie, and John Hurley, eds. 2012. *Transformation of the Employment Structures in the EU and USA*. New York: Palgrave Macmillan.

Folbre, Nancy. 2002. *The Invisible Heart: Economics and Family Values*. New York: New Press.

———. 2006. "Demanding Quality: Worker/Consumer Coalitions and 'High Road' Strategies in the Care Sector." *Politics and Society* 34(1): 11–31.

Gaggl, Paul, and Sylvia Kaufmann. 2015. "The Cyclical Component of Labor Market Polarization and Jobless Recoveries in the US." Working paper no. 14.03. Gerzensee: Swiss National Bank.

Gautié, Jérôme, and John Schmitt, eds. 2009. *Low-Wage Work in the Wealthy World*. New York: Russell Sage Foundation.

Gittleman, Maury B., and David R. Howell. 1995. "Changes in the Structure and Quality of Jobs in the United States: Effects by Race and Gender, 1973–1990." *ILR Review* 48(3): 420–40.

Goos, Maarten, and Alan Manning. 2007. "Lousy and Lovely Jobs: The Rising Polarization of Work in Britain." *Review of Economics and Statistics* 89(1): 118–33.

Goos, Maarten, Alan Manning, and Anna Salomons. 2009. "Job Polarization in Europe." *American Economic Review: Papers and Proceedings* 99(2): 58–63.

———. 2014. "Explaining Job Polarization: Routine-Biased Technological Change and Offshoring." *American Economic Review* 104(8): 2509–26.

Goos, Maarten, Emilie Rademakers, Anna Salomons, and Marieke Vandeweyer. Forthcoming. "Job Polarization: Its History, An Intuitive Framework and Some Empirical Evidence." In *The Oxford Handbook of Job Quality*, edited by Christopher Warhurst, Christopher Mathieu, and Rachel E. Dwyer. Oxford: Oxford University Press.

Hirsch, Barry T., and Edward J. Schumacher. 2004. "Match Bias in Wage Gap Estimates Due to Earnings Imputation." *Journal of Labor Economics* 22(3): 689–722.

Howell, David R. 2013. "The Austerity of Low Pay: US Exceptionalism in the Age of Inequality." *Social Research: An International Quarterly* 80(3): 795–816.

Howell, David R., Ellen Houston, and William Milberg. 2001. "Skill Mismatch, Bureaucratic Burden, and Rising Earnings Inequality in the U.S.: What Do Hours and Earnings Trends by Occupation Show?" In *Power, Employment and Accumulation: Social Structures in Economic Theory and Practice*, edited by Jim Stanford, Lance Taylor, and Ellen Houston. Armonk, N.Y.: M. E. Sharpe.

Howell, David R., and Arne L. Kalleberg. 2019. "Declining Job Quality in the United States: Explanations and Evidence." *RSF: The Russell Sage Foundation Journal of the Social Sciences* 5(4): 1–53. DOI: 10.7758/RSF.2019.5.4.01.

Hunt, Jennifer, and Ryan Nunn. 2018. "Is Employment Polarization Informative About Wage Inequality and Is Employment Really Polarizing?" Working paper. New Brunswick, N.J.: Rutgers University.

Kalleberg, Arne L. 2011. *Good Jobs, Bad Jobs: The Rise of Polarized and Precarious Employment Systems in the United States, 1970s to 2000s*. New York: Russell Sage Foundation.

Kochar, Rakesh. 2014. "Latino Jobs Growth Driven by U.S. Born: Immigrants No Longer the Majority of Hispanic Workers." Washington, D.C.: Pew Research Center.

Kristal, Tali. 2013. "The Capitalist Machine: Computerization, Workers' Power, and the Decline in Labor's Share Within U.S. Industries." *American Sociological Review* 78(3): 361–89.

Krueger, Alan B. 2017. "Where Have All the Workers Gone?: An Inquiry into the Decline of the U.S. Labor Force Participation Rate." *Brookings Papers on Economic Activity* 2017(2): 1–87. Washington, D.C.: Brookings Institution Press.

Krueger, Alan B., and Lawrence H. Summers. 1988. "Efficiency Wages and the Inter-Industry Wage Structure." *Econometrica* 56(2): 259–94.

Liu, Yujia, and David B. Grusky. 2013. "The Payoff to Skill in the Third Industrial Revolution." *American Journal of Sociology* 118(5): 1330–74.

López, Gustavo, Kristen Bialik, and Jynnah Radford. 2018. "Key Findings About U.S. Immigrants." Washington, D.C.: Pew Research Center. Accessed March 12, 2019. http://www.pewresearch.org/fact-tank/2018/11/30/key-findings-about-u-s-immigrants.

Manning, Alan. 2003. *Monopsony in Motion: Imperfect Competition in Labor Markets*. Princeton, N.J.: Princeton University Press.

McCall, Leslie. 2011. "Women and Men as Class and Race Actors: Comment on England." *Gender and Society* 25(1): 94–100.

Meyer, Peter B., and Anastasiya M. Osborne. 2005. "Proposed Category System for 1960–2000 Census Occupations." *BLS* working paper no. 383. Washington: U.S. Department of Labor.

Milkman, Ruth, and Rachel E. Dwyer. 2002. "Growing Apart: The 'New Economy' and Job Polarization in California, 1992–2000." The State of California Labor Series. Berkeley: University of California Institute for Labor and Employment.

Mishel, Lawrence, John Schmitt, and Heidi Shierholz. 2013. "Don't Blame the Robots: Assessing the Job Polarization Explanation of Growing Wage Inequality." Washington, D.C.: Economic Policy Institute.

Mouw, Ted, and Arne L. Kalleberg. 2010. "Occupations and Wage Inequality in the United States." *American Sociological Review* 75(3): 402–31.

National Bureau of Economic Research (NBER). 2017. "U.S. Business Cycle Expansions and Contractions." Accessed March 12, 2019. https://www.nber.org/cycles.html.

——. 2019. "CPS Merged Outgoing Rotation Groups." Accessed April 10, 2019. https://www.nber.org/data/morg.html.

Oesch, Daniel, and Jorge Rodriguez Menés. 2011. "Upgrading or Polarization? Occupational Change in Britain, Germany, Spain, and Switzerland, 1990–2008." *Socio-Economic Review* 9(3): 503–31.

Organization for Economic Co-operation and Development (OECD). 2014. *OECD Employment Outlook 2014*. Paris: OECD Publishing. DOI: 10.1787/empl_outlook-2014-en.

Osterman, Paul, and Beth Shulman. 2011. *Good Jobs America: Making Work Better for Everyone*. New York: Russell Sage Foundation.

Piketty, Thomas, and Emmanuel Saez. 2006. "The Evolution of Top Incomes: A Historical and International Perspective." *American Economic Review* 96(2): 200–205.

Pugh, Allison J. 2015. *The Tumbleweed Society: Working and Caring in an Age of Insecurity*. New York: Oxford University Press.

Rothstein, Jeffrey S. Forthcoming. "The Steady but Uneven Decline in Manufacturing Job Quality." In *The Oxford Handbook of Job Quality*, edited by Christopher Warhurst, Christopher Mathieu, and Rachel E. Dwyer. Oxford: Oxford University Press.

Sassen, Saskia. 2001. *The Global City: New York, London, Tokyo*. Princeton, N.J.: Princeton University Press.

Tomaskovic-Devey, Donald. 2017. "Market Concentration and Structural Power As Sources of Industrial Productivity." In *Industries, Firms, and Jobs*, edited by George Farkas and Paula England. New York: Routledge.

Tomaskovic-Devey, Donald, and Ken-Hou Lin. 2011. "Income Dynamics, Economic Rents, and the Financialization of the U.S. Economy." *American Sociological Review* 76(4): 538–59.

Tomaskovic-Devey, Donald, and Sheryl Skaggs. 2002. "Sex Segregation, Labor Process Organization, and Gender Earnings Inequality." *American Sociological Review* 108(1): 102–28.

U.S. Census Bureau. 2018. "Poverty Thresholds, 2017." Accessed March 12, 2019. https://www.census.gov/data/tables/time-series/demo/income-poverty/historical-poverty-thresholds.html.

Weeden, Kim. 2002. "Why Do Some Occupations

Pay More Than Others? Social Closure and Earnings Inequality in the United States." *American Journal of Sociology* 108(1): 55–101.

Wright, Erik Olin. 1997. *Class Counts: Comparative Studies in Class Analysis*. Cambridge: Cambridge University Press.

———. 2019. *How to Be an Anti-capitalist for the Twenty-First Century*. Verso: London.

Wright, Erik Olin, and Rachel E. Dwyer. 2003. "The Patterns of Job Expansions in the United States: A Comparison of the 1960s and 1990s." *Socio-Economic Review* 1(3): 289–325.

The Geography of Polarization, 1950 to 2015

TOM VANHEUVELEN AND KATHERINE COPAS

In this article, we ask where affluent and economically insecure households reside. We examine the economic conditions of the tails of wage distributions in local areas to make sense of trends in geographical residence. Using census and American Community Survey data covering 1950 to 2015, we draw two main conclusions. From 2000 onward, economic polarization coincided with two kinds of geographic residential patterns: polarized and poor labor markets. We also find divergence in the link between geographical location and wages across the wage distribution. We question whether the concentration of affluent and poor households in polarized places signify moves to better economic opportunity by low-wage workers. Our results illustrate the geographical consequences of low-wage rent destruction and highlight implications for future work addressing geographical stratification.

Keywords: wage inequality, local labor markets, poverty, affluence, low-wage work

The rise of low-paid and nonstandard work in the United States, largely a feature of the middle- and low end of the labor market, has co-occurred with the rapid growth of top-end pay (Atkinson, Piketty, and Saez 2011). These changes reflect a variety of polarizations well documented in the stratification literature: occupational polarization, or the hollowing out of the middle of the occupational distribution and the bifurcation of employment into good and bad jobs (Goos and Manning 2007; Kalleberg 2013), wage polarization, or the takeoff of top pay and the stagnation and decline of real wages at the middle and the bottom of the earnings distribution (Piketty, Saez, and Zucman 2017). They also reflect a variety of polarizations across otherwise similar firms via contested markets, typified by the recent growth of monopsony (Manning 2003), an emphasis on core competency versus outsourced labor (Weil 2014) and the growth of firm-level inequality and industrial segmentation (Song et al. 2015; Abowd, McKinney, and Zhao 2018; Wilmers 2017). Across these manifestations of polarization is a common argument that contemporary changes to low-paid and economically insecure

Tom VanHeuvelen is assistant professor of sociology at the University of Minnesota. **Katherine Copas** is a PhD candidate of sociology at the University of Illinois at Urbana-Champaign.

© 2019 Russell Sage Foundation. VanHeuvelen, Tom, and Katherine Copas. 2019. "The Geography of Polarization, 1950 to 2015." *RSF: The Russell Sage Foundation Journal of the Social Sciences* 5(4): 77–103. DOI: 10.7758/ RSF.2019.5.4.03. Direct correspondence to: Tom VanHeuvelen at tvanheuvelen@gmail.com, Department of Sociology, 909 Social Sciences Building, 267 19th Ave. S, Minneapolis, MN 55455; and Katherine Copas at kcopas2@illinois.edu, 3059 Lincoln Hall, 702 S. Wright St., Urbana, IL 61801.

work are inextricably entwined with contemporary changes in the concentration of economic affluence.

This article situates wage polarization in geographical space and asks where those in affluent and economically insecure households reside. Although class-based segregated residence has long been central to stratification research (Lee and Marlay 2007; Reardon and Bischoff 2011), studies frequently restrict focus to the largest metropolitan areas and late into the contemporary era of rising inequality. In contrast, and motivated by Douglas Massey and Mary Fischer (2003), we extend analytical focus to the local labor market level, examining change in residence patterns from 1950 to 2015 in 722 commuting zones that cover the entire contiguous United States constructed from sixteen waves of census and American Community Survey (ACS) microdata. Then, exploiting the large and locally representative samples of these data, we assess geographical variation in the economic conditions at the tails of local earnings distributions to develop an understanding of the mechanisms behind shifting residence patterns.

Our findings can be summarized by two main points. First, wage polarization has increasingly resulted in two types of labor markets: polarized and poor. In the past fifteen years, affluent and poor households have sorted into the same labor markets, and a large concentration of poor households tends to push out affluent ones. Households in between have become separated from affluent ones and more integrated with poor households. Second, geography is increasingly important for the fortunes of the affluent, and increasingly unimportant for the fortunes of the poor. We are in a unique period of the post–World War II era: the wage differences across labor markets among low-wage workers have never been more similar, whereas the wage differences across labor markets among high-wage workers have never been more different. Low wages differed by a factor of two in 1960, but by only 35 percent today. Within this period, the United States experienced an abrupt shift from Keynesian economics to neoliberal Reaganomics. The subsequent deregulation, deindustrialization, and union-busting decreased

workers' power, especially those with lower levels of educational attainment and employed in lower-wage jobs. Furthermore, contingent work for less-educated workers has grown more uniform across labor markets. In total, we are skeptical that the recent connection between affluence and poverty in certain labor markets is due to the pull of brighter economic fortunes for lower-paid and lower-skill workers. Instead, our findings support recent arguments of the dependence of affluent households on a stock of local low-paying labor (Mazzalari and Ragusa 2013; Wilmers 2017) as well as an underexamined geographical consequence of the removal of protections and power among middle- and low-pay workers.

We argue that recent changes to wage polarization have had negative consequences for low-wage workers, not only those far removed from affluent labor markets, but increasingly those inside them as well. Our results have three main implications. First, we show the geographical consequences of wage polarization, especially for low-wage workers. Scholars have argued that contemporary changes in the labor market have destroyed many of the rents enjoyed by low-wage workers (Sørensen 2000): job security, livable wages, union membership, internal labor markets, and employment benefits, for example (Cappelli and Keller 2013; Kalleberg 2013; Weeden and Grusky 2014; Weil 2014; VanHeuvelen 2018b). Our work extends this line of research to place-based wage rents. Bad jobs are increasingly bad everywhere, suggesting that low-paid workers have fewer places to turn for brighter economic opportunities. Second, our results present an important challenge to rosier arguments of the positive agglomeration externalities among densely populated "brain hubs" (Moretti 2012). A resonant claim in recent years among geographical stratification research has been that urban agglomeration and the high wages of high-paid workers in such places tend to have widely experienced benefits (Glaeser et al. 2009; Glaeser 2012): one of the more lucrative and desirable choices for all residents is to attract the affluent. Our findings suggest that much of the work that developed these conclusions focused on a unique historical era of unusually large agglomeration wage benefits for low-wage workers. Recent decades have seen a broadly shared deterioration of pay for lower-wage workers and a growing division between the top and the bottom, particularly in affluent areas. Third, our work speaks to popular concern over the increasingly divergent fortunes across American labor markets. Some places, such as densely populated global cities along the coasts, are pulling apart economically, politically, and socially from others, such as small towns that rely on a few manufacturing or agricultural employers (Holzer et al. 2011), leading some to suggest policies like relocation vouchers for low-income workers (Strain 2014; Hsieh and Moretti 2015; Lindsey and Teles 2018). Our findings suggest that such recommendations might overemphasize differences at the top end of the wage distribution and may not recognize long-run historical leveling occurring at the low end of the labor market. Although economic fortunes have grown in a small number of large and affluent labor markets, places are becoming more uniform for many, particularly those in low-paying and insecure work.

BACKGROUND

The recent upswing of U.S. inequality has been driven by occupational polarization, or the growth of high- and low-paying jobs concurring with the hollowing out of middle-paying jobs (Wright and Dwyer 2003; Dwyer and Wright 2019; Mouw and Kalleberg 2010) and wage polarization, or the concurrent takeoff of top pay alongside the stagnation and decline of median and lower wages (Piketty, Saez, and Zucman 2017). At the same time, scholars note that low-paying jobs are frequently precarious and insecure, defined by uncertain working hours, lower work quality, less occupational authority and autonomy, fewer benefits, and greater prevalence of part-time work (Kalleberg 2013). How do these polarizations and changes to precarity occur across geographical space? Underneath macrolevel economic trends are widely diverse local labor markets, such as densely populated cities tightly connected to global markets, agricultural and ranching communities, and rust belt communities adapting to deindustrializa-

tion and import competition (Moller, Alderson, and Nielsen 2009). In the following section, we discuss reasons to anticipate why wage polarization may occur unevenly across local labor markets, resulting in uneven economic consequences for low-paid workers.

The Case for Between-Place Polarization

On the one hand, wage polarization may lead to labor market polarization, in that the bifurcation of employment into good and bad jobs might aggregate up to labor market bifurcation into cities with better and worse economic opportunities for the local workforce (compare Florida 2014; Glaeser 2012; Lindsey and Teles 2018; Moretti 2012). Sociologists have shown intra-metropolitan income segregation to have grown rapidly over the past thirty-five years, driven primarily by changing residential patterns of high- and low-income households (Reardon and Bischoff 2011). This research tradition assesses many dimensions of segregation, but primarily focuses on neighborhoods in the largest labor markets (Massey 1996; Lee and Marlay 2007; Owens 2012; Wilson 2011). Yet segregation does not exclusively occur among neighborhoods of large cities. For example, Daniel Lichter, Domenico Parisi, and Michael Taquino show that racial segregation occurs across "places" within metropolitan statistical areas (2015). Similarly, Enrico Moretti documents the importance of large and densely populated "brain hubs," such as Silicon Valley, Seattle, Washington, New York City, and Stamford, Connecticut, that draw highly educated workers (2012), partially due to desirable cultural amenities (Florida 2014) and partially to higher potential earnings through agglomeration economies (Glaeser and Gottlieb 2009; Moretti 2012).[1] Cooperation, serendipity, network connections, job switching, and information sharing are facilitated in these urban areas, allowing knowledge workers to be more efficient, raising productivity and thus pay. Such brain hubs have largely pulled away from less populated cities and towns, which have declined in population, returns to skill, and local job opportunities. Relatedly, many smaller cities built

1. Moretti and Glaeser also identify the importance of within-career upward wage mobility for low-wage workers in more affluent areas. Our research is unable to assess this component of their arguments.

around a small set of manufacturing industries have lost a significant proportion of this core employment due to globalization and import competition (Holzer et al. 2011; Autor, Dorn, and Hanson 2013), whereas agricultural communities struggle to retain employment and college-educated residents (Lichter and Schafft 2016).

If income and employment polarizations correspond with labor market polarization, what consequences might this have for lower-wage work in affluent areas? Some research suggests that the factors leading to the beneficial wage-boosting agglomeration externalities enjoyed by more highly educated and skilled workers extend to low-wage workers. For example, Moretti shows that wage growth among high school educated workers was greater in cities with larger mean wages for college-educated workers (2012; see also Glaeser and Gottleib 2009; De La Roca and Puga 2017).[2] If economic fortunes for the affluent have diverged across areas, then lower- and middle-wage workers across such places might have similarly diverged, those in affluent labor markets pulled up via the same mechanisms detailed in agglomeration theories. Furthermore, thriving labor markets might allow for broadly improved employment opportunities for all workers. Given that these areas are typically denser in population, industries, and job opportunities, they might have more favorable employment opportunities for both more highly and less-skilled workers, allowing for improved matching between firm and worker, wage-boosting job mobility, and more employment opportunities immediately following job loss (Sorensen and Sorenson 2007; Mouw and Kalleberg 2010; De La Roca and Puga 2017). All these may boost not only wages, but also worker leverage and thus job quality.

Alternatively, the least skilled workers might be pushed out of good labor markets to poorer but more affordable areas through such factors as rising housing costs (Ganong and Shoag 2017). Similarly, economic changes that result

in the economic divergence of labor markets might exacerbate pay inequality at the low end by pushing wages down outside affluent and populous areas. For example, David Autor and his colleagues show the geographically uneven consequences of import competition with China, which hit especially hard in areas heavily reliant on a smaller set of employers and industries (Autor, Dorn, and Hanson 2013). Less-educated and lower-paid workers incurred the brunt of the pecuniary consequences, experiencing large cumulative wage declines over time and higher probabilities of repeat exposure to import competition across job switches. Furthermore, shocks such as deindustrialization have broadly rippling consequences, as many related industries, such as services and construction, experience related economic hardship. Scholars have shown that the most vulnerable workers in areas that experience such economic shocks are the least likely to migrate to better opportunities (Wozniak 2010; Moretti 2012). Thus, migration may occur unevenly, leaving behind the least skilled and most vulnerable workers in declining areas. The resulting negative economic conditions might translate into lower pay, worse job quality, and fewer benefits for low-skill and low-pay workers. Low pay across labor markets might also be exacerbated through the contemporary dynamics of economic polarization.

The Case for Within-Place Polarization

Alternatively, the concentration of affluence in labor markets may co-occur alongside a broadly shared growth of low-wage work, which would necessarily result in wage polarization both within and between places. Contemporary affluent households might depend on a stock of low-wage workers. For example, Francesca Mazzolari and Giuseppe Ragusa argue that high-earning households rely on the outsourcing of domestic services, such as childcare, cooking, cleaning, and transportation, to low-paid—frequently female immigrant—workers (2013).

2. Our research is similar to work by Moretti and Glaeser in focusing on how agglomeration economies—which largely benefit highly paid workers—affect the entire local wage distribution. Ours differ from theirs primarily by examining these spillover effects in a longer historical series, and by examining related issues of job quality for less-educated workers.

GEOGRAPHY OF POLARIZATION 81

Similarly, Jesper Sorensen and Olav Sorenson find horizontal and vertical differentiation among Danish labor markets to be key for generating inequality (2007). Nathan Wilmers extends their analysis by arguing that high-income consumers generate inequality within industries through the demand of status or quality differentiation (2017). For example, high-income consumers frequently demand variety of choice of restaurants, which generates demand for many lower-paid and insecure workers to staff these suites of choices. If high-income consumption relies on low-paid and insecure service and production workers to provide outsourced domestic care and choice among cultural amenities, then one might anticipate that the two poles of the labor force to coreside in the labor markets where the affluent locate.[3]

Similarly, changes to organizational norms might result in the growth of highly and low-paid workers in the same area. David Weil identifies the growing importance of a managerial focus on *core competency*, or workplace fissuring (2014). Low-skill labor is viewed as a cost to be temporarily incurred. Firms outsource low-skill labor to external companies that face great pressure to reduce wages in order to minimize costs. These changes resulted in declining pay and benefits for outsourced workers (Dube and Kaplan 2010). Many services, such as cleaning, cooking, and security, require in person presence for the completion of occupational tasks, and there is little reason to suspect that brain hubs, which frequently house large and profitable global firms, are somehow immune from the pressures to fissure. Thus, affluent areas with large stocks of skilled workers employed in the core competency of high-paying firms might coreside in areas with workers experiencing declining wage standards.

There is additional theoretical reason to expect diverging geographic trajectories across top and bottom ends of the labor market. Aage Sørensen details the importance of *rent destruction*, or the removal of benefits and protections that push wages above market levels, among labor for the contemporary rise of inequality (2000). He argues that the destruction of rents won during the New Deal and immediately following World War II—unionization, minimum wages, internal labor markets, ideals of worker protection, and job security, for example—should result in "less positional inequality, but more inequality overall . . . the destruction of rents in the labor market has created a labor market with fewer structural supports for the returns to labor" (2000, 1553).[4] That is, there should be fewer predictable locations of relatively higher wages for middle- and lower-wage workers despite growing wage inequality. Much research on low-paid and contingent work has followed such argumentation, finding that a significant reason for growing economic insecurity is the destruction of protective rents among the lower end of the labor market (for example, Western and Rosenfeld 2011; Van-Heuvelen 2018b). If broadly experienced rent destruction drives the contemporary growth of low-paid and precarious work, then recent trends should correspond with less geographical variation of rents, resulting in low-wage convergence across areas. Simply put, bad jobs might be increasingly bad across labor markets, leading to a convergence of economic fortunes of low-wage workers across labor markets that are more and less affluent.

Sociologists provide additional theoretical reason to expect that the mechanisms of high- and low-wage work may lead to within-place polarization. Kim Weeden and David Grusky note the importance of rent creation at the top end of the labor market and its independence from low-wage rent destruction (2014). For example, occupational closure and barriers to college degrees keep the supply of skill artificially

3. An important counterargument to the discussion in this section is that brain hubs might grow more polarized over time as low-wage workers select into these areas based on their possibility for upward wage attainment over their careers (see De La Roca and Puga 2017). Such a possibility is not testable with our census data and beyond the scope of the current project, but presents a compelling alternative mechanism to the ones focused on in this article. Future research is needed that focuses on differential selection.

4. For example, the decline in labor union membership and power results in lower between-group inequality between union and non-union members, but increases overall inequality in the labor market.

RSF: THE RUSSELL SAGE FOUNDATION JOURNAL OF THE SOCIAL SCIENCES

low relative to demand, increasing wage returns. Winner-take-all markets and growing market power of a smaller number of firms similarly should concentrate occupational location of high-wage work, increasing the concentration and pay of high-wage workers in a smaller number of areas. From this perspective, the fortunes of high- and low-paid workers are segmented across relatively isolated spaces of the labor market, where workers are more or less successful in creating, or maintaining, rents. In this case, rent creation among top wages in brain hubs need not couple tightly with local rent creation among low wages.

Demographic Changes and Geographical Polarization

Care is needed to ensure that wage differences across labor markets are not confounded by group-based differences in wage setting and location of residence. The era under consideration includes several substantial policy and demographic changes, including the civil rights movement and subsequent backlash, the gender revolution and upward educational and occupational attainment of women, and changes to immigration laws that partially account for growing racial and ethnic diversity. These policies have resulted in well-documented wage differences across sex and racial-ethnic groups that result partially from discriminatory practices and barriers to social networks and skill development (compare Pedulla and Mueller-Gastell 2019). Previously research illustrates that such wage differences play out differently in different labor markets due to structural factors such as workforce casualization, deindustrialization, and occupational segregation (McCall 2002) as well as local demographic composition (Huffman and Cohen 2004). Similarly, residential patterns have changed substantially over time. Smaller cities and rural areas have seen an influx of Hispanic immigrants (Lichter et al. 2010; Massey 2010), and African American migration to the southern United States has increased substantially over the past two decades (Frey 2014). These patterns, along with the well-established segregation patterns

documented by stratification scholars and demographers, may provide important understanding of the mechanisms driving results (Holliday and Dwyer 2009; Wilson 2011). We therefore pay special consideration to how results vary across gender, race, and nativity groups.

DATA

We use sixteen waves of U.S. Census and American Community Survey microdata (Ruggles et al. 2019). Individuals and households are sorted into 722 local labor markets, *commuting zones* (CZ), which cover the entire contiguous United States (Tolbert and Sizer 1996; VanHeuvelen 2018a). Census definitions of local labor markets, CZs are county clusters grouped together based on census journey to work data. Briefly, commuting is greater between work and home across the counties of a single CZ than across counties of two separate CZs (for example, in California, more workers commute between San Francisco and San Mateo counties than between San Mateo and Santa Barbara counties). CZs have become increasingly common in geographical studies of labor markets and economic inequality (Autor and Dorn 2013; Autor, Dorn, and Hanson 2013; Bloome 2014; Chetty et al. 2014; Charles, Hurst, and Schwartz 2018; VanHeuvelen 2018a). We use Dorn's (2009) publicly available codes to construct 1990 definition commuting zones for years 1950, 1970, 1980, 1990, 2000, and 2005–2009. We then extend his sorting logic to "Minipuma" identifiers in year 1960 and updated public use micro areas (PUMA) definitions for pooled years 2011–2015.[5] In total, we have eight repeated observations of 722 local labor markets, resulting in 5,776 CZ-year observations.

Commuting zones are a useful labor market definition for this study. Most important, they cover all areas of the United States. This advantage overcomes limitations of many income segregation and polarization studies that select on either data availability or labor market population size. The current research thus reconciles studies of urban (Patillo and Robinson 2016) and rural (Lichter and Schafft 2016) labor

---

5. We label 2011–2015 as 2010 for simplicity.

markets. Furthermore, CZs are more fine-grained than state-level measurements (Ganong and Shoag 2017). A pear farmer in Washington State's Yakima Valley might not consider herself in the same labor market—or face the same changes in cost of living and economic opportunity—as a childcare provider in Seattle, for example. CZs are also defined through the lived experience of workers based on residence and occupational location, a benefit over definitions of labor markets based on political jurisdictions, such as counties or states. Many workers in Washington, D.C., commute from nearby counties, such as Fairfax County in Virginia and Montgomery County in Maryland. Additionally, a variety of microlevel measurements, such as employment status and wage distributions, can be computed as a CZ-level characteristic, an advantage over aggregated categories available through the census. However, the commuting zone definition has important drawbacks. Perhaps most critically, we cannot measure census tract or neighborhood segregation, or income segregation, across places within a commuting zone (Dwyer 2007; Lichter, Parisi, and Taquino 2015). For example, the New York City commuting zone includes the five boroughs as well as surrounding commuter counties, such as Westchester County. Although this reflects the location of residence and work in the overall New York City labor market, the meaningful fine-grained income segregation that occurs across counties, places, blocks, and buildings cannot be detected. Our study is therefore best understood as complementary to city-level segregation studies, providing a context for how economic polarization plays out across the full distribution of U.S. labor markets.

Measures of Affluence

We use four variables to examine affluence. First, we measure the local concentration of affluent *households*, which we conceptualize as those at or above the 95th percentile of the national household year-specific income distribution.[6] To account for variation of household size, we normalize income by the square root of household members. Household income includes total money income of all household members age fifteen or more during the previous year: wage and salary income, business and farm incomes, social security income, welfare and public assistance, interest, dividend, and rental income, and other money income.[7] Measures are thus post-transfer, pre-tax. We compute the percentage of households in a CZ defined as affluent over the total number of households in that zone. Second, we measure the normalized household income at the local 95th percentile. Third, we shift focus to *individual wages* and measure the local level of the 95th wage percentile. Wages are constructed by dividing a worker's total pre-tax wage and salary income (inclusive of wages, salaries, commissions, cash bonuses, tips, and other monetary income received from an employer) by annual hours worked. Top-coded wage incomes are multiplied by 1.5, wages are bottom-coded to half the year-specific federal minimum wage, and wages are adjusted to 2009 dollars using the personal consumption expenditure index (VanHeuvelen 2018a). Fourth, we measure the wage bill share of the top 5 percent of wage earners in a CZ. This is measured as the total wage income of those at or above the 95th percentile, divided by the total annual wages earned in a commuting zone.

Definitions of Low-Paid and Insecure Work

We use four variables to measure local low-paid and insecure work. First, we measure the rate of *relative poverty*, identified as a *household* earning less than half the median national household income. These measures are normalized by the square root of household mem-

6. In main results, we do not normalize incomes by local cost of living, which has typically been computed through some relative measure of household rent. Rebecca Diamond shows that local cost of living and local concentration of amenities, such as availability of green space, cultural activities, and public transportation, tend to wash one another out when computing local wage and inequality levels (2016). We do replicate results adjusting for local cost of living.

7. Specific categories vary by year. We replicated results using only salary and wages, but results were similar.

bers.[8] Second, to measure low pay, we measure the local *individual wage* at the 10th percentile. Third, we measure the wage bill share of the 10th percentile and below of workers relative to total wages earned in a commuting zone. Fourth, we measure the proportion of employed prime-age men and women (separately) who work part time, defined as working twenty hours a week or less or twenty-six weeks a year or less, and have a high school degree or less.[9] Descriptive statistics are listed in table 1. We also examine how wage results are affected by local variation in cost of living. Details are provided in corresponding sections in the results section.[10]

Controls

Because geographical sorting could be driven by a variety of factors, including local industries, demographics, educational attainment, population density, and policy legacies, we include several characteristics of local labor market when estimating regression models. These are noted in table 1.

METHODS

Regression results come from two-way fixed-effects regression models. We include fixed effects for both year and commuting zone. Results are weighted by the logged number of households in a commuting zone. We use ro-bust standard errors and test all regression main results using bootstrapped and jack-knifed standard errors. Several other analyses are descriptive in nature. We discuss specific methodological decisions for all such analyses.[11]

RESULTS

Figure 1 shows the relationship, by year, of the percentage of households that are affluent, defined as at or above the 95th percentile of the country-level normalized household income, and that are poor, defined as half or less than the national median normalized household income. Markers are weighted by the logged household count in a commuting zone. Among the many notable patterns, we highlight four. First, in all years, CZs with the highest concentration of affluent households tend to be those with the lowest concentration of poor households. Simple correlations between these percentages range from –0.77 (1960) to –0.60 (2000). At the same time, substantial heterogeneity exists across the least poor CZs in terms of the concentration of affluent households. Among such CZs, nearly the entire range of affluence concentration is observable. Second, the poorest commuting zones are unique in their consistent low concentration of affluent households.[12] Such places, like eastern Kentucky, where President Lyndon Johnson announced

---

8. Unfortunately, tax information from the gold standard tax measurement system, NBER's TAXSIM, is not available at the state level prior to 1977 (Brady, Baker, and Finnigan 2013; Young et al. 2016), and so our measure of relative poverty comes from post-transfer, pre-tax measures.

9. In sensitivity analyses, we measure the proportion of workers in home production substitute industries (Mazzolari and Ragusa 2013). We also replicated the results of Moretti (2012) by examining the CZ-median high school and college wages. Results reinforced main conclusions below. We follow the logic of Liu and Nazareno, this issue, who show that the negative consequences of precarious work are largely concentrated among less-educated workers (2019).

10. We replicated all results with and without foreign-born workers. We reach the same substantive conclusions across these sampling decisions.

11. The results are intended to *descriptively* assess changes across labor markets over time. Our research design is not robust enough to make strong causal claims about the relationship between local labor market conditions and wage attainment. In this article, we draw on the strengths of examining inequality trends over a long period using a full set of local labor markets, rather than develop a stronger and narrower causal identification between a treatment and an inequality outcome. All results should be read with the understanding of this trade-off.

12. We find that areas with high average poverty have consistently low levels of relative affluence, and that maximum levels of affluence concentration among poor areas reach the median value of affluence concentration of the whole sample.

Table 1. Descriptive Statistics

		1950	1960	1970	1980	1990	2000	2005–2009	2011–2015
Percent affluent	Mean	3.53	2.90	2.89	3.25	2.41	2.82	2.70	2.90
	SD	2.13	1.42	1.20	1.32	1.39	1.38	1.47	1.44
Percent relative poverty	Mean	35.70	33.16	30.79	27.97	29.87	28.54	28.57	28.28
	SD	11.28	12.02	7.69	6.88	7.83	6.78	6.60	6.18
Population density	Mean	3.15	3.21	3.24	3.36	3.38	3.47	3.48	3.51
	SD	1.35	1.38	1.44	1.44	1.48	1.52	1.56	1.56
Wage: 10th percentile	Mean	0.92	1.12	1.48	1.56	1.51	1.68	1.67	1.66
	SD	0.19	0.26	0.20	0.13	0.13	0.11	0.11	0.10
Wage: 95th percentile	Mean	2.56	2.85	3.16	3.23	3.24	3.37	3.44	3.48
	SD	0.15	0.15	0.12	0.11	0.12	0.14	0.16	0.15
Wage bill share: bottom 10 percent	Mean	0.04	0.03	0.02	0.02	0.02	0.02	0.01	0.02
	SD	0.01	0.02	0.00	0.00	0.00	0.00	0.00	0.00
Wage bill share: top 5 percent	Mean	0.10	0.09	0.10	0.12	0.14	0.15	0.16	0.17
	SD	0.03	0.02	0.01	0.01	0.01	0.02	0.02	0.02
Part-time work: prime-age high school men	Mean	0.07	0.09	0.06	0.06	0.08	0.07	0.08	0.09
	SD	0.03	0.04	0.02	0.02	0.02	0.02	0.02	0.02

Source: Authors' compilation based on 1950–2000 census and 2005–2015 American Community Survey data (Ruggles et al. 2019).
Note: 722 repeated observations across eight time periods. Percent affluent and percent poverty computed as local percentage of households at or above 95th percentile of national household income distribution, or at or below half of national median income. Wage and wage bill share information computed from local wage distributions in commuting zones. Control variables in regression models include: median household income, percent employment in manufacturing, in service, and in agriculture, percent of individuals age twenty-five and older with a college degree, educational heterogeneity (Moller et al. 2009), population density, female labor-force participation, percent of population over age sixty-five, percent population black, percent of households headed by a single mother, abstract task occupational concentration, and routine intensive occupational concentration. Descriptive statistics of controls available on request. For ease of presentation, we refer to the 2005–2009 combination of years as "2005," and 2011–2015 as "2010." N = 5,776.

Figure 1. Relationship Between Percentage of Affluent and Poor Households

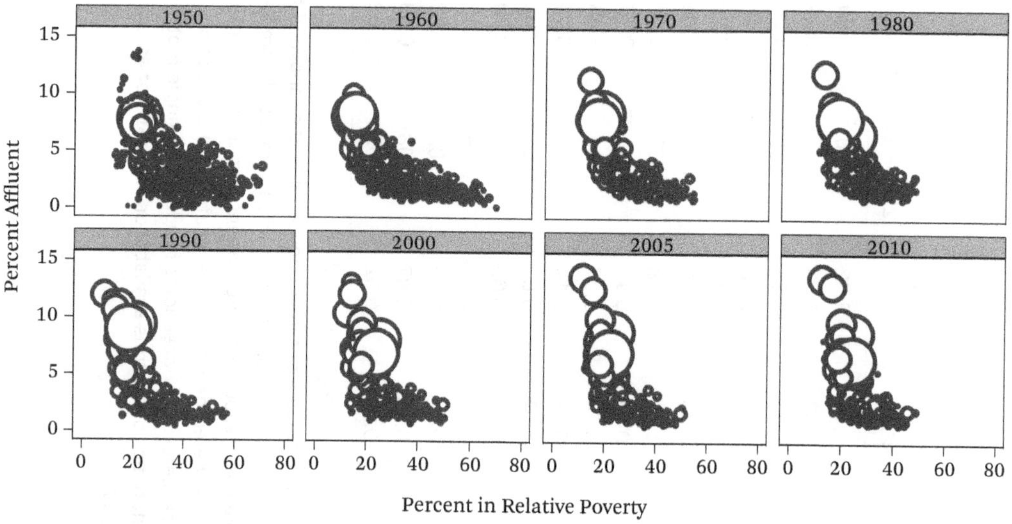

Source: Authors' compilation based on 1950–2000 census and 2005–2015 American Community Survey data (Ruggles et al. 2019).
Note: A total of 722 commuting zones. Percent affluent computed as the number of households at or above the nation-level 95th household income percentile over the total number of households in a commuting zone. Percent relative poverty is the number of households in a commuting zone at or below half the nation-level median household income. Markers are weighted by the number of households in a commuting zone. For ease of interpretation, in figures we label years 2005–2009 as "2005" and 2011–2015 as "2010."

the War on Poverty, have very high rates of poverty and little connection to affluence. Third, affluent areas have growing poverty.[13] In 1990, for example, the lowest CZ poverty rates were at 9.5 percent. By 2015, the lowest poverty rate was 13.5 percent. Fourth, one can observe from 2000 onward the separation of three labor markets as unique in their concentration of affluence: Washington, D.C., San Jose, California, and San Francisco, California.[14]

How has wage polarization occurred across geographical space? Figure 2 uses the logic of Massey and Fischer (2003) to examine change in CZ segregation of affluent households, poor households, and middle-income households, or those in between affluent and poor. These three groups do not perfectly capture income segregation across the whole of the income distribution, potentially masking income segregation occurring between and within these poles. For example, Sean Reardon and Kendra Bischoff measure income segregation as occurring across income binned into year-specific groups ranging from fifteen to twenty-five (2011). Yet results highlight the geographical consequences of wage polarization at the tails of the distribution, and notably, we reach the same conclusions when comparing across

13. The very large relative poverty rates reflect the income convergence between the South and the rest of the country during the early and mid-twentieth century (Lindert and Williamson 2016; Ganong and Shoag 2017).

14. Other intuitive labor markets with large numbers of affluent respondents, such as New York City and Seattle, have high concentrations of affluent workers. New York City has the fourth highest concentration in the most recent wave, and Seattle is in the top twenty. Because commuting zones incorporate many surrounding smaller cities (for example, the Seattle commuting zone includes less-affluent surrounding areas, such as Kent, Everett, Renton, Bremerton, and Tacoma), some of the concentration of affluent workers in some city centers is diffused by these broader labor market definitions.

Figure 2. Relative Change in Segregation of Affluent, Poor, and In-Between Households

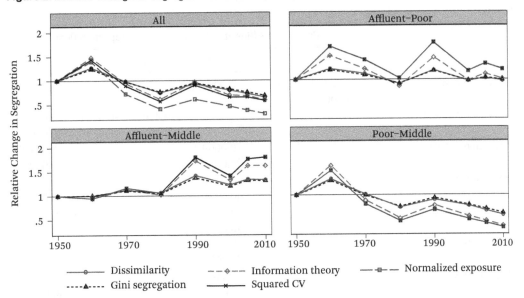

Source: Authors' compilation based on 1950–2000 census and 2005–2015 American Community Survey data (Ruggles et al. 2019).
Note: A total of 722 commuting zones. Segregation measures computed from household counts at the commuting zone level and estimated separately by year. All segregation measures normalized to equal 1 in 1950 to ease interpretation. *Affluent* refers to households at or above the nation-level 95th household income percentile. *Poor* refers to households at or below half the nation-level household median income. *Middle* refers to all other households. Substantively similar results used when comparing income deciles and ventiles.

household income deciles and ventiles. We also reach the same conclusions if we adjust local measurements of income based on cost of living (Moretti 2013). We include five common indices of evenness and exposure used in neighborhood-level segregation studies: the dissimilarity segregation index, Gini segregation index, information theory segregation index, squared coefficient of variation segregation index, and (n-group) normalized exposure segregation index. For interpretability of trends across indices, figure 2 shows changes relative to levels normalized to one at 1950.

Figure 2 shows that CZ-level segregation of affluent, middle-income, and poor households declined substantially over time, which reflects Massey's and Fischer's findings (2003). Overall, households in these three income groups are increasingly integrated in the same local labor markets. However, comparisons of paired groups reveal important heterogeneity. The overall trends are driven primarily by the de-

clining CZ-level segregation of poor and middle-income households. In contrast, aside from year-to-year fluctuation, the segregation of poor and affluent households has remained relatively constant, although affluent-poor segregation declined in recent decades relative to the 1990 high-water mark. At the same time, we observe increasing separation across labor markets of affluent and middle-income households. These results suggest two countervailing types of labor market sorting: some places are becoming increasingly polarized, becoming more defined by a concentration of affluent and poor households, whereas other areas are becoming increasingly isolated from high-income earners.

To better understand the nature of such geographical sorting, we present the results from two-way fixed-effects regression models predicting the proportion of affluent and poor households in table 2. That is, models predict the proportion affluent using the proportion

Table 2. Fixed-Effects Regression Models Predicting Proportion Affluent and Proportion in Relative Poverty

	Proportion Affluent			Proportion Poor		
	(1)	(2)	(3)	(4)	(5)	(6)
Proportion poor	−0.095***	−0.0031	0.0002			
	(0.005)					
Proportion affluent				−2.419***	−0.0231	0.0184
				(0.090)	(0.078)	(0.086)
Proportion X 1960			−0.0008			−1.0470***
			(0.006)			(0.090)
Proportion X 1970			−0.0235***			−0.4748***
			(0.007)			(0.085)
Proportion X 1980			−0.0323***			−0.1911*
			(0.007)			(0.088)
Proportion X 1990			−0.0066			−0.3167***
			(0.008)			(0.095)
Proportion X 2000			−0.0109			0.0458
			(0.008)			(0.094)
Proportion X 2005–2009			−0.0206*			0.1672
			(0.008)			(0.088)
Proportion X 2011–2015			−0.0280***			0.4193***
			(0.008)			(0.089)
Commuting zone fixed effects?	Yes	Yes	Yes	Yes	Yes	Yes
Year fixed effects?	Yes	Yes	Yes	Yes	Yes	Yes
Controls?	No	Yes	Yes	No	Yes	Yes
N	5,776	5,776	5,776	5,776	5,776	5,776

Source: Authors' compilation based on 1950–2000 census and 2005–2015 American Community Survey data (Ruggles et al. 2019).

Note: Robust standard errors in parentheses. Models include controls for manufacturing employment, agriculture employment, service employment, proportion twenty-five and older with a college degree, educational heterogeneity, population density, population growth, median household income, proportion age sixty-five and older, proportion black, proportion Hispanic, proportion immigrant, female labor-force participation. Controls computed from IPUMS.

*p < .05; **p < .01; ***p < .001 (two-tailed tests)

poor, and vice versa. Models control for year and CZ fixed effects and use robust standard errors. Thus, results show how change in affluence concentration associates with change in poverty concentration, and vice versa.[15]

Models 1 and 4 show simple associations from regression models that include fixed effects but not control variables. In both cases, we observe significant and negative associations. Growth in affluence is associated with a decline in the proportion of poor households,

and growth of poor households associates with a decline in the proportion of affluent households. Yet the main coefficients in models 2 and 5 are both negative and statistically insignificant when controls are included in models. Sensitivity tests show significance to be removed with the addition of median household income. Median household income is highly significant and positively associated with affluence and negatively associated with poverty. However, we observe significant and diverging

15. We reach the same substantive conclusions if we use measures of poverty and affluence adjusted by local cost of living.

Figure 3. Year-Specific Coefficients from Fixed-Effects Models

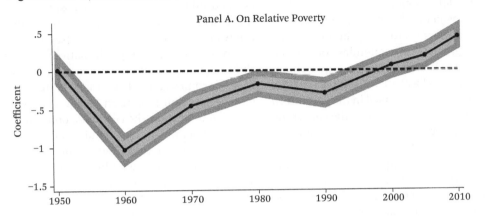

Panel A. On Relative Poverty

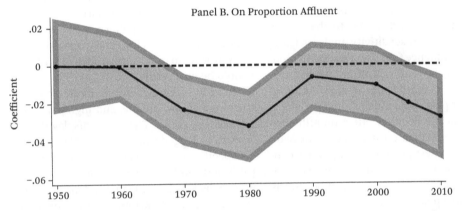

Panel B. On Proportion Affluent

Source: Authors' compilation based on 1950–2000 census and 2005–2015 American Community Survey data (Ruggles et al. 2019).
Note: Coefficients follow fixed-effects (commuting zone FEs) regression models in table 2. Affluence (top panel) and poverty (bottom panel) coefficients are interacted with time period indicators. Shaded areas represent 95 percent confidence intervals.

trends over time in models 3 and 6. To ease interpretation, these are presented in figure 3, which shows year-specific coefficients for proportion affluent on proportion poor (top panel) and vice versa (bottom panel). First (top panel), we observe that prior to 2000, the presence of affluent households had a negative and statistically significant association with relative poverty. That is, growth in the proportion of affluent households tended to correspond with declining rates of relative poverty. However, this negative association shrunk substantially in magnitude between 1960 and 1990, and since 2000, it has reversed: growth in the rate of affluent households corresponds with growth in

relative poverty. Results from models 1 and 2 largely reflect the combination of these opposite associations.

Turning attention to the bottom panel, we observe that growth in the proportion of poverty generally corresponds with a declining proportion of affluent households. Although some years, 1950, 1960, 1990, and 2000, have insignificant coefficients, all point in the same negative direction, in contrast to figure 2. Notably, though the positive association in the top panel from 2000 onward has grown in magnitude, the negative association in the bottom panel has as well. Since 2000, the magnitude of this negative association has increased by 170 percent, from

−0.01 to −0.027 (difference of the two coefficients, $p < .001$, two-tailed test).

These results highlight two main conclusions. First, whereas the wage-boosting influence of agglomerated economies could be effectively argued to raise lower-wage households out of poverty in local areas from 1960 to 1990, this association has reversed in the past fifteen years. In the contemporary era, the concentration of affluence corresponds with an increasingly polarized labor market. This finding is suggestive of contemporary high-income households relying on a low-paid and insecure stock of workers. In contrast, areas with large stocks of low-earning households are becoming locked out of the polarized economy, and high-earning households are increasingly sorting out of these labor markets. We further assess these arguments in sensitivity analyses using recentered influence function regression models separately by year, examining the associations across percentiles of the distribution of affluence or poverty as independent variables. We find that the negative effect on affluence concentration is greatest in most recent years among the highest percentiles of poverty concentration. Simply put, labor market wage polarization appears to be resulting in two forms of geographic polarization.

Economic Conditions Across a Polarized Geography

Thus far, our results suggest that poor households have become more concentrated alongside affluent ones, and that many labor markets are increasingly segregated from affluence and hold large stocks of poor households. These findings, however, lend themselves to starkly different interpretations. Edward Glaeser, Matt Resseger, and Kristina Tobio (2009) and Enrico Moretti (2012), for example, note that such associations might be spurious if less-skilled workers sort into agglomerated areas to take advantage of rosier economic opportunities.

That is, the contemporary copresence of poverty and affluence misidentifies a positive wage trajectory for low-wage workers seeking opportunity in trickle-down "brain hubs" (see also De La Roca and Puga 2017). Alternatively, these shifts might represent a broadly shared leveling of low incomes across labor markets through rent destruction (Sørensen 2000). A critical question is whether the economic opportunities at the bottom and the middle of the wage distribution are more favorable in brain hubs, which based on the geographical stratification literature, we understand as places with higher concentration of affluence, (possibly) lower concentration of poverty, and population density.[16] Is this favorable wage comparison growing alongside the growing polarization of these labor markets? If the patterns detected in figures 2, 3, and 4 reflect low-paid workers increasingly moving to opportunity, such opportunity should be observable.

To address these questions, figure 4 presents the range of low, middle, and high pay across commuting zones. The y-axes display the difference in logged wages across CZs at similar CZ-specific percentiles of wage distributions (10th, 50th, and 95th). Panels show between-CZ wage gaps (clockwise from top-left) of the CZ-specific wage levels, across affluence concentration, across poverty concentration, and among the most and least densely populated CZs.[17] For example, the dark solid line in the top-right panel in year span from 2011 to 2015 shows the wage difference at the 10th percentile of CZs with dense concentrations of affluent households—Washington, D.C., San Francisco, California, and San Jose, California—against wages at the 10th percentile of CZs with few affluent households—Hazard, Kentucky, Poplar Bluff, Missouri, and Jena, Louisiana.

As anticipated, densely populated labor markets, labor markets with a higher concentration of affluent households, and labor markets with fewer poor households tend to have higher rel-

16. We cannot track individuals over time who move from one labor market to another, nor can we track the wage trajectories of lower-wage workers who move into more affluent labor markets. Larger stocks of poor households could conceivably reflect lower wage workers selecting into labor markets with greater opportunity for upward wage mobility. We discuss this in more detail in the conclusion.

17. We compute population-weighted means of commuting zones that are in the top or bottom 5th percentiles of each CZ-level distribution by year, and then measure the gap among low-, middle-, and high-paid work.

Figure 4. Change in Wage Differences Across CZs at High-, Middle-, and Low-Wage Levels

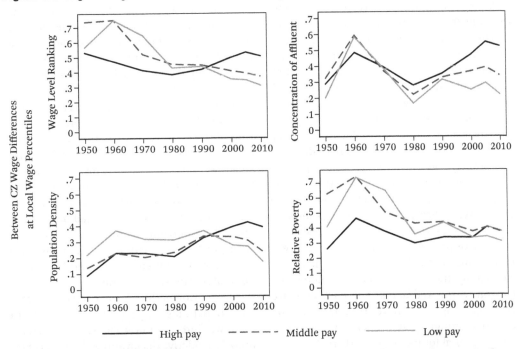

Source: Authors' compilation based on 1950–2000 census and 2005–2015 American Community Survey data (Ruggles et al. 2019).

Note: Percentiles represent locations in CZ-specific wage distributions. Lines represent difference in wages at specific percentiles across CZs, specifically those at or above the 95th percentile minus those at or below the 5th percentile. For example, the solid black line in the lower left indicates the difference in wages at the 95th percentile between the most densely populated CZs (such as New York City and Newark, New Jersey) and the least densely populated CZs (such as Lakeview, Oregon, and Jordan, Montana). High pay refers to wages at the 95th percentile, middle pay refers to wages at the 50th percentile, and low pay refers to wages at the 10th percentile.

ative wages for lower-, middle-, and higher-income respondents (Glaeser, Resseger, and Tobio 2009; Moretti 2012). That is, wages across the whole distribution tend to be higher in affluent and agglomerated labor markets. However, a historical assessment of these comparisons leads to a critical complicating conclusion: low pay has become increasingly similar across commuting zones, whereas high pay has diverged. For example, the top-left panel shows the gaps across the whole distribution of percentiles. In this panel, we observe that the relative wage gap across CZs at the 10th percentile has declined substantially over time. Whereas low wages varied on average by 0.7 across CZs in 1960, this gap declined by approximately 60 percent over time to under 0.3. In 1960, wages among CZs with the highest 10th percentile

wages—Cleveland, Ohio, Chicago, Illinois, Newark, New Jersey, and Buffalo, New York, for example—were higher by a factor of two relative to wages with the lowest 10th percentile wages—West Liberty, Kentucky, Greenville, Mississippi, and Cordele, Georgia, for example ($(e^{0.7}-1)*100 = 101.4$ percent). In 2011–2015, wages among CZs with the highest 10th percentile wages—Minneapolis, Minnesota, San Francisco, California, Washington, D.C., and Boston, Massachusetts, for example—were only 35 percent ($(e^{0.29}-1)*100 = 33.6$ percent) greater than 10th percentile wages in the lowest-paying CZs—Greenville, Mississippi, Gallup, Arizona, Crystal City, Texas, and Valdosta, Georgia, for example.

In contrast, the gap in high wages across CZs has grown from about 0.35 (in 1970, or approximately 42 percent) to more than 0.5 in 2011–2015 (approximately 65 percent). This panel shows 1980 as an important pivot point for increasing wage differentiation for high wages, coinciding with the well-documented economic transition to neoliberal politics and industrial relations. Remarkably, the geographical range of high pay is as high today as it was in 1949, prior to southern income convergence with the North (Lindert and Williamson 2016). Similar patterns are observed across affluence and poverty concentration, as well as population density. We considered whether results might be driven by specific regions or age groups. We replicated figure 4 among southern- and nonsouthern CZs, and among restricted samples of prime-age workers.[18] Across these replications we reached the same results. Considered together, results lead to a general conclusion: compared across the past sixty-five years, geography has never been more consequential for high-wage workers and never less consequential for low-wage workers.[19]

Even if the wage gains for low-wage workers in affluent areas have deteriorated in recent decades, might we nevertheless still observe greater relative advantage of low-wage workers in more affluent places relative to poorer ones? Although place-based wage benefits have declined, they are nonetheless present. Perhaps these small gaps are consequential for raising the relative standing of low-paid work in affluent labor markets. To assess this question, we examine the wage bill share of those in the bottom 10 percent and top 5 percent in local areas, shown in figure 5.[20] These are computed as the proportion of the total wage and salary incomes held by those in the bottom 10 percent of a CZ-specific distribution, and the propor-

tion of the top 5 percent, over the CZ-specific total sum of wages and incomes. We assess wage bill shares across the logged percentage of affluent households, the percentage of poor households, and population density using locally weighted regression lines estimated separately by year.[21]

We observe no meaningful variation of the wage bill held by those in the bottom 10 percent of the earnings distribution across affluence, poverty, or density distributions. Instead, we observe a general loss over time of the already small holdings of those with low wages. Such workers held about 4 percent of wages in 1950, which by 2010 had declined to around 1.5 percent. In contrast, we observe clear positive associations for high-pay wage bill shares in affluence hubs and in densely populated areas. In contrast, from 1980 onward, variation of the top wage bill held across areas depending on poverty rates is scant. In total, we find that low-wage workers increasingly face relative disadvantage in terms of total earnings held in densely populated, affluence concentrated areas. Any wage boosts afforded to low-wage workers in these areas could well be offset by the larger relative wage share disadvantage.

Cost of Living
How might results of figure 4 be driven by variation in cost of living? Housing is substantially more expensive in San Francisco and New York City than in many rural areas of the South and Midwest, for example. This might level some of the differences we observe across areas. We follow the logic of Moretti (2012) and partially adjust wages based on the year-specific adjusted gross rent of a two- or three- bedroom apart-

---

18. Year 1960 is excluded in these replications because no nativity information is available.

19. We also examined counterfactual differences between the lagged wage level at the 50th percentile of less-affluent commuting zones relative to the 25th percentile in more-affluent CZs, to simulate the potential wage change of a typical individual relocating from a more- to a less-affluent CZ. We found that since 2000, middle wages in less-affluent CZs have grown more than lower wages in affluent CZs. The reverse was the case prior to 2000. We take this as additional supportive evidence that moving to more affluent CZs has become a riskier proposition for anyone but high wage workers. Figures are available on request.

20. We replicated these results at the household level and reached similar conclusions.

21. We show the logged percentage because of the skewed distribution of affluence concentration across commuting zones.

Figure 5. Wage Bill Share Across Affluence, Population Density, and Relative Poverty

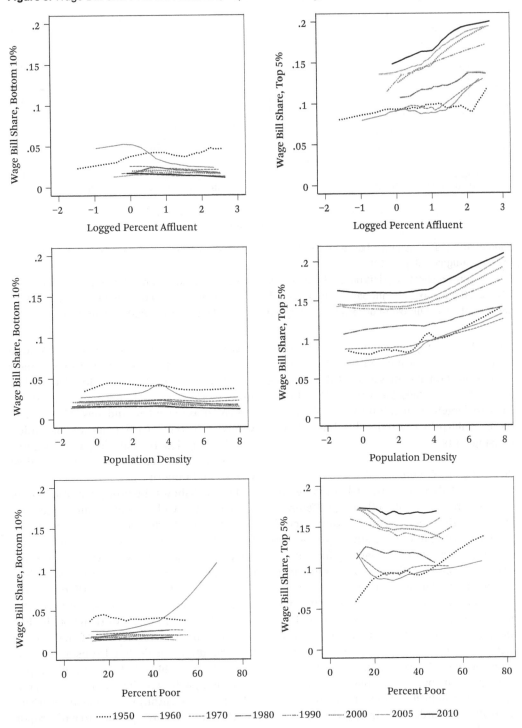

Source: Authors' compilation based on 1950–2000 census and 2005–2015 American Community Survey data (Ruggles et al. 2019).
Note: Lines computed from locally weighted regressions of wage bill against variables indicated along the x-axis, separately by year. Bandwidth = 0.3.

Figure 6. Replication of Figure 4, by Sex, Race-Ethnicity, and Nativity Groups

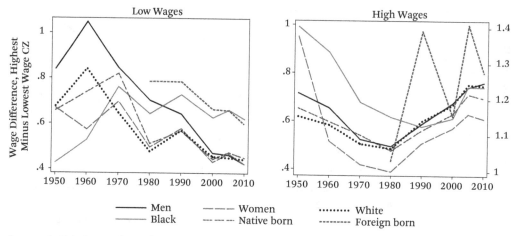

Source: Authors' compilation based on 1950–2000 census and 2005–2015 American Community Survey data (Ruggles et al. 2019).

Note: Figures replicate top left panel of figure 4, which shows the maximum difference of wages across 722 CZs. Right y-axis of right panel is for foreign-born individuals. Foreign born begins in year 1980 because of small number of observations of foreign born workers in years 1950 through 1970.

ment. We then replicate figure 4, which is included in the online appendix.[22] Although the separation of top incomes across CZs is attenuated in between 2005–2009 and 2011–2015, results are largely similar. It is thus unlikely that these results primarily reflect local variation of housing costs.

Replication by Group

Care is needed to ensure that labor market differences are not simply reflecting differences in wage setting and residence patterns across gender, racial-ethnic, and nativity groups. Figure 6 replicates figure 4 separately for workers by race, sex, and nativity status. Overall results are largely similar, suggesting that results are not primarily driven by heterogeneity in results across groups. A few of the deviations from main results are notable. For low-paid workers, men experienced the largest relative convergence across CZs over time. Geographic pay gaps grew for low-income black workers between 1949 and 1970 and then declined slightly from 1990 onward. Of course, given the substantial social and political changes during these decades (Mandel and Semyonov 2016), it is unsurprising to observe differences in trends

between white and black workers. Among highly paid workers, we observe substantially greater geographical variation for black and female workers in early decades, but trends largely converge in 1990 and onward. Again, divergence in these earlier decades is understandable against the backdrop of substantial and legally codified discrimination against women and minorities.

Figure 7 shows the group composition of low pay in CZs with the lowest and highest levels of low pay, by decade. A few trends are notable. White workers have been consistently underrepresented in low-paid work, the difference especially pronounced before 1980 in low-paying CZs. Conversely, black, Hispanic, and female workers have been consistently overrepresented among low-paid work in both higher- and lower-paying CZs. Black and female worker representation has declined substantially between 1950 and 2000, but remains disproportionately high. Low-paying CZs have grown rapidly in the concentration of Hispanic workers, but this has not corresponded to a disproportionate concentration of Hispanic workers in low-paid work in low-paying CZs. In total, although figures 6 and 7 illustrate important

22. The online appendix is available at https://www.rsfjournal.org/content/5/4/77/tab-supplemental.

Figure 7. Percent of Workers Above and Below 10th Wage Percentile

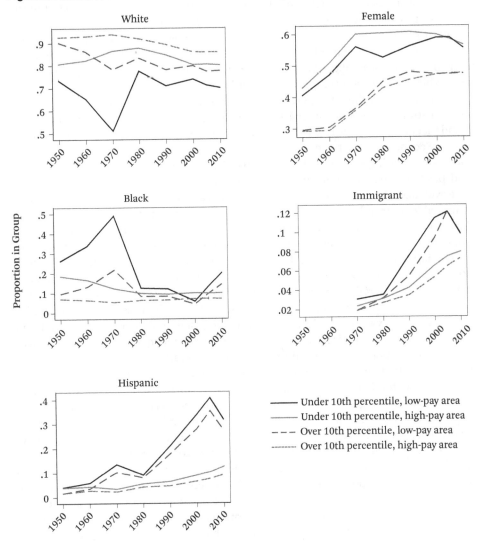

Source: Authors' compilation based on 1950–2000 census and 2005–2015 American Community Survey data (Ruggles et al. 2019).

group-based heterogeneity in low- and high-wage work, results do not cleanly point to group-based geographical differences in wage setting as primarily driving the results.

Precarious Work

What about job quality? Although pay might be leveling across geographical areas, perhaps benefits in affluence hubs accrue through job quality.[23] We examine this possibility by examining the rate of part-time work among prime-age men and women with a high school degree or less.[24] Unfortunately, census and ACS data do not have information on the multiple dimensions of job quality, precariousness, and contingency (Cappelli and Keller 2013; Kalle-

23. Unfortunately, census and ACS data do not have consistent measurements of work precarity across the eras assessed.

24. We also examined all prime-age workers and workers with a college degree. Results are substantively similar. We exclude years 1950 and 1960 because of the nature of female employment in these years. Trends in

berg 2013). We therefore use part-time work among prime-age workers with a high school degree or less as a proxy for the broader system of contingent work.

Figure 8 replicates the methods of figure 5 but uses part-time work as an outcome. A few results are notable. First, we observe gendered shifts in part-time work over time. The percentage of male part-time workers has increased over time, and that of female part-time workers has decreased. Second, we observe declining variation across commuting zones based on affluence and poverty concentration. In early years, we see evidence that part-time work was less concentrated in more affluent areas, in areas with lower poverty (for men), and in more densely populated areas. Yet especially since 2000, the associations across CZs have flattened, so that the proportion of part-time employment has become generally uniformly distributed across areas. Comparing across year-specific lowess lines, we observe clear longitudinal growth of male part-time work in more affluent and less poor areas, and little change in part-time female employment in more affluent areas. In total, these results suggest that not only have low wages leveled across CZs in recent decades, but that risk of precarious employment has also become more evenly distributed. Simple correlations by year illustrate these points as well. For example, the negative association between proportion affluence and male part-time work changed from a maximum of –0.48 in 1960 to essentially 0 in 2005–2009 and 2011–2015. For women, it changed from –0.12 in 1950 and –0.17 in 1990 to 0.04 in 2011–2015. The positive association between poverty and male part-time work decreased from a high of 0.73 in 1960 to a low of around 0.25 in 2005–2009 and 0.3 in 2011–2015. Similarly, we replicated fixed-effects regression models from table 2 predicting part-time work and found an emerging positive and significant association between part-time work and affluence, percentage in poverty,[25] and population density, since the year 2000, and a significant decline in the magnitude of the positive association between poverty and part-time work following 1990. Overall, these findings are suggestive that geographical leveling has occurred for both wage levels and employment precarity.[26]

CONCLUSION

In this research, we ask how wage polarization occurred across local labor markets in the contiguous United States. We examine several dimensions of affluence and low pay across 722 local labor markets, commuting zones, covering the entire contiguous United States, from 1950 to 2015. We first examine the geographical patterns of the residence of affluent and poor households. We then assess the geographical variation of low- and high-end pay. Simply put, our results call into question how beneficial urban agglomeration has been for lower-paid workers in recent decades.

We draw two main conclusions. First, household sorting across labor markets, particularly from 2000 onward, has increasingly resulted in two types of labor markets: polarized and poor. Commuting zones with higher rates of poverty tended to separate from affluent households, and local concentration of affluence has become associated with growth of poverty. Furthermore, affluent and middle-income households have increasingly segregated into different labor markets. Overall, wage polarization has coevolved with two types of labor market polarizations, one internal to labor markets where the affluent live, and one between labor markets, poorer places being increasingly separated from affluent households.

---

these years do not refute main conclusions discussed in the text (for a more inclusive and multidimensional set of measurements of precarious and insecure work relations, see, in this issue, Lambert, Henly, and Kim 2019; Liu and Nazareno 2019; Pedulla and Mueller-Gastell 2019).

25. Specifically, the inverse of percentage poor.

26. We find one contradictory piece of evidence to our general conclusions: areas with high poverty and with low affluence concentration have higher proportions of prime-age less-educated men not in the labor force. Thus, although the economic conditions of the low end of the labor market are converging across labor markets, access to any form of employment in poorer areas have increased for less-educated men.

Figure 8. Percent Prime-Age High School or Less Working Part Time

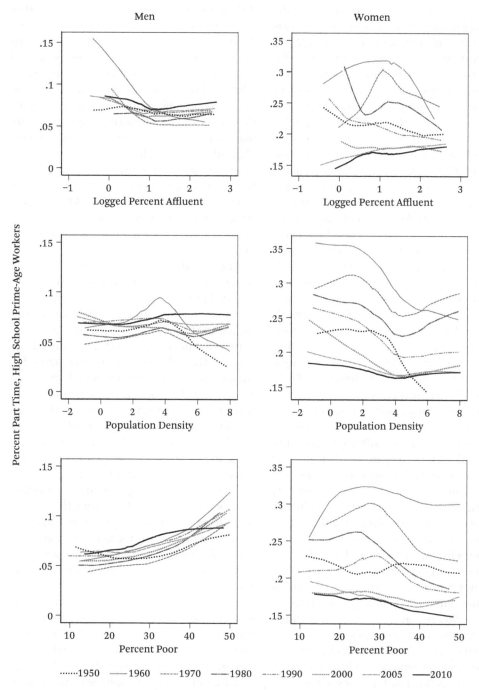

Men

Women

Percent Part Time, High School Prime-Age Workers

Logged Percent Affluent

Logged Percent Affluent

Population Density

Population Density

Percent Poor

Percent Poor

······1950 ——1960 -----1970 ——1980 ----1990 ········2000 ——2005 ——2010

Source: Authors' compilation based on 1950–2000 census and 2005–2015 American Community Survey data (Ruggles et al. 2019).
Note: Lines computed from locally weighted regressions of the percent of prime-aged part-time workers in a commuting zone against variables indicated along the x-axis, separately by year. Bandwidth = 0.6.

These findings support recent arguments of the contemporary interdependence of affluence and low-paid labor. For example, Wilmers uses the example of restaurant workers (2017). An important cultural taste of modern affluence is the selection of a dining choice from many restaurants. Such a choice requires the employment of multiple low-paid jobs, such as line cooks and wait staff. Similarly, Mazzolari and Ragusa highlight the reliance of high-earning households on outsourced domestic work, jobs that typically fall to lower-paid, frequently immigrant labor (2013). In sensitivity analyses, we find that affluence concentration was positively correlated with home substitution industry employment, but not similar nontradable industries. These contrasting correlations emerged after 1990, which roughly corresponds with our results. We also find home substitution employment to uniformly have lower mean, median, and 90th percentile wages relative to workers with a high school degree or less outside home substitution industries. In total, our results support recent arguments of the emergence of a reliance of affluent households on poorer ones.

At the same time, commuting zones with large stocks of poor households have consistently been isolated from affluent households. And growth of poverty, particularly from 2000 onward, associates negatively with the proportion of affluent households. As a sensitivity analysis, we estimated recentered influence function regressions predicting the proportion of affluent households with the proportion of poor households, and we found that the coefficient of poverty was significantly more negative at higher quantiles of the poverty distribution. Thus, entrenched poverty contributes to pushing affluence away. Combined with the earlier results, these findings suggest a broad polarization occurring across local labor markets. Local places tend to be either polarized, increasingly defined by the coresidence of affluent and poor households, or excluded from affluence and largely defined by poverty.

Our second main conclusion is that geography is becoming increasingly important for high-end pay and increasingly unimportant for low-end pay. We find that low-wage differences across commuting zones declined considerably

between 1950 and today, whereas geographical differences in high-end pay are as large as they have ever been in the post–World War II era. Although less-skilled workers do tend to earn higher wages in richer, more densely populated places, the magnitude of these benefits has declined substantially over time. We also document the broadly shared emergence of part-time work for less-educated workers, which we use as a proxy for contingent employment, along dimensions of brain hubs. Thus, not only have low wages converged across places, but so has the risk of precarious work for low-wage workers. In total, we observe starkly diverging trends. Geography is increasingly important for the rich and increasingly unimportant for the poor.

These findings add an additional wrinkle to recent research on low-paying work. Removal of protective rents for workers increases overall inequality, but removes inequality attached to structural positions. Just as the decline of labor union power has reduced the importance of between-group inequality between union and non-union members but increased overall inequality (Western and Rosenfeld 2011) and earnings volatility (VanHeuvelen 2018b), changes to economic markets, social policies, organizational management practices, and social norms—we argue—have led to a reduction of between-place inequality for low-wage workers, but greater overall inequality between the top and the bottom. If economic opportunities, rents, and power resources are being removed among the lower-paid segment of the labor market, it makes intuitive sense that one should observe convergence of wage setting across areas.

Relatedly, Weeden and Grusky note the asymmetric rent destruction and creation occurring at the bottom and top ends of the labor market (2014). That trends of high and low pay diverge suggests that these patterns play out to create contrasting geographical consequences at the tails of the labor market. These changes might create additional challenges for lower-paid workers in affluent areas. Sociologists and social psychologists have noted the importance of relative economic standing for happiness, well-being, and senses of self-worth (for example, Alderson and Katz-Gerro 2016). It may be that the positive wage gains of low-wage workers in affluent areas correspond with negative social status and psychological burdens.

These findings cast doubt on some of the rosier claims made by scholars of geographical inequality. Moretti, for example, argues that the agglomeration-induced wage gains made by highly skilled workers in brain hubs had widely shared benefits (2012). Similarly, Glaeser and his colleagues argue that the coresidence of poor and affluent households in the same labor market misidentifies contemporary polarization with the poor being drawn to locations of economic opportunity (Glaeser et al. 2009; Glaeser 2012). We confirm their general findings that low wages tend to be higher in affluent areas than in poorer areas. Yet, when we extend historical focus across the whole of the post–World War II era, a leveling of these wage-boosting effects is clearly observable. Whereas low wages differed by 100 percent across labor markets in 1960, they differ by only roughly 35 percent today. That such leveling has occurred at the same time that the affluent have concentrated in fewer places and witnessed a dramatic growth in their wages suggests a slowdown of the broadly shared benefits of urban agglomeration. We suggest that divergence of rent construction and rent destruction across the wage distribution better explain contemporary trends than urban agglomeration (Weeden and Grusky 2014).

We did not find clear evidence that results were primarily driven by group composition across commuting zones based on sex, race-ethnicity, or nativity. Rather, we find that the overall trends applied to many groups. It is beyond the scope of the current research to explain why some group trends, such as the gap for low pay across CZs for black workers, diverge from others. However, we believe future research on these topics would be of great use.

We are skeptical of policies that attempt to reinvigorate declining geographical mobility (Molloy et al. 2011, 2017). Think tanks and popular stories highlight the sharply diverging economic trajectories of rural and urban areas (for example, Strain 2014; Hsieh and Moretti 2015; Lindsey and Teles 2018), leading some to argue that financially incentivizing geographical mobility out of low-income areas into urban cores would be a silver bullet to the problem of low-wage work, and more generally, economic growth. All that seems to be stopping individuals is the cost to move, local housing costs, or perhaps cultural attachment to place. Our findings suggest that such a focus might place too much emphasis on the upper and upper-middle end of the wage distribution. A critical and often overlooked trend is that bad jobs are increasingly bad wherever one looks. Attempts to shift low-skill workers from one labor market to another might not adequately address the broad leveling of rents among such workers.

Our focus was on the dynamics of polarization across all labor markets of the United States. An important shortcoming of this focus is that it ignores the critical dynamics of wage setting and segregation that occur within large U.S. labor markets. Reardon and Bischoff, for example, find growing income segregation leading to greater income inequality among large cities in recent decades (2011). Lichter and colleagues find increasing place-based segregation within large urban areas (2015). There could well be important heterogeneity occurring below the overall trends we assess. More generally, scholars have thoroughly documented the different challenges of reducing poverty in rural and urban areas (Lichter and Schafft 2016; Patillo and Robinson 2016). Future research might fruitfully assess the qualities of low-wage workers and poor households across labor markets and over time. What occupations and householding characteristics define low-wage workers in affluent and poor places, and what are the wage differences of low-wage workers, adjusted for demographic and occupational characteristics? It might be that wages are higher in affluent areas for low-wage workers when comparing workers with similar age profiles, occupational, and industry characteristics. Similarly, the composition of poor households across areas can reveal important local risk profiles for poverty reduction policy decisions.

Several additional caveats are in order. If more affluent areas have higher rates of development, investment, cultural amenities, public services, and industrial concentration, then these places may offer more lucrative opportunities for workers across the life course. Furthermore, if affluent areas have broader educational and vocational training opportunities, low-wage workers in these areas might be better positioned for upward mobility (Schultz 2019). Additionally, densely populated cities may offer benefits to low-wage minority workers. For example, Devah Pager's audit studies in New York City revealed companies that discriminated more and less against minority applicants (2016). The simple presence of a greater stock of employers in larger areas might allow for greater opportunities to find those who do not discriminate as intensely.

Our study follows labor markets, not individuals, over time, meaning that we might miss important upward wage attainment dynamics for lower-wage workers in more affluent labor markets. We cannot track wage and labor market residence changes at the individual-level with these census data, making this question beyond the scope of the current study. Yet variation in mobility trends across labor markets is an important mechanism of agglomeration identified by both Glaeser and Moretti, and such variation may well offset some of the convergence among low wages that we have documented in this article. Conversely, sensitivity analyses show that labor markets with contemporary high concentration of affluent households also tend to have higher levels of wage inequality. And Raj Chetty and his colleagues show local inequality has dampened intergenerational income mobility in recent decades, suggesting that the current takeoff of top pay might similarly depress upward individual-level wage mobility in these labor markets (2014). Nevertheless, such an argument is speculative, and so future longitudinal work at the individual level is needed to qualify results presented here.

The recent push for minimum wage to be set at living wages and some localities' adoption of $15 minimum wages is an important development to be examined as future waves of ACS data become available. The Economic Policy Institute identifies forty-two localities that have a minimum wage mandate above state levels (2018). When passed in locations with a high concentration of affluence, such as Seattle, Washington, D.C., New York City, the San Francisco metropolitan area, and Chicago, these policies may assist in raising the standard of living for low-wage workers in these areas. It may be that future research detects a policy-driven, rather than agglomeration-driven, reversal of the trends documented here. Future research would do well to assess how such local minimum wage policy changes affect the long-run trends documented here.

In total, we argue that wage polarization is a manifestation of negative labor market outcomes for low-wage workers, not only those far removed from affluent labor markets, but increasingly those inside them as well. Geographical location of residence remains important for economic opportunity, but this has become increasingly restricted to the choice of highly paid workers. Overall, our study has demonstrated the important geographical consequences and implications of contemporary changes to low-paying and contingent work.

REFERENCES

Abowd, John M., Kevin L. McKinney, and Nellie L. Zhao. 2018. "Earnings Inequality and Mobility Trends in the United States: Nationally Representative Estimates from Longitudinally Linked Employer-Employee Data." *Journal of Labor Economics* 36(S1): S183–300.

Alderson, Arthur S., and Tally Katz-Gerro. 2016. "Compared to Whom? Inequality, Social Comparison, and Happiness in the United States." *Social Forces* 95(1): 25–54.

Atkinson, Anthony B., Thomas Piketty, and Emmanuel Saez. 2011. "Top Incomes in the Long Run of History." *Journal of Economic Literature* 49(1): 3–71.

Autor, David, H., and David Dorn. 2013. "The Growth of Low-Skill Service Jobs and the Polarization of the US Labor Market." *American Economic Review* 103(5): 1553–97.

Autor, David, H., David Dorn, and Gordon H. Hanson. 2013. "The China Syndrome: Local Labor Market Effects of Import Competition in the United States." *American Economic Review* 103(6): 2121–68.

Bloome, Deirdre. 2014. "Income Inequality and Intergenerational Income Mobility in the United States." *Social Forces* 93(3): 1047–80.

Brady, David, Regina S. Baker, and Ryan Finnigan. 2013. "When Unionization Disappears: State-Level Unionization and Working Poverty in the

United States." *American Sociological Review* 78(5): 872–96.

Cappelli, Peter H., and J. R. Keller. 2013. "A Study of the Extent and Potential Causes of Alternative Employment Arrangements." *ILR Review* 66(4): 874–901.

Charles, Kerwin Kofi, Erik Hurst, and Mariel Schwartz. 2018. "The Transformation of Manufacturing and the Decline in US Employment." *NBER* working paper no. w24468. Cambridge, Mass.: National Bureau of Economic Research.

Chetty, Raj, Nathaniel Hendren, Patrick Kline, and Emmanuel Saez. 2014. "Where Is the Land of Opportunity? The Geography of Intergenerational Mobility in the United States." *Quarterly Journal of Economics* 129(4): 1553–623.

De La Roca, Jorge, and Diego Puga. 2017. "Learning by Working in Big Cities." *Review of Economic Studies* 84(1): 106–42.

Diamond, Rebecca. 2016. "The Determinants and Welfare Implications of US Workers' Diverging Location Choices by Skill: 1980–2000." *American Economic Review* 106(3): 479–524.

Dorn, David. 2009. "Essays on Inequality, Spatial Interaction, and the Demand for Skills." PhD diss., University of St. Gallen.

Dube, Arindrajit, and Ethan Kaplan. 2010. "Does Outsourcing Reduce Wages in the Low-Wage Service Occupations? Evidence from Janitors and Guards." *ILR Review* 63(2): 287–306.

Dwyer, Rachel E. 2007. "Expanding Homes and Increasing Inequalities: US Housing Development and the Residential Segregation of the Affluent." *Social Problems* 54(1): 23–46.

Dwyer, Rachel E., and Erik Olin Wright. 2019. "Low-Wage Job Growth, Polarization, and the Limits and Opportunities of the Service Economy." *RSF: The Russell Sage Foundation Journal of the Social Sciences* 5(4): 56–76. DOI: 10.7758/RSF.2019 .5.4.02.

Economic Policy Institute. 2018. "Minimum Wage Tracker." Accessed November 15, 2018. https:// www.epi.org/minimum-wage-tracker.

Florida, Richard. 2014. *The Rise of the Creative Class, Revisited.* New York: Basic Books.

Frey, William. 2014. *Diversity Explosion: How New Racial Demographics Are Remaking America.* Washington, D.C.: Brookings Institute.

Ganong, Peter, and Daniel Shoag. 2017. "Why Has Regional Income Convergence in the US De- clined?" *Journal of Urban Economics* 102 (November): 76–90.

Glaeser, Edward L. 2012. *Triumph of the City: How Our Greatest Invention Makes Us Richer, Smarter, Greener, Healthier, and Happier.* New York: Penguin.

Glaeser, Edward L., and Joshua D. Gottlieb. 2009. "The Wealth of Cities: Agglomeration Economies and Spatial Equilibrium in the United States." *Journal of Economic Literature* 47(4): 983–1028.

Glaeser, Edward L., Matt Resseger, and Kristina Tobio. 2009. "Inequality in Cities." *Journal of Regional Science* 49(4): 617–46.

Goos, Maarten, and Alan Manning. 2007. "Lousy and Lovely Jobs: the Rising Polarization of Work in Britain." *Review of Economics and Statistics* 89(1): 118–33.

Holliday, Amy L., and Rachel E. Dwyer. 2009. "Suburban Neighborhood Poverty in US Metrolitan Areas in 2000." *City & Community* 8(2): 155–76.

Holzer, Harry, Julia Lane, David Rosenblum, and Fredrik Andersson. 2011. *Where Are All the Good Jobs Going? What National and Local Job Quality and Dynamics Mean for U.S. Workers.* New York: Russell Sage Foundation.

Hsieh, Chang-Tai, and Enrico Moretti. 2015. "Why Do Cities Matter? Local Growth and Aggregate Growth." *NBER* working paper no. 21154. Cambridge, Mass.: National Bureau of Economic Research.

Huffman, Matt, and Philip Cohen. 2004. "Racial Wage Inequality: Job Segregation and Devaluation Across U.S. Labor Markets." *American Journal of Sociology* 109(4): 902–36.

Kalleberg, Arne L. 2013. *Good Jobs, Bad Jobs: The Rise of Polarized and Precarious Employment Systems in the United States 1970s to 2000s.* New York: Russell Sage Foundation.

Lambert, Susan J., Julia R. Henly, and Jaeseung Kim. 2019. "Precarious Work Schedules as a Source of Economic Insecurity and Institutional Distrust." *RSF: The Russell Sage Foundation Journal of the Social Sciences* 5(4): 218–57. DOI: 10.7758/RSF .2019.5.4.08.

Lee, Barrett A., and Matthew Marlay. 2007. "The Right Side of the Tracks: Affluent Neighborhoods in the Metropolitan United States." *Social Science Quarterly* 88(3): 776–89.

Lichter, Daniel T., Domenico Parisi, and Michael C. Taquino. 2015. "Toward a New Macro-

Segregation? Decomposing Segregation Within and Between Metropolitan Cities and Suburbs." *American Sociological Review* 80(4): 843–73.

Lichter, Daniel T., Domenico Parisi, Michael C. Taquino, and Steven Grice. 2010. "Residential Segregation in New Hispanic Destinations: Cities, Suburbs, and Rural Communities Compared." *Social Science Research* 39(2): 215–30.

Lichter, Daniel T., and Kai A. Schafft. 2016. "People and Places Left Behind: Rural Poverty in the New Century." *The Oxford Handbook of the Social Science of Poverty*, edited by David Brady and Linda M. Burton. Oxford: Oxford University Press.

Lindert, Peter H. and Jeffrey G. Williamson. 2016. *Unequal Gains: American Growth and Inequality Since 1700*. Princeton, N.J.: Princeton University Press.

Lindsey, Brink, and Steven Teles. 2018. *The Captured Economic: How the Powerful Enrich Themselves, Slow Down Growth, and Increase Inequality*. Oxford: Oxford University Press.

Liu, Cathy Yang, and Luísa Nazareno. 2019. "The Changing Quality of Nonstandard Work Arrangements: Does Skill Matter?" *RSF: The Russell Sage Foundation Journal of the Social Sciences* 5(4): 104–28. DOI: 10.7758/RSF.2019.5.4.04.

Mandel, Hadas, and Moshe Semyonov. 2016. "Going Back in Time? Gender Differences in Trends and Sources of the Racial Pay Gap, 1970 to 2010." *American Sociological Review* 81(5): 1039–68.

Manning, Alan. 2003. *Monopsony in Motion: Imperfect Competition in Labor Markets*. Princeton, N.J.: Princeton University Press.

Massey, Douglas S. 1996. "The Age of Extremes: Concentrated Poverty and Affluence in the 21st Century." *Demography* 33(4): 395–412.

———. 2010. *New Faces in New Places: The Changing Geography of American Immigration*. New York: Russell Sage Foundation.

Massey, Douglas S., and Mary J. Fischer. 2003. "The Geography of Inequality in the United States, 1950–2000." *Brookings-Wharton Papers on Urban Affairs* (2003): 1–40.

Mazzolari, Francesca, and Giuseppe Ragusa. 2013. "Spillovers from High-Skill Consumption to Low-Skill Labor Markets." *Review of Economics and Statistics* 95(1): 74–86.

McCall, Leslie. 2002. *Complex Inequality: Gender, Class and Race in the New Economy*. New York: Routledge.

Moller, Stephanie, Arthur S. Alderson, and Francois

Nielsen. 2009 "Changing Patterns of Income Inequality in US Counties, 1970–2000." *American Journal of Sociology* 114(4): 1037–101.

Molloy, Raven, Christopher L. Smith, and Abigail Wozniak. 2011. "Internal Migration in the United States." *Journal of Economic Perspectives* 25(3): 173–96.

———. 2017. "Job Changing and the Decline in Long-Distance Migration in the United States." *Demography* 54(2): 631–53.

Moretti, Enrico. 2012. *The New Geography of Jobs*. Boston, Mass.: Houghton Mifflin Harcourt.

———. 2013. "Real Wage Inequality." *American Economic Journal: Applied Economics* 5(1): 65–103.

Mouw, Ted, and Arne Kalleberg. 2010. "Do Changes in Job Mobility Explain the Growth of Wage Inequality Among Men in the United States, 1977–2005?" *Social Forces* 88(5): 2053–77.

Owens, Ann. 2012. "Neighborhoods on the Rise: A Typology of Neighborhoods Experiencing Socioeconomic Ascent." *City and Community* 11(4): 345–69.

Pager, Devah. 2016. "Are Firms That Discriminate More Likely to Go Out of Business?" *Sociological Science* 3: 849–59.

Pattillo, Mary, and John N. Robinson III. 2016. "Poor Neighborhoods in the Metropolis." *The Oxford Handbook of the Social Science of Poverty*, edited by David Brady and Linda M. Burton. Oxford: Oxford University Press.

Pedulla, David S., and Katariina Mueller-Gastell. 2019. "Nonstandard Work and the Job Search Process: Application Pools, Search Methods, and Perceived Job Quality." *RSF: The Russell Sage Foundation Journal of the Social Sciences* 5(4): 130–58. DOI: 10.7758/RSF.2019.5.4.05.

Piketty, Thomas, Emmanuel Saez, and Gabriel Zucman. 2017. "Distributional National Accounts: Methods and Estimates for the United States." *Quarterly Journal of Economics* 133(2): 553–609.

Reardon, Sean F., and Kendra Bischoff. 2011. "Income Inequality and Income Segregation." *American Journal of Sociology* 116(4): 1092–153.

Ruggles, Steven, Sarah Flood, Ronald Goeken, Josiah Grover, Erin Meyer, Jose Pacas, and Matthew Sobek. 2019. IPUMS USA: Version 9.0 [data set]. Minneapolis, MN: IPUMS. DOI: 10.18128/D010 .V9.0.

Schultz, Michael A. 2019. "The Wage Mobility of Low-Wage Workers in a Changing Economy,

1968 to 2014." *RSF: The Russell Sage Foundation Journal of the Social Sciences* 5(4): 159–89. DOI: 10.7758/RSF.2019.5.4.06.

Song, Jae, David J. Price, Fatih Guvenen, Nicholas Bloom, and Till Von Wachter. 2015. "Firming Up Inequality." *NBER* working paper no. w21199. Cambridge, Mass.: National Bureau of Economic Research.

Sørensen, Aage B. 2000. "Toward a Sounder Basis for Class Analysis." *American Journal of Sociology* 105(6): 1523–58.

Sorensen, Jesper B., and Olav Sorenson. 2007. "Corporate Demography and Income Inequality." *American Sociological Review* 72(5): 766–83.

Strain, Michael R. 2014. "A Jobs Agenda for the Right." *National Affairs* 18 (Winter). Accessed February 12, 2019. https://www.nationalaffairs.com/publications/detail/a-jobs-agenda-for-the-right.

Tolbert, Charles M., and Molly Sizer. 1996. "U.S. Commuting Zones and Labor Market Areas." Staff report no. AGES870721. Washington: Economic Research Service, U.S. Department of Agriculture.

VanHeuvelen, Tom. 2018a. "Recovering the Missing Middle: A Mesocomparative Analysis of Within-Group Inequality, 1970–2011." *American Journal of Sociology* 123(4): 1064–116.

———. 2018b. "Moral Economies or Hidden Talents? A Longitudinal Analysis of Union Decline and Wage Inequality, 1973–2015." *Social Forces* 97(2): 495–30.

Weeden, Kim A., and David B. Grusky. 2014. "Inequality and Market Failure." *American Behavioral Scientist* 58(3): 473–91.

Weil, David. 2014. *The Fissured Workplace*. Cambridge, Mass.: Harvard University Press.

Western, Bruce, and Jake Rosenfeld. 2011. "Unions, Norms, and the Rise in U.S. Wage Inequality." *American Sociological Review* 76(4): 513–37.

Wilmers, Nathan. 2017. "Does Consumer Demand Reproduce Inequality? High-Income Consumers, Vertical Differentiation, and the Wage Structure." *American Journal of Sociology* 123(1): 178–231.

Wilson, William Julius. 2011. *When Work Disappears: The World of the New Urban Poor*. New York: Vintage.

Wozniak, Abigail. 2010. "Are College Graduates More Responsive to Distant Labor Market Opportunities?" *Journal of Human Resources* 45(4): 944–70.

Wright, Eric Olin, and Rachel Dwyer. 2003. "The Patterns of Job Expansions in the USA: A Comparison of the 1960s and 1990s." *Socio-Economic Review* 1(3): 289–325.

Young, Cristobal, Charles Varner, Ithai Z. Lurie, and Richard Prisinzano. 2016. "Millionaire Migration and Taxation of the Elite: Evidence from Administrative Data." *American Sociological Review* 81(3): 421–46.

The Changing Quality of Nonstandard Work Arrangements: Does Skill Matter?

CATHY YANG LIU AND LUÍSA NAZARENO

This article explores the implications of nonstandard employment for types of workers and their change over time. Using data from 1995, 2005, and 2017, we trace the evolving forms of nonstandard employment over the last decade and the associated job-quality patterns for workers with different skills, measured by education levels and occupation tasks. We find that nonstandard employment reduces earnings and weekly work schedule but does not affect the likelihood of feeling insecure about job continuity for workers in general. However, a closer examination reveals considerable variation along these three dimensions: highly educated nonstandard workers have lower earnings and fewer working hours than traditional workers over time and nonstandard routine occupation workers tend to feel greater job insecurity. Variations across gender and race-ethnicity are also discussed.

Keywords: nonstandard work arrangements, job quality, skills

Since the 1970s, demographic and institutional changes such as globalization and market liberalization have led to an internal reorganization of enterprises' business models with direct consequences to employment. Technological advancements and automation also played a role in the changing nature of work by creating new jobs while making others obsolete. The polarization between good and bad jobs, as well as the flexibilization of employment contracts, raised concerns over the impacts of such changes for workers and their families (Weil 2014; Kalleberg, Reskin, and Hudson 2000; Autor 2015a; Abraham et al. 2017).

New forms of work, characterized by higher flexibility and looser ties between workers and employers, started to spread in the United States and elsewhere in the 1990s. Such non-

Cathy Yang Liu is professor of public policy at Andrew Young School of Policy Studies, Georgia State University. **Luísa Nazareno** is a PhD student of public policy at Andrew Young School of Policy Studies, Georgia State University.

© 2019 Russell Sage Foundation. Liu, Cathy Yang, and Luísa Nazareno. 2019. "The Changing Quality of Nonstandard Work Arrangements: Does Skill Matter?" *RSF: The Russell Sage Foundation Journal of the Social Sciences* 5(4): 104–28. DOI: 10.7758/RSF.2019.5.4.04. We thank the editors of this volume, the reviewers, and colleagues who participated in the Russell Sage Foundation and W. K. Kellogg Foundation's conference on Changing Job Quality: Causes, Consequences, and Challenges, June 2018, for their insightful comments and suggestions. We appreciate the financial support from the Kauffman Foundation Future of Work program. Direct correspondence to: Cathy Yang Liu at cyliu@gsu.edu, 14 Marietta St. NW #329, Atlanta, GA 30303; and Luísa Nazareno at luisa.nazareno@gmail.com, 14 Marietta St. NW, Atlanta, GA 30303.

standard arrangements, also labeled as marked-mediated arrangements, nontraditional employment relations, or flexible arrangements, are frequently associated with higher insecurity and precarity of work (Kalleberg 2000). Recently, the emergence of work enabled by technological advancements and online platforms has contributed to the debate between flexibility and insecurity that characterizes nonstandard employment. The Great Recession has also intensified insecurity and job-quality concerns in the economy (Howell and Diallo 2008; Holzer et al. 2011; Kalleberg 2009). In this context, it is important to understand the temporal trends and effects of a changing workplace on job quality and worker well-being in order to formulate effective public policy.

To date, the consequences of these employment changes are mixed. On the one hand, the increasing insecurity and precarity of jobs raise concerns regarding the quality of work and impacts on workers' lives and families (Kalleberg 2011; Harris and Krueger 2015). New organizational strategies of firms, such as outsourcing, have been empirically associated with wage penalties to workers, reduction of benefits and unionization, and income inequality (Dube and Kaplan 2010; Goldschmidt and Schmieder 2017). On the other hand, the inherent flexibility of alternative employment and the emergence of new arrangements provide employees with tools to deal with increasing family responsibilities, income volatility, as well as complement their earnings (Farrell and Greig 2016a, 2016b; McKinsey & Company 2015; Golden 2008).

The ability to take advantage of the benefits of nonstandard arrangements and avoid their downsides varies among workers. Existing literature suggests that higher skills increase the odds of benefiting from flexibility given their leveraging power (Golden 2008; Kalleberg 2011, 2003), and that low-skill workers tend to be more vulnerable to precarity and segregation (Kalleberg 2011; Kalleberg, Reskin, and Hudson 2000; Catanzarite 2000). The distinctions among those groups as well as across different types of alternative arrangements, skill levels, and industry sectors are significant (Liu and Kolenda 2012). However, research on the implications of nonstandard work arrangements for workers with different skills is inadequate.

This article addresses the question by distinguishing job-quality patterns between standard and nonstandard employment arrangements for workers with different skills from 1995 to 2017. We are interested in how job quality in traditional and nonstandard employment differs for low-skill, middle-skill, and high-skill workers, as well as how such differences change over time. Although job quality is a multidimensional and broad concept, we focus on three dimensions: earnings, working hours, and expectations regarding job continuity. We measure skill level using two approaches: educational attainment and job task content.

Our results establish the overall negative effects of nonstandard employment on job quality for workers in general, though the exact effects vary by skill. We find stronger effects on high-skill workers, who worked fewer hours and received fewer earnings over time. Low-skill workers in alternative arrangements worked fewer hours, but the gap seems to be gradually closing. For these workers, the wage penalty showed up only when measured as workers in manual nonroutine occupations, but not when measured as low-educated. Meanwhile, evidence is not convincing of differences in wages or work schedules for middle-skill workers in alternative arrangements, despite their feeling increasingly insecure about their job continuity in the future, a fact not shared by the other classes of workers.

The findings for earnings and expectations are robust for all workers and male-only samples, but the difference in the weekly hours worked in nonstandard arrangements disappear or increase if female workers are excluded. Such difference indicates that there might be some self-selection of workers who need to combine paid and unpaid work for family or other reason who opt for such arrangements. We also find evidence of differences in pay and hours worked by race-ethnicity, but a closer look at how such differences interact with nonstandard emloyment is pending. These areas require future investigation.

CONCEPTUALIZING NONSTANDARD
EMPLOYMENT ARRANGEMENT

The conceptualization of nonstandard employment distinguishes from traditional nine-to-five work arrangements in which workers are expected to work full time for an indefinite period within the employers' place of business and under their supervision. Such arrangements were labeled with different terms over time, such as alternative arrangements, market-mediated arrangements, nontraditional employment relations, flexible arrangements, and atypical employment, among others (Kalleberg 2000). This essay uses nonstandard and alternative arrangements interchangeably.

In 1995, the Bureau of Labor Statistics (BLS) and the Census Bureau launched the Contingent Work Supplement (CWS) to the Current Population Survey (CPS), a survey designed specifically to provide detailed information on workers with nonstandard employment arrangements. The CWS defines *alternative work arrangements* as those "arranged through an employment intermediary such as a temporary help firm," or involving jobs that the "place, time, and quantity of work are potentially unpredictable" (Polivka 1996, 7).[1] The CWS operationalizes alternative employment in the following categories: independent contractors (including consultants and freelancers), on-call workers and day laborers, temporary help workers (those paid by temporary help agencies regardless of whether their job is temporary), and workers provided by contract firms (BLS 2005).

Workers under alternative employment arrangements include individuals performing varying tasks. Some of these jobs—such as independent contractors in farms and construction, on-call workers as substitute teachers and performance artists—have existed in the United States for decades; the growth of temporary help started in the aftermath of the World War II (Polivka 1996). Contract-out workers gained

momentum after the 1970s as a result of the restructuring of the global economy and the adoption of new corporate strategies (Weil 2014). In the past decade, new arrangements enabled by online platforms (also known as gig work) have attracted attention as one of the fastest growing segments of the labor markets (Farrell and Greig 2016a; Abraham et al. 2017).

NONSTANDARD ARRANGEMENTS
AND JOB QUALITY

Institutional and demographic changes have had significant impacts on employment from the second half of the twentieth century. The workforce became larger and more diversified through increasing female participation, rising educational attainment, and easier access to global labor markets (Kalleberg 2011; Goldin, Katz, and Kuziemko 2006). At the same time, the search for flexibility and costs reduction originated new business models, in which big enterprises shed employment to networks of smaller firms while setting strict standard controls for their performance and blurring the relationship between workers and employers—a scenario Weil 2014 describes as a "fissuring workplace." Moreover, technological advancements, such as automation and computerization, progressively substituted workers performing routine tasks that characterized many of the middle-skill occupations (Autor 2015a, 2015b).

Following these changes, recent decades saw a growing polarization between good and bad jobs and a hollowing of the middle occupations. A good job features relatively high earnings, training and promotion opportunities over time, fringe benefits, some worker control over schedule and work content and duration, stability, occupational health, and safety (Kalleberg 2011; Bernhardt et al. 2015; Clark 2005). Conversely, bad jobs are those with lower payments, fewer opportunities and benefits, and more insecurity. Jobs in between are relatively

---

1. Contingent and nonstandard employment are overlapping yet different concepts in the CWS. *Contingent* is "any job in which an individual does not have an explicit or implicit contract for long-term employment or one in which the minimum hours worked can vary in a nonsystematic manner" (Polivka and Nardone 1989, 11). The key distinction is that contingent workers either do not expect their jobs to last or have a temporary job. As a result, not all workers in alternative arrangements are contingent, and not all contingent workers are in alternative arrangements.

stable and well paid but do not require a high level of skills from workers, such as those in the big corporations and manufactures of the twentieth century. In this context, by the end of the century, education has become the great divide between workers with better and worse jobs, and between high- and low-paid occupations (Fischer and Hout 2016).

Job quality is, therefore, central to the discussion, but measuring it is somewhat challenging given its multidimensional and subjective nature. Often, given data availability, its operationalization captures only some dimensions. Arne Kalleberg, Barbara Reskin, and Ken Hudson, for instance, operationalize the "badness" of a job based on the share of low-wage workers, and workers with no pension and health insurance (2000). In this essay, we focus on three of the dimensions suggested by the literature: earnings, hours worked, and future expectations.

Nonstandard work arrangements have mixed implications for workers. On the one hand, higher flexibility allows workers to deal with personal and family responsibilities, increase work-life satisfaction, as well as their ability to deal with income volatility and complement earnings (Farrell and Greig 2016a; Golden 2008). In particular, the growing willingness of workers to engage in the emerging gig economy supports the notion that they value flexibility (Donovan, Bradley, and Shimabukuro 2016). On the other hand, the flip side of flexibility is insecurity, which tends to be greater for workers with alternative work arrangements who are likely positioned at the periphery of organizations with weaker linkages to the organizational core (Kalleberg, Reskin, and Hudson 2000; Kalleberg 2012, 2003). Job insecurity further intensified after the Great Recession (Holzer 2011).

The implication of nonstandard employment would vary for workers with different skills. The literature suggests that higher skills increase the odds of benefiting from flexibility given its greater leverage power (Golden 2008) and that the correlation between worker skills and job quality over time is increasing (Holzer

2011; Holzer et al. 2011). Having more portable skills elevates workers' likelihood of being employed in diverse organizations and therefore, having relatively more stability in occupations (Kalleberg 2003).

Overall, higher skills are assets that employers value and, consequently, increase the bargaining power of workers (Kalleberg 2011; Catanzarite 2000; Carnoy, Castells, and Benner 1997). Inversely, low-skill workers have less bargaining power and are more easily replaced, thus tend to be more vulnerable to worsening labor market conditions regardless of employment arrangement (Kalleberg 2011). For instance, the outsourcing of typical low-skill occupations such as janitorial, security, and cleaning services have been empirically associated with significant wage and benefit penalties in the United States and Germany (Dube and Kaplan 2010; Goldschmidt and Schmieder 2017).[2] Middle-skill workers make up a large share of the workforce. Given the elimination of many middle-skill jobs by automation, the displacement of workers and mismatch between skills and jobs are both growing (Autor 2015b; Holzer et al. 2011). To our knowledge, research on the effects of nonstandard employment particular to these workers is inadequate.

Workers in alternative arrangements are substantially diverse, and industries with higher contingency rates tend to have a higher share of low-skill workers (Liu and Kolenda 2012). Within the four types of alternative arrangements, the distribution of skills varies. On-call, temporary, and contracted-out workers tend to have higher shares of low-skill workers than standard arrangements, and independent contractors tend to have higher shares of high-skill workers than any of the other nonstandard and standard arrangements (Katz and Krueger 2019; Hippel et al. 2006). Such complexities call for a deeper understanding of the effects of nonstandard employment on job quality for different works. This article contributes to this discussion by testing how the impacts on job quality vary for workers with different skills and how such effects change over time.

2. Outsourcing is a growing trend, but independent from work arrangements as discussed here. The example is only an illustration of the higher vulnerability of low-skill workers in general.

DATA AND METHODOLOGY

Our analysis made use of the 1995, 2005, and 2017 CWS surveys to trace the changing job quality of nonstandard employment over two decades. The Bureau of Labor Statistics and the Bureau of Census introduced the CWS in 1995 to gather detailed information on workers in alternative work arrangements (Census Bureau 1995, 2005, 2017). The survey was carried out in 1995, 1997, 1999, 2001, 2005, and 2017. The recent release of CWS data offers an opportunity to update what is known about nonstandard workers.

Our samples comprise civilian individuals age sixteen and older who worked for either pay or profit in the week previous to the interview: 54,122 observations in 1995, 42,537 in 2005, and 46,144 in 2017. For each year, we used a dummy variable to distinguish between workers in standard versus nonstandard work arrangements. Nonstandard workers include those who are independent contractors, on-call, day laborers, temporary help agency workers, or contracted workers; others are defined as standard workers by a 2005 CWS technical note (BLS 2005). We did not break nonstandard arrangements further in our analysis due to the reduced sample size of some categories.

We operationalized skills through qualifications and occupations, the two most commonly used indirect indicators of skills (Eurostat 2016). We used educational attainment as a signal of worker skills as follows: low-, high-, and middle-skill workers correspond to workers with less than a high school degree, workers with a bachelor's degree or higher, and workers in between, respectively. This approach has the advantage of readily available information, but it is limited when skills are acquired not only through formal education, but also through on-the-job training, and genetic inheritance, such individual characteristics (Becker 1994).

Complementing the first approach, we also categorize workers' skills by the content of the tasks and qualifications required for them to perform their occupations. We follow the skill-biased technological change literature and divided occupations according to cognitive versus manual, and routine versus nonroutine tasks (Acemoglu and Autor 2010; Jaimovich and Siu 2014; Foote and Ryan 2014).[3] Low-, middle-, and high-skill occupations are, respectively, nonroutine manual occupations, routine occupations, and nonroutine cognitive occupations.[4] Nonroutine manual occupations are essentially service occupations, whereas nonroutine cognitive include managers, professionals, and technicians. Routine occupations are the ones in the middle of the skills distribution, including cognitive jobs (such as sales, and office and administrative support) and manual ones (blue-collar jobs) (Jaimovich and Siu 2014).[5]

We capture skills by first running models controlling for educational attainment and occupations for each year. Second, we stratify workers by educational levels and run models controlling for task content of occupations. Third, we stratify by occupations controlling for education. In all models, the variable of interest is the dummy for nonstandard work arrangement, which captures varying job quality for different workers.[6]

Job quality is a multidimensional concept, as discussed earlier, and we focus on three dimen-

---

3. "The distinction between cognitive and manual jobs is straightforward, characterized by differences in the extent of mental versus physical activity. The distinction between routine and non-routine jobs is based on the work of Autor, Levy, and Murnare (2003). If the tasks involved can be summarized as a set of specific activities accomplished by following well-defined instructions and procedures, the occupation is considered routine. If instead the job requires flexibility, creativity, problem-solving, or human interaction skills, the occupation is non-routine" (Jaimovich and Siu 2014, 8),

4. For a full description of the classification of occupations, see Jaimovich and Siu 2014, A2.

5. Workers in farming, fishing, and forestry were not considered in the analysis. These totaled 1,331 in 1995, 265 in 2005, and 398 in 2017.

6. For the correspondence of our two measures of skills, see table A1. In all years, around 73 percent of highly educated workers were performing high-skill jobs (nonroutine cognitive occupations), however the correspondence is worse for middle- and low-skill workers. To the former, 60 percent of middle-educated workers were

Table 1. Workers by Employment Arrangement

Employment Arrangement	1995		2005		2017	
	Frequency	Percent	Frequency	Percent	Frequency	Percent
Standard	48,757	90.1	37,884	89.1	41,307	89.5
Nonstandard	5,365	9.9	4,653	10.9	4,837	10.5
Independent contractors, consultants, and freelancers	3,348	62.4	2,948	63.4	3,082	63.7
On-call workers and day laborers	867	16.2	826	17.8	761	15.7
Paid by temporary help agencies	522	9.7	366	7.9	413	8.5
Contracted out	628	11.7	512	11.0	582	12.0
Total	54,122	100	42,537	100	46,144	100

Source: Authors' compilation based on CWS 1995, 2005, and 2017 (U.S. Census Bureau 1995, 2005, 2017).
Note: Data weighted using CWS supplement weights.

sions: hourly earnings, weekly hours worked, and expected job continuity. We used the logarithm of the hourly earnings from the main job to test the hypothesis that nonstandard employment has a depressing effect on earnings. We calculated hourly earnings by dividing weekly earnings[7] by the total hours worked weekly at the main job. We trimmed the extreme values of hourly earnings below $1 and above $100 following the literature (Lemieux 2010; Spletzer and Handwerker 2014; Schmitt 2003).

The second dependent variable is total weekly hours worked in all jobs, a variable created by adding total hours worked on the main job and all other jobs combined. We used it to test the hypothesis that nonstandard workers have different work schedules from comparable traditional workers. Because both earnings and hours worked are interval variables, we used ordinary least squares to test the first and the second hypotheses.

To test whether nonstandard employment caused higher insecurity, the last dependent variable was a dummy for expected job continuity, coded one for workers who said that they could continue to work at their current job as long as they wished, provided that the economy did not change and their job performance was adequate, and zero otherwise. To test this hypothesis, we used logistic regressions. All models include standard demographic control variables for race-ethnicity, sex, age, marital status, and nativity.

Finally, to test the robustness of our results, we ran all models for male workers only. The rationale for the test is to capture potential unobservable factors that may result in self-selection of workers in nonstandard work arrangements, such as the willingness to combine paid and unpaid work in their schedules.

DESCRIPTIVE STATISTICS
Nonstandard workers remained roughly 10 percent of the workforce during the entire period (table 1). Around 63 percent of the nonstandard workers remained as independent contractors, independent consultants, and freelancers. On-call workers and day laborers, and temporary help agency employees' shares decreased slightly from 16.2 percent to 15.7 percent and from 9.7 percent to 8.5 percent respectively from 1995 to 2017. Contracted workers experienced a slight growth from 11.7 percent to 12.0 percent.

---

performing routine occupations in 1995 and 2005, dropping to 54 percent in 2017. To the latter, the correspondence fluctuated from 41 percent in 1995 to 32 percent in 2005 and 35 percent in 2017.

7. Due to the rotation groups methodology, CWS included information only on earnings of workers who were on rotation groups four and eight in February of each year. For the remaining workers, we used the earnings information from the earnings files, where available.

Table 2. Share of Workers by Skill Level and Employment Arrangement

	1995		2005		2017	
	Standard	Non-standard	Standard	Non-standard	Standard	Non-standard
Skills as educational attainment						
Low education	11.8	11.1	10.8	11.2	8.1	9.6
Middle education	62.0	58.7	59.0	56.8	54.1	52.7
High education	26.2	30.3	30.2	32.0	37.8	37.7
Skills as occupational tasks content						
Nonroutine manual	17.9	17.5	15.6	16.6	17.2	19.5
Routine	49.5	48.0	49.2	45.9	41.9	40.0
Nonroutine cognitive	32.6	34.6	35.3	37.5	40.9	40.6

Source: Authors' compilation based on CWS 1995, 2005, and 2017 (U.S. Census Bureau 1995, 2005, 2017).
Note: Data weighted using CWS supplement weights. N in 1995, 2005, and 2015 are, respectively, 54,122, 41,829, and 46,144.

CWS 2017 data portray a pattern that contradicts previous findings that the share of nonstandard workers reached 15 percent in 2015 driven mostly by the growth on contract-out workers (Katz and Krueger 2019). These estimates used the Rand-Princeton Contingent Worker Survey (RPCWS) data, a survey inspired on CWS and intended to fill its ten-year void. A possible explanation for the differences in estimates between CWS 2017 and RPCWS 2015 are the surveys' designs, which may have led to comparisons that are possible in concept but not in practice (see Abraham et al. 2017).[8]

Breaking down both the standard and nonstandard workers by their educational attainment levels, we see that all three levels are well represented in the nonstandard workforce (table 2), consistent with previous studies (Liu and Kolenda 2012; Hippel et al. 2006). More than half of all workers are in the middle-educated category—those with a high school diploma but without a college degree. Although their share is decreasing, they remain the largest section of the U.S. workforce and make up 53 percent of standard workers and 54 percent of nonstandard workers in 2017. Highly educated workers—the fastest growing share of the workforce—were equally represented in standard and nonstandard work arrangements in 2017 (roughly 38 percent). Meanwhile, low-educated workers in traditional arrangements experienced an overall decline during these twenty years from 12 percent to around 8 percent, but the drop in nonstandard arrangements accounted for 1.5 percentage points only.

By measuring skills through occupational task content, we observe a decline in the routine occupations in both standard and nonstandard work arrangements from nearly 50 percent in 1995 to 40 percent in 2017, illustrating the hollowing of the middle-skill occupations' thesis (Kalleberg 2011; Autor 2015b; Acemoglu and Autor 2010; Foote and Ryan 2014). Although nonroutine manual occupations re-

8. Abraham and her colleagues discuss some items that may have turned the Rand data incomparable to CWS, such as: internet-based survey rather than interviews; in RPCWS respondents answer questions about themselves whereas in CWS they answer to all members of the household; the sample of respondents of RPCWS was assembled from a variety of sources with unknown nonresponse rates, which may lead to a lesser representativeness of the U.S. population, and so on (2017). The authors also point to the stability in the share of nonstandard arrangements found in the General Social Survey 2002, 2006, 2010, and 2014 as grounds for caution in comparing the Rand survey and CWS.

Table 3. Demographic Characteristics of Workers by Employment Arrangement

	1995		2005		2017	
	Standard	Non-standard	Standard	Non-standard	Standard	Non-standard
Mean age	38.2	41.1	40.3	43.5	41.7	46.2
Female (share)	47.7	37.9	47.8	38.5	47.9	38.1
Married (share)	60.3	64.6	58.4	62.9	54.5	58.8
Foreign born (share)	10.0	10.0	15.2	15.6	17.3	20.1
Race-ethnicity (share)						
White	77.6	82.3	70.2	75.5	63.5	65.0
Black	10.9	8.1	10.6	7.9	11.6	10.5
Hispanic	8.5	6.9	13.0	12.4	16.6	16.9
Other	3.0	2.7	6.2	5.3	8.3	7.7

Source: Authors' compilation based on CWS 1995, 2005, and 2017 (U.S. Census Bureau 1995, 2005, 2017).
Note: Data weighted using CWS supplement weights. N in 1995, 2005, and 2015 are, respectively, 54,122, 41,829, and 46,144.

mained relatively stable in standard arrangements over the period, in the nonstandard group it increased by 2 percentage points up to 19 percent in 2017. Nonroutine cognitive occupations grew steadily from around 33 percent in 1995 to roughly 40 percent in 2017.

Educational attainment is a common measure of skills' supply (it corresponds to each individual worker characteristic); occupations provide a measure of demand for skills (tasks are essentially a job characteristic). The increase of educational levels accompanied by the decrease in middle-skill occupations (routine) and stability of low-skill occupations (nonroutine manual) supports the hypothesis of a skill mismatch between workers and jobs (Eurostat 2016; Holzer 2011).

Demographic Characteristics
Table 3 provides a demographic overview of workers, displaying the variables we used as controls in the empirical analysis. Female workers made up nearly half of the standard workforce but remained less represented among nonstandard workers over the period (roughly 38 percent). In the three observation years, workers were on average older in nonstandard than in standard arrangements, and such differences became even larger in 2017.

Regarding racial-ethnic composition, the share of white workers has declined over the period, dropping by 14 percentage points in standard and 17 percentage points in nonstandard arrangements from 2005 to 2017. The share of African American workers in the nonstandard workforce grew by 2.5 percentage points over the period but remained at around 11 percent in standard arrangements. Further, the growing participation of Hispanic and other racial-ethnical groups reflect an increasingly diverse workforce. In 2017, Hispanic workers accounted for roughly 17 percent of standard and nonstandard workers, a growth of 195 and 245 percent from 1995 respectively. Other racial-ethnic groups also registered greater shares in the workforce, increasing from 3 percent in 1995 to 8.3 percent in 2017 for standard workers and from 2.7 percent to 7.7 percent among nonstandard workers during the same period.

Finally, although the foreign-born shares were similar between two types of workers in 1995 (around 10 percent) and 2005 (around 15 percent), their share in nonstandard employment exceeded that in standard employment in 2017. Like the racial-ethnical composition, foreign-born individuals have experienced considerable growth in the period.

Indicators of Job Quality

Table 4 provides the comparison of job-quality indicators for workers with different skills in standard and nonstandard work arrangements. Hourly earnings of workers in nonstandard arrangements were higher for low- and middle-educated workers, and those in routine occupations. Although we do not explore each alternative arrangements in detail in this article, we should expect to see considerable variation in earnings across alternative arrangements as some tend to pay better than others (Kalleberg 2003). Low- and middle-educated workers worked more hours in alternative arrangements over the years, whereas the opposite is true for high-skill workers in both measures.

The share of workers who feel uncertain about their job continuity fluctuated over time among nonstandard workers but remained relatively stable among traditional workers. Among highly educated workers in 1995 and 2005, as well as workers in routine occupations in 2005 and 2017, a significantly lower share of workers in nonstandard arrangements expect jobs to continue. Although the literature suggests increasing insecurity and anxiety in the labor markets in general in the aftermath of the Great Recession (Holzer et al. 2011), our data suggest that this phenomenon is particularly related to nonstandard workers in routine occupations, which may be a consequence of automation-related job losses.

REGRESSION RESULTS

We start this section by presenting the effects of nonstandard employment on job quality, assuming those are the same across skill levels. For workers with similar skills (both measured as educational attainment and occupation task content) and demographic characteristics, nonstandard work had a growing depressing effect on earnings over time of roughly 3 percent in 1995 to 7 percent in 2017 (see table 5).[9] Likewise, the differences in work schedules increased

over the period. Workers in nonstandard arrangements worked 0.7 fewer hours than traditional workers in 1995 and 1.2 fewer hours in 2017. Nonstandard employment also decreased confidence in job continuity. The log-odds of expecting job continuity were smaller for comparable nonstandard than standard workers in 1995 and 2005, growing from −0.3 to −0.4, but in 2017 was no longer significant.

As expected, higher skills increased expected earnings. Low- and middle-educated workers' predicted earnings were less than comparable highly educated workers over the entire period.[10] Similarly, workers performing nonroutine manual occupations (representing low skills) and routine occupations (middle skills) earned less than comparable workers performing nonroutine cognitive occupations (high skills). High-skill workers, measured by both education and occupation task content, had longer work schedules in all years.

Demographic variables have the expected signs regarding earnings and hours worked. Both earnings and hours worked increased with age, but at a decreasing rate. Females earned approximately 26 percent less and worked six fewer hours than comparable males in 1995; these differences decreased to 20 percent and 4.4 hours in 2017, respectively. Black and Hispanic workers earned less than comparable white workers, but the data revealed diverging trends, the gap increasing from roughly 10 to 12 percent less for blacks and decreasing from 7 to 5 percent less for Hispanics from 1995 to 2017. Meanwhile, workers of other races and ethnicities had higher expected earnings than whites in 2017. Blacks and Hispanics have higher expected weekly working hours, but the differences have decreased from 2005 to 2017. Further analysis of the interactions between such differences and nonstandard employment is needed to understand the underlying dynamics. However, like skills, demographic characteristics of individuals did not seem to affect expectations, except in the case of foreign-born

9. Due to limited space, we do not show the coefficients for demographics control variables in most tables. Full results are available on request.

10. We use the terms *comparable* and *similar* to denote that all other variables in the model are held constant. In this case, a comparable worker has similar demographic characteristics, same type of work arrangement (standard or nonstandard), and similar occupation.

Table 4. Job Quality by Skill Level and Employment Arrangement

	1995		2005		2017	
	Standard	Nonstandard	Standard	Nonstandard	Standard	Nonstandard
Panel A. Skills as educational attainment						
Low-educated						
Mean hourly earnings	8.1*	8.9	10.9*	12.0	14.4*	17.6
Mean weekly hours (all jobs)	34.6	34.5	35.4*	36.0	34.4*	36.7
Expect job to continue (%)	96.5	93.7	94.6	91.8	96.2	94.2
Middle-educated						
Mean hourly earnings	11.3*	12.6	15.9*	18.0	19.8*	21.0
Mean weekly hours (all jobs)	39.4*	40.0	39.4*	39.8	38.9*	39.4
Expect job to continue (%)	96.8	96.6	96.1	95.3	96.3	95.9
Highly educated						
Mean hourly earnings	18.4*	19.3	26.0	26.0	32.4*	31.4
Mean weekly hours (all jobs)	43.3*	42.1	42.3*	40.6	41.7*	38.2
Expect job to continue (%)	96.6*	94.2	95.9*	93.0	96.4	96.3
Panel B. Skills as occupational tasks content						
Nonroutine manual occupation						
Mean hourly earnings	7.9	8.0	12.1	12.1	15.8	16.1
Mean weekly hours (all jobs)	35.1	34.0	35.9	34.5	35.3	35.4
Expect job to continue (%)	96.9	96.4	95.9	95.7	96.1	97.8
Routine occupation						
Mean hourly earnings	11.6*	13.6	15.9*	18.5	20.2*	22.0
Mean weekly hours (all jobs)	39.7*	41.0	39.6*	40.7	39.4	39.7
Expect job to continue (%)	96.8	95.4	95.8*	93.5	96.4*	93.7
Nonroutine cognitive occupation						
Mean hourly earnings	17.3*	18.3	24.6	25.0	31.7	31.3
Mean weekly hours (all jobs)	42.7*	41.8	42.0*	40.6	41.6*	39.3
Expect job to continue (%)	96.6	95.3	95.9	94.0	96.4	96.8

Source: Authors' compilation based on CWS 1995, 2005, and 2017 (U.S. Census Bureau 1995, 2005, 2017).

Note: Data weighted using CWS supplement weights.

*Standard and nonstandard workers' means statistics are significantly different at least at the 0.05 level in two-tailed t-tests of means (nonweighted).

Table 5. Job Quality of Workers in Standard and Nonstandard Work Arrangements

	Log Weekly Hourly Earnings (Main Job)			Weekly Hours Worked (All Jobs)			Expected Continuity		
	1995	2005	2017	1995	2005	2017	1995	2005	2017
Nonstandard arrangement	-0.03***	-0.04***	-0.07***	-0.69***	-0.71***	-1.25***	-0.27*	-0.37***	-0.11
	(0.01)	(0.01)	(0.01)	(0.17)	(0.18)	(0.17)	(0.15)	(0.14)	(0.15)
Low education	-0.42***	-0.50***	-0.46***	-4.01***	-3.95***	-4.31***	0.05	-0.12	0.04
	(0.02)	(0.01)	(0.01)	(0.20)	(0.22)	(0.22)	(0.12)	(0.12)	(0.14)
Middle education	-0.27***	-0.29***	-0.29***	-1.47***	-1.32***	-1.05***	0.17**	0.05	-0.00
	(0.01)	(0.01)	(0.01)	(0.13)	(0.14)	(0.12)	(0.08)	(0.08)	(0.07)
Nonroutine manual occupation	-0.44***	-0.41***	-0.41***	-4.16***	-3.40***	-3.75***	0.21**	0.12	-0.02
	(0.01)	(0.01)	(0.01)	(0.17)	(0.18)	(0.16)	(0.10)	(0.11)	(0.10)
Routine occupation	-0.19***	-0.22***	-0.26***	-1.30***	-1.06***	-1.26***	0.11	0.01	-0.00
	(0.01)	(0.01)	(0.01)	(0.13)	(0.14)	(0.13)	(0.07)	(0.08)	(0.08)
Demographic controls	Yes	Yes	Yes	Yes	Yes	Yes	Yes	Yes	Yes
Observations	18,957	35,855	38,330	50,679	38,994	43,597	45,338	35,822	39,404

Source: Authors' compilation based on CWS 1995, 2005, and 2017 (U.S. Census Bureau 1995, 2005, 2017).
Note: Data weighted using CWS supplement weights. Table reports results of OLS regressions on the hourly earnings and weekly hours worked, and results of Logit regressions on expected job continuity. Standard errors (for OLS models) and robust standard errors (for logit) in parentheses.
*$p < .1$; **$p < .05$; ***$p < .01$

Figure 1. Effects of Nonstandard Work Arrangements on Job Quality of Workers

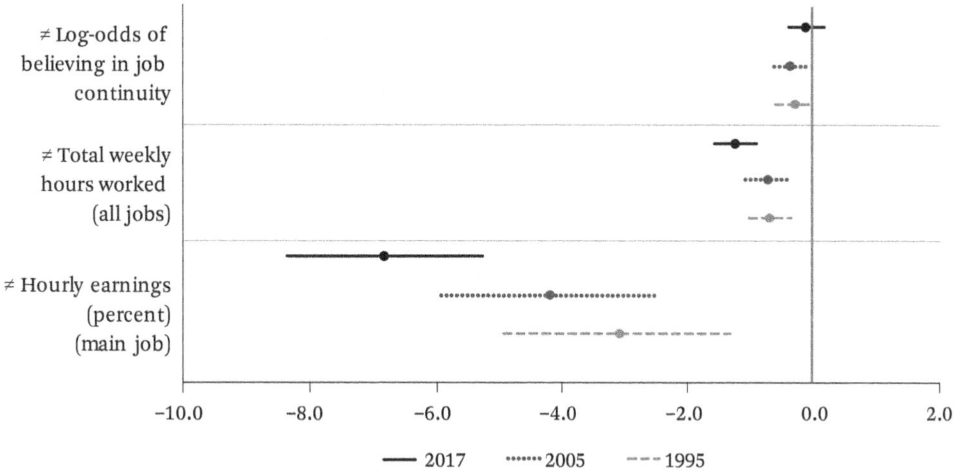

Source: Authors' compilation based on CWS 1995, 2005, and 2017 (U.S. Census Bureau 1995, 2005, 2017).
Note: Coefficients and confidence intervals on nonstandard employment (dummy) obtained from OLS regressions on hourly earnings and weekly hours worked, and logit regressions on expected job continuity. Models control for education, occupation, and demographics.

workers, who were less likely to expect their job to continue, holding the remaining variables constant.[11]

In summary, we find overall evidence that workers in nonstandard employment arrangements have shorter working schedules and feel more insecure about their job continuity, than workers with similar skills and demographic characteristics in traditional arrangements (figure 1). Differences in earnings are increasing, though a further investigation would require more information on nonpecuniary benefits. Next, we drop the assumption that the effect of nonstandard employment is the same across skill levels by stratifying our models.

Nonstandard Employment Effects by Educational Attainment Levels
Nonstandard employment arrangements did not significantly affect earnings of comparable low- and middle-educated workers in 1995 and 2005 but had a positive effect for the former and a negative effect for the latter in 2017 (table 6). For highly educated workers, nonstandard employment represented an increasing wage pen-

alty over the years, growing from roughly –6 to –12 percent from 1995 to 2017. Highly educated workers in nonstandard arrangements also worked significantly fewer hours than their counterparts in traditional arrangements, and the difference expanded from 1.4 to 3.2 hours less over time. The effect was not significant for low- and middle-educated workers in most years, except for low-educated workers in 1995. Finally, there is not enough evidence of differences regarding job continuity expectations between standard and nonstandard workers in the stratified models, except for highly educated workers in 2005.

Within all educational levels, tasks content performed in each occupational group significantly differentiated workers' earnings and weekly schedules (see table A3). Workers in nonroutine manual occupations earned less and worked fewer hours than those in nonroutine cognitive occupations over time, and the difference steadily decreased at all educational levels. Distinctly, the earnings gap between routine occupations (the "middle" jobs) and the reference group slightly increased for workers

11. For full models' results, see table A2.

Table 6. Effects of Nonstandard Work Arrangements on Job Quality of Workers by Education

	Low-Educated			Middle-Educated			Highly Educated		
	1995	2005	2017	1995	2005	2017	1995	2005	2017
Log hourly earnings (main job)	-0.01	0.01	0.06**	-0.02	-0.00	-0.05***	-0.06***	-0.13***	-0.12***
Observations	1,982	3,323	2,759	11,544	21,334	20,839	5,431	11,198	14,732
Weekly hours worked (all jobs)	-1.38**	-1.07*	-0.65	-0.23	-0.12	-0.10	-1.37***	-1.80***	-3.19***
Observations	5,457	3,770	3,233	31,187	23,260	23,647	14,035	11,964	16,717
Expected job continuity	-0.66	-0.42	-0.50	-0.09	-0.22	-0.10	-0.41	-0.59**	-0.03
Observations	5,015	3,550	2,863	28,169	21,521	21,572	12,154	10,751	14,969
Occupational and demographic controls	Yes	Yes	Yes	Yes	Yes	Yes	Yes	Yes	Yes

Source: Authors' compilation based on CWS 1995, 2005, and 2017 (U.S. Census Bureau 1995, 2005, 2017).

Note: Data weighted using CWS supplement weights. Table reports coefficients for the nonstandard employment dummy in each regression. Coefficients from OLS regressions on the hourly earnings and weekly hours worked, and logit regressions on expected job continuity. Standard errors (for OLS models) and robust standard errors (for logit) in parentheses.

*p < .1; **p < .05; ***p < .01

in all models. We find no evidence that occupations differentiated workers regarding future expectations.

Therefore, stratifying workers by education levels showed that nonstandard employment is consistently associated with all three indicators of job quality for highly educated workers. One possible explanation for such significant effects is that this is the group who prefers and can afford to have more flexibility and fewer hours worked to combine job and household responsibilities (Goldin, Katz, and Kuziemko 2006). If that is the case, the effects we found should not be interpreted as indicators of precarity.

Nonstandard Employment Effects by the Content of Tasks Performed in Occupations

The stratification of workers by occupational tasks content paints a slightly different picture. Figure 2 illustrates the summary findings of the stratification by education and occupations. In line with the previous stratification, nonstandard employment significantly reduced the earnings of high-skill workers (now taken as those in nonroutine cognitive occupations) by 4 percent in 1995, and 13 percent in 2017 (table 7). Unlike low-educated workers, nonstandard employment represented a wage penalty of roughly 4 percent for those in nonroutine manual occupations over the entire period. Regarding weekly schedule, the conclusions are similar and indicate that low- and high-skill workers tend to work fewer hours in nonstandard arrangements than comparable traditional workers.

An important distinction from the previous stratification concerns future expectations for middle-skill workers: those performing routine jobs are increasingly less secure about their job continuity—which may be a consequence of the reduction of middle-skill jobs (Jaimovich and Siu 2014; Foote and Ryan 2014). Within all occupations, education is significantly and positively related to earnings. Over time, the work schedule increased with education for similar workers in all occupational categories, but education does not significantly differentiate workers performing similar tasks (see table A4).

Robustness Check

Due to the higher flexibility of nonstandard arrangements, it is possible that our findings are partially influenced by self-selection of workers who might need to combine paid and unpaid work and who are less worried about work schedule, wage differentials, or job continuity. Evidence indicates, for instance, that highly educated female workers experience a discontinuity in their careers following motherhood and move to jobs with reduced earnings and work schedules (Bertrand, Goldin, and Katz 2010).

To test such a hypothesis, we ran all models for male workers only, given that women are still those who carry most of the housework (Blau and Kahn 2000). Conclusions remained unchanged regarding hourly earnings and work expectations. Important differences, however, were found in work schedule, and we report those in table 8.

First, the full model (which assumed the same effect for all workers) predicted that nonstandard workers had reduced weekly work schedules, but the opposite is true when considering males only. Second, we previously found that low and highly educated workers worked fewer hours in nonstandard arrangements, whereas evidence of differences for middle-educated workers was insufficient. In the males-only models, we do not find significant differences for low- and high-skill workers (there is variation across years for the latter), but middle-educated workers have longer schedules. Finally, stratifying by occupation task content, we find similar inconclusive evidence of different working schedules for low- and high-skill workers (nonroutine manual and cognitive occupations), but middle-skill workers (routine occupations) have longer schedules in nonstandard arrangements.

Therefore, some self-selection of workers in nonstandard arrangements to combine paid and unpaid work across skill levels seems plausible. By restricting the sample to males, the reduced work schedule effect disappears for low- and high-skill workers, whereas for middle-skill workers, nonstandard employment represents an increase in the number of hours worked.

Table 7. Effects of Nonstandard Work Arrangements on Job Quality of Workers by Occupational Tasks

	Nonroutine Manual Occupation			Routine Occupation			Nonroutine Cognitive Occupation		
	1995	2005	2017	1995	2005	2017	1995	2005	2017
Log hourly earnings (main job)	-0.04*	-0.05**	-0.04**	-0.01	0.01	-0.02*	-0.04**	-0.11***	-0.13***
Observations	3,283	5,345	6,220	9,097	17,202	16,088	6,577	13,308	16,022
Weekly hours worked (all jobs)	-1.48***	-1.58***	-0.64	0.08	0.19	-0.39	-1.56***	-1.67***	-2.50***
Observations	8,687	5,980	7,226	24,784	18,807	18,061	17,208	14,207	18,310
Expected job continuity	-0.15	-0.02	0.65*	-0.41*	-0.46**	-0.59***	-0.19	-0.43*	0.13
Observations	8,043	5,580	6,478	22,249	17,562	16,623	15,046	12,680	16,303
Educational and demographic controls	Yes	Yes	Yes	Yes	Yes	Yes	Yes	Yes	Yes

Source: Authors' compilation based on CWS 1995, 2005, and 2017 (U.S. Census Bureau 1995, 2005, 2017).

Note: Data weighted using CWS supplement weights. Table reports coefficients for the nonstandard employment dummy in each regression. Coefficients from OLS regressions on the hourly earnings and weekly hours worked, and logit regressions on expected job continuity. Standard errors (for OLS models) and robust standard errors (for logit) in parentheses.

* $p < .1$; ** $p < .05$; *** $p < .01$

Figure 2. Effects of Nonstandard Work Arrangements on Job Quality by Skill

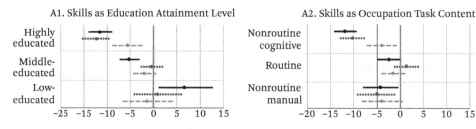

Panel A. Percent Difference in Hourly Earnings (Main Job)

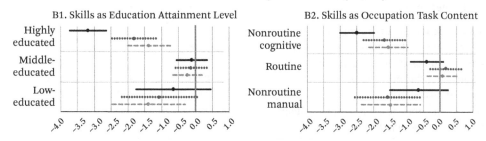

Panel B. Difference in Weekly Hours Worked (All Jobs)

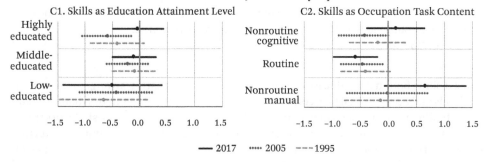

Panel C. Difference in Job Continuity Expectations

Source: Authors' compilation based on CWS 1995, 2005, and 2017 (U.S. Census Bureau 1995, 2005, 2017).

Note: Panels A and B obtained from OLS regressions. Panel C obtained from logit regressions. For A1, B1, and C1, models control for occupation task content and demographics. For A2, B2, and C2, models control for education attainment and demographics.

DISCUSSION AND CONCLUSION

In a context of changing nature of employment driven by technological and institutional transformations, identifying and monitoring their effects on workers is a necessary task to inform public policy. Nonstandard arrangements raise concerns over employment quality and workers' well-being, given that these jobs are often associated with higher insecurity and fewer benefits and protections to workers (Kalleberg 2011) despite offering more flexibility and new

tools to deal with volatility (Golden 2008; Farrell and Greig 2016a; Abraham et al. 2017).

Nonstandard employment arrangements should have different implications for different types of workers. This article contributes to this literature by providing evidence on the differentiating effects of nonstandard work on job quality of workers with different skills in 1995, 2005, and 2017. Our analysis focused on three indicators of job quality: earnings, hours worked, and expected job continuity. We op-

Table 8. Gender Differences in Effects of Nonstandard Employment on Weekly Hours Worked

	1995	2005	2017
Full model			
All workers	-0.69***	-0.71***	-1.25***
Males only	0.97***	0.70***	-0.09
Stratified by educational attainment			
All low-educated	-1.38**	-1.07*	-0.65
Low-educated males	-0.09	-0.07	-0.74
All middle-educated	-0.23	-0.12	-0.10
Middle-educated males	1.27***	0.97***	0.76***
All highly educated	-1.37***	-1.80***	-3.19***
Highly educated males	0.87**	0.48	-1.38***
Stratified by occupation task content			
All workers in nonroutine manual occupation	-1.48***	-1.58***	-0.64
Males in nonroutine manual occupation	-0.84	-0.30	-0.31
All workers in routine occupation	0.08	0.19	-0.39
Males in routine occupation	1.63***	1.17***	0.14
All workers in nonroutine cognitive occupation	-1.56***	-1.67***	-2.50***
Males in nonroutine cognitive occupation	0.46	0.14	-0.47

Source: Authors' compilation based on CWS 1995, 2005, and 2017 (U.S. Census Bureau 1995, 2005, 2017).
Note: Data weighted using CWS supplement weights. Table reports coefficients for the nonstandard employment dummy obtained from OLS regressions on weekly hours worked.
*$p < .1$; **$p < .05$; ***$p < .01$

erationalized skills both using educational attainment levels and occupational task content. Our general finding is that workers in nonstandard employment receive increasingly lower earnings and work fewer hours than comparable workers in traditional arrangements. No evidence indicates differences in expectations of job continuity. However, the effects are heterogeneous for subgroups of workers.

Earnings-wise, nonstandard employment is increasingly reducing the earnings of high-skill workers whereas, for middle-skill workers, the wage penalty was significant only in 2017. For low-skill workers, on the other hand, the skills' operationalization pointed to different conclusions: in alternative arrangements, nonroutine manual workers received 5 percent lower earnings over the entire period and low-educated workers earned 7 percent more in 2017. The positive difference seem to be a growing trend.

Regarding weekly hours worked, high-skill workers in alternative arrangements are increasingly working fewer hours than comparable traditional workers. Low-skill workers are also working fewer hours, but the overtime trend seems to close the gap. For middle-skill workers, no evidence suggests different schedules by employment arrangement. The reduced working schedules are at least partly explained by self-selection of workers who may need to combine paid and unpaid work—by restricting the samples to male workers, the differences in working hours disappear for low- and high-skill workers, and middle-skill workers work longer hours in alternative arrangements.

Finally, we did not find evidence of nonstandard employment being associated with lower expectations of job continuity, except for workers in routine occupations, who are increasingly feeling insecure about the future. This is in line with the literature stressing the reduction of middle jobs in the U.S. economy due to automation and institutional changes (Weil

2014; Acemoglu and Autor 2010). Insecurity for routine occupations may also have increased in the aftermath of the Great Recession because job losses were concentrated in the middle segment (Foote and Ryan 2014).

High-skill workers are the fastest growing share of the workforce and, in theory, are in the best position to benefit from the flexibility and protect themselves against insecurity (Golden 2008; Kalleberg 2011; Holzer 2011). We find that in nonstandard arrangements they receive increasingly fewer earnings and work fewer hours. Such differences may be explained by self-selection of workers who prefer or can afford to be in such a position. If that is the case, they should not be interpreted as indicators of job precarity.

Low-skill workers, on the contrary, are more vulnerable to worsening working conditions. These workers have worse jobs regarding earnings and working hours, and, in the educational operationalization, least expectations regarding continuity of their jobs. Therefore, although we confirm the literature that associates lower skills with worse jobs (Kalleberg 2011; Holzer et al. 2011; Catanzarite 2000; Fischer and Hout 2016), we do not find that

nonstandard employment has a worsening effect. Rather, it seems that low-skill workers are in equally bad jobs regardless of work arrangement, at least according to the dimensions we assessed.

Although our analysis provides nuanced evidence on the association between skills and nonstandard employment quality, more research is needed to further unpack the underlying dynamics. In particular, differences between types of nonstandard employment need clarification, the mechanisms that lead workers to nonstandard arrangements (self-selection versus lack of alternatives), as well as the inclusion of other dimensions of job quality such as health insurance, pensions, and paid vacation. A closer examination of how nonstandard employment would affect workers with different race-ethnicity and immigrant status can also reveal important variations. Evidence is convincing that the slow adjustments of legislation in the face of new arrangements have opened the room for misclassification of workers and reduction of their rights (Harris and Krueger 2015; Weil 2014). A better understanding of these workers will help inform future policy design.

Table A1. Correspondence of Skill Measurement: Education Levels and Occupation's Task Content

| Occupation Task Content | Education Attainment Level | | | | | | | | |
| | 1995 | | | 2005 | | | 2017 | | |
	Low	Middle	High	Low	Middle	High	Low	Middle	High
Nonroutine manual	41.3	19.4	4.0	32.3	18.1	5.0	35.5	22.2	6.7
Routine	53.3	59.8	23.3	62.3	59.8	22.8	56.8	54.2	20.6
Nonroutine cognitive	5.5	20.8	72.8	5.4	22.1	72.2	7.7	23.6	72.8
Total	100	100	100	100	100	100	100	100	100

Source: Authors' compilation based on CWS 1995, 2005, and 2017 (U.S. Census Bureau 1995, 2005, 2017).

Note: Data weighted using CWS supplement weights. N in 1995, 2005 and 2015 are, respectively, 54,122, 41,829, and 46,144.

Table A2. Job Quality of Workers in Standard and Nonstandard Work Arrangements

	Log Weekly Hourly Earnings (Main Job)			Weekly Hours Worked (All Jobs)			Expected Continuity		
	1995	2005	2017	1995	2005	2017	1995	2005	2017
Nonstandard arrangement	-0.03***	-0.04***	-0.07***	-0.69***	-0.71***	-1.25***	-0.27*	-0.37***	-0.11
	(0.01)	(0.01)	(0.01)	(0.17)	(0.18)	(0.17)	(0.15)	(0.14)	(0.15)
Low Education	-0.42***	-0.50***	-0.46***	-4.01***	-3.95***	-4.31***	0.05	-0.12	0.04
	(0.02)	(0.01)	(0.01)	(0.20)	(0.22)	(0.22)	(0.12)	(0.12)	(0.14)
Middle Education	-0.27***	-0.29***	-0.29***	-1.47***	-1.32***	-1.05***	0.17**	0.05	-0.00
	(0.01)	(0.01)	(0.01)	(0.13)	(0.14)	(0.12)	(0.08)	(0.08)	(0.07)
Nonroutine manual occupation	-0.44***	-0.41***	-0.41***	-4.16***	-3.40***	-3.75***	0.21**	0.12	-0.02
	(0.01)	(0.01)	(0.01)	(0.17)	(0.18)	(0.16)	(0.10)	(0.11)	(0.10)
Routine occupation	-0.19***	-0.22***	-0.26***	-1.30***	-1.06***	-1.26***	0.11	0.01	-0.00
	(0.01)	(0.01)	(0.01)	(0.13)	(0.14)	(0.13)	(0.07)	(0.08)	(0.08)
Female	-0.26***	-0.23***	-0.20***	-6.10***	-5.00***	-4.44***	-0.09	-0.02	0.04
	(0.01)	(0.01)	(0.01)	(0.10)	(0.11)	(0.10)	(0.06)	(0.06)	(0.06)
Black	-0.10***	-0.12***	-0.12***	-0.22	0.81***	0.49***	-0.18*	-0.26**	-0.16
	(0.01)	(0.01)	(0.01)	(0.16)	(0.18)	(0.16)	(0.10)	(0.11)	(0.10)
Latino	-0.07***	-0.06***	-0.05***	0.26	1.34***	0.32**	-0.04	-0.14	-0.11
	(0.02)	(0.01)	(0.01)	(0.20)	(0.19)	(0.16)	(0.13)	(0.10)	(0.11)
Other race-ethnicity	-0.02	-0.00	0.03***	-0.60*	0.66***	-0.63***	0.14	0.17	0.11
	(0.02)	(0.01)	(0.01)	(0.31)	(0.25)	(0.20)	(0.16)	(0.15)	(0.13)
Foreign born	-0.06***	-0.04***	-0.04***	0.69***	0.15	-0.03	-0.34***	-0.56***	-0.22**
	(0.02)	(0.01)	(0.01)	(0.19)	(0.18)	(0.16)	(0.11)	(0.10)	(0.10)
Married	0.05***	0.04***	0.07***	-0.37***	-0.03	-0.18	-0.01	-0.02	0.11
	(0.01)	(0.01)	(0.01)	(0.11)	(0.12)	(0.11)	(0.07)	(0.07)	(0.07)
Age	0.05***	0.05***	0.04***	1.49***	1.32***	1.20***	-0.00	-0.00	-0.00
	(0.00)	(0.00)	(0.00)	(0.02)	(0.02)	(0.02)	(0.00)	(0.00)	(0.00)
Age²	-0.00***	-0.00***	-0.00***	-0.02***	-0.01***	-0.01***			
	(0.00)	(0.00)	(0.00)	(0.00)	(0.00)	(0.00)			
Constant	1.71***	2.12***	2.54***	16.60***	17.47***	19.42***	3.38***	3.33***	3.42***
	(0.04)	(0.03)	(0.02)	(0.47)	(0.51)	(0.46)	(0.13)	(0.13)	(0.12)
Observations	18,957	35,855	38,330	50,679	38,994	43,597	45,338	35,822	39,404

Source: Authors' compilation based on CWS 1995, 2005, and 2017 (U.S. Census Bureau 1995, 2005, 2017).

Note: Data weighted using CWS supplement weights. Table reports the results of OLS regressions on the hourly earnings and weekly hours worked, and results of Logit regressions on expected job continuity. Standard errors (for OLS models) and robust standard errors (for logit) in parentheses.

*p < .1; **p < .05; ***p < .01

Table A3. Effects of Nonstandard Work Arrangements on Job Quality of Workers Stratified by Educational Levels

	Low-Educated			Middle-Educated			Highly Educated		
	1995	2005	2017	1995	2005	2017	1995	2005	2017
Panel A. OLS regression on log hourly earnings (main job)									
Nonstandard arrangement	-0.01	0.01	0.06**	-0.02	-0.00	-0.05***	-0.06***	-0.13***	-0.12***
	(0.03)	(0.03)	(0.03)	(0.01)	(0.01)	(0.01)	(0.02)	(0.02)	(0.01)
Nonroutine manual occupation	-0.37***	-0.36***	-0.35***	-0.42***	-0.38***	-0.36***	-0.56***	-0.44***	-0.50***
	(0.05)	(0.04)	(0.04)	(0.02)	(0.01)	(0.01)	(0.04)	(0.03)	(0.02)
Routine occupation	-0.16***	-0.15***	-0.18***	-0.16***	-0.20***	-0.22***	-0.23***	-0.26***	-0.31***
	(0.05)	(0.04)	(0.04)	(0.01)	(0.01)	(0.01)	(0.02)	(0.01)	(0.01)
Observations	1,982	3,323	2,759	11,544	21,334	20,839	5,431	11,198	14,732
Panel B. OLS regression on weekly hours worked (all jobs)									
Nonstandard arrangement	-1.38**	-1.07*	-0.65	-0.23	-0.12	-0.10	-1.37***	-1.80***	-3.19***
	(0.55)	(0.57)	(0.56)	(0.22)	(0.23)	(0.23)	(0.32)	(0.34)	(0.28)
Nonroutine manual occupation	-4.79***	-5.92***	-4.33***	-4.02***	-3.29***	-3.58***	-4.05***	-3.23***	-3.66***
	(0.69)	(0.81)	(0.73)	(0.19)	(0.22)	(0.20)	(0.50)	(0.48)	(0.33)
Routine occupation	-1.70**	-2.65***	-1.52**	-1.29***	-1.14***	-1.28***	-1.80***	-1.05***	-1.39***
	(0.67)	(0.78)	(0.70)	(0.15)	(0.17)	(0.17)	(0.23)	(0.25)	(0.20)
Observations	5,457	3,770	3,233	31,187	23,260	23,647	14,035	11,964	16,717
Panel C. Logit regression on expected job continuity									
Nonstandard arrangement	-0.66	-0.42	-0.50	-0.09	-0.22	-0.10	-0.41	-0.59**	-0.03
	(0.41)	(0.34)	(0.46)	(0.21)	(0.20)	(0.20)	(0.25)	(0.24)	(0.24)
Nonroutine manual occupation	-0.06	-0.45	0.52	0.18	0.09	-0.14	0.14	0.26	-0.08
	(0.44)	(0.53)	(0.49)	(0.13)	(0.14)	(0.13)	(0.30)	(0.28)	(0.21)
Routine occupation	-0.22	-0.56	0.01	0.07	-0.03	-0.09	0.25*	0.08	0.16
	(0.42)	(0.51)	(0.45)	(0.10)	(0.11)	(0.11)	(0.14)	(0.14)	(0.13)
Observations	5,015	3,550	2,863	28,169	21,521	21,572	12,154	10,751	14,969

Source: Authors' compilation based on CWS 1995, 2005, and 2017 (U.S. Census Bureau 1995, 2005, 2017).

Note: Data weighted using CWS supplement weights. All models control for demographic characteristics. Table reports coefficients for the nonstandard employment dummy in each regression. Coefficients from OLS regressions on the hourly earnings and weekly hours worked, and Logit regressions on expected job continuity. Standard errors (for OLS models) and robust standard errors (for logit) in parentheses.

*p < .1; **p < .05; ***p < .01

Table A4. Effects of Nonstandard Work Arrangements on Job Quality of Workers Stratified by the Content of Tasks Performed in Occupation

	Nonroutine Manual Occupation			Routine Occupation			Nonroutine Cognitive Occupation		
	1995	2005	2017	1995	2005	2017	1995	2005	2017
Panel A. OLS regression on log hourly earnings (main job)									
Nonstandard arrangement	-0.04*	-0.05**	-0.04**	-0.01	0.01	-0.02*	-0.04**	-0.11***	-0.13***
	(0.02)	(0.02)	(0.02)	(0.01)	(0.01)	(0.01)	(0.02)	(0.02)	(0.01)
Low education	-0.33***	-0.50***	-0.40***	-0.39***	-0.46***	-0.41***	-0.50***	-0.55***	-0.53***
	(0.04)	(0.03)	(0.02)	(0.02)	(0.02)	(0.02)	(0.05)	(0.04)	(0.04)
Middle education	-0.19***	-0.27***	-0.22***	-0.22***	-0.25***	-0.25***	-0.30***	-0.31***	-0.34***
	(0.04)	(0.02)	(0.02)	(0.02)	(0.01)	(0.01)	(0.01)	(0.01)	(0.01)
Observations	3,283	5,345	6,220	9,097	17,202	16,088	6,577	13,308	16,022
Panel B. OLS regression on weekly hours worked (all jobs)									
Nonstandard arrangement	-1.48***	-1.58***	-0.64	0.08	0.19	-0.39	-1.56***	-1.67***	-2.50***
	(0.45)	(0.50)	(0.45)	(0.24)	(0.25)	(0.25)	(0.30)	(0.32)	(0.27)
Low education	-4.96***	-5.10***	-5.29***	-3.31***	-3.78***	-3.72***	-3.20***	-2.44***	-4.04***
	(0.59)	(0.61)	(0.53)	(0.27)	(0.29)	(0.29)	(0.66)	(0.76)	(0.65)
Middle education	-1.60***	-1.53***	-1.14***	-1.24***	-1.42***	-0.96***	-1.68***	-1.28***	-1.10***
	(0.54)	(0.53)	(0.41)	(0.20)	(0.21)	(0.19)	(0.18)	(0.20)	(0.17)
Observations	8,687	5,980	7,226	24,784	18,807	18,061	17,208	14,207	18,310
Panel C. Logit regression on expected job continuity									
Nonstandard arrangement	-0.15	-0.02	0.65*	-0.41*	-0.46**	-0.59***	-0.19	-0.43*	0.13
	(0.33)	(0.37)	(0.37)	(0.22)	(0.20)	(0.20)	(0.26)	(0.23)	(0.26)
Low education	0.18	-0.27	0.46	-0.04	-0.14	-0.31*	0.19	0.43	-0.03
	(0.33)	(0.33)	(0.30)	(0.18)	(0.17)	(0.19)	(0.40)	(0.50)	(0.43)
Middle education	0.34	-0.06	0.06	0.08	0.01	-0.18	0.17	0.07	0.09
	(0.31)	(0.29)	(0.23)	(0.13)	(0.14)	(0.13)	(0.10)	(0.11)	(0.11)
Observations	8,043	5,580	6,478	22,249	17,562	16,623	15,046	12,680	16,303

Source: Authors' compilation based on CWS 1995, 2005, and 2017 (U.S. Census Bureau 1995, 2005, 2017).

Note: Data weighted using CWS supplement weights. All models control for demographic characteristics. Table reports coefficients for the nonstandard employment dummy in each regression. Coefficients from OLS regressions on the hourly earnings and weekly hours worked, and Logit regressions on expected job continuity. Standard errors (for OLS models) and robust standard errors (for logit) in parentheses.

*p < .1; **p < .05; ***p < .01

REFERENCES

Abraham, Katharine G, John C. Haltiwanger, Kristin Sandusky, and James R Spletzer. 2017. "Measuring the Gig Economy: Current Knowledge and Open Issues." Paper presented at the IZA Labor Statistics Workshop "The Changing Structure of Work." Bonn (June 30, 2017). Accessed February 15, 2019. http://conference.iza.org/conference_files/Statistic_2017/abraham_k16798.pdf.

Acemoglu, Daron, and David Autor. 2010. "Skills, Tasks and Technologies: Implications for Employment and Earnings." *NBER* working paper no. 16082. Cambridge, Mass.: National Bureau of Economic Research.

Autor, David. 2015a. "Polanyi's Paradox and the Shape of Employment Growth." Paper presented at the 2014 Federal Reserve Bank of Kansas City: Economic Policy Symposium, Reevaluating Labor Market Dynamics. Jackson Hole, Wyom. (August 21–23, 2014). DOI: 10.3386/w20485.

———. 2015b. "Why Are There Still So Many Jobs? The History and Future of Workplace Automation." *Journal of Economic Perspectives* 29(3): 3–30. DOI: 10.1257/jep.29.3.3.

Autor, David H., Frank Levy, and Richard J. Murnane. 2003. "The Skill Content of Recent Technological Change: An Empirical Exploration." *Quarterly Journal of Economics* 118(4): 1279–333.

Becker, Gary S. 1994. *Human Capital: A Theoretical and Empirical Analysis, with Special Reference to Education*, 3rd ed. Chicago: University of Chicago Press.

Bernhardt, Annette, Rosemary Batt, Susan Houseman, and Eileen Appelbaum. 2015. "Domestic Outsourcing in the U.S.: A Research Agenda to Assess Trends and Effects on Job Quality." Paper prepared for the Future of Work Symposium, U.S. Department of Labor. Washington (December 2015). Accessed February 15, 2019. https://www.dol.gov/asp/evaluation/completed-studies/Future_of_work_research_agenda_to_assess_trends_and_effects_on_job_quality.pdf.

Bertrand, Marianne, Claudia Goldin, and Lawrence F. Katz. 2010. "Dynamics of the Gender Gap for Young Professionals in the Financial and Corporate Sectors." *American Economic Journal: Applied Economics* 2: 228–55.

Blau, Francine D., and Lawrence M. Kahn. 2000. "Gender Differences in Pay." *Journal of Economic Perspectives* 14(4): 75–99.

Bureau of Labor Statistics (BLS). 2005. "Contingent and Alternative Employment Arrangements, February 2005." Washington: U.S. Department of Labor. Accessed February 15, 2019. https://www.bls.gov/news.release/archives/conemp_0727 2005.pdf.

Carnoy, Martin, Manuel Castells, and Chris Benner. 1997. "Labour Markets and Employment Practices in the Age of Flexibility: A Case Study of Silicon Valley." *International Labour Review* 136(1): 27–48.

Catanzarite, Lisa. 2000. "Brown-Collar Jobs: Occupational Segregation and Earnings of Recent-Immigrant Latinos." *Sociological Perspectives* 43(1): 45–75. http://journals.sagepub.com/doi/pdf/10.2307/1389782.

Clark, Andrew E. 2005. "Your Money or Your Life: Changing Job Quality in OECD Countries." *British Journal of Industrial Relations* 43(3): 377–400. doi:10.1111/j.1467–8543.2005.00361.x.

Donovan, Sarah A, David H Bradley, and Jon O. Shimabukuro. 2016. "What Does the Gig Economy Mean for Workers?" *CRS* report no. R44365. Washington, D.C.: Congressional Research Service. Accessed February 15, 2019. https://fas.org/sgp/crs/misc/R44365.pdf.

Dube, Arindrajit, and Ethan Kaplan. 2010. "Does Outsourcing Reduce Wages in the Low-Wage Service Occupations? Evidence from Janitors and Guards." *Industrial and Labor Relations Review* 63(2). DOI: 10.1177/001979391006300206.

Eurostat. 2016. "Statistical Approaches to the Measurement of Skills—The State of Play in Europe within the European Statistical System." Luxembourg: European Union. DOI:10.2785/652037.

Farrell, Diana, and Fiona Greig. 2016a. "Paychecks, Paydays, and the Online Platform Economy Big Data on Income Volatility." New York: JP Morgan-Chase. Accessed February 15, 2019. https://www.jpmorganchase.com/corporate/institute/document/jpmc-institute-volatility-2-report.pdf.

———. 2016b. "The Online Platform Economy: What Is the Growth Trajectory?" New York: JP Morgan-Chase. Accessed February 15, 2019. https://www.jpmorganchase.com/corporate/institute/document/ope-growth-trajectory.pdf.

Fischer, Claude S., and Michael Hout. 2016. *Century of Difference: How America Changed in the Last One Hundred Years*. New York: Russell Sage Foundation.

Foote, Christopher L, and Richard W. Ryan. 2014. "Labor Market Polarization Over the Business

Cycle." *NBER Macroeconomics Annual* 29(1): 371–413. DOI: 10.1086/680656.

Golden, Lonnie. 2008. "Limited Access: Disparities in Flexible Work Schedules and Work-at-Home." *Journal of Family and Economic Issues* 29(1): 86–109. DOI: 10.1007/s10834-007-9090-7.

Goldin, Claudia, Lawrence F. Katz, and Ilyana Kuziemko. 2006. "The Homecoming of American College Women: The Reversal of the College Gender Gap." *Journal of Economic Perspectives* 20(4): 133–56. DOI:10.1257/jep.20.4.133.

Goldschmidt, Deborah, and Johannes F. Schmieder. 2017. "The Rise of Domestic Outsourcing and the Evolution of the German Wage Structure." *Quarterly Journal of Economics* 132(3): 1165–217. DOI: 10.1093/qje/qjx008.

Harris, Seth D., and Alan B. Krueger. 2015. "A Proposal for Modernizing Labor Laws for Twenty-First-Century Work: The Independent Worker." Washington, D.C.: Brookings Institute. http://www.hamiltonproject.org/assets/files/modernizing_labor_laws_for_twenty_first_century_work_krueger_harris.pdf.

Hippel, Courtney von, Venkat Bendapudi, Judith Tansky, David B. Greenberger, Stephen L. Mangum, and Robert L. Heneman. 2006. "Operationalizing the Shadow Workforce: Toward an Understanding of the Participants in Nonstandard Employment Relationships." In *The Shadow Workforce: Perspectives on Contingent Work in the United States, Japan and Europe*, edited by Sandra E. Gleason. Kalamazoo, Mich: Upjohn Institute.

Holzer, Harry J. 2011. "Raising Job Quality and Worker Skills in the US : Creating More Effective Education and Workforce Development Systems in States." *Hamilton Project* discussion paper no. 2011-10. Washington, D.C.: Brookings Institute.

Holzer, Harry J., Julia I. Lane, David B. Rosenblum, and Frederik Andersson. 2011. *Where Are All the Good Jobs Going?: What National and Local Job Quality and Dynamics Mean for U.S. Workers*. New York: Russell Sage Foundation.

Howell, David, and Mamadou Diallo. 2008. "The Importance of Accounting for Job Quality: Charting U.S. Economic Performance with Alternative Labor Market Indicators." *Challenge* 51(1): 26–44. DOI:10.2753/0577-5132510102.

Jaimovich, Nir, and Henry E. Siu. 2014. "The Trend Is the Cycle: Job Polarization and Jobless Recover-

ies." Working paper. University of Zurich. Accessed February 15, 2019. http://www.nirjaimovich.com/assets/jpjr.pdf.

Kalleberg, Arne L. 2000. "Nonstandard Employment Relations: Part-Time, Temporary and Contract Work." *Annual Review of Sociology* 26: 341–65. http://www.annualreviews.org/doi/pdf/10.1146/annurev.soc.26.1.341.

———. 2003. "Flexible Firms and Labor Market Segmentation: Effects of Workplace Restructuring on Jobs and Workers." *Work and Occupations* 30(2). DOI: 10.1177/0730888403251683.

———. 2009. "Precarious Work, Insecure Workers: Employment Relations in Transition." *American Sociological Review* 74(2): 1–22.

———. 2011. *Good Jobs, Bad Jobs: The Rise of Polarized and Precarious Employment Systems in the United States, 1970s–2000s*. New York: Russell Sage Foundation.

———. 2012. "Job Quality and Precarious Work: Clarifications, Controversies, and Challenges." *Work and Occupations* 39(4): 427–48. doi:10.1177/0730888412460533.

Kalleberg, Arne L., Barbara F. Reskin, and Ken Hudson. 2000. "Bad Jobs in America: Standard and Nonstandard Employment Relations and Job Quality in the United States." *American Sociological Review* 65(2): 256–78. Accessed February 15, 2019. https://www.jstor.org/stable/pdf/2657440.pdf.

Katz, Lawrence F., and Alan B. Krueger. 2019. "The Rise and Nature of Alternative Work Arrangements in the United States, 1995–2015." *ILR Review* 72(2): 382–416.

Lemieux, Thomas. 2010. "What Do We Really Know About Changes in Wage Inequality?" In *Labor in the New Economy*, edited by Katharine G. Abraham, James R. Spletzer, and Michael J. Harper. Chicago: University of Chicago Press.

Liu, Cathy Yang, and Ric Kolenda. 2012. "Counting and Understanding the Contingent Workforce: Using Georgia as an Example." *Urban Studies* 49(5): 1003–25. DOI: 10.1177/0042098011408139.

McKinsey & Company. 2015. "A Labor Market That Works: Connecting Talent with Opportunity in the Digital Age." New York: McKinsey Global Institute. http://www.mckinsey.com/global-themes/employment-and-growth/connecting-talent-with-opportunity-in-the-digital-age.

Polivka, Anne E. 1996. "Contingent and Alternative Work Arrangements Defined." *Monthly Labor Re-*

view 119(3): 3–9. https://www.bls.gov/mlr/1996/10/art1full.pdf.

Polivka, Anne E., and Thomas Nardone. 1989. "On the Definition of 'Contingent Work'." *Monthly Labor Review* 112(12): 9–16. Accessed February 15, 2019. https://stats.bls.gov/mlr/1989/12/art2full.pdf.

Schmitt, John. 2003. "Creating a Consistent Hourly Wage Series from the Current Population Survey's Outgoing Rotation Group, 1979–2002." Washington, D.C.: Center for Economic and Policy Research. Accessed February 15, 2019. http://ceprdata.org/wp-content/cps/CEPR_ORG_Wages.pdf.

Spletzer, James R., and Elizabeth W. Handwerker. 2014. "Measuring the Distribution of Wages in the United States from 1996 Through 2010 Using the Occupational Employment Survey." *Monthly Labor Review*, May. Accessed February 15, 2019. https://www.bls.gov/opub/mlr/2014/article/measuring-the-distribution-of-wages-in-the-united-states-from-1996-through-2010 -using-the-occupational-employment-survey.htm.

U.S. Bureau of the Census (Census Bureau). 1995. "Current Population Survey, February 1995: Contingent Worker Supplement (ICPSR 6736)." Ann Arbor, Mich.: Inter-university Consortium for Political and Social Research [distributor], 2005-12-06. DOI: 10.3886/ICPSR06736.v2.

———. 2005. "Current Population Survey, February 2005: Contingent Worker Supplement (ICPSR 4311)." Ann Arbor, Mich.: Inter-university Consortium for Political and Social Research [distributor], 2012-10-24. DOI:10.3886/ICPSR04311.v2.

———. 2017. "Current Population Survey, May 2017: Contingent Worker Supplement (ICPSR 37191)." Ann Arbor, Mich.: Inter-university Consortium for Political and Social Research [distributor], 2018-11-29. DOI: 10.3886/ICPSR37191.v1.

Weil, David. 2014. *The Fissured Workplace: Why Work Became So Bad for So Many and What Can Be Done to Improve It*. Cambridge, Mass.: Harvard University Press.

PART II
New Labor Market Dynamics and Outcomes

Nonstandard Work and the Job Search Process: Application Pools, Search Methods, and Perceived Job Quality

DAVID S. PEDULLA AND KATARIINA MUELLER-GASTELL

Millions of workers labor in nonstandard employment relationships, such as part-time and temporary jobs. Yet little is known about how the job search process is influenced by such positions. This article examines the ways that job seekers' application pools and search processes are shaped by nonstandard employment relationships. Among our findings is evidence that job seekers are more likely both to perceive nonstandard positions as being below their skill level and to receive job offers for those positions, presenting many workers with a complex trade-off between obtaining a job and working in a position that is poorly matched to their skill level. Together, our findings demonstrate how the job search process is shaped by nonstandard employment relationships with broad consequences for labor market inequality.

Keywords: nonstandard work, job search, labor markets, inequality

The U.S. economy has faced numerous changes in recent decades, including the increased use of technology in the workplace, the decline of organized labor and unionization, the polarization of job quality, as well as the utilization of nonstandard employment relationships (Clawson and Clawson 1999; Hyman 2018; Kalleberg 2000, 2009, 2011; Smith 1997). Indeed, millions of workers in the United States now labor in part-time and temporary positions (Bureau of Labor Statistics 2018a, 2018b; Katz and Krueger 2016). In response, a significant body of scholarship has emerged to understand the underlying forces that drive the prevalence and use of nonstandard labor (Autor 2003; Kalleberg, Reynolds, and Marsden 2003). Researchers have also examined the consequences of nonstandard labor for workers' material and subjective well-being as well as their career trajectories (Epstein et al. 1999; Kalleberg, Reskin,

David S. Pedulla is assistant professor in the Department of Sociology at Stanford University. Katariina Mueller-Gastell is a PhD candidate in the Department of Sociology at Stanford University.

© 2019 Russell Sage Foundation. Pedulla, David S., and Katariina Mueller-Gastell. 2019. "Nonstandard Work and the Job Search Process: Application Pools, Search Methods, and Perceived Job Quality." *RSF: The Russell Sage Foundation Journal of the Social Sciences* 5(4): 130–58. DOI: 10.7758/RSF.2019.5.4.05. Data collection for the project was conducted jointly with Devah Pager and generous support for this research came from the Russell Sage Foundation (85-13-01) to both Pedulla and Pager as well as the following funding to Pager: NSF (CAREER0547810) and NIH (1K01HD053694). We thank Arne Kalleberg, David Howell, three anonymous reviewers, and participants in the RSF conference on Changing Job Quality: Causes, Consequences, and Challenges for valuable feedback on earlier versions of this manuscript. Direct correspondence to: David S. Pedulla at dpedulla@stanford.edu, Department of Sociology, Stanford University, Building 120, Room 132, 450 Serra Mall, Stanford, CA 94305.

and Hudson 2000; Pedulla 2016). This research has provided valuable insights into the causes and consequences of nonstandard employment in the United States and beyond.

Limited scholarship, however, has investigated the ways that the prevalence of nonstandard employment relations shape the job search process. Yet, given that these positions occupy a large role in the economy, interesting questions emerge about who applies for these jobs and the methods used to find nonstandard employment. Additionally, questions arise about how workers perceive the quality of the nonstandard positions to which they apply and why they might submit applications for these types of positions. In this article, we address four sets of issues at the nexus of nonstandard employment and the job search process.

The first set of questions centers on the application pools to which job seekers submit applications. Scholars have found compelling evidence of racial and ethnic, gender, age, and other sociodemographic differences in the workers who actually labor in nonstandard employment positions (Bureau of Labor Statistics 2018b; Katz and Krueger 2016). Yet we have limited information about whether workers from different sociodemographic backgrounds are more likely to apply for part-time and temporary positions. It is possible that these groups of workers are more likely to be in nonstandard jobs due to the positions for which they receive job offers rather than due to the positions for which they actually submit applications. Thus, this article explores sociodemographic differences in the employment relationships of the job openings to which job seekers submit applications.

Additionally, we ask whether job seekers' application pools focus on one employment relation type—full time, standard, or nonstandard—or whether their application pools are better characterized by a mixed status, whereby a single job seeker applies for multiple job types. Specifically, we ask whether job seekers apply for full-time, standard positions, and nonstandard positions simultaneously. It is possible that during the search for work, individuals know what type of job they want and search entirely for jobs that have a single type of employment relationship. However, given

the prevalence of nonstandard employment, job seekers' application pools may in fact be more complex.

Second, we probe the search methods that are used during the job search process and how these relate to applications for nonstandard positions. The search methods—network-based, informal methods versus formal methods, for example—may differ between applications to standard and nonstandard positions. Perhaps workers are more likely to rely on family, friends, and acquaintances to find out about nonstandard positions but use the internet and other formal sources to learn about full-time, standard jobs. Understanding these issues will assist in better conceptualizing the matching process between workers and job openings in the labor market, where nonstandard jobs make up a significant share of the available positions.

Third, we examine how job seekers perceive the quality of the nonstandard positions to which they apply. Part-time and temporary jobs tend to be of lower quality. On average, they offer lower wages and are less likely to provide health and pension benefits than full-time, standard positions (Kalleberg, Reskin, and Hudson 2000), although variation in these positions is significant. Yet we know little about how job seekers perceive the quality of the nonstandard jobs to which they are submitting applications. Thus, we examine whether job seekers perceive nonstandard jobs to which they submit applications as being beneath their skill level, an important component of job quality.

Finally, we ask whether applying for nonstandard jobs may be a way for workers to get a toehold in the labor market. It is possible that employers are less stringent about their requirements for hiring for nonstandard positions and, thus, workers may be more likely to receive job offers for positions that are part time or temporary than they would be for full-time, permanent, standard jobs. If job seekers are more likely both to receive job offers from nonstandard positions and to perceive these jobs as beneath their skill level, an important trade-off emerges for job seekers: getting a job versus using their skills.

To date, many of these issues have been largely absent from conversations on nonstandard employment relationships. This gap in the literature is due in part to data limitations. Addressing these topics requires having detailed information about whether the individual applications submitted by job seekers are for standard or nonstandard jobs. Surveys with information about the applications submitted by individual job seekers are limited and even fewer collect information about the employment relationship that corresponds to the jobs to which the individual applied. We draw on an original data set that contains this information to address these issues.

THE JOB SEARCH PROCESS AND NONSTANDARD WORK

A significant body of scholarship has pointed to the many changes that have occurred in the U.S. economy over the past decades. Often referred to as the "new economy," researchers note how the economic landscape in the contemporary United States is generally characterized by the relative decline of manufacturing jobs and the rise of service-sector jobs, the increased use of technology in the workplace, the outsourcing of production, the globalization of trade, the polarization of job quality, and the rise and prevalence of nonstandard employment relationships (Autor 2003; Hollister 2011; Kalleberg 2000; Smith 1997; Wright and Dwyer 2003; Clawson and Clawson 1999; Kim and Sakamoto 2008). This final aspect of the "new economy" is our central focus. Despite questions about the extent of the rise of nonstandard work (Bernhardt 2014)—such as part-time and temporary agency employment—we know that millions of workers work in such positions in the United States (Bureau of Labor Statistics 2018a; Katz and Krueger 2016), making our understanding of how these types of positions intersect with job searching important.

Before moving on to the ways that nonstandard employment relationships may shape the job search process, it is useful to define what we mean by nonstandard employment. Throughout this article, we focus on two types

of nonstandard work: part-time work and temporary employment.[1] Part-time work is the most common type of nonstandard employment and refers to individuals who work fewer than thirty-five hours per week (Kalleberg 2000). Roughly 17 percent of the U.S. labor force is in a part-time position (Bureau of Labor Statistics 2018a). Among those in part-time positions, approximately a quarter are involuntarily working part time, preferring a full-time position. Part-time employment shows some occupation and industry variation. Individuals in service, sales, and office occupations as well as those in the wholesale and retail trade and hospitality and leisure industries are more likely to be in part-time positions (Bureau of Labor Statistics 2018c, 2018d).

By contrast, temporary employment has to do with the time horizon for an individual's employment, rather than the number of hours that they work per week. Thus, temporary employment can be full time or part time. It can also be structured in multiple ways. One common type of temporary work is Temporary Help Agency (THA) employment, when the worker is on the payroll of one company (the temp agency) but performs their daily work at another company. Importantly, the THA is also the legal employer of the temp worker (Autor 2003). Among THA workers, 46 percent would prefer a permanent position, indicating that a significant proportion of THA workers are involuntarily in those positions (Bureau of Labor Statistics 2018b). Not all temporary workers, however, are employed by temp agencies. Companies can hire workers directly on a temporary basis with the mutual understanding that the worker's involvement at the company will be discontinued at some point in the future.

An important feature of some temporary positions—both agency based and those that are directly through companies—is that these positions can sometimes become permanent. According to a study by the American Staffing Association, roughly half of temporary workers perceived temping as a pathway to permanent

1. The rise of part-time employment over the past thirty years has been limited, although rates of involuntary part-time work did increase during the Great Recession (Dunn 2018). And, though Temporary Help Agency (THA) employment has remained relatively stable since the mid-1990s, THA employment increased significantly between the late 1970s and mid-1990s (Autor 2003; Bureau of Labor Statistics 2018b).

employment. They also find that roughly one-third of temporary workers end up receiving an offer for a permanent position from the employer for which they temped (American Staffing Association 2017). In our analysis, we distinguish between temporary positions that are unlikely to become permanent and those that have the potential to become permanent.

It is important to note that our analysis does not cover applications for all types of nonstandard employment. For example, we do not have information about whether applications were submitted for on-call jobs, "gig" work, or independent contracting positions.[2] Yet, we are able to examine two key types of nonstandard work: part-time employment and temporary employment. Next, we move on to thinking about how the job search process may be shaped by these positions in the economy. To begin, we discuss how key sociodemographic characteristics of workers may shape the types of jobs to which they apply.

The Sociodemographic Concentration of Nonstandard Work

Research documenting the ways that nonstandard work is unevenly distributed across the population is significant. Women, for example, are much more likely than men to work part time, particularly among prime-age workers. More than 70 percent of part-time workers between the ages of twenty-five and fifty-four in the United States are women (Bureau of Labor Statistics 2018a). Historically, part-time work was largely seen as a way for women to balance paid employment with their disproportionate role in childcare and housework (Kalleberg 2000; Tilly 1992; Epstein et al. 1999). And, although the gender gap in part-time work has declined over time, it remains pronounced. The gender gap for THA employment, by contrast, is limited (Bureau of Labor Statistics 2018b; Katz and Krueger 2016).

In terms of part-time work—particularly involuntary part-time work—there are also racial disparities. Among prime-age workers in part-time positions, black men and black women are more likely than white men and white women, respectively, to involuntarily be working part time (Bureau of Labor Statistics 2018a). Racial disparities are also significant in temporary agency employment, African Americans being three times as likely and Hispanic workers nearly twice as likely as whites to work through a temp agency (Katz and Krueger 2016). Thus, in general, workers of color are more likely to be involuntarily working part time and employed through temporary help agencies.

Age also structures workers' experiences of nonstandard employment. Despite similar overall rates of part-time work for individuals of different ages, differences are significant in terms of whether they are working part time voluntarily or involuntarily. Among part-time workers, prime-age workers (twenty-five to fifty-four-year-olds) are more likely to involuntarily work part time and less likely to voluntarily work part time than both younger and older workers (Bureau of Labor Statistics 2018a). Additionally, workers between twenty and twenty-four are relatively more likely to be working through temporary help agencies (Bureau of Labor Statistics 2018b). However, older workers are only slightly more likely to be in THA positions than mid-career individuals (Bureau of Labor Statistics 2018b).

Estimates also indicate that education matters in determining who labors in nonstandard positions. Insofar as nonstandard positions are less desirable, workers with more education may be able to avoid these types of employment relationships (Kalleberg, Reskin, and Hudson 2000). Indeed, evidence is significant that workers with a bachelor's degree or higher are less likely to be in THA positions (Bureau of Labor Statistics 2018b). Nonetheless, at least for vol-

---

2. It is unclear exactly how applications for independent contracting positions would be captured with our data collection strategy, given that an individual who is an independent contractor generally bids to work on a project rather than applying for a job in the sense that we are considering here. Other types of nonstandard employment—such as on-call work—were not included in the item on the survey instrument asking about the employment relationship of the position for which the job seeker applied. The item asked only whether a position was full time, part time, temporary that has the possibility to become permanent, or temporary that is unlikely to become permanent.

untary part-time work, variation by educational attainment is limited (Dunn 2018). The gender gap in part-time work, however, persists across all levels of education (Dunn 2018).

Some of these patterns are likely stronger among intersections of social positions. For example, women's employment is more likely than men's to "sag" during the transition to marriage and family formation (Goldin and Mitchell 2017). Additionally, women are more likely than men to work part time, due in part to the gendered demands of caretaking and household labor (Kalleberg 2000; Epstein et al. 1999). Married women may therefore be particularly likely to apply for part-time positions. Additionally, race and gender may intersect to produce divergent likelihoods of applying for nonstandard positions (Browne and Misra 2003). Thus, we also examine whether intersectional patterns exist among the applications submitted by job seekers.

Many of these findings are based on surveying job incumbents about their positions. In other words, the estimates are drawn from the workers who actually labor in these positions. Outstanding questions exist, however, about whether workers differentially *apply* for nonstandard positions along the same sociodemographic axes as they work in those positions. We might imagine that the association between one's demographic group and the types of jobs one applies to would be strongest among workers who voluntarily work in those positions. By contrast, we may expect a weaker correlation between demographic characteristics and application type among groups who are involuntarily in those positions. Regardless, if we see differences between the types of workers who apply for nonstandard positions and the types of workers who are incumbents in nonstandard positions, it may point to processes on the demand side of the labor market that are allocating workers to different types of employment relationships.

Job Searching in the New Economy

Given the prevalence of nonstandard positions in the economy and the large proportion of workers who are in these positions, workers' job searches necessarily include these types of jobs. To date, however, little research has docu-

mented how the job search process is influenced by nonstandard positions. One aim of this article is to document the ways that part-time and temporary positions are involved in shaping the structure of job seekers' application pools as well as the processes by which they find employment.

In terms of the structure of individuals' application pools, two entirely different types of job seekers are possible: those who apply solely for full-time, standard positions and those who apply solely for nonstandard positions. It is easy to imagine a worker who knows that they are looking for a full-time, permanent job and, thus, discards any job postings or job leads that are not for a full-time, permanent position. Similarly, it would not be surprising if a job seeker who was solely looking for part-time jobs to assist with balancing various work and nonwork demand—such as caring for a child or elderly parent—limited their search to part-time positions.

It is also possible, however, that many job seekers' goals and preferences are less clear cut. They may be open to different types of positions—including nonstandard jobs—or they may at least not screen out nonstandard positions if they appear to be a reasonable fit on other dimensions (such as occupation or location). If this is the case, then the structure of job seekers' application pools may be mixed, whereby they submit applications for multiple types of positions—both full-time, standard positions and nonstandard positions—at the same time. As a descriptive exercise, it is interesting to see which type of search most accurately reflects reality.

If, indeed, some individual workers are applying for different types of positions at the same time, this is one important way that nonstandard employment influences the labor market, complicating workers' application pools. The existence of these mixed application pools would also raise questions about whether workers with those mixed pools are different from the workers applying for positions with only one type of employment relationship. Existing theoretical perspectives on job search provide insights about what types of workers may be more likely to apply for mixed application pools.

Workers face myriad challenges during the job search process. From discrimination to high levels of competition to figuring out a job and organization that is a good fit, job searching can be challenging (Bertrand and Mullainathan 2004; Pager, Western, and Bonikowski 2009; Pedulla 2018; Rivera 2012). Workers who are facing challenges may expand their job search to include additional occupations, company types, or potentially employment relations. Devah Pager and David Pedulla, for example, find that African Americans include a greater range of occupational categories and characteristics in their application pools than observationally similar whites (2015). They also present evidence that concerns about discrimination underlie this racially distinct search behavior. Beyond discrimination, workers who are struggling to find employment, a process that can be filled with feelings of demoralization and self-blame (Sharone 2014), may become less stringent in their search criteria (Krueger and Mueller 2016). As a worker spends more time unemployed, for example, they may loosen their job search criteria and begin to apply for jobs, regardless of whether they are full-time, standard positions or part time or temporary. Thus, there are reasons to think that individuals who face discrimination and other challenges in the labor market may be more likely to have heterogeneous or mixed application pools.

Network-Based Job Search
One of the central concerns in sociological scholarship on job search has been the methods that individuals use to find work. Of particular interest has been the network-based, informal channels through which people find out about jobs (Granovetter 1973; Mouw 2003; for reviews, see Castilla, Lan, and Rissing 2013; Trimble and Kmec 2011). Network-based job search can consist of multiple channels, including friends, family, acquaintances, and coworkers (present or former). Scholars have also drawn the distinction between strong and weak network ties, whereby the latter are likely to be more beneficial for job seekers, in part because they are likely to connect the job seeker with nonredundant information about job leads (Granovetter 1973; Yakubovich 2005). These

types of network-based job search methods are contrasted against more formal channels, such as internet-based search. Indeed, network-based search is quite important in understanding the job matching process given that approximately 50 percent of jobs are found through some sort of informal channel (Corcoran, Datcher, and Duncan 1980; Granovetter 1973; Mouw 2003).

Network-based job search may be successful for many reasons (Fernandez, Castilla, and Moore 2000; Kmec 2006). First, it can provide a job seeker with key resources, such as information about the opening. Additional resources may include the network alter—the *referrer* in the job search context (Smith 2005; Marin 2012)—putting in a good word for the job seeker at the company or putting the job seeker in touch with someone at the company (Castilla, Lan, and Rissing 2013). Second, network-based job search may have a signaling function. When a job seeker is referred by someone for a given job posting, that individual is putting their reputation on the line for the job seeker and, at least in some way, vouching for them. Thus, employers may interpret job seekers with a referral as a positive signal about their ability, status, and potential productivity (Castilla, Lan, and Rissing 2013).

Network-based job search could intersect with nonstandard work in multiple, competing ways. On the one hand, nonstandard types of positions may be less likely to be posted in formal places. It is even possible that many nonstandard positions are not posted at all or are quickly generated for a specific project, particularly in the case of temporary employment. Thus, network-based search may provide valuable information about these types of nonstandard job openings that would not be otherwise available to job seekers. In this case, we could expect that nonstandard job applications would be more likely to have been submitted after hearing about the opening through a network-based channel.

By contrast, it is also possible that workers are not as open with their social networks about looking for part-time work and temporary employment. Thus, the alters in one's network may not share information with a job seeker about positions that are not full time and permanent. In this case, we may expect to see that job seekers are less likely to apply for nonstandard jobs that they heard about through their network connections and more likely to find these openings through formal mechanisms. Of course, it is also possible that the search methods job seekers use when applying for standard and nonstandard positions will not differ.

Perceptions of Job Quality: Are Nonstandard Jobs Below a Worker's Skill Level?

There are multiple ways to think about and measure job quality. On many key dimensions, scholars have documented that part-time and temporary jobs are of lower quality, on average, than full-time, standard positions. For example, 44.2 percent of men and 35.2 percent of women in temporary help agency positions have low wages, compared with 11.2 percent of men and 16.0 percent women in regular full-time jobs (Kalleberg, Reskin, and Hudson 2000). Similarly, part-time workers are more likely than full-time workers to have low wages. Arne Kalleberg, Barbara Reskin, and Kenneth Hudson also present compelling evidence that access to important benefits—such as health insurance and pensions—is much lower among nonstandard workers (2000). Beyond these material aspects of job quality, qualitative scholarship has probed the lived experiences of workers in nonstandard jobs. For both part-time and temporary employment, research in this area has documented significant stigma and devaluation for the workers who labor in these positions (Henson 1996; Rogers 1995; Smith 1998). Evidence also indicates that temporary employment is correlated with psychological morbidity and, in some cases, more negative workplace attitudes (for a review, see Virtanen et al. 2005; Broschak, Davis-Blake, and Block 2008).[3] Yet, variation in job quality is significant within categories of nonstandard employment (Haley-Lock 2009), such as the distinction between *retention* and *secondary* part-time work (Tilly 1996).

The material and subjective experiences of workers while they are in nonstandard positions have been examined, but data limitations have made it difficult to explore how workers perceive nonstandard positions to which they might apply before they actually take on those positions. In this article, we examine one such perception: the skill level of the job. Specifically, we examine whether the lower quality of nonstandard jobs found among job incumbents also translates to workers' perceptions of these jobs before they work in them. In other words, do workers' perceptions of a job application's skill level correlate with the employment relationship of the position?

A Toehold in the Labor Market?

Debate in the literature has been significant about whether nonstandard jobs can serve as stepping stones to future employment opportunities or whether they trap workers, making it difficult for them to advance into better positions down the road (Addison, Cotti, and Surfield 2009; Addison and Surfield 2009; Autor and Houseman 2010; Fuller 2011; Pedulla 2016). Another way to conceptualize this issue, however, is to consider whether it is easier for workers to obtain job offers when applying for nonstandard positions compared to full-time, standard jobs. Rather than asking about the future consequences of nonstandard work—the "stepping stone" versus "dead end" comparison—we could consider whether nonstandard jobs offer a "toehold" in the labor market.

This may be the case for multiple reasons. Employers may be less selective in hiring decisions for nonstandard jobs since the individual will not be a permanent employee or will be working fewer hours per week than if they were full time. Additionally, with some types of nonstandard workers, it is easier to terminate or fire the individual than it is if they are a full-time permanent worker (Autor 2003). Thus, employers and hiring managers may be less stringent in the selection criteria or more likely to take a risk on a worker for a temporary position because they can easily let the worker go if they are not working out. If, indeed, this is the case,

---

3. Joseph Broschak, Alison Davis-Blake, and Emily Block offer insights into the complexity of the workplace attitudes of temporary agency and retention part-time workers (2008). In some cases, workers in these positions do not report more negative workplace attitudes.

then nonstandard positions may serve as a point of entry for workers into the labor market. If obtaining a job offer for a nonstandard position is easier than obtaining an offer for a full-time, standard job, then these types of positions may enable workers to enter the labor market and gain some experience, which may prove useful down the road. However, insofar as nonstandard positions are of poorer quality or limit workers' future labor market opportunities (Pedulla 2016), an easy entry point into nonstandard positions may not be beneficial for workers' longer-term careers.

DATA AND METHODS

To address these issues, we draw on original panel data, which we call the National Longitudinal Study of Job Search (NLSJS). The NLSJS follows a national sample of 2,060 job seekers over eighteen months. The data were collected in collaboration with Gfk (formerly Knowledge Networks). The sampling design for the Gfk panel—referred to as KnowledgePanel—is based on a combination of random-digit dial methods and address-based sampling methods. Their sampling frame covers approximately 97 percent of all U.S. households (Knowledge Networks 2011).

In total, the NLSJS consists of nine survey waves, which were conducted between February 8, 2013, and November 30, 2014. The first seven waves were conducted roughly six weeks apart over approximately eight months. The eighth wave was conducted one year after the baseline. The final survey (wave nine) took place approximately eighteen months after the baseline survey. The target population for the NLSJS was non-institutionalized adults ages eighteen through sixty-four who were residing in the United States and who had looked for work over the previous four weeks. The NLSJS also oversampled African American respondents.[4] For our analyses, we limit our sample to job seekers who reported at the baseline survey that they wanted to work at least thirty-five hours per week in the job for which they were searching.[5] This sample restriction is important because it removes individuals who would ideally like to work part time. Thus, it is important to remember that the individuals in our analytic sample want to be working full time.

The NLSJS collected detailed information about many aspects of the job seekers' experiences, such as sociodemographic and background characteristics, employment histories and experiences, as well as job search behaviors. Important for our purposes, respondents at each wave were asked to provide information about the five most recent jobs they had applied to in the past four weeks. Then, they were asked a series of questions about each job opening that they listed, including whether the job opening was for a full-time position, a part-time position, a temporary position with the possibility of becoming permanent, or a temporary position that was unlikely to become permanent; and the search method through which the job seeker heard about the opening (family member, friend, online, and so on). Thus we are able to analyze the pools of applications submitted by each job seeker to examine whether application pools are segregated or mixed in terms of employment relations,

---

4. To recruit participants for the NLSJS, Gfk sampled 19,509 of its KnowledgePanel members and sent email invitations to this group to screen them for eligibility. Of those 19,509 individuals, 11,231 (57.6 percent) completed the screening items. We screened individuals for eligibility on two items. First, the respondent had to provide informed consent. Second, the respondent had to have been looking for work in the four weeks prior to participating in the survey. Of the 11,231 respondents who completed the screening items, 2,092 (18.6 percent) were eligible to participate in the NLSJS. Of those eligible, 2,060 (98.5 percent) completed the survey. Similar descriptions of these data appear in working papers that use these data (see, for example, Pedulla and Pager 2017).

5. Information about desired work hours was gathered through an item that asked, "Assuming you could find suitable work, how many hours per week would you prefer to work on this job?" Individuals with missing data on this item are included in the sample and a dummy variable is included in all models to indicate whether or not the job seeker had missing data on this item. Results are similar when individuals with missing data on this item are excluded. The sign of coefficients for our findings remain consistent, though statistical significance is lost in some instances.

how applications for nonstandard jobs are correlated with key demographic characteristics, and what search methods are used to apply for nonstandard jobs.

Variable Construction

For our analyses, one key measure is the employment relationship of the position for each application submitted by a respondent. As noted, for each job application that they listed, survey respondents were asked to select "all that apply" from the following choices: full time, part time, temporary position that is unlikely to become permanent, and temporary position with the possibility of becoming permanent. These categories are not mutually exclusive. Our classification structure for the employment relationship of a given application is as follows. Applications that respondents indicated were both full time and one of the three other categories are classified as mixed positions. This category includes, for example, individual job openings that are temporary full-time positions as well as positions that could be full time or part time. Beyond mixed applications, though, we are interested in whether the pool of applications submitted by a job seeker was mixed. A respondent's application pool is coded as a mixed application pool if an applicant applied to both full-time, permanent positions and any other kind of job during their job search.[6] The application pool measure is at the level of the respondent, not the application.

To capture the search methods used for each application, respondents were asked how they found out about each job opening to which they applied. Specifically, they were asked about each application: how did you hear about the position with [employer name]? They were then told to select all options that apply from a list of potential sources (for example, family, friends, online search). In our analyses, we separately compare the four network-based job search methods—family member, friend, acquaintance, and employer or coworker—to formal job search methods. We combine all formal types of job search—newspaper ad, online search, employment agency, help wanted sign, and directly contacting the employer. Given that these job search methods are not mutually exclusive, if a respondent used both a network-based search method (such as friend or family member) and a formal method (such as searching online) in applying to a position, we consider their search method to be whichever network-based method they selected.[7]

To capture how long individuals have been unemployed, we asked respondents how long they had been unemployed in the twenty-four months prior to the baseline survey. We use this item to capture individuals' unemployment duration (in weeks) leading up to baseline. This variable is coded as 0 for anyone who was employed at baseline (regardless of whether they were unemployed at some point in the twenty-four months before baseline). Some respondents who indicated they were unemployed at the time of the baseline survey did not answer the question about unemployment duration. We coded these respondents as having the mean unemployment duration on this variable and include in our models an indicator variable for whether they were missing on the unemployment duration item.

We also analyze whether nonstandard positions are perceived as requiring lower skills than full-time, standard positions. For each application, respondents were asked which of the following options best describes the position with the employer to which they were applying: a position that is below my level of skill or experience, a position that is appropriate for my level of skill or experience, or a position that is above my level of skill or experience. We used these responses to code whether each position is below the applicant's skill level. The variable

6. As a robustness check, we operationalized mixed application pools as the proportion of applications submitted that were to full-time positions. When we use this variable, all our findings remain equivalent in sign, magnitude, and significance level. In supplemental analyses, we also coded mixed application pools as those that included at least three applications to a full-time position alongside an application to a nonstandard position, while limiting the sample to only those applicants that applied to at least five positions overall. With this threshold, our results remain qualitatively similar, but statistical significance levels change in some instances.

7. We obtain similar results when alternative coding schemes are used for this variable.

is coded 1 if the respondent selected that the application was for a position below their skill level, and 0 otherwise.

In one set of analyses, we also examine whether nonstandard applications are more likely to result in job offers than applications for full-time, standard positions. Our "job offer" outcome variable is taken from an item that asked respondents at each wave whether they had received an offer from any of the companies—by name—that they had applied to in that wave as well as any of the companies that they had applied to in previous waves. This item is then used to create a variable that captures, for each application, whether the application resulted in a job offer.[8]

Standard sociodemographic variables were collected by Gfk from their panel members. We use these items to capture respondents' gender, age, race-ethnicity, educational attainment, and marital status.[9] These sociodemographic characteristics are included as covariates in the models. The survey also collected information about respondents' occupations in their current or most recent job, which we control for. Specifically, respondents indicated their most recent job title on the survey in an open text format. Then, trained coders at the University of Wisconsin Survey Center classified these open-text responses into three-digit Standard Occupational Classification (SOC) codes for occupation. In our analyses, we use the two-digit SOC codes for major occupational categories. All models control for job seekers' prior occupation.[10]

Two additional controls are included in our models. First, we control for the intensity of respondents' job search. Specifically, we con-trol for the number of applications that respondents reported submitting over the four weeks prior to each survey wave (logged to adjust for skew). Additionally, we control for the number of waves that a respondent was in the sample. Descriptive information about our sample is presented in table 1.

Results

Our results proceed as follows. First, we examine the application pools of job seekers by looking at sociodemographic differences in who applies for each type of nonstandard position. We then explore whether individuals submit applications to more than one type of job (for example, full time, standard and nonstandard). We then examine the prevalence and predictors of these types of mixed application pools. Next, we examine whether different job search methods are used for nonstandard job applications relative to full-time, standard job applications. Then, we examine the perceived quality of job seekers' applications for nonstandard positions relative to full-time, standard jobs. Finally, we examine whether nonstandard applications are more likely to result in job offers than applications submitted for full-time, standard positions.

Sociodemographic Differences in Applying for Nonstandard Work

We begin by examining demographic differences in submitting applications for positions with particular types of employment relationships. For these analyses, each observation captures one of the applications that the job seeker submitted. Each application is nested within a given survey wave and each survey wave is

8. If a respondent listed a company name that was illegible or something other than a company name (such as the occupation or industry), that application was not presented to respondents when asking them about job offers in future waves because they would be unlikely to be able to identify the application. When we limit our analyses of job offers just to applications where the company name was carried forward to future waves, all findings regarding job offers hold. Additionally, in the survey, we asked respondents at each wave whether they had received a job offer from a company that they had not previously listed. For this set of applications, we did not ask about the employment relationship of the position and, thus, those offers are not included in these analyses.

9. We recode marital status into three categories: never married, married or cohabiting, and divorced, separated, or widowed.

10. The only models where controls for previous occupation are not explicitly entered are those where we include respondent-specific fixed effects.

Table 1. Summary Statistics of Analytic Sample

	Mean	SD	Observations
Age (years)	40.81	13.21	1,390
Woman	0.45	0.50	1,390
Race-ethnicity			
White, non-Hispanic	0.61	0.49	1,390
Black, non-Hispanic	0.17	0.37	1,390
Other, non-Hispanic	0.04	0.19	1,390
Hispanic	0.15	0.36	1,390
Two or more races, non-Hispanic	0.04	0.18	1,390
Marital status			
Married or cohabiting	0.56	0.50	1,390
Never married	0.30	0.46	1,390
Separated, divorced, or widowed	0.14	0.35	1,390
Employment at baseline			
Unemployed	0.33	0.47	1,386
Full-time employed	0.55	0.50	1,386
Alternative employment arrangement	0.12	0.32	1,386
Weeks unemployed at baseline (all respondents)	22.20	57.63	1,390
Weeks unemployed at baseline for those unemployed	63.33	82.72	429
Number of applications sent by applicant	11.71	8.77	1,390

Source: Authors' calculations.
Note: Respondents can report at most five job applications in each survey wave. The maximum possible number of applications for any single respondent is thus forty-five across the nine survey waves. Respondents who sent no applications are excluded from the sample. Four respondents did not indicate their employment status. Of the 452 respondents who reported they were unemployed, twenty-three did not provide an estimate of the duration of unemployment in the baseline survey.

nested within a given respondent. We use a multinomial logistic regression model, with standard errors clustered by respondent, to examine the sociodemographic correlates of applying for a nonstandard job. We move through five key sociodemographic groups—gender, race-ethnicity, age, marital status, and education—and then examine potential interactive effects between these different characteristics. In the model, the omitted category for the dependent variable is an application for a full-time, standard position. The findings are presented in table 2.

Gender   In terms of gender, we find that women are significantly more likely than men to apply for part-time jobs relative to full-time jobs. However, no gender differences are discernable in applying for temporary-to-permanent nor

temporary positions. Women are, however, more likely than men to submit an application for a position that could take on multiple employment relationships (for example, a job that could be either part time or full time, or a position that is temporary, but full time).

Race-ethnicity   The lack of statistically significant differences between the types of applications submitted by non-Hispanic white workers and workers of color is striking. Indeed, black workers are no more or less likely to apply for part-time or temporary-to-permanent positions than white workers are. In addition, they are marginally statistically significantly less likely to apply for temporary positions. This is quite surprising given that African Americans are significantly overrepresented in temporary jobs in the broader economy. Additionally, we see that

Table 2. Multinomial Logistic Regression Model of Type of Position Applied to

Ref = Full Time, Standard	Part Time	Temporary-to-Permanent	Temporary	Mixed
Woman	0.678***	0.0404	−0.0476	0.369**
	(0.112)	(0.172)	(0.241)	(0.143)
Ref = white, non-Hispanic				
Black, non-Hispanic	−0.124	−0.148	−0.478+	−0.0117
	(0.149)	(0.208)	(0.256)	(0.170)
Other, non-Hispanic	−0.130	0.400	−0.0926	−0.596+
	(0.378)	(0.325)	(0.467)	(0.343)
Hispanic	0.304+	0.264	0.193	0.188
	(0.160)	(0.207)	(0.352)	(0.185)
Two or more races, non-Hispanic	−0.580*	−0.173	−1.170**	−0.0765
	(0.283)	(0.491)	(0.419)	(0.302)
Ref = age 35–44				
18–24	1.213***	0.597*	0.270	0.961***
	(0.199)	(0.302)	(0.365)	(0.247)
25–34	0.253	0.0243	−0.102	0.527*
	(0.180)	(0.264)	(0.463)	(0.218)
45–54	0.195	0.0417	0.354	0.584**
	(0.181)	(0.239)	(0.287)	(0.206)
55–64	0.434*	0.209	0.700*	−0.0114
	(0.199)	(0.240)	(0.316)	(0.215)
Ref = never married				
Married or cohabiting	−0.140	−0.342+	−0.0832	−0.362*
	(0.127)	(0.193)	(0.273)	(0.155)
Separated, divorced, or widowed	−0.224	0.0495	−0.0461	−0.360
	(0.186)	(0.242)	(0.397)	(0.257)
Ref = some college				
Less than high school	0.0339	−0.0723	−0.432	0.369
	(0.205)	(0.326)	(0.370)	(0.280)
High school	0.0928	0.111	−0.572*	0.254
	(0.138)	(0.203)	(0.243)	(0.186)
College or higher	−0.820***	−0.336+	−0.421	−0.681***
	(0.139)	(0.179)	(0.281)	(0.155)
Weeks unemployed (log)	0.0683**	0.112**	−0.00715	0.143***
	(0.0260)	(0.0380)	(0.0458)	(0.0317)
Constant	−2.308***	−3.049***	−4.085***	−2.799***
	(0.372)	(0.444)	(0.802)	(0.389)
Occupation controls	Yes	Yes	Yes	Yes
Wave fixed effects	Yes	Yes	Yes	Yes
Clusters	1390			
Observations	16,271			

Source: Authors' calculations.

Note: Standard errors in parentheses. All standard errors clustered on applicant. Respondents who did not report their weeks of unemployment in the baseline survey are coded as being unemployed for the mean number of weeks for their baseline employment status. The model contains a separate indicator variable for whether this information was missing for the respondent. Occupation controls include the twenty-three categories of the SOC system for the previous occupation held by the applicant. The model also includes controls for the number of applications submitted by a respondent, the number of survey waves they participated in, and whether they did not indicate how many hours they would prefer to work in a week.

+$p < .1$; *$p < .05$; **$p < .01$; ***$p < .001$

Hispanic workers are marginally significantly more likely than non-Hispanic white workers to apply for part-time positions, but show no differences in applying for temporary positions. In general, it is surprising that the racial and ethnic differences found among incumbents in nonstandard positions in existing scholarship—particularly temporary work—do not appear in the application pools of job seekers.

Age   In terms of age, existing research suggests that non-prime-age workers—individuals younger than twenty-five and older than fifty-four—are more likely to be in nonstandard employment. Therefore, it is likely that both younger and older job seekers will be more likely to apply for nonstandard positions than workers at the peak of their careers. Our data provide general support for this prediction.

Younger workers, between the ages of eighteen and twenty-four, are more likely than workers between thirty-five and forty-four to apply for part-time positions, temporary-to-permanent positions, and mixed positions (all relative to full-time standard positions). For older workers, evidence indicates that workers between fifty-five and sixty-four are more likely to apply for part-time positions and for temporary positions (than for full-time positions) than middle-aged workers, aged thirty-five to forty-four. Thus, in general, non-prime-age workers are more likely to submit applications to nonstandard positions, particularly part-time positions, than workers in the middle of their careers. These findings are generally consistent with the age composition of incumbents in nonstandard positions.

Marital Status   Limited differences emerge in the types of applications submitted by workers with different marital statuses. Although, workers who are married or cohabiting are marginally significantly less likely than never married workers to apply for temp-to-perm positions

and significantly less likely to apply for mixed positions.

Education   In terms of education, key differences emerge. We see that having completed college or more—versus having just some college—is associated with being less likely to apply for part-time jobs and positions that offer multiple potential employment relationships and marginally significantly less likely to apply for temporary-to-permanent positions. This suggests that people higher on the educational attainment ladder are more likely to be focused on full-time, standard employment during their job search.

Interactive Effects   We next explore possible interactions between key sociodemographic characteristics. The full models for these analyses are presented in table A1. First, we examine whether the relationship between gender and submitting applications for nonstandard employment is shaped by a worker's marital status.[11] Our findings indicate that the relationship between being a woman and applying for a part-time position is stronger among married or cohabiting women than women who have never been married.

Second, we were interested in whether gender intersected with race-ethnicity to shape the likelihood of applying for nonstandard employment. Overall, we see limited evidence of this. In general, the interactions between the gender of the job seeker and the race-ethnicity of the job seeker are not statistically significant. However, the data demonstrate that the relationship between being a woman and applying for a temporary-to-permanent job is weaker among black women than among white women. Thus, instances where gender and race intersect to shape whether applicants apply for nonstandard positions are limited.

Together, these findings provide some evidence that the demographic differences that are found among incumbents in nonstandard

---

11. We also examined the interaction between being a woman and having a child twelve years old or younger living in the household. The interaction is not statistically significant in predicting part-time applications, compared to full-time, standard applications. The only case where the interaction term is statistically significant is in predicting applications for temporary-to-permanent positions relative to full-time, standard applications. In this case, the interaction term is negative.

positions are mirrored in the application pools that job seekers submit. One important finding that diverges from this pattern, however, is the relationship between race and ethnicity and nonstandard employment. While black and Hispanic workers tend to be overrepresented in nonstandard positions, particularly temporary employment, they do not appear more likely to apply for these positions.

Mixed Application Pools

Our next set of analyses explore the diversity of application pools by the type of employment relationship within the same individual. Specifically, we ask whether individual applicants submit pools of applications that contain more than one employment relationship. This could mean that an individual, for example, applies for both full-time and part-time positions during their job search. Descriptively, our data indicate that these types of mixed application pools are quite common. Of the respondents in our sample, 55.18 percent have mixed application pools, applying for standard and nonstandard positions alongside one another. Indeed, only about one-third (33.38 percent) applied solely for full-time, standard jobs. Roughly 11 percent applied solely for nonstandard positions. Thus, for more than half of the job seekers in our sample, their application pools consisted of applications for multiple types of positions.

Next, we examine the demographic predictors of whether an individual's application pool contains mixed application types. To do this, we generated a three-category variable for whether a respondent's application pool contained only full-time, standard applications; a mix of full-time, standard and nonstandard positions; or only nonstandard positions. In table 3, we estimate a multinomial logit model where the dependent variable is the three-category variable capturing the employment relationships of respondents' application pools. The omitted category for the dependent variable is having an application pool that is only full-time, standard positions. The full set of controls discussed is also included in the models. For these analyses, there is only one observation per respondent in the data set. Additionally, it is important to remember that the job seekers in our analytic sample indicated that they wanted to work at least thirty-five hours per week and that the unemployment rate during the data collection period was still relatively high (Bureau of Labor Statistics 2018e).

The results from in table 3 reveal that mixed application pools are far from randomly distributed across job seekers. Women, on average, are more likely to have mixed application pools—relative to full-time, standard application pools—than men. Black workers are marginally statistically significantly more likely than white workers to apply for mixed application pools, relative to full-time standard application pools.[12] Additionally, both younger workers (eighteen to twenty-four) and older workers (fifty-five to sixty-four) are significantly more likely to have mixed application pools than middle-age workers. Highly educated individuals—those with at least a bachelor's degree—are less likely to apply for more than one job type, compared to individuals with just some college. Finally, workers who have been unemployed for longer durations are more likely to have mixed application pools.

Together, the findings in table 3 suggest that individuals who belong to groups that may experience less advantage in the labor market—such as women, less educated workers, and workers who have been unemployed for longer periods of time—are more likely to apply for multiple job types, including nonstandard positions alongside their search for full-time, standard jobs. These analyses document two important patterns about how the job search process is shaped by the prevalence of nonstandard employment. First, mixed application pools are common: more than half of the individuals in our sample apply to more than one job type across their set of applications. Second, mixed application pools are not randomly distributed and are correlated with key sociodemographic characteristics.

12. In a model where race-ethnicity is the only predictor of application pool type, the coefficient for being black rather than white is large, positive, and statistically significant ($p<.001$) in predicting having a mixed application pool.

Table 3. Multinomial Logistic Regression Model of Whether the Respondent Applied to Both Full-Time and Nonstandard Positions

	Mixed Application Pool	Nonstandard Positions Only
Woman	0.417**	0.772***
	(0.156)	(0.219)
Ref = white, non-Hispanic		
Black, non-Hispanic	0.398+	−0.285
	(0.203)	(0.325)
Other, non-Hispanic	−0.359	0.168
	(0.364)	(0.544)
Hispanic	0.204	0.715**
	(0.210)	(0.265)
Two or more races, non-Hispanic	0.314	−0.178
	(0.406)	(0.699)
Ref = age 35–44		
18–24	1.018***	1.513***
	(0.302)	(0.430)
25–34	0.274	0.654+
	(0.218)	(0.355)
45–54	0.234	0.760*
	(0.218)	(0.361)
55–64	0.474*	1.202***
	(0.228)	(0.365)
Ref = never married		
Married or cohabiting	−0.270	−0.224
	(0.175)	(0.249)
Separated, divorced, or widowed	−0.324	−0.370
	(0.250)	(0.362)
Ref = some college		
Less than high school	0.526	1.168*
	(0.447)	(0.507)
High school	−0.164	0.0644
	(0.207)	(0.280)
College or higher	−0.855***	−0.451+
	(0.172)	(0.254)
Weeks unemployed (log)	0.203***	0.213**
	(0.0464)	(0.0670)
Constant	−1.984***	−2.158***
	(0.373)	(0.563)
Occupation controls	Yes	Yes
Observations	1,390	

Source: Authors' calculations.

Note: Standard errors in parentheses. Respondents who did not report their weeks of unemployment in the baseline survey are coded as being unemployed for the mean number of weeks for their baseline employment status. The model contains a separate indicator variable for whether this information was missing for the respondent. Occupation controls include the twenty-three categories of the SOC system for the previous occupation held by the applicant. The model includes controls for the number of applications submitted by a respondent, the number of survey waves they participated in, and whether they did not indicate how many hours they would prefer to work for in a week.

$+p < .1$; $*p < .05$; $**p < .01$; $***p < .001$

Table 4. Multinomial Logit Model of Type of Informal Job Search Method Used

Ref = Formal Search Only	Family	Friends	Acquaintance	Colleague or Employer
Ref = full time, standard				
Part time	-0.00729	0.269**	0.418**	0.103
	(0.163)	(0.0987)	(0.139)	(0.199)
Temporary to permanent	0.388+	0.367*	0.743***	0.239
	(0.227)	(0.175)	(0.210)	(0.278)
Temporary	0.642*	0.102	0.881***	0.679**
	(0.307)	(0.230)	(0.238)	(0.251)
Mixed	-0.122	0.0825	-0.377+	0.223
	(0.211)	(0.129)	(0.208)	(0.213)
Weeks unemployed (log)	0.0673+	-0.0732**	-0.0614+	-0.0388
	(0.0398)	(0.0253)	(0.0328)	(0.0368)
Constant	-1.744***	-0.690*	-2.344***	-3.058***
	(0.423)	(0.296)	(0.379)	(0.427)
Demographic controls	Yes	Yes	Yes	Yes
Occupation controls	Yes	Yes	Yes	Yes
Wave fixed effects	Yes	Yes	Yes	Yes
Clusters	1,371			
Observations	14,945			

Source: Authors' calculations.

Note: Standard errors in parentheses. All standard errors clustered on applicant. Demographic controls include gender, race-ethnicity, age, marital status, and educational attainment. Respondents who did not report their weeks of unemployment in the baseline survey are coded as being unemployed for the mean number of weeks for their baseline employment status. The model contains a separate indicator variable for whether this information was missing for the respondent. Occupation controls include the twenty-three categories of the SOC system for the previous occupation held by the applicant. The model also includes controls for the number of applications submitted by a respondent, the number of survey waves they participated in, and whether they did not indicate how many hours they would prefer to work for in a week.

+$p < .1$; *$p < .05$; **$p < .01$; ***$p < .001$

Nonstandard Work and Search Methods

In the next set of analyses, we examine variation in the search methods through which individuals find out about job openings with different employment relationships. It is possible that applications submitted for nonstandard positions—part-time, temporary, temporary-to-permanent jobs—are more likely than full-time job applications to be the result of informal, network-based job search practices, such as hearing about the opening from family, friends, acquaintances, or employers or coworkers. However, it is also possible that the often lower pay and lower status that come with nonstandard positions make it so that individuals use formal channels for these types of positions and reserve network-based search for full-time, standard positions.

Here we examine whether people are more or less likely to hear about nonstandard job openings through their family, friends, acquaintances, and coworkers or employers. Table 4 presents the results of a multinomial logistic regression model, where whether the job opening was heard about through family, friends, acquaintances, or coworkers or employers (relative to through a formal channel) is regressed on the employment relationship of the application and a host of sociodemographic variables and additional controls.[13]

13. For these analyses, we have excluded applications to positions that were heard of through more than one network-based channel (such as through both a friend and a family member).

The findings reveal that acquaintances—the quintessential weak ties—play a particularly important role in the job searches of individuals who are applying for nonstandard positions. For part-time, temporary-to permanent, and temporary positions, job seekers are more likely to have heard about the opening from acquaintances than from formal channels. Although family is significantly more likely than formal methods to lead to applications for temporary positions, there is no association between part-time work and hearing about the opening through family. Openings for part-time positions as well as temporary-to-permanent positions are more likely to be heard about from friends than from formal channels. Workers are also more likely to hear about temporary positions from coworkers or employers. Thus there is some variation in the types of positions heard about through network-based channels. Further, acquaintances appear to be particularly useful types of ties through which individual hear about nonstandard job openings. Future scholarship would be well served to further probe the mechanisms driving these different processes.

The Perceived Skill Level of Nonstandard Applications

Our previous analyses examined the job search process: who applies for nonstandard jobs, what do application pools look like, and what types of methods are utilized to apply for those positions. Next, we turn to issues of perceived job quality. Specifically, we examine whether job seekers are more likely to perceive applications for nonstandard positions to be below their skill level relative to positions for full-time, standard jobs.

Table 5 presents estimates from logistic regression models where the dependent variable is whether the job seeker perceives the application to be for a position that is beneath their skill level. The key explanatory variable is the employment relationship of the position. Model 1 is a logistic regression model with the full set of sociodemographic covariates and other controls. A clear pattern emerges: applications to part-time positions, temp-to-perm positions, temporary positions, and mixed status applications (relative to full-time positions) are more likely to be perceived as below the applicant's skill level.

Table 5. Logistic Regression Models of Whether Job Is Perceived to Be Below One's Skill Level

	(1)	(2)
	Below Skill	Below Skill
Ref = full time, standard		
Part time	0.973***	1.149***
	(0.0929)	(0.0772)
Temporary to permanent	0.613***	0.671***
	(0.137)	(0.111)
Temporary	0.498*	0.853***
	(0.195)	(0.146)
Mixed	0.497***	0.608***
	(0.116)	(0.0964)
Woman	−0.0737	
	(0.0999)	
Ref = white, non-Hispanic		
Black, non-Hispanic	0.00626	
	(0.127)	
Other, non-Hispanic	−0.173	
	(0.259)	

Table 5. (*continued*)

	(1)	(2)
	Below Skill	Below Skill
Hispanic	0.179	
	(0.141)	
Two or more races, non-Hispanic	0.583**	
	(0.209)	
Ref = age 35–44		
18–24	−0.310[+]	
	(0.186)	
25–34	−0.229	
	(0.159)	
45–54	0.194	
	(0.144)	
55–64	0.303*	
	(0.142)	
Ref = never married		
Married or cohabiting	−0.0727	
	(0.119)	
Separated, divorced, or widowed	−0.181	
	(0.152)	
Ref = some college		
Less than high school	−0.203	
	(0.250)	
High school	−0.308*	
	(0.128)	
College or higher	−0.229*	
	(0.107)	
Constant	−1.754***	
	(0.256)	
Wave fixed effects	Yes	Yes
Occupation controls	Yes	No
Respondent fixed effects	No	Yes
Clusters	1,386	739
Observations	15,993	11,025

Source: Authors' calculations.

Note: Standard errors in parentheses. Standard errors in model 1 are clustered on applicant. Occupation controls include the twenty-three categories of the SOC system for the previous occupation held by the applicant. Additionally, model 1 includes controls for the number of applications submitted by a respondent, the number of survey waves they participated in, and whether they did not indicate how many hours they would prefer to work for in a week. Applications where the respondent did provide information about the perceived skill level of the position are excluded from the analysis.

$^+p < .1$; $^*p < .05$; $^{**}p < .01$; $^{***}p < .001$

Model 2 is also a logistic regression model but includes respondent-specific fixed effects. Including respondent-specific fixed effects enables us to compare perceptions of a job's skill level for applications for standard and nonstandard jobs for the same individual. Thus the model removes concerns about time-invariant unobserved individual heterogeneity. The findings in model 2 closely parallel those in model 1, with nonstandard applications being positively correlated with perceptions of the position being below the applicant's skill level. The findings in table 5 thus provide compelling evidence that applications submitted to nonstandard positions are perceived by job applicants to be beneath their level of skill.

Next, we examined whether these skill perceptions vary by workers' sociodemographic characteristics (the results are presented in table A2). Two key findings emerge from these analyses. First, the association between part-time work and perceiving that a job is below one's skill level is weaker for women than for men. Given that respondents in our analytic sample desire a full-time job, this finding suggests that women are able to find part-time work that is a better match for their skill level. For men, this is more of a challenge. This finding is consistent with the idea that part-time work is more normatively "appropriate" for women than it is for men. Second, we find that black workers are more likely than white workers to perceive the temporary jobs that they apply to as being below their skill level. This in particularly interesting because black workers are no more likely than white workers to apply for temporary jobs. Moreover, they are no more likely to perceive full-time, standard jobs as being below their skill level. Thus, this finding suggests that when black workers apply to temporary positions, they are particularly likely to apply for jobs that are highly at odds with their

skill set. Although this could point to the particular challenges the black workers face in the labor market, such as discrimination, future work would be well served to further investigate what may be driving this pattern.

A Foot in the Door? Nonstandard Applications and Job Offers

Our final set of analyses pivot toward a distinct issue: can nonstandard jobs provide a toehold for workers in the labor market? In other words, are applications for nonstandard positions more likely to result in job offers? In table 6, we address this question. For each application submitted over the survey period, we collected information about whether it resulted in a job offer. After a respondent listed an application, we asked at that wave and then in all future waves whether it had led to a job offer. Thus we are able to examine whether applications submitted for nonstandard positions, relative to standard positions, are more likely to result in a job offer.[14]

Model 1 in table 6 is similar to the previous models we presented—a logistic regression model, with standard errors clustered by respondent, and controls included for a broad set of sociodemographic variables and other covariates. The findings show that applications submitted for any type of nonstandard position (with the exception of mixed applications, which is marginally statistically significant) are more likely to result in a job offer than applications submitted for full-time, standard jobs.[15] Also, we find evidence that, net of a broad set of controls, black workers are less likely to receive job offers than their white counterparts.

Given the structure of our data, we are also able to address this question using a within-person comparison approach. In other words, we can look at whether—for the same job seeker—they are more likely to receive job of-

---

14. At each wave, we also asked respondents whether they had received a job offer for a position that was not previously listed and then asked a series of questions about each of those positions. Unfortunately, given time limitations in the survey, we were not able to include an item about the type of position (for example, part time, temporary) for the set of job offers received for applications not previously listed. Our analyses of job offers thus do not include all job offers respondents received.

15. We examined whether the association between nonstandard work and job offers was moderated by the search method (for example, family, friends, acquaintances). We did not find supporting evidence.

Table 6. Logistic Regression Models of Whether an Application Resulted in an Offer

	(1)	(2)
	Got offer	Got offer
Ref = full time, standard		
Part time	0.389***	0.371**
	(0.108)	(0.124)
Temporary to permanent	0.615***	0.817***
	(0.161)	(0.169)
Temporary	1.100***	0.996***
	(0.156)	(0.190)
Mixed	0.255+	0.0274
	(0.144)	(0.149)
Woman	0.0367	
	(0.103)	
Ref = white, non-Hispanic		
Black, non-Hispanic	−0.349*	
	(0.150)	
Other, non-Hispanic	0.188	
	(0.364)	
Hispanic	−0.306*	
	(0.134)	
2+ races, non-Hispanic	0.349	
	(0.376)	
Ref = age 35–44		
18–24	0.295+	
	(0.173)	
25–34	0.272	
	(0.173)	
45–54	−0.0136	
	(0.170)	
55–64	−0.00293	
	(0.183)	
Ref = never married		
Married or cohabiting	0.219+	
	(0.119)	
Separated, divorced, or widowed	0.150	
	(0.162)	
Ref = some college		
Less than high school	0.378	
	(0.397)	
High school	−0.362*	
	(0.158)	
College or higher	−0.0650	
	(0.113)	
Constant	−1.797***	
	(0.296)	
Occupation controls	Yes	Yes
Wave fixed effects	Yes	Yes

(continued)

Table 6. (*continued*)

| | (1) | (2) |
	Got offer	Got offer
Respondent fixed effects	No	Yes
Clusters	1,390	552
Observations	16,271	7,467

Source: Authors' calculations.
Note: Standard errors in parentheses. Standard errors in model 1 are clustered on applicant. Occupation controls include the twenty-three categories of the SOC system for the previous occupation held by the applicant. Model 1 also includes controls for the number of applications submitted by a respondent, the number of survey waves they participated in, and whether they did not indicate how many hours they would prefer to work for in a week.
$^{+}p < .1; ^{*}p < .05; ^{**}p < .01; ^{***}p < .001$

fers for applications submitted to nonstandard positions. Given that more than half of the respondents have mixed application pools, this approach provides us with a large group of job seekers to analyze with this approach. Model 2 in table 6, which includes individual-level fixed effects, demonstrates that this within-person analysis produces similar results. The same worker is more likely to receive job offers for nonstandard positions than they are for full-time, standard job openings.

There may be some questions about whether respondents actually end up taking the offers that they receive for nonstandard positions. Our data support the idea that they do. Respondents report that they plan to accept roughly 85 percent of the job offers that they receive. This pattern is similar across the different types of employment relationships. Indeed, a test for differences in proportions of offers that were planned to be accepted indicates that no statistically significant variation across types of applications. The idea of nonstandard positions providing a path to employment that is easier than obtaining a full-time, standard position and providing a toehold for workers therefore has some support. Yet, as the previous analyses demonstrated, these nonstandard positions are also more likely to be perceived to be below a worker's skill level. The quality of these nonstandard jobs may thus be a concern, resulting in a complicated trade-off for workers between obtaining a job and the quality of that job.

DISCUSSION AND CONCLUSION

The starting point for this article was the observation that millions of workers labor in nonstandard jobs, such as part-time or temporary positions. Yet little is known about how the job search process—a key social and economic process—is shaped by these types of positions. We have drawn on panel data about the job search process to examine the ways that job seekers' application pools are influenced by nonstandard employment relationships, the types of search methods that are used to apply for nonstandard positions, the perceived quality of those jobs, and whether applications for nonstandard positions are more likely to result in job offers than applications for full-time, standard positions.

Our findings shed new light on this important set of issues. First, our findings point to the ways that applications for nonstandard positions are unevenly distributed throughout the population. Women are far more likely than men to apply for part-time positions, even though our sample is limited to individuals indicating that they would like to find a job where they would work at least thirty-five hours per week. This aligns with the pattern that women are much more likely than men to actually labor as incumbents in part-time positions. Additionally, younger workers are more likely to apply for part-time jobs and individuals with higher levels of education are less likely to apply for part-time positions. Interestingly, though, we generally do not find that workers of color are significantly more likely than white workers to apply for nonstandard positions. This lack of a finding is surprising, given that workers of color are overrepresented in non-standard positions. Although beyond the scope of our data, it is possible there may be some demand-side process that steers workers of color into nonstandard jobs. This issue—which could be a mechanism driving inequalities between white workers and workers of color—would be valuable for future research to explore.

Second, we find evidence that fully half of the job seekers in our sample submitted mixed application pools—sets of applications that included both full-time, standard positions as well as an application for at least one other type of job, such as part-time or temporary work. We also find that mixed application pools are more common among workers who are disadvantaged on some axis of inequality in the labor market. For example, women, less-educated workers, and people who have been unemployed for longer durations of time are more likely to have mixed application pools. This finding suggests that applying for both full-time, standard jobs and other types of positions simultaneously may be an adaptive strategy deployed by workers who know that they may experience challenges obtaining a new job. Future scholarship would be well served to further explore this issue.

Our findings also reveal that job search methods are intertwined with the type of position that a job seeker applies to. Across the board, job seekers are significantly more likely to hear about nonstandard job openings through weak ties—that is, their acquaintances. It is possible that this finding emerges due to nonstandard positions being less likely to be posted in formal places, making one's networks—particularly one's acquaintances who are likely to have nonredundant information about potential jobs—important in hearing about openings for these types of positions. This finding is intriguing and speaks to the importance of future work that unpacks why these correlations emerge.

Our results also show that workers perceive the quality of nonstandard positions—mea-sured as the position being perceived below the worker's skill level—as worse than standard jobs. This finding holds across different types of nonstandard positions and model specifications, even when we net out time-invariant individual-level characteristics. Yet our findings also indicate that nonstandard employment can serve as a toehold for workers in the labor market. Job seekers are more likely to receive job offers for applications submitted for non-standard types of positions than for full-time, standard jobs. Workers are also equally likely to accept nonstandard positions and standard, full-time positions. Juxtaposing these findings, a likely conflict emerges for workers. They can apply for nonstandard positions as a way to increase their likelihood of getting a job offer. But, they are then more likely to be in a position that is below their skill level, which can have negative consequences for their future labor market opportunities (Pedulla 2016). And, the evidence on whether nonstandard jobs—particularly temporary positions—can serve as stepping stones to better employment opportunities in the United States is mixed (Autor and Houseman 2010; Addison and Surfield 2009). Existing scholarship suggests that these effects may vary in important ways by the sociodemographic characteristics of the worker (Pedulla 2014, 2016). Thus, trade-offs for workers when deciding whether to apply for and work in nonstandard positions are very real, and these positions have the potential to keep workers stuck in a less desirable segment of the labor market.

Together, our findings provide new insights about job searching in a labor market where nonstandard jobs are a key component of the economic landscape. We uncover a complex set of job search processes, where many workers appear to be hedging their bets on labor market success by applying for both full-time, standard and nonstandard positions simultaneously. This strategy appears to have some payoff because applications for nonstandard positions are more likely to result in job offers than positions for full-time, standard positions. Negative repercussions, however, are also possible, given that these nonstandard positions may not fully utilize workers' skills. Our results also highlight the importance of jointly considering nonstandard employment relations and job search processes. By bringing these two often separate literatures together we can gain new insights into the nature of nonstandard work as well as the contours of the job search process. As scholarship contin- ues to move forward on both of these issues, additional attention to how the job search process shapes and is shaped by nonstandard employment will advance our understanding of these key aspects of the labor market.

Table A1. Multinomial Logit Model of Type of Position Applied To

Ref = Full Time, Standard	Part Time	Temporary-to-Permanent	Temporary	Mixed
Woman	0.392+	0.109	−0.517	0.00742
	(0.217)	(0.287)	(0.358)	(0.269)
Ref = white, non-Hispanic				
Black, non-Hispanic	0.0215	0.344	−0.295	−0.415+
	(0.233)	(0.269)	(0.370)	(0.250)
Other, non-Hispanic	−0.450	0.465	−0.474	−0.609
	(0.456)	(0.362)	(0.649)	(0.381)
Hispanic	0.515*	0.0447	0.00653	0.242
	(0.249)	(0.275)	(0.416)	(0.280)
Two or more races, non-Hispanic	−0.606+	0.00388	−1.218*	−0.0788
	(0.326)	(0.634)	(0.541)	(0.388)
Ref = age 35-44				
18-24	1.255***	0.685*	0.422	0.938***
	(0.200)	(0.291)	(0.363)	(0.243)
25-34	0.260	0.0716	−0.0438	0.503*
	(0.178)	(0.259)	(0.450)	(0.212)
45-54	0.204	0.0546	0.382	0.623**
	(0.181)	(0.242)	(0.294)	(0.206)
55-64	0.469*	0.228	0.716*	0.0229
	(0.201)	(0.247)	(0.315)	(0.212)
Ref = never married				
Married or cohabiting	−0.477**	−0.418+	−0.256	−0.626**
	(0.183)	(0.250)	(0.363)	(0.221)
Separated, divorced, or widowed	−0.501+	0.111	−0.305	−0.443
	(0.268)	(0.297)	(0.478)	(0.404)
Ref = some college				
Less than high school	0.130	−0.0996	−0.263	0.382
	(0.218)	(0.318)	(0.384)	(0.279)
High school	0.141	0.172	−0.477+	0.254
	(0.139)	(0.204)	(0.248)	(0.184)
College or higher	−0.839***	−0.317+	−0.424	−0.682***
	(0.138)	(0.175)	(0.283)	(0.150)
Weeks unemployed (log)	0.0388	0.108**	−0.0181	0.146***
	(0.0257)	(0.0370)	(0.0409)	(0.0315)
Woman X married or cohabiting	0.619*	0.194	0.470	0.517+
	(0.247)	(0.342)	(0.406)	(0.280)
Woman X separated, divorced, or widowed	0.487	−0.189	0.641	0.167
	(0.341)	(0.451)	(0.698)	(0.484)
Woman X black, non-Hispanic	−0.255	−1.047**	−0.303	0.610+
	(0.295)	(0.376)	(0.468)	(0.326)

Table A1. (*continued*)

Ref = Full Time, Standard	Part Time	Temporary-to-Permanent	Temporary	Mixed
Woman X other, non-Hispanic	0.681	−0.229	1.158	0.0980
	(0.726)	(0.731)	(0.847)	(0.751)
Woman X Hispanic	−0.376	0.355	0.527	−0.0573
	(0.325)	(0.399)	(0.712)	(0.365)
Woman X two or more races, non-Hispanic	0.0161	−0.554	0.302	0.121
	(0.609)	(0.803)	(0.869)	(0.555)
Constant	−1.856***	−2.681***	−2.944***	−2.231***
	(0.229)	(0.296)	(0.402)	(0.281)
Wave fixed effects	Yes	Yes	Yes	Yes
Clusters	1,390			
Observations	16,271			

Source: Authors' calculations.

Note: Standard errors in parentheses. All standard errors clustered on applicant. Respondents who did not report their weeks of unemployment in the baseline survey are coded as being unemployed for the mean number of weeks for their baseline employment status. The model contains a separate indicator variable for whether this information was missing for the respondent. Occupation controls include the twenty-three categories of the SOC system for the previous occupation held by the applicant. The model also includes controls for the number of applications submitted by a respondent, the number of survey waves they participated in, and whether they did not indicate how many hours they would prefer to work for in a week.

$^{+}p < .1; {}^{*}p < .05; {}^{**}p < .01; {}^{***}p < .001$

Table A2. Logit Models of Whether an Application Is Perceived as Below Skill, with Interactions

	(1)	(2)
	Below Skill	Below Skill
Ref = full time, standard		
Part time	1.154***	1.078***
	(0.133)	(0.115)
Temporary to permanent	0.684***	0.827***
	(0.188)	(0.171)
Temporary	0.447+	0.375
	(0.249)	(0.237)
Mixed	0.599***	0.672***
	(0.158)	(0.161)
Woman	0.0309	-0.0765
	(0.117)	(0.0995)
Part time X woman	-0.353*	
	(0.178)	
Temporary to permanent X woman	-0.183	
	(0.263)	
Temporary X woman	0.151	
	(0.406)	
Mixed X woman	-0.221	
	(0.233)	
Ref = white, non-Hispanic		
Black, non-Hispanic	0.00246	0.0880
	(0.127)	(0.158)
Other, non-Hispanic	-0.170	-0.0300
	(0.257)	(0.308)
Hispanic	0.172	0.298+
	(0.141)	(0.177)
Two or more races, non-Hispanic	0.581**	0.729***
	(0.210)	(0.202)
Ref = age 35–44		
18–24	-0.311+	-0.292
	(0.186)	(0.185)
25–34	-0.233	-0.216
	(0.159)	(0.158)
45–54	0.198	0.193
	(0.144)	(0.144)
55–64	0.302*	0.305*
	(0.142)	(0.140)
Ref = never married		
Married or cohabiting	-0.0601	-0.0690
	(0.120)	(0.120)
Separated, divorced, or widowed	-0.180	-0.175
	(0.152)	(0.151)
Ref = some college		
Less than high school	-0.209	-0.220
	(0.250)	(0.253)
High school	-0.309*	-0.317*
	(0.127)	(0.129)
College or higher	-0.235*	-0.229*
	(0.107)	(0.107)
Part time X black, non-Hispanic		-0.179
		(0.232)

Table A2. (*continued*)

	(1)	(2)
	Below Skill	Below Skill
Part time X other, non-Hispanic		−0.517
		(0.447)
Part time X Hispanic		−0.268
		(0.269)
Part time X two or more races, non-Hispanic		−0.255
		(0.343)
Temporary to permanent X black, non-Hispanic		−0.608[+]
		(0.323)
Temporary to permanent X other, non-Hispanic		−0.788
		(0.776)
Temporary to permanent X Hispanic		−0.255
		(0.386)
Temporary to permanent X two or more races, non-Hispanic		−0.990
		(0.735)
Temporary X black, non-Hispanic		1.131*
		(0.444)
Temporary X other, non-Hispanic		0.218
		(0.757)
Temporary X Hispanic		−0.269
		(0.621)
Temporary X two or more races, non-Hispanic		0.140
		(0.848)
Mixed X black, non-Hispanic		−0.459
		(0.289)
Mixed X other, non-Hispanic		−0.191
		(0.380)
Mixed X Hispanic		−0.264
		(0.308)
Mixed X two or more races, non-Hispanic		−0.606
		(0.493)
Constant	−1.791***	−1.803***
	(0.258)	(0.257)
Occupation controls	Yes	Yes
Wave fixed effects	Yes	Yes
Clusters	1,386	1,386
Observations	15,993	15,993

Source: Authors' calculations.

Note: Standard errors in parentheses. All standard errors clustered on applicant. Respondents who did not report their weeks of unemployment in the baseline survey are coded as being unemployed for the mean number of weeks for their baseline employment status. Each model contains a separate indicator variable for whether this information was missing for the respondent. Occupation controls include the twenty-three categories of the SOC system for the previous occupation held by the applicant. Each model includes controls for the number of applications submitted by a respondent, the number of survey waves they participated in, and whether they did not indicate how many hours they would prefer to work for in a week.

$^+p < .1$; $^*p < .05$; $^{**}p < .01$; $^{***}p < .001$

REFERENCES

Addison, John T., Chad Cotti, and Christopher J. Surfield. 2009. "Atypical Work: Who Gets It, and Where Does it Lead? Some U.S. Evidence Using the NLSY79." *IZA discussion paper no. 4444.* Bonn: Institute of Labor Economics.

Addison, John T., and Christopher J. Surfield. 2009. "Does Atypical Work Help the Jobless? Evidence from a CAEAS/CPS Cohort Analysis." *Applied Economics* 41(9): 1077–87.

American Staffing Association (ASA). 2017. "ASA Annual Economic Analysis: 2017 Staffing Industry Playbook." Accessed July 23, 2018. www.americanstaffing.net/playbook.

Autor, David. 2003. "Outsourcing at Will: The Contribution of Unjust Dismissal Doctrine to the Growth of Employment Outsourcing." *Journal of Labor Economics* 21(1): 1–42.

Autor, David, and Susan Houseman. 2010. "Do Temporary-Help Jobs Improve Labor Market Outcomes for Low-Skilled Workers? Evidence from 'Work First'." *Applied Economics* 2 (July): 96–128.

Bernhardt, Annette. 2014. "Labor Standard and the Reorganization of Work: Gaps in Data and Research." *IRLE working paper no. 100-14.* Berkeley: University of California.

Bertrand, Marianne, and Sendhil Mullainathan. 2004. "Are Emily and Greg More Employable than Lakisha and Jamal? A Field Experiment on Labor Market Discrimination." *American Economic Review* 94(4): 991–1013.

Broschak, Joseph P., Alison Davis-Blake, and Emily S. Block. 2008. "Nonstandard, Not Substandard: The Relationship Among Work Arrangements, Work Attitudes, and Job Performance." *Work and Occupations* 35(1): 3–43.

Browne, Irene, and Joya Misra. 2003. "The Intersection of Gender and Race in the Labor Market." *Annual Review of Sociology* 29: 487–513.

Bureau of Labor Statistics. 2017. "Women in the Labor Force: A Databook." *BLS report no. 1071.* Washington: U.S. Department of Labor.

——. 2018a. "Household Data Annual Averages. 8. Employed and Unemployment Full- and Part-Time Workers by Age, Sex, Race, and Hispanic or Latino Ethnicity." Accessed December 12, 2018. http://www.bls.gov/cps/cpsaat08.htm.

——. 2018b. "Contingent and Alternative Employment Arrangements, May 2017." Washington: U.S. Department of Labor. Accessed December 12, 2018. https://www.bls.gov/news.release/conemp.nr0.htm.

——. 2018c. "Household Data Annual Averages. 21. Persons at Work in Nonagricultural Industries by Class of Worker and Usual Full- or Part-time Status." Accessed December 12, 2018. http://www.bls.gov/cps/cpsaat21.htm.

——. 2018d. "Household Data Annual Averages. 23. Persons at Work by Occupation, Sex, and Usual Full- or Part-time Status." December 12, 2018. http://www.bls.gov/cps/cpsaat23.htm.

——. 2018e. "Charting the Labor Market: Data from the Current Population Survey (CPS)." Accessed December 12, 2018: https://www.bls.gov/web/empsit/cps_charts.pdf.

Castilla, Emilio J., George J. Lan, and Ben A. Rissing. 2013. "Social Networks and Employment: Mechanisms (Part 1)." *Sociology Compass* 7(12): 999–1012.

Clawson, Dan, and Mary Ann Clawson. 1999. "What Has Happened to the U.S. Labor Movement? Union Decline and Renewal." *Annual Review of Sociology* 25: 95–119.

Corcoran, Mary, Linda Datcher, and Greg Duncan. 1980. "Information and Influence Networks in Labor Markets." In *Five Thousand American Families: Patterns of Economic Progress*, edited by Greg Duncan and James Morgan. Ann Arbor, Mich.: Institute for Social Research.

Dunn, Megan. 2018. "Who Chooses Part-Time Work and Why?" *Monthly Labor Review* March: 1–25. Accessed February 15, 2019. https://www.bls.gov/opub/mlr/2018/article/who-chooses-part-time-work-and-why.htm.

Epstein, Cynthia Fuchs, Carroll Seron, Bonnie Oglensky, and Robert Sauté. 1999. *The Part-Time Paradox: Time Norms, Professional Life, Family and Gender.* New York: Routledge.

Fernandez, Roberto M., Emilio J. Castilla, and Paul Moore. 2000. "Social Capital at Work: Networks and Employment at a Phone Center." *American Journal of Sociology* 105(5): 1288–356.

Fuller, Sylvia. 2011. "Up and On or Down and Out? Gender, Immigration and the Consequences of Temporary Employment in Canada." *Research in Social Stratification and Mobility* 29(2): 155–80.

Goldin, Claudia, and Joshua Mitchell. 2017. "The New Life Cycle of Women's Employment: Disappearing Humps, Sagging Middles, Expanding

Tops." *Journal of Economic Perspectives* 31(1): 161–82.

Granovetter, Mark S. 1973. "The Strength of Weak Ties." *American Journal of Sociology* 78(6): 1360–80.

Haley-Lock, Anna. 2009. "Variation in Part-Time Job Quality Within the Nonprofit Human Service Sector." *Nonprofit Management & Leadership* 19(4): 421–42.

Henson, Kevin Daniel. 1996. *Just a Temp*. Philadelphia, Pa.: Temple University Press.

Hollister, Matissa. 2011. "Employment Stability in the U.S. Labor Market: Rhetoric Versus Reality." *Annual Review of Sociology* 37: 305–24.

Hyman, Louis. 2018. *Temp: How American Work, American Business, and the American Dream Became Temporary*. New York: Viking.

Kalleberg, Arne L. 2000. "Nonstandard Employment Relations: Part-time, Temporary and Contract Work." *Annual Review of Sociology* 26: 341–65.

———. 2009. "Precarious Work, Insecure Workers: Employment Relations in Transition." *American Sociological Review* 74(1): 1–22.

———. 2011. *Good Jobs, Bad Jobs: The Rise of Polarized and Precarious Employment Systems in the United States, 1970s–2000s*. New York: Russell Sage Foundation.

Kalleberg, Arne L., Barbara F. Reskin, and Kenneth Hudson. 2000. "Bad Jobs in America: Standard and Nonstandard Employment Relations and Job Quality in the United States." *American Sociological Review* 65(2): 256–78.

Kalleberg, Arne L., Jeremy Reynolds, and Peter V. Marsden. 2003. "Externalizing Employment: Flexible Staffing Arrangements in US Organizations." *Social Science Research* 32(4): 525–52.

Katz, Lawrence F., and Alan B. Krueger. 2016. "The Rise and Nature of Alternative Work Arrangements in the United States, 1995–2015." *NBER* working paper no. w22667. Cambridge, Mass.: National Bureau of Economic Research.

Kim, ChangHwan, and Arthur Sakamoto. 2008. "The Rise of Intra-Occupational Wage Inequality in the United States, 1983–2002." *American Sociological Review* 73(1): 129–57.

Kmec, Julie A. 2006. "White Hiring Agents' Organizational Practices and Out-Group Hiring." *Social Science Research* 35(3): 668–801.

Knowledge Networks. 2011. "Knowledge Networks Methodology." Palo Alto, Calif.: Knowledge Networks.

Krueger, Alan B., and Andreas I. Mueller. 2016. "A Contribution to the Empirics of Reservation Wages." *American Economic Journal: Economic Policy* 8(1): 142–79.

Marin, Alexandra. 2012. "Don't Mention It: Why People Don't Share Job Information, When They Do, and Why It Matters." *Social Networks* 34(2): 181–92.

Mouw, Ted. 2003. "Social Capital and Finding a Job: Do Contacts Matter?" *American Sociological Review* 68(6): 868–98.

Pager, Devah, and David S. Pedulla. 2015. "Race, Self-Selection, and the Job Search Process." *American Journal of Sociology* 120(4): 1005–54.

Pager, Devah, Bruce Western, and Bart Bonikowski. 2009. "Discrimination in a Low-Wage Labor Market: A Field Experiment." *American Sociological Review* 74(5): 777–99.

Pedulla, David S. 2014. *Non-Standard, Contingent, and Precarious Work in the "New Economy."* PhD diss., Princeton University.

———. 2016. "Penalized or Protected? Gender and the Consequences of Nonstandard and Mismatched Employment Histories." *American Sociological Review* 81(2): 262–89.

———. 2018. "How Race and Unemployment Shape Labor Market Opportunities: Additive, Amplified, or Muted Effects?" *Social Forces* 96(4): 1477–506.

Pedulla, David S., and Devah Pager. 2017. "Race and Networks in the Job Search Process." Working Paper. Stanford, Calif.: Stanford University.

Rivera, Lauren A. 2012. "Hiring as Cultural Matching: The Case of Elite Professional Service Firms." *American Sociological Review* 77(6): 999–1022.

Rogers, Jackie Krasas. 1995. "Just a Temp: Experience and Structure of Alienation in Temporary Clerical Employment." *Work and Occupations* 22(2): 137–66.

Sharone, Ofer. 2014. *Flawed System, Flawed Self: Job Searching and Unemployment Experiences*. Chicago: University of Chicago Press.

Smith, Sandra Susan. 2005. "'Don't Put My Name on It': Social Capital Activation and Job-Finding Assistance Among the Black Urban Poor." *American Journal of Sociology* 111(1): 1–57.

Smith, Vicki. 1997. "New Forms of Work Organization." *Annual Review of Sociology* 23: 315–39.
———. 1998. "The Fractured World of the Temporary
Worker: Power, Participation, and Fragmentation
in the Workplace." *Social Problems* 45(4): 411–30.
Tilly, Chris. 1992. "Dualism in Part-Time Employment." *Industrial Relations* 31(2): 330–47.
———. 1996. *Half a Job: Bad and Good Part-Time Jobs
in a Changing Labor Market*. Philadelphia, Pa.:
Temple University Press.
Trimble, Lindsey B., and Julie A. Kmec. 2011. "The
Role of Social Networks in Getting a Job." *Sociology Compass* 5(2): 165–78.

Virtanen, Marianna, Mika Kivimäki, Matti Joensuu,
Pekka Virtanen, Marko Elovainio, and Jussi
Vahtera. 2005. "Temporary Employment and
Health: A Review." *International Journal of Epide-
miology* 34(3): 610–22.
Wright, Erik Olin, and Rachel E. Dwyer. 2003. "The
Patterns of Job Expansions in the USA: A Com-
parison of the 1960s and 1990s." *Socio-Economic
Review* 1: 289–325.
Yakubovich, Valery. 2005. "Weak Ties, Information,
and Influence: How Workers Find Jobs in a Local
Russian Labor Market." *American Sociological
Review* 70(3): 408–21.

The Wage Mobility of Low-Wage Workers in a Changing Economy, 1968 to 2014

MICHAEL A. SCHULTZ

How are changes in the low-wage labor market affecting the mobility of workers out of low-wage work? I investigate changes in the wage mobility of workers starting employment spells in low wages using the Panel Study of Income Dynamics from 1968 to 2014 and discrete-time event history analysis. About half of all low-wage workers move to better wages within four years. Effects on mobility rates are significant by age, gender, race, education, occupation, and job characteristics. Mobility rates out of low-wage work have declined since the late 1990s. Little progress has been made in closing the gaps in mobility for women and nonwhites over time. I find evidence for the decline of firm internal labor markets and lower mobility for part-time workers over time.

Keywords: occupations, labor markets, inequality, time

The last decade for the U.S. labor market was tumultuous. Low-wage and nonstandard work have expanded since the turn of the century (Howell and Kalleberg 2019). A weak labor market in the early 2000s was punctured by the Great Recession in 2008. A long and slow recovery followed. Looking further back, the U.S. labor market has changed substantially since the 1970s (Kalleberg 2011). Women have entered the labor force in large numbers, deindustrialization hit hard in the 1980s and quickened the service transition. Union membership declined steadily, and the education expansion continues to lead to a more-educated labor force. Companies restructured and changed hiring practices, resulting in the decline of firm internal labor markets.

What are the consequences of these changes for low-wage workers' chances of moving to better wages? Research reveals the increasing economic insecurity of Americans since the 1970s (Western et al. 2012). Increases are documented in the life-course risk of poverty (Sandoval, Rank, and Hirschl 2009), income instability (Hacker 2006; Western et al. 2016; Latner 2018), and occupational mobility during a worker's

Michael A. Schultz is a doctoral candidate in sociology at the University of North Carolina at Chapel Hill.

© 2019 Russell Sage Foundation. Schultz, Michael A. 2019. "The Wage Mobility of Low-Wage Workers in a Changing Economy, 1968 to 2014." *RSF: The Russell Sage Foundation Journal of the Social Sciences* 5(4): 159–89. DOI: 10.7758/RSF.2019.5.4.06. I am grateful to Arne Kalleberg and Ted Mouw for many conversations that led to this article. I would like to thank David Howell, conference participants, and the three anonymous reviewers for constructive feedback. The collection of data used in this study was partly supported by the National Institutes of Health under grant number R01 HD069609 and R01 AG040213 and the National Science Foundation under award numbers SES 1157698 and 1623684. Direct correspondence to: Michael A. Schultz at schultzm @live.unc.edu, 155 Hamilton Hall, CB#3210, Chapel Hill, NC 27599

career (Jarvis and Song 2017). In these analyses, the 1990s are a pivotal turning point. A growing literature analyzes the mobility of workers out of low-wage work (Knabe and Plum 2010; Aertz and Gürtzgen 2012; Mouw and Kalleberg 2018). However, studies of mobility out of low-wage work that include change over time are rare (Mouw and Kalleberg 2018; Campbell 2012; Bernhardt et al. 2001). Most research on this topic in the United States includes data from little more than a decade and consequently offers little attention to changes over time (Connolly, Gottschalk, and Newman 2003; Boushey 2005; Andersson, Holzer, and Lane 2005; Salverda and Mayhew 2009). New analyses are needed to understand how the macro changes up through the Great Recession in the U.S. labor market since the 1970s changed mobility patterns for low-wage workers.

This article contributes to closing this gap in the literature by analyzing mobility rates for U.S. workers entering low wages between 1968 and 2013. Longitudinal data come from the nationally representative Panel Study of Income Dynamics (PSID). Mobility rates over time are estimated using discrete-time event history models for entering in low-wage work from better wages or unemployment. Two research questions motivate this study. How have mobility rates out of low-wage work changed since the late 1960s? Are changes in mobility rates over time explained by changes in the low-wage labor market's occupational structure, the behavior of firms, or the demographic and skills of low-wage workers?

LITERATURE REVIEW

David Howell and Arne Kalleberg, in their introduction to this issue, describe three prominent accounts for how the U.S. labor market has changed since the 1970s (2019). I draw on the two polar accounts, the perfect competition model with its interest in skill-biased technological change (SBTC), and the institutional model to formulate hypotheses for how macro changes in the economy may have affected mobility rates out of low-wage work. Changes in mobility rates over time are likely due to two factors: changes in the characteristics of low-wage workers (demographics and education),

or changes in the characteristics of available jobs (occupation and work hours).

The institutional account argues that the characteristics of the available jobs have worsened (Kalleberg 2011). The growth of the service sector has resulted in occupational polarization (Dwyer and Wright 2019; Goos, Manning, and Salomons 2009; Massey and Hirst 1998), including a growth of jobs at the low end in personal services (Wren 2013). The theory is these jobs are worse than previously available jobs because they are non-union (Boushey 2005; Brady, Baker, and Finnigan 2013; VanHeuvelen 2018), more likely to be part time (Kalleberg 2011), have nonstandard work arrangements (Kalleberg, Reskin, and Hudson 2000; Kalleberg 2000), and are less likely to be linked to occupational and internal labor markets (Cappelli 1999; Andersson, Holzer, and Lane 2005; Farber 2010; Handwerker 2018). The result is an expected increase in the low-wage labor market, or at least an expansion of the lowest mobility parts of the low-wage labor market. Previously better-paying jobs and acceptable low-wage jobs have become dead-end, undesirable jobs. The institutional account predicts lower mobility out of low-wage work since the 1970s due to worsening job characteristics. Institutional theorists recommend improving the conditions of these bad jobs through regulation (such as a $15 minimum wage or mandatory health insurance coverage) or government transfers (such as the highly successful Earned Income Tax Credit).

In contrast, the perfect competition account argues that the skills of low-wage workers are not keeping up with the up-skilling of jobs resulting from technological change, including the introduction of the computer (Goldin and Katz 2008; Acemoglu and Autor 2011; for a critique, see Card and DiNardo 2002). The focus of SBTC theorists is on the middle-skill jobs primarily in the middle of the wage distribution that have become automated or deskilled because of technological change. David Autor and David Dorn find that local labor markets with high levels of middle-skill, routine nonmanual work in 1980 had greater expansions of low-skill, low-end service work in the following decades than otherwise comparable markets

(2013). The low-wage labor market is thought to be expanding to receive this influx of semi-skilled workers who did not have enough skills to obtain jobs further up the skill ladder. The perfect competition model expects mobility out of low-wage work to either be the same because SBTC mainly affects middle-skill jobs, or lower because of overcrowding in the low-wage labor market. The emphasis on workers' skills leads to the recommendation to invest in education and training to increase the skills of workers to match the available jobs.

Labor Market Changes and the Mobility Out of Low Wages

Research distinguishes between the composition of the labor market in terms of demographics and education, on the one hand, and the structure of the labor market in terms of occupational characteristics and firm behavior, on the other. Numerous previous labor market studies have shown that older workers, non-white racial groups, women, and women with children experience weaker labor market outcomes than their education and labor-force experience would predict (Boushey 2005; Knabe and Plum 2010; Andersson et al. 2005; Cockx and Picchio 2012; Campbell 2012; Kronberg 2013; Wilson and Roscigno 2016; Ren 2019). If the demographic change in the low-wage labor market is toward groups that face more stigma in the labor market, mobility rates could decrease over time.

The jobs that have declined due to occupational polarization are often thought of as predominantly male manufacturing jobs. However, research has shown that predominantly female office and clerical support occupations have in fact seen some of the largest declines (Mouw and Kalleberg 2010; Autor and Dorn 2013). This leaves the expected gender transformation of the low-wage labor market unclear. The United States as a whole has become more racially diverse since the 1970s, which should be reflected in the low-wage labor market. The wage gaps for women (England 2010) and blacks (Semyonov and Lewin-Epstein 2009) have closed since the 1970s. They did so partly in response to the declining wage position of white men. Similarly, gaps in mobility rates out

of low-wage work by gender and race could decline because of fewer opportunities for white men rather than more opportunities for women and blacks. On the other hand, the program of mass incarceration begun in the 1970s disproportionately affected blacks and could result in lower mobility out of low wages as a consequence of less access to stable jobs (Pager 2007).

Many young workers enter low-wage work as they complete their education and transition to the labor market and move quickly to higher wages (Salverda and Mayhew 2009). Colin Campbell reports that 76 percent of young workers in low-wage jobs move to better wages in eight years (2012); William Carrington and Bruce Fallik report 65 percent (2001). The lengthening of young adulthood and the longer transition from school to work in recent years make it likely that more young workers are entering low-wage work than in the past (Smith, Crosnoe, and Chao 2016; Maume and Wilson 2015). All else being equal, more young workers should increase mobility rates out of low wages overall.

Low-wage workers in their prime earning years (thirty-four to fifty-four) are significantly less mobile out of low wages, and mobility declines with age in the United States (Salverda and Mayhew 2009). Ted Mouw and Kalleberg find that among an older sample (mean age of thirty-nine) without a college degree, only 13 percent moved out of low-wage jobs within three years (2018).

The lower mobility rate of prime-age workers can be explained several ways. Prime-age low-wage workers are more likely to have either accumulated a job history in low-wage work and or experienced spells of unemployment. An underappreciated finding in the comparative literature is the high rates of movement in the United States between low wages and unemployment and vice versa (Mason and Salverda 2010). Consequently, analysis of mobility out of low wages that do not properly account for unemployment spells may be picking up the wage-scarring effects of unemployment (Gangl 2006). Low-wage job experience for prime-age workers may be stigmatized by employers and equivalent in employer's minds to unemployment.

Another possible explanation is that prime-age workers may experience a low rate of wage mobility because they are less educated than young workers. Because of ongoing educational expansion, young workers are more likely to have higher education than older workers and thus are more likely to move out of low wages. From a human capital perspective, where education and labor market experience are proxy for a worker's skill, the higher likelihood of remaining in low wages is because workers with less education are less skilled (Autor and Dorn 2013). The returns to labor market experience for less-educated workers declined significantly by the 1980s, making the longer labor market experience of prime-age workers of little value (Bernhardt et al. 2001; French, Mazumder, and Taber 2005).

Alternatively, from a positional good and credentialism perspective, what matters is a worker's education credentials relative to other workers in the labor market (Sørensen 1983; Frank 1985; Kalleberg 2007; Horowitz 2018). Workers with fewer educational credentials would be screened out by employers offering higher wages. This effect is compounded for less-educated prime-age workers because they are more likely to have less education relative to the labor market as a whole and less likely to update their credentials with further training. An increase in young, more-educated workers into the low-wage labor market would result in a reduction in the mobility rate for less-educated workers from a positional good perspective. The overall mobility rate for low-wage workers could increase, decrease, or stay the same depending on whether the proportion of young educated workers is larger, smaller, or stays the same relative to the proportion of prime-age workers with less education.

Occupations in the low-wage labor market are not equal in providing routes to higher wages (Boushey 2005; Holmes and Tholen 2013; Mouw and Kalleberg 2018). Mouw and Kalleberg (2018) use a novel measure of skill similarity based on the movement of workers between occupations to advance the occupation- and task-specific human capital literature (Kambourov and Manovskii 2009; Gathmann and Schönberg 2010; Yamaguchi 2012; Sanders 2014). They find more mobility due to returns

to occupational experience for low-wage workers from manual (construction and machine operators) and skilled service (bartenders, cooks, receptionists, and sales workers) than among low-end service occupations (food service workers and cleaners). Similarly, David Maume and George Wilson find that the lower wage growth of 2000s cohort of young workers in the National Longitudinal Study of Youth (NSLY) relative to the 1980s cohort is partially explained by their higher employment in low-end service occupations (2015). A shift in the composition of the low-wage labor market toward low-end service work would result in decreased mobility rates over time.

Deindustrialization and the transition to the service economy resulted a decline of the middle and a growth in high-end occupations, whether defined by skills or by wages (Massey and Hirst 1998; Goos, Manning, and Salomons 2009; Holmes and Tholen 2013; Kalleberg 2011; Dwyer and Wright 2019). These studies of occupational polarization also find a growth in low-skill and low-wage occupations. Jennifer Hunt and Ryan Nunn reveal that the growth in low-end occupations is likely an artifact of this literature's primary method of differentiating between high, medium, and low-wage occupations using the occupational mean or median wages (2019; see also Mishel, Shierholz, and Schmitt 2013). This approach hides the variation in wages across occupations. Variation in wages within occupation has grown substantially since the 1980s even though the explanatory power of occupations in explaining wage inequality has grown more (Mouw and Kalleberg 2010).

Unions raise wages not only for union workers (VanHuevelan 2018), but also for non-unionized workers (Brady, Baker, and Finnigan 2013). Their decline could lead to an expansion of the low-wage labor market, or more likely to wages in manual occupations sharing workers with industries such as manufacturing that were union strongholds and de-unionized. Heather Boushey finds that working for a union does increase the odds of mobility out of low-wage work (2005). Formal pay scales and firm job ladders pushed by unions likely lead to an increase in wage returns to experience in union jobs (Freeman and Medoff 1984).

Finally, changes in firm behavior since the 1970s have resulted in increased flexibility in staffing arrangements, including the decline of the firm internal labor market (Kalleberg and Berg 1987; Cappelli 1999; Kalleberg 2000; Farber 2010; Kalleberg and Mouw 2018) and the disconnection of lower-skill workers from firm internal labor markets through domestic outsourcing (Weil 2014; Bernhardt et al. 2016; Handwerker and Spletzer 2015). Labor markets based on promotion within firms are unlikely to have gone away completely, particularly in government and union jobs (Newman 2008; Holmes and Tholen 2013). Researchers have found that changing firms rather than building tenure within the firm is a primary route out of low-wage work (Bernhardt et al. 2001; Andersson, Holzer, and Lane 2005, Bolvig 2005; Newman 2008; Heinze and Gürtzgen 2010; Pavlopoulos et al. 2014). Some firms pay higher wages because of either lower industry competition or through employing fewer higher skilled workers. Elizabeth Handwerker finds that increased establishment occupational concentration over time explains a substantial portion of the growing between-establishment inequality (2018). Firm mobility to a high-premium firm may be more difficult to achieve in recent years because firms have outsourced lower-paid work such as janitorial and food services to firms specializing in providing these services.

The growth of low-end service occupations in industries such as retail and hospitality led to an increase in part-time work and temporary work (Kalleberg 2000, 2011; Wren 2013). Less-skilled temporary workers are more likely to move to unemployment (Gash 2008). Part-time workers may share the experience of job instability with temporary workers as companies turn to the greater use of nonstandard employment relationships in order to protect their core workers (Kalleberg, Reynolds, and Marsden 2003; Pedulla 2013). Temporary and part-time workers have less opportunity to get occupational and firm experience and have lower mobility rates. The extent to which part-time work is a form of nonstandard work arrangements is unclear because it could be an individual choice for flexibility (Kalleberg 2007, 2011). A decline in mobility out of low-wage work among part-time workers over time could be a result of changing preferences for flexibility or a signal that part-time work is a soft form of temporary work and should receive more attention (Kalleberg 2003; Lambert, Henly, and Kim 2019).

In sum, the overall trend in mobility rates out of low-wage work over time is likely attributable to a combination of the changes in the demographic and educational composition of the low-wage labor market and structural changes in occupational characteristics and firm behavior. Untangling the overall trend requires paying particular attention to changes in the size and mobility rates of six groups: young, educated workers; prime-age, less-educated workers; workers in low-end service occupations; part-time workers; workers with multiple years of occupational experience; and workers with more years spent unemployed.

Mobility Out of Low-Wage Work in the United States

Table 1 presents a summary of research on the mobility of low-wage workers in the United States using longitudinal survey data. A few features stand out. Most studies are limited to less than a decade or to two birth cohorts in analyses of the NSLY. Only two more recent studies cover a longer period, but they analyze young workers and workers persistently in low wages respectively (Campbell 2012; Mouw and Kalleberg 2018). The one study analyzing all low-wage workers (ages sixteen to sixty-five) analyzes year-to-year transitions (Salverda and Mayhew 2009). Both of the analyses of young workers (ages sixteen to twenty-four) use the PSID.

A difficulty in comparing study results arises from the different definitions used for low-wage work ranging from minimum wages (Carrington and Fallik 2001; Boushey 2005) to $5 wage growth (Connolly, Gottschalk, and Newman 2003). The Organization for Economic Cooperation and Development defines low-wage work at two-thirds of the median hourly wage for full-time workers (OECD 2018). In contrast, a landmark comparative multicountry study used two-thirds of the hourly median wage for all workers (Gautié and Schmitt 2010). Others have suggested that two-thirds of the mean

Table 1. Studies of Mobility Out of Low-Wage Work in Using Longitudinal Survey Data

Author and Year	Time Period	Age at t0	Observation Window	Survey	Low-Wage Threshold or Approach	Model
Mouw and Kalleberg (2018)	1996–2011	All employed	2.5 years	SIPP	Two-thirds of the median for selection into low-wages and three-quarters of the median for mobility out	Discrete-time event history analysis and conditonal logit to identify stepping-stone occupations
Maume and Wilson (2015)	1979–2010	18–30	Up to 12 years	NSLY79, NSLY97	Wage growth of individuals by latent class based on wage profile	Latent class trajectory models followed by ordinal logits to predict latent class membership
Campbell (2012)	1969–2005	23–24	8 years	PSID	Three-quarters of the median hourly wage	Logit for probability of being in low-wages at two through eight years
Salverda and Mayhew (2009)	1995–2001	16–65	1 year	PSID	Two-thirds of the median hourly wage	Five probit for one-year transitions
Andersson, Holzer, and Lane (2006)	1993–2001	25–54	Up to 10 years	LEHD, nine states	Workers persistently in the bottom quartile between 1993 and 1995	Logit for probability of escaping low wages in 1999 to 2001

Boushey (2005)	1992–2003	24–54	2 years	SIPP	Minimum wage	Logit for probability of remaining in low wages two years later
French, Mazumder, and Taber (2005)	1983–2003	18–28	4 years	SIPP	Wage growth for young workers never enrolled in school	Regression to explain changes in wage growth
Connolly, Gottschalk, and Newman (2003)	1986–2000	18–40	4 years	SIPP	Wage growth of individuals in poverty households	Descriptive analysis of mean wage growth and probit to predict greater than $5 wage growth
Carrington and Fallick (2001)	1979–1994	14–22	Up to 15 years	NSLY79	Minimum wage	Probit for post-education year-to-year probability of remaining in minimum wages
Bernhardt, Morris, Handcock, and Scott (2001)	1966–1994	14–34	Up to 15 years	NLSM66, NSLY79	By educational group, of particular interest here are the low educated	Growth curve model with person random effects predicting wage growth over age

Source: Author's compilation.

rather than of the median is the most appropriate measure, given rising income inequality in the top half of the distribution but not in the bottom (Howell and Kalleberg 2019).

Most workers in the United States move out of low-wage work within the first few years. Wiemer Salverda and Ken Mayhew observe that 41.1 percent of low-wage workers escape to better wages in one year (2009). Young workers move out more quickly (Carrington and Fallik 2001; Campbell 2012). Mobility is lower for workers in persistently low-wage jobs, 27 percent in six years (Andersson, Holzer, and Lane 2005), and for low-wage workers in poverty households, 18 percent in four years (Connolly, Gottschalk, and Newman 2003).

Evidence indicates that the mobility out of low wages is cyclical and follows the economic cycle (French, Mazumder, and Taber 2005; Campbell 2012). Salverda and Mayhew find more movement between low-wage work and unemployment in the United States compared to similar countries in Western Europe (2009; Mason and Salverda 2010). Consequently, economic downturns may affect mobility out of low-wage work more in the United States. Helen Connolly and her colleagues find similar rates of mobility in the early and late 1990s (2003); Mouw and Kalleberg find lower mobility in the 2000s relative to the 1990s (2018).

A longer time frame is needed to untangle the effect of the economy from the long-term trend in mobility out of low-wage work. The current literature covers the entire period from 1980 through the late 2000s together. However, a patchwork of measures of low-wage work and approaches to modeling mobility make comparisons across time from the current literature infeasible. I begin to address this gap in the literature by providing an analysis of mobility out of low-wage work from 1968 to 2014.

Mobility and Selection

A central concern of the low-wage mobility literature is properly accounting for selection into low-wage work (Cappellari 2002; Aertz and Gürtzgen 2012; Mosthaf, Shnabel, and Stephani 2011; Cockx and Picchio 2012). Unobserved characteristics may be biasing estimates of mobility. The most common approach, following Mark Stewart and Joanna Swaffield (1999), is to use instrumental variables, usually parental background or social class. Alternative approaches include combining James Heckman and Burton Singer's mass points approach (1984) while restricting the sample to labor market entrants (Pavlopoulos and Fouarge 2010) and modeling the movement of workers between pairs of occupations conditional on the occupation's skill similarity (Mouw and Kalleberg 2018). Differences in country and time period make comparisons of mobility rates using alternative methodological approaches to selection difficult (Knabe and Plum 2010; McKnight et al. 2016).

DATA AND METHODS

The Panel Study of Income Dynamics is the longest-running nationally representative longitudinal survey in the United States. The original sample consists of approximately five thousand households selected in 1968 and their descendants. The survey was conducted annually through 1997 and biannually afterward. A key benefit of the PSID over the NSLY is that the sample is representative of the age structure and is not restricted to specific birth cohorts. When weighted to account for attrition and immigration since 1968, the PSID has been found comparable to the Current Population Survey (CPS) for poverty (Grieger, Danziger, and Schoeni 2009), and wage inequality (Heathcote, Perri, and Violante 2010).

I use all survey years of the PSID from 1968 to 2015 to select the analytic sample. Job and earnings information were collected for household heads and their spouses. The reference period for labor market earnings is the prior calendar year. I reconstruct each worker's occupational biography using all available information on current or (if unemployed) last and previous jobs. I then match job-year observations to the worker's hourly wages for that year calculated from the worker's total labor income and annual work hours. I use actual annual hours for salaried workers as well as hourly workers to reflect the increase in overwork (Cha and Weeden 2014). I top-code average weekly working hours at sixty hours a week and top- and bottom-code hourly wages at the 1st and 99th percentile.

I model mobility out of low-wage work using

discrete-time event history analysis to account for truncation and model time-varying covariates (Allison 1982; Mills 2011). Event history models are estimated using logistic regression, making the cross-group comparisons of coefficients biased due to heteroskedasticity (Mood 2010). I report the average marginal effects calculated over the sample because they remain unbiased for across group comparisons (Mood 2010) and facilitate interpretation of logistic regression (Williams 2012; Long and Mustillo 2018). Regression coefficients are available on request.

The baseline hazard for mobility is modeled using a cubic polynomial of the time since the start of the worker's current employment spell. Workers enter the analytic sample when they are observed starting to earn low wages between 1968 and 2013. I exclude all workers in low-wage jobs in their first observation in the sample. The exception are workers age twenty-five who enter the sample at the earliest possible age regardless of employment status and wages in the previous year. I follow workers who enter the sample until their first observation in a job with an hourly wage above the low-wage threshold, until they truncate due to sample attrition, or until the end of the observation window in 2014. I model mobility by employment spells because the probability of mobility out of low wages is higher for the unemployed who are pulled into low-wage work during tight labor markets. Workers who exit to unemployment remain in the sample. If they return to employment, they will contribute another employment spell to the analysis.

A comparison with the CPS reveals that the PSID underreports young low-wage workers (ages fifteen to twenty-four). The PSID collects job and wage information only for household heads and spouses. The missing young, low-wage workers are likely still members of their parents' or guardians' household. As a consequence, I limit my analysis to young-adult workers (twenty-five to thirty-four) and prime-age workers (thirty-five to fifty-four) who enter low-wage employment spells. About a third of all low-wage workers are younger than twenty-five

and about 6 percent are older than sixty-five (see figure O1).[1]

Workers who achieve wages above the low-wage threshold and then return to low wages are added back to the sample. A person-level random effect and a count of the number of times the worker has achieved mobility and returned to low wages are included to account for correlation between mobility spell outcomes from the same worker. The worker's employment status in the year before entering a low-wage employment spell is included to capture a worker's prior work history. The variable differentiates between coming from unemployment or better wages or being a young entrant who is newly able to enter the sample by turning twenty-five. Two variables continue counting across employment spells that do not end in mobility. The first is a count of years employed in low wages since entering the sample. The second is a count of the number of years unemployed or out of the labor force for more than four months. These choices reduce some of the error associated with unmeasured duration dependence in low-wage work by capturing as much of a worker's low-wage employment history as possible.

The primary results presented use the two-thirds of the median hourly wage for full-time workers. In a secondary analysis, I switch to the alternative two-thirds of the mean low-wage threshold for all workers. In a third set of models, I analyze the mobility of low-wage workers earnings below the lower threshold based on the median ($12.87 on average in 2015 dollars) to above the higher threshold based on the mean ($15.43 on average in 2015 dollars). The hourly wage thresholds are calculated from the CPS using similar measures of annual earnings and annual hours (for the low-wage thresholds in each year, see table O1). I group the years workers start a low-wage employment spell into thirteen entry periods following the economic cycle between 1968 and 2013 (see table O2). For example, the entry periods since 2000 are 2001 to 2003, 2004 to 2006, 2007 to 2009, and 2010 to 2013 (for more information on the methods, see the online appendix).

---

1. The online appendix includes the methodology as well as tables and figures designated in text with a leading O (https://www.rsfjournal.org/content/5/4/159/tab-supplemental).

Key Independent Variables

In line with the established literature on changes in the labor market across time, I distinguish between four sets of covariates: demographic, education and labor market experience, occupational, and firm characteristics. The demographic characteristics include age, race, gender, marital status, the presence of children, and the presence of children under six in the household. Age at the start of the employment spell is coded as a categorical variable with two groups, young adult (twenty-five to thirty-four), and prime age (thirty-five to fifty-four). I differentiate between racial groups using a variable for whites and nonwhites. Gender is a bounded by the limitation of the survey data to the male-female binary. Marital status is a three-category variable differentiating people who are never married, married, and previously married. The presence of children in the household and having a child under six are 0–1 variables, indicating the presence or absence of these children. Education is measured using a four-category variable of educational credentials (less than high school degree or equivalent, high school degree, some college, four-year college degree, or higher degree). The labor-force experience is captured using variables for employment status prior to entering low-wage work, years worked in low wages, and a count of years unemployed for four months or longer.

The occupation characteristics included in the primary analysis are working part-time hours (less than thirty-five hours a week), years of occupational experience, current occupation, and the occupation at the start of the low-wage employment spell. Current occupation is a time-varying variable. When considered with the fixed variable for occupation at spell start, the two occupation variables allow for an assessment of the effect of occupational moves on the odds of mobility. I differentiate between four large occupations: low-end service, manual, clerical, and mid-tier service, and professional and technical, aggregated using required occupational skills and environments from O*Net (onetonline.org). Workers build occupational experience by staying in the same occupation or moving to an occupation requiring similar skills. I follow Mouw and Kalleberg (2018) and use a measure of occupational skill similarity derived from workers moving between occupations in the CPS (for more detail on these measures, see the online appendix).

The only firm characteristic available for both household heads and spouses at the start of the survey is industry. Detailed industries are grouped into eight categories based on the 1990 census classification system: agriculture and mining; manufacturing and utilities; wholesale and retail trade; finance, insurance, and business services; personal services and entertainment; health care and social assistance; education and public administration; and other professional, scientific, and technical. Beginning with the 1981 wave, firm experience is available for heads and spouses. This PSID-generated variable is a count of all firm experience across periods of unemployment. From this measure, I derive variables for changing firms and a count of the number of firm changes since entering the sample. Measures of whether the individual worker is in job covered by a union (0–1) or works for the government at any level (0–1) become available for heads and spouses with the 1979 wave. I test the inclusion all of these variables in a supplementary analysis of the years from 1981 to 2014.

RESULTS

Figure 1 compares the trend in the size of the U.S. low-wage labor market in the PSID and CPS for workers between twenty-five and sixty-four years old using two alternative low-wage thresholds: two-thirds of the median hourly wage for full-time workers and two-thirds of the mean hourly wage for all workers (hereafter the median and mean threshold respectively). The size of the low-wage labor market is mostly stable from 1968 to 2014. About one-quarter of all workers in the United States are in low wages across this period using the median threshold (see Mason and Salverda 2010 for a consistent finding). The trend is dynamic. The percentage of low-wage workers swung down in the late 1970s, then came up slowly through the 1980s. The Great Recession brought the share of low-wage work to 28 percent.

In contrast, using the mean threshold, the low-wage labor market grew steadily, from 27

Figure 1. Size of U.S. Low-Wage Labor Market, 1967–2015

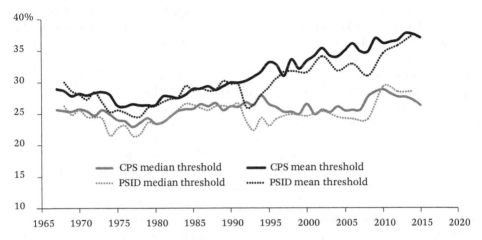

Source: Author's calculations based on the PSID (2018) and CPS (Flood et al. 2018).
Note: The median low-wage threshold refers to two-thirds of the median wage for full-time workers. The mean threshold is two-thirds of the mean wage for all workers.

percent in the 1970s to 37 percent in the early 2010s. The inflation-adjusted median hourly wage has been stable over this period. The mean hourly has increased, reflecting the growing inequality between the middle and top half of the wage distribution (Kalleberg 2011). The growth in the low-wage labor market over time when using the two-thirds of the mean threshold for all workers is partially due to the increasing threshold (see table O1).

The occupational composition of the low-wage labor market in the United States changed only minimally since the 1970s using the median hourly wage threshold (see figure O2). Most of the change occurred in the early 2000s. The proportion of low-wage workers in low-end service work stayed near 45 percent through the early 2000s before increasing to 52 percent by the early 2010s. A corresponding decrease occurred among clerical and mid-tier service workers and manual workers. Manual workers made up about 25 percent of all low-wage workers through the early 2000s before dropping to 20 percent. The decline in share for clerical and mid-tier service was slower and steadier, reaching 20 percent by 2000 and dropping to 15 percent by 2015. Workers in professional and technical occupations made up 15 percent of low-wage workers in 2015, almost double their share in 1968. Since 1980, the proportion of

manual workers in low-wage work increased from 20 percent to 30 percent (see figure O3). The proportion of workers in low-end service (46 percent) and professional and technical (11 percent) occupations in low wages held steady even as these occupations grew significantly over the period. About 22 percent of all clerical and mid-tier workers are in low wages.

The detailed occupations with the largest number of low-wage workers in low-end services are the typical occupations associated with low-wage work: 69.1 percent of housekeepers, 81.7 percent of childcare workers, 48.2 percent of retail salespeople, and 64.5 percent of servers (for the top ten largest detailed occupations in each of the four aggregate occupations, see table A1). Among the detailed manual occupations with the largest number of low-wage workers are sewing machine operators (66.5 percent), laborers and freight movers (37.7 percent), automotive service mechanics (25.4 percent), and construction laborers (34.7 percent).

What kind of professional and technical workers, many whom typically have a college degree, are in low-wage work? A small portion of workers in predominantly female occupations, including 12.7 percent of elementary school teachers and 37 percent of kindergarten and preschool teachers. The same pattern holds for clerical and mid-tier service. It is predominantly female occupations including bookkeepers (23.8 percent), office clerks (35.1 percent), and word processors (23.6 percent) that have the most low-wage workers in this aggregate occupation. The smaller percentage of workers in low wages in these occupations indicates that workers may be able to move out of low wages by staying in the same or moving to a similar occupation.

On average over the entire period from 1968 to 2014, 41.8 percent of workers entering low-wage jobs between the ages of twenty-five to fifty-four move to higher wages within two years, 55.4 percent in four years, and 62.9 percent in six years using the median threshold and the Kaplan-Meier method (Allison 1982). Cumulative mobility rises to 56.5, 70.3, and 77.7 percent in two, four, and six years for the about 10 percent of workers entering low wages in professional and technical occupations. Cumulative mobility goes down to 30.2, 43.2, and 51.5 percent for the majority of low-wage workers who start low-wage employment spells in low-end service occupations. Low-wage workers first observed in clerical and mid-tier service occupations experience mobility rates closer to those entrants to professional and technical occupations (50, 65.8, and 72.9 percent in two, four, and six years). Entrants into manual workers split the difference between these low- and high-end occupations with cumulative mobility similar to the rate for all low-wage workers (46, 59, and 65.8 percent in two, four, and six years). Prime-age entrants (age thirty-five to fifty-four) move out of low wages at similar rates on average to young adult (age twenty-five to thirty-four) entrants (43.3 to 40.3, 55.8 to 55.1, and 62.7 to 63.4 percent, at two, four, and fix years respectively).

Overall mobility out of low-wage work has declined in the 2001 to 2014 period relative to the 1968 to 1985 period (-2 percent at two years, -1.9 at four, -1.7 at six) and the higher mobility during the 1986 to 2000 period (-3.7, -4.5, and -4.8 percent at two, four, and six years since entering low wages) using the Kaplan-Meier method. The decline in mobility in the 2001 to 2014 period is strongest among for low-wage entrants into manual workers (-7.2, -7.3, and -6.4 percent at two, four, and six years) and into clerical and mid-tier service occupations (-3,

-5.1, and -4.9 percent at two, four, and six years). Low-wage entrants into professional and technical occupations have increased their mobility in the most recent period relative to the 1968 and 1985 period.

Descriptive Statistics by Employment Spell

The value of analyzing mobility using employment spells is to capture the negative effects of unemployment on mobility while accounting for the increased probability of mobility when the unemployed return to work. Experiencing an unemployment spell of longer than four months is common for low-wage workers (21.8 percent in two years, 39 percent in four years, 49.4 percent in six years). As expected, low-wage entrants into professional and technical occupations have the fewest unemployment spells (15, 30.5, and 36.4 percent by two, four, and six years); entrants into low-end service occupations have the most (24.2, 41.3, and 51.9 percent by two, four, and six years). Low-wage workers in the most recent period, from 2001 to 2014, have the fewest moves to unemployment (14.6 to 24.6, 29.7 to 42.8, and 39.7 to 52 percent by two, four, and six years) relative to the 1968 to 1985 period despite overall lower mobility out of low wages in the most recent period. They also return to low-wage employment more quickly in the more recent period (57.7 to 42.8, 73.1 to 53.5, and 79.3 to 58.7 percent by two, four, and six years).

The demographic and educational characteristics of entrants into low wages has changed since the late 1960s (see table A2). The employment-spell nature of these statistics results in workers who are most at risk for becoming unemployed produce more entrances into low-wage employment spells. Historically, more women than men have entered employment spells in low-wage work using the median threshold (for the median threshold, see table O2). Since 2000, parity has been higher; men and women are entering low-wage work at similar rates. The change is primarily driven by more men entering low-wage manual (50.9 percent between 1968 and 1985 to 23.4 percent between 2001 and 2013) and low-end service occupations (78.8 percent to 63.6 percent). The small share of women in manual occupations between 1968 and 1985 was likely concentrated in the most low-paid jobs, such as textiles, and makes up a disproportionate share of manual workers in low wages. Nonwhite workers grew as a proportion of entrants into low-wage work, almost doubling from the 1968 to 1985 period (17.4 percent) to the most recent period after 2000 (31.5 percent). The largest growth in the share of nonwhite workers occurred among low-wage workers in professional and technical occupations; the largest concentration remains in manual and low-end service occupations.

The age composition of entrants into low wages has become older as more prime-age workers (age thirty-five to fifty-four) enter low-wage employment spells (51.4 percent between 1968 and 1985 to 60.1 percent between 2001 and 2013). This corresponds with a growth in workers entering low-wage jobs from employment in better wages (41.8 percent between 1968 and 1985 to 50.3 percent between 2001 and 2013). The proportion coming from unemployment or out of the labor force declined correspondingly because the share of young entrants has remained stable at around 10 percent.

Most workers entering low-wage work after 2001 have a high school degree, the same as in the late 1970s, but their share drops 10 percent, from 44.8 to 35.2 percent. The decline in the proportion of workers entering low-wage work with less than a high school education has been significant (26.4 to 12.2 percent) and is highest in manual occupations (44.6 to 19.4 percent). This is offset by a share of entrants with some college and, to a lesser extent, with a bachelor's degree or higher. Workers with at least a four-year college degree are most likely to be among the small share of entrants in low-wage professional and technical occupations (54.1 percent between 2001 and 2013). The share of entrants with a college degree has grown among entrants into the clerical and mid-tier occupations (12.5 percent between 1968 and 1985 to 20.1 percent between 2001 and 2013) and service and low-end service occupations (4.2 percent between 1968 and 1985 to 13.6 percent between 2001 and 2013).

The starting wages for entrants into low-wage jobs has declined about 4 percent across occupations relative to the median between 1968 to 1985 and 2000 to 2013 (53.2 percent to 49.7 percent). This decline is on average about 60 cents in 2015 dollars. The share of workers entering low-wage work in a low-end service occupation who started in part-time hours declined over time (40.7 percent to 28.3 percent), and increased among entrants into professional and technical occupations (18.6 percent to 27.1 percent). The measure of weekly hours can include hours from multiple jobs. As a result, if low-wage workers are more likely to have second jobs in the more recent period in order to reach full-time hours, it would show up as a decline in part-time work. The share of part-time work is lowest among entrants into manual occupations, 12.4 percent between 2001 and 2013.

Occupational experience is low and remains low for low-wage entrants across time (1.3 years from 1986 to 2000). This indicates that entrants into low wages have accrued little occupational experience or are changing occupations to others with different skill and task profiles where accrued experience is less transferable. The industries in which entrants into low wages are finding jobs are mostly stable over time. The most notable change is the decline in the share of entrants into the manufacturing and utilities industry corresponding to deindustrialization.

In the more restricted 1981 to 2014 sample, the proportion of workers entering low-wage work in a job covered by a union increased from 8.9 percent between 1968 and 1985 to 11.4 percent between 2000 and 2013. The increase is particularly strong for professional and technical occupations and for clerical and mid-tier service occupations; the share for entrants into manual occupations has declined. The share of entrants into government employment is stable overall but masks both an increase among entrants into professional and technical and clerical and mid-tier service occupations, and a decline among manual occupations. The greater proportion of workers entering union jobs may be in the public sector, where unionization rates have declined less (Kalleberg 2011). The greater proportion in low wages would indicate that the strength of these unions in raising wages may have declined, especially in the context of tighter government budgets.

Many workers start an employment spell in low wages with no firm experience. The high average firm experience (3.6 years) indicates a substantial portion of workers with greater

Figure 2. Mobility Rate Across Employment Spell by Entry Period and Occupation

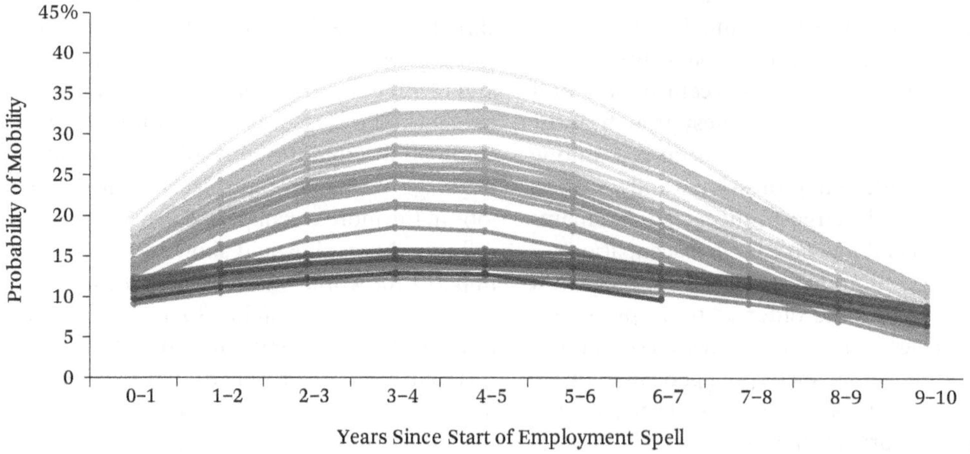

Source: Author's calculations based on the PSID (2018).
Note: Using median threshold (two-thirds of the median age for full-time workers). Compiled from the four baseline models (m0) by starting occupation.

than five or ten years' of experience entering low-wage jobs. The growth in this metric over time fits with more workers falling into low wages from higher wages due to the declining value of their wages relative to inflation. At the same time, the average number of firm changes in a mobility spell doubles over time. The greater churn in the low-wage labor market between firms in the 2001 to 2014 period, combined with fewer entrants into low-wage jobs coming from four months or more of unemployment, indicates both the availability of low-wage work and its insecurity in recent years.

Predicting Mobility Out of Low Wages

The mobility rates out of low wage for workers age twenty-five to fifty-four vary across time. Significant variation is uncovered when accounting for starting occupation, as seen in figure 2. In this section, I present results from final discrete-time event history models with all of the covariates using the median threshold, describing the characteristics that significantly effect mobility (see figure A2) and the degree to which these effects have changed over time (see figure 3). I primarily refer to the effects for all low-wage workers. Where significant, I note variation by the occupation and age group that workers started in when they entered a low-

wage employment spell. When comparing effects of covariates across time, I follow the descriptive analysis and analyze effects for the three periods, from 1968 to 1985, 1986 to 2000, and 2001 to 2014.

Cumulative mobility over the employment spell is similar to the Kaplan-Meier estimates of mobility since entering low-wage work (see figure A1). Mobility out of low-wage work at two, four, and six years is marginally lower over the employment spell because workers moving to unemployment contribute multiple employment spells. Workers coming from unemployment on average have a 4.4 percent lower probability of mobility out of low wages relative to workers coming from better wages (for all of the average marginal effects, see table O3). The effect of coming from a better-wage job on mobility out of low wages is significantly higher from 2000 to 2014, at 6.5 percent, up from 3.9 percent in the first period. Each move to unemployment and subsequent count of years in unemployment or out of the labor force reduces the probability of moving out of low wages in the next employment spell on average by 2.9 percent. The average effect at two years of unemployment has declined from a high of 3.8 percent between 1968 and 1985 to 3.1 percent between 2001 and 2014. However, the effect at

Figure 3. Significant Changes in Average Marginal Effects for Covariates over Time

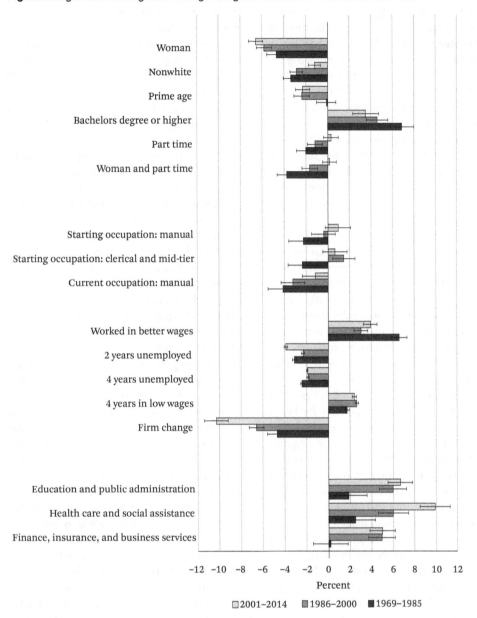

Source: Author's calculations based on the PSID (2018).
Note: Using median threshold (two-thirds of the median wage for full-time workers). Reference categories: woman (man), nonwhite (white), prime age (young adult), bachelor's or higher (high school diploma), part-time (full-time), starting and current occupation (professional and technical), firm change
(same firm), worked in better wages (unemployed), industry (agriculture and mining).

four years of unemployment increased from 1.9 percent to 2.4 percent from the first to the most recent of the three periods.

Young entrants (twenty-five years old and entering the sample in low wages) have no ob-served years in unemployment by definition. Thus the predicted probability of being a young entrant is 2.9 percent plus the coefficient for young entry, which is insignificant for all low-wage workers. Young entry reduces mobility for young-adult low-wage entrants (age twenty-five to thirty-four), indicating an age effect where older workers coming from unemployment in this age category have a higher probability of mobility (3.2 percent) than those entering the sample at age twenty-five. Prime-age workers had significantly less mobility in the first two periods, through 2000 (–2.2 percent), but not from 2001 to 2014.

Women (relative to men) and nonwhites (relative to whites) have lower mobility rates. For all low-wage workers, the average marginal effect of gender is three times larger for women (–4.5 percent) than for being nonwhite (–1.5 percent). Nonwhites have a lower probability of mobility out of low-wage work among prime-age workers and among entrants into manual occupations (–2.3 and –2.6 percent respectively). The effect for women is not significant among entrants into the predominantly female mid-tier service occupations and is stronger for young adults, entrants into low-end service occupations, and entrants into manual occupations (–5.5, –4.8, and –6.5 percent respectively). The average penalty for being a woman declined over time from a high of 6.5 percent between 1968 and 1985. The penalty for being nonwhite, however, increased over time. The change is due to the increase in the negative effect of being nonwhite among entrants into low-end service occupations in the most recent period. It is now on par with the constant effect over time for entrants into manual occupations. Married workers experience a higher probability of mobility than never-married workers. The effect of being married is two times stronger among entrants into low-wage manual occupations (2.4 percent). Being a woman with a child under age six in the household reduces the probability of mobility by 1.9 percent. The effect is two times as strong for low-wage entrants in professional and technical occupations.

Education effects are large. Among all low-wage workers, a college degree increases the probability of mobility by 5.4 percent over a high school degree. The effect doubles for low-wage entrants into professional and technical occupations and is insignificant for low-wage entrants into manual occupations. Young-adult workers benefit more from a college degree

than prime-age workers on average (6.4 to 3.1 respectively). Entrants with less than a high school degree have a lower probability of moving out of low wages (–4.2 percent) relative to those with a high school degree; the effect for having completed some college is about half that of a college degree (2.6 percent). The negative effect for not having a high school degree lowers mobility out of low wages for entrants into clerical and mid-tier occupations (–13.5 percent) in particular. The average marginal effect of having a bachelor's or higher degree on mobility out of low-wage work almost doubled in the period from 2001 to 2014 relative to 1968 to 1985 and 1986 to 2000 in the model for all low-wage workers. The increased value of a bachelor's degree for mobility out of low-wage work is significant only for workers starting in low-end service occupations among the occupation and age models.

The effect is positive for greater employment experience in low wages on mobility, particularly for young-adult entrants where the effect is three times greater. The value at four years of low-wage experience has declined from 2.5 percent in the 1968 to 1985 period to 1.8 percent in the 2001 to 2014 period. Higher occupational experience increases the probability for mobility, but the effect is much lower (0.5 percent per year), indicating that general labor-force experience matters more for mobility than occupation-specific experience. A worker would need to build up seven years of occupational experience in their low-wage job to match the increased probability of mobility that comes from moving to an occupation with little or no skill similarity to their current job.

The effect of part-time work hours varies across time. In the earliest period, from 1968 to 1985, working part-time hours has little effect on mobility. In the next period, from 1986 to 2000, the sign turns negative. In the most recent period, from 2001 to 2014, part-time hours lower the probability of mobility by 2 percent. The switch-in sign for part-time work is primarily driven by young-adult workers and is stronger for a woman working part time.

The average marginal effects for starting occupation and current occupation need to be interpreted together. Starting an employment spell in a low-end service occupation, relative to a professional or technical one, significantly lowers the probability for mobility out of wages (–2.1 percent). The negative effect of remaining in a low-end service occupation for workers starting a spell in this occupation is three times greater than moving to a professional and technical occupation. For these workers, moving to a manual occupation is little better than staying in a low-end service occupation. Moving up the occupational hierarchy from manual to clerical or mid-tier service and professional or technical occupations increases the probability of mobility. Only low-wage entrants into manual work increase their probability of mobility by staying in a manual occupation (0.9 percent) relative to moving to a professional or technical one. The negative effect of starting in a manual occupation relative to a professional or technical one is three times larger in the most recent period (2001 to 2014) and two times larger for a clerical or mid-tier occupation than in the first period (1968 to 1985).

The largest effects are for industry. Working in low wages in personal services and entertainment is no different than working in agriculture or mining, an industry with low mobility. Workers in health care and social assistance, education and public administration, and manufacturing and utilities have about a 7.5 percent higher probability of mobility out of low wages. Wholesale and retail trade as well as other professional, scientific, and technical industries have smaller effects more similar in size to having a college degree instead of a high school degree (4.9 and 3.5 respectively). The industry effects are strongest for professional and technical workers. Three industries see significant declines in their positive effects on mobility in the most recent period, from 2001 to 2014: finance, insurance, and business services; health care and social assistance; and education and public administration. The decline in mobility over time may reflect the decline in firm internal labor markets in the large institutions that dominate these industries, including hospitals, schools, and local government.

A supplemental analysis from 1981 to 2014 incorporates additional job and firm measures. Working in a job covered by a union increases the probability of mobility by 8.2 percent. The positive effect for working in a government job is 2.4 percent. The effect for firm experience is small but significant (1 percent for ten years of experience). The effect for firm changes on the probability of mobility attenuates over time. Changing firms decreased the probability of mobility out of low-wage work by 10.3 percent between 1981 and 1985. The effect diminishes by half to –4.7 percent in the most recent period, 2001 to 2014. The significance of this effect and its decline over time are driven by its significance among the largest share of low-wage workers, those entering low-end service occupations.

Explaining Mobility Rates Across Time

The second research question is whether demographic, education, occupational, and firm characteristics explain the different mobility rates across time. I use a stepwise series of discrete-time event history models to test the effect of including new sets of variables on the period effects. The baseline model (m0) includes only the effect of entry period on the hazard for the employment spell, along with a control variable for the number of previous successful exits from low wages. The second model (m1) adds demographic variables, followed by education and human capital variables, including the count of unemployment and employment status in the previous year (m2), then occupational variables (m3), and finally firm variables (m4). The base category for the entry period is from 1993 to 1996, a period with a tightening labor market when unemployment dropped from 7 percent to 5.5 percent.

Figures 4 and 5 present the average marginal effect of each entry period for each of the five model specifications for workers starting low-wage employment spells in low-end service and manual occupations. Most of the effects of entry period are not significantly different for professional and technical occupations and clerical and mid-tier service occupations; the overall entry period effects for all low-wage workers closely matches the trend for low-end service workers (see figures O4 through O6). The method here is to test whether the inclusion of each new set of variables explains the entry period effects and moves the effect toward zero in all periods. For example, if including education and human capital variables re-

Figure 4. Average Marginal Effect of Entry Period on Mobility, Low-End Service Entrants

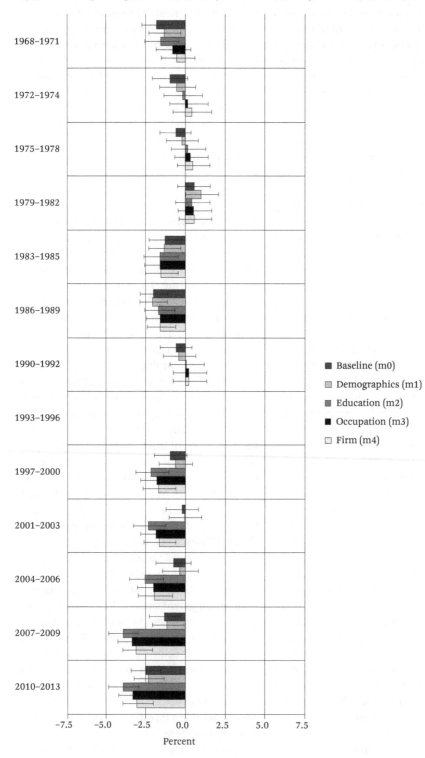

Source: Author's calculations based on the PSID (2018).
Note: Using median threshold (two-thirds of the median wage for full-time workers).

Figure 5. Average Marginal Effect of Entry Period on Mobility, Manual Entrants

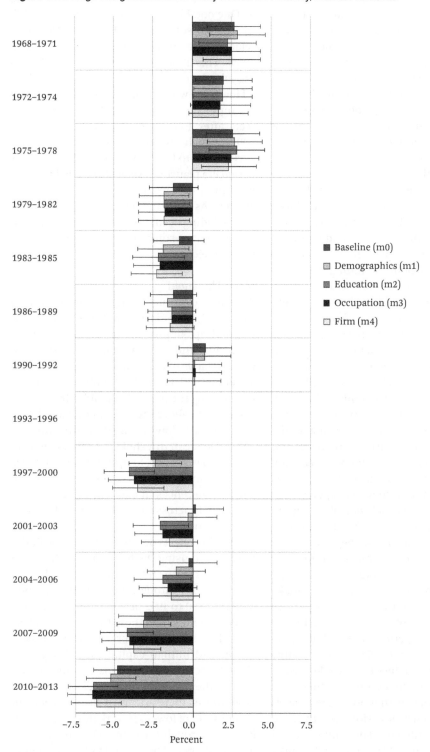

■ Baseline (m0)
□ Demographics (m1)
■ Education (m2)
■ Occupation (m3)
□ Firm (m4)

Source: Author's calculations based on the PSID (2018).
Note: Using median threshold (two-thirds of the median wage for full-time workers).

moves these effects, then the interpretation is that higher (or lower) mobility rates in a given period were due to the workers' favorable (or unfavorable) education and human capital characteristics. The reverse is true if including these variables increases the entry period effects (moving them away from zero). This indicates that higher (or lower) mobility rate in the previous model is despite more unfavorable (or favorable) educational and human capital worker characteristics.

Starting with the analysis of low-end service occupations, only the 1986 to 1989 and the 2010 to 2013 entry periods have significantly lower mobility than the 1993 to 1996 reference period in the baseline (m0) and the second model including demographics (m1). Both are periods of high unemployment. Including education human capitals variables (m2) has a significant effect. All entry periods after 1997 have significantly lower mobility than the reference period. These significant negative effects vary in size from 2.1 in the 1997 to 2000 period to 2.5 percent in the 2004 to 2006 period to 3.9 from 2007 to 2009 and 2010 to 2013. This negative effect indicates that entrants with similar education, unemployment and work experience, and coming from better wages are doing worse in the more recent period. Further analysis (not shown), reveals that the variables for years unemployed, years in low-wage work, and status prior to entering the employment spell mostly drive this effect, not the inclusion of education.

Adding occupational (m3) and firm (m4) characteristics attenuates the negative effects of entry period among entrants into low-end service occupations. The attenuation is small (on average 0.4 percent), but enough to make the smaller effects for the three entry periods from 1997 to 2006 not significantly different from the reference period after including occupational characteristics. The similarly large effects for the periods since the Great Recession (2007 onward) remain significant. Including firm characteristics further attenuates the effects in these two recent periods, but these effects remain significant. The supplemental analysis from 1981 to 2014 with the inclusion of additional job and firm experience variables does not change this result.

The mobility rates for low-wage entrants into manual occupations is similar (see figure 5). One notable difference is the higher mobility in the first three periods, from 1968 to 1978 relative to the 1980s, the late 1990s, and the late 2000s. This fits with the decline in manufacturing jobs during the 1980s. As in the model for all low-wage workers, including education and unemployment history results in stronger effects after 1997. The exception is the early 2000s, which remain similar to the reference period (1993 to 1996). The housing boom in this period is a plausible explanation for why mobility is not lower in this period among manual workers. As in the model for all low-wage workers, including occupational (m3) and firm (m4) characteristics somewhat attenuates the entry period effects.

Mean Threshold

Switching to the higher mean-derived low-wage threshold, cumulative mobility out of low wages drops approximately 2 to 3 percent at two, four, and six years since entering low wages relative to the median using the Kaplan-Meier method. Most of the mobility out of low wages using the mean threshold is from workers entering above the median threshold. Mobility from below the median threshold to above the mean threshold is approximately 10 percent lower at two, four, and six years relative to the mean (see figures O7 and O8). The occupation differences in cumulative mobility remain stable across these alternative threshold specifications.

Mobility effects over time are marginally different when using the higher mean threshold (see figures O9 to O12). The entry periods from the late 1960s through the early 1980s, along with the 1990 to 1992 period have significantly higher mobility than those from the late 2000s for all low-end service workers. When the education and human capital variables are included, these earlier periods become significantly different from the reference period. In other words, there is a much clearer decline in mobility out of low-wage work from higher mobility up through the early 1990s and a steady decline afterward punctured by lower mobility after the Great Recession. The same patterns hold for mobility from below the median threshold to above the mean, although the period effect sizes are half as large because the base level probability of mobility is lower. Manual workers have significantly higher probability rates above the mean from 1968 to 1978 using the mean threshold. The same minimal attenuation of entry period effects for the period after the late 1990s found using the median threshold with the inclusion of occupation and firm characteristics occurs when using the mean threshold.

DISCUSSION AND CONCLUSION

Mobility out of low-wage work is modeled for thirteen entry periods from 1968 to 2013 for entrants age twenty-five to fifty-four into low wages for all workers, young and prime-age workers, and by four large aggregate occupations. More than half of all workers entering a low-wage employment spell move above the two-thirds of the median low-wage threshold for full-time workers in four years. However, it takes seven years for half of these workers entering low wages below the median threshold to move above the higher two-thirds of the mean low-wage threshold.

Mobility out of low-wage work has declined for entrants into low wages since the late 1990s to the end of the study period in the early 2010s. Workers entering low-wage employment during the Great Recession (2007 to 2009) and the years afterward (2010 to 2013) experienced 3.7 and 4 percent lower probabilities of mobility. These effects are similar in size to the negative effect of being a woman relative to being a man and the positive effect of having a college degree relative to having a high school diploma. These Great Recession effects are the largest period effects by a factor of two since the late 1960s.

In the baseline analysis of mobility out of low wages, the effect of entry period on mobility is minimal. A larger portion of entrants into low-wage work in the 2000s are prime age, nonwhite, and men. These demographic changes explain little of the change in mobility rates over time. The negative effect on mobility out of low wages from the late 1990s onward is revealed when controlling for the work and unemployment history. This period effect is found in the Kaplan-Meier life table analysis based on time since first entering low wages and is not an artifact of the employment-spell design.

This indicates that the probabilities of mobility out of low-wage work are lower since the late 1990s even though low-wage workers have more labor market experience, less unemployment history, higher education, and are more likely to have fallen into low wages from better wages. Consistent with other research, I find that the returns to labor market experience for achieving mobility have decreased and that the negative effects of unemployment have increased when comparing the 2000 to 2014 period with prior years. My findings add to the growing evidence of increased insecurity among workers at the bottom since the 1990s (Hacker 2006; Sandoval, Rank, and Hirschl 2009; Western et al. 2016; Latner 2018).

The institutional account would explain the lower returns to education and experience for low-wage workers mobility as a consequence of worsening occupational and firm characteristics (Howell and Kalleberg 2019). I find some evidence for this argument in the attenuation of the entry period effects since the late 1990s after including occupational and firm characteristics. The lowest mobility out of low wages is among entrants into and movers to low-end service occupations and the share of low-wage workers in these occupations has grown, particularly since 2000.

The decline of the higher mobility out of low wages in education, health, and business services is evidence of a decline in firm internal labor markets due to the large institutions that dominate these industries. In addition, part-time work is now a stronger hindrance to mobility out of low-wage work. More attention should be paid to part-time work as a form of insecurity in the new economy. In the supplemental analysis from 1981 to 2014, I find a decline in the negative effect of firm changes over time, further evidence for a decline in internal labor markets and their subsequent use as a route to mobility. These findings indicate that institutional changes have contributed to reducing pathways to mobility for low-wage workers.

The perfect competition model claims that the education and skills of workers are not keeping up with the available jobs (Autor and Dorn 2013). The low-wage labor market since the 2000s is more skilled than in the past. College-educated workers have increased their share in the low-wage labor market and are moving out of low-wage work more quickly. The more-educated group that remains is the growing share with some college education. This group has doubled in low-end service occupations since the 1968 to 1985 period. Additionally, the lower mobility rate for prime-age workers compared to young adults goes away in the 2001 to 2014 period. When combined with the increase in low-wage workers coming from better wages, the evidence is consistent with the account of the perfect competition model that a decline in middle-skill jobs pushes more semi-skilled workers into the low-wage labor market.

The stability in the size of the low-wage labor market across time in the United States using the median threshold is a caution to the over-interpretation of the occupational polarization literature. Low-end service occupations have increased as a share of the low-wage labor market, but have long been dominant. The new trend is an increase in the percentage of workers in low-end service occupations that are not in low wages. This analysis does not find an increase in mobility out of low-end service occupations over time, suggesting that these higher-paid forms are not accessible to workers in low wages in the same occupation. The size of the low-wage labor market has increased when using the higher two-thirds of the mean threshold reflecting the growing insecurity of the lower middle class. However, these workers are less likely to be in the low-end service occupations typically associated with low-wage work. Rather, it is workers higher up the occupation and skill ladder, like elementary school teachers, who are added to the low-wage labor market when using the mean threshold.

I find positive effects for time employed in low wages and increases in occupational experience on mobility out of low-wage work. This counteracts the narrative that only low-wage workers who are younger, have more education, or are temporarily in low wages between spells of working in higher pay move out. Some workers use low-wage work as a stepping stone (Knabe and Plum 2010; Cockx and Picchio 2012; Mouw and Kalleberg 2018). They are thus able to build occupational experience and move to another occupation requiring a similar set of tasks where their previous experience applies.

However, this is a slow process. In contrast, low-wage workers who are able to move occupations with little or no skill similarity to their previous low-wage occupation increase their probability of mobility similar to having some college education over a high school degree. Similarly, working in a union job and a government job have large positive effects on the probability of mobility, in line with research on the wage benefits of unions (Boushey 2005; Brady et al. 2013; VanHeuvelen 2018).

The consistent negative effects for women and nonwhites on mobility since 1968 reveals how little progress has been made for these groups in the low-wage labor market. The closing of the gender pay gap (Kronberg 2013) and the progress made on racial pay gaps (Ren 2019) have not resulted in a closing of mobility rates out of the low-wage labor market. Men and whites are moving up and out at higher rates even after accounting for education, experience, and various occupational and firm characteristics. Although the probability of mobility out of low-wage work has narrowed for women, the negative effect of being a woman is similar in size to the positive effect of having a college degree relative to a high school degree. I find that the penalty for being nonwhite on mobility out of low-wage work has worsened since the late 1960s. A plausible explanation is the disparate impact of criminal records among nonwhites as part of mass incarceration (Pager 2007).

Future research on mobility out of low-wage work over time should use more detailed occupations and industries contextualized in geographically bound labor markets. A finer grained analysis may provide a clearer story about changes in occupational and industry structure that are central to the institutional narrative and be able to identify the changes that began to occur in the 1990s. Selection should be taken seriously and use new methods to account for duration dependence and unemployment spells. Most studies of the wage mobility of low-wage workers use a threshold approach or follow the workers for only a short period after they secure higher wages. The intragenerational mobility literature would benefit from a deeper understanding of the wage growth of low-wage workers, particularly once they move to higher wages.

Table A1. Top Ten Detailed Occupations by Large Occupation

Occupations	Percent in Low Wages
Professional and technical	
Farmers, ranchers, and other agricultural managers	60.9
Elementary and middle school teachers	12.7
Preschool and kindergarten teachers	37.0
Other teachers and instructors	25.6
Sales representatives, wholesale and manufacturing	9.4
Real estate brokers and sales agents	22.7
Designers	26.3
Legislators	7.6
Accountants and auditors	6.7
Artists and related workers	33.0
Clerical and mid-tier service	
Managers, all other	14.2
Logisticians	2.5
Miscellaneous agricultural workers (such as conservation workers)	80.8
Bookkeeping, accounting, and auditing clerks	23.8
Teacher assistants	55.3
Office and administrative support workers, all other	22.5
Office clerks, general	35.1
Shipping, receiving, and traffic clerks	27.2
First-line supervisors of office and administrative support workers	10.8
Word processors and typists	26.5
Manual	
Production workers, all other	24.9
Sewing machine operators	66.5
Laborers and freight, stock, and material movers, hand	37.7
Miscellaneous assemblers and fabricators	28.2
Inspectors, testers, sorters, samplers, and weighers	27.9
Operating engineers and other construction equipment operators	25.0
Automotive service technicians and mechanics	25.3
Construction laborers	34.7
Packaging and filling machine operators and tenders	4.3
Motor vehicle operators	38.0
Low-end service	
Maids and housekeeping cleaners	69.1
Childcare workers	81.7
Retail salespersons	48.2
Nursing, psychiatric, and home health aides	63.3
Chefs and head cooks	68.6
Waiters and waitresses	64.5
Janitors and building cleaners	46.3
Cashiers	70.8
Driver, sales workers, and truck drivers	22.1
Hairdressers, hairstylists, and cosmetologists	57.6

Source: Author's calculations based on the PSID (2018).

Note: Using median threshold (two-thirds of the median wage for full-time workers).

Table A2. Descriptive Characteristics of Entrants and Jobs in Three Periods

	All Entrants			Professional-Technical		
	1968–1985	1986–2000	2001–2013	1968–1985	1986–2000	2001–2013
N	6,068	9,324	6,879	658	1,328	1,265
Female	66.4%	60.0%	55.4%	51.1%	55.7%	59.6%
Nonwhite	17.4	24.0	31.5	8.2	15.5	17.8
Prime age (thirty-five to fifty-four)	51.4	56.8	60.1	44.8	59.4	59.3
Marital status						
Never married	7.6%	17.4%	27.7%	12.4%	17.4%	26.6%
Married	67.0	47.5	43.0	71.9	53.5	50.6
Child(ren) in the household						
Yes	66.1%	57.2%	54.3%	59.7%	53.0%	52.9%
Under age six	27.4	25.4	25.7	27.8	24.0	25.2
Woman with a child under age six	25.0	26.0	27.3	29.7	25.7	25.5
Education						
Less than high school	26.4%	14.6%	12.2%	7.4%	4.3%	3.1%
High school diploma	44.1	42.2	35.2	25.9	21.1	14.0
Some college	17.9	26.2	31.2	24.9	30.8	28.9
Bachelor's or higher	11.6	17.0	21.4	41.8	43.7	54.1
Employment status before entry						
Unemployed	48.3%	45.8%	38.8%	37.6%	37.6%	35.6%
Working, better wages	41.8	45.8	50.3	51.7	56.0	55.5
Young entry	10.0	8.4	10.9	10.7	6.5	9.0
Years observed in low wages	0.8	1.1	1.0	0.4	0.8	0.7
Years observed in unemployment	0.8	1.3	0.9	0.4	0.9	0.7
Average starting wage (median=100)	53.2	50.5	49.7	55.5	52.0	52.0
Part-time hours	27.0%	23.4%	24.2%	18.6%	23.9%	27.1%
Woman and part-time hours	37.4%	33.7%	32.9%	30.8%	33.8%	36.0%
Average occupational experience	1.2	1.3	1.4	1.1	1.2	1.1
Industry						
Agriculture and mining	11.1%	12.8%	12.5%	22.8%	12.1%	10.8%
Manufacturing and utilities	21.9	18.3	16.6	7.2	8.9	8.9
Wholesale and retail trade	23.6	22.2	23.0	11.8	7.9	8.5
Finance, insurance, and business services	8.7	10.2	10.4	10.9	13.7	12.6
Personal services and entertainment	9.9	9.5	9.8	3.4	3.9	7.0
Health care and social assistance	9.0	9.0	10.2	10.0	14.0	9.5
Education and public administration	11.8	12.8	11.1	23.4	23.6	26.0
Other professional, scientific, and technical	4.1	5.2	6.4	10.6	16.0	16.7
Only from 1981 onward						
N	1,855	6,983	5,162	195	890	897
Union job	8.9%	9.8%	11.4%	5.0%	8.2%	13.4%
Government job	15.1%	15.7%	15.3%	17.2%	23.5%	25.8%
Average firm experience	3.6	3.6	4.1	3.1	3.5	3.9
Average firm count	1.5	3.3	4.4	1.5	3.4	4.5

Source: Author's calculations based on the PSID (2018).

Note: Using median threshold (two-thirds of the median wage for full-time workers).

Clerical-Mid-Tier			Manual			Low-End Service		
1968–1985	1986–2000	2001–2013	1968–1985	1986–2000	2001–2013	1968–1985	1986–2000	2001–2013
1,327	1,995	1,149	1,607	2,295	1,441	2,476	3,706	3,024
70.7%	69.0%	72.0%	50.9%	32.5%	23.4%	78.8%	71.4%	63.6%
11.7	20.7	30.7	21.6	29.2	38.0	22.9	27.1	35.4
52.0	61.2	61.5	49.3	52.0	64.3	55.0	55.3	57.4
6.1%	14.5%	23.2%	6.4%	19.3%	27.6%	7.6%	18.2%	30.3%
67.9	50.4	47.0	69.0	45.1	43.5	63.1	44.2	37.1
66.8%	55.5%	56.8%	67.7%	55.3%	53.3%	67.2%	61.4%	54.4%
24.1	22.2	24.7	30.8	25.7	25.2	27.7	28.0	26.6
19.6	20.8	26.1	27.0	24.3	18.6	26.6	30.0	30.6
15.3%	7.0%	7.7%	44.6%	24.9%	19.4%	31.3%	18.8%	15.1%
44.4	39.9	32.8	44.9	51.1	50.5	50.6	48.4	38.9
27.7	35.0	39.4	7.7	19.4	24.6	14.0	22.0	32.5
12.5	18.1	20.1	2.7	4.6	5.6	4.2	10.9	13.6
43.6%	40.0%	38.4%	44.3%	40.2%	35.6%	58.4%	56.6%	42.5%
46.9	52.7	51.7	45.2	52.2	55.8	31.8	32.8	43.9
9.5	7.2	9.9	10.6	7.6	8.6	9.8	10.6	13.6
0.6	0.8	0.8	0.7	0.8	1.0	1.1	1.5	1.2
0.7	1.0	0.8	0.7	1.1	0.9	1.1	1.9	1.1
56.1	53.5	52.5	54.9	51.2	50.3	49.1	47.4	47.0
24.0%	19.0%	26.4%	13.8%	10.2%	12.4%	40.7%	33.5%	28.3%
31.9%	26.1%	32.3%	20.6%	16.7%	15.1%	49.6%	43.0%	35.3%
1.2	1.2	1.5	1.1	1.2	1.5	1.4	1.4	1.4
13.7%	14.5%	11.5%	15.8%	27.7%	29.7%	1.6%	3.5%	4.3%
16.2	14.8	11.9	61.1	47.3	43.6	8.0	8.6	7.8
20.2	19.3	12.7	10.9	10.4	13.9	38.8	37.5	40.2
13.4	13.3	14.0	5.9	7.6	10.0	5.9	8.0	7.9
4.4	4.1	4.2	1.7	1.1	1.2	21.6	20.5	18.3
11.1	11.2	12.6	0.1	0.5	0.1	12.5	9.9	15.1
15.0	16.6	23.2	3.9	5.0	1.0	9.5	9.7	3.6
6.1	6.2	9.9	0.7	0.3	0.5	2.1	2.2	2.7
409	1,479	986	518	1,797	1,084	733	2,817	2,195
6.7%	10.8%	11.7%	16.9%	14.0%	13.4%	7.3%	7.5%	9.2%
20.5%	19.7%	25.8%	9.6%	12.0%	5.6%	13.6%	12.2%	9.8%
4.1	3.8	4.7	4.4	4.3	4.6	2.9	3.1	3.5
1.5	3.4	4.5	1.5	3.0	4.4	1.5	3.4	4.3

Figure A1. Cumulative Mobility Out of Low-Wage Work Across Employment Spells

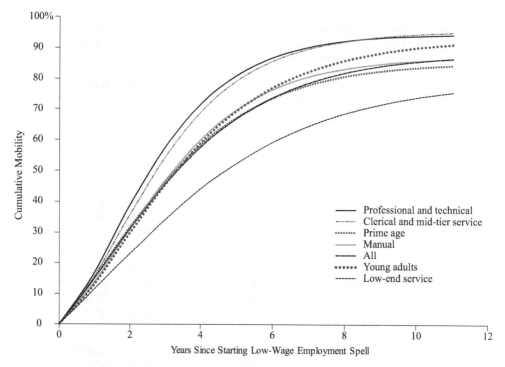

Source: Author's calculations based on the PSID (2018).

Note: Results from the full model (m4) using the median wage threshold (two-thirds of the median wage for full-time workers).

Figure A2. Significant Average Marginal Effects for Mobility for All Low-Wage Workers

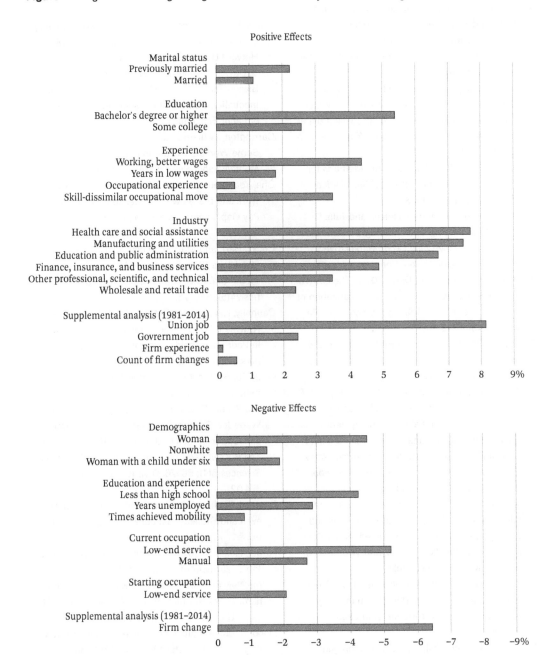

Source: Author's calculations based on the PSID (2018).

Note: Results from the full model (m4) using the median wage threshold (two-thirds of the median wage for full-time workers). Reference categories: woman (man), nonwhite (white), marital status (never married), child under six (without a child under six), education (high school diploma), worked in better wages (unemployed), starting and current occupation (professional and technical), firm change (same firm), industry (agriculture and mining).

REFERENCES

Acemoglu, Daron, and David Autor. 2011. "Skills, Tasks and Technologies: Implications for Employment and Earnings." In *Handbook of Labor Economics*, vol. 4B, edited by Orley Ashenfelter and David Card. Amsterdam: Elsevier.

Aertz, Bodo, and Nicole Gürtzgen. 2012. "What Explains the Decline in Wage Mobility in the German Low-Wage Sector?" *ZEW* discussion paper no. 12-041. Mannheim: Centre for European Economic Research.

Allison, Paul D. 1982. "Discrete-Time Methods for the Analysis of Event Histories." *Sociological Methodology* 13(1): 61–98.

Andersson, Fredrick, Harry J. Holzer, and Julia I. Lane. 2005. *Moving Up or Moving On: Who Advances in the Low-Wage Labor Market?* New York: Russell Sage Foundation.

Autor, David H., and David Dorn. 2013. "The Growth of Low-Skill Service Jobs and the Polarization of the US Labor Market." *American Economic Review* 103(5): 1553–97.

Bernhardt, Annette, Rosemary Batt, Susan Houseman, and Eileen Appelbaum. 2016. "Domestic Outsourcing in the U.S.: A Research Agenda to Access Trends and Effects on Job Quality." *IRLE* working paper no. 102-16. Berkeley, Calif.: Institute for Research on Labor & Employment.

Bernhardt, Annette, Martina Morris, Mark S. Handcock, and Marc A. Scott. 2001. *Divergent Paths: Economic Mobility in the New American Labor Market.* New York: Russell Sage Foundation.

Bolvig, Iben. 2005. "Within- and Between-Firm Mobility in the Low-Wage Labour Market." In *Job Quality and Employer Behaviour*, edited by Stephen Bazen, Claudio Lucifora, and Wiemer Salverda. New York: Basingstoke.

Boushey, Heather. 2005. "No Way Out: How Prime-Age Workers Get Trapped in Minimum Wage Jobs." *Working USA: The Journal of Labor and Society* 8(6): 659–70.

Brady, David, Regina Baker, and Ryan Finnigan. 2013. "When Unionization Disappears. State-Level Unionization and Working Poverty in the United States." *American Sociological Review* 78(5): 872–96.

Campbell, Colin. 2012. "Low-Wage Mobility During the Early Career." *Research in Social Stratification and Mobility* 30(2): 175–85.

Cappellari, Lorenzo. 2002. "Do the 'Working Poor' Stay Poor? An Analysis of Low Pay Transitions in Italy." *Oxford Bulletin of Economics and Statistics* 64(2): 87–110.

Cappelli, Peter. 1999. *The New Deal at Work: Managing the Market-Driven Workforce.* Boston, Mass.: Harvard Business School Press.

Card, David, and John E. DiNardo. 2002. "Skill-Biased Technological Change and Rising Wage Inequality: Some Problems and Puzzles." *Journal of Labor Economics* 20(4): 733–83.

Carrington, William J., and Bruce C. Fallik. 2001. "Do Some Workers Have Minimum Wage Careers?" *Monthly Labor Review* 124(5): 17–27.

Cha, Youngjoo, and Kim A. Weeden. 2014. "Overwork and the Slow Congruence in the Gender Pay Gap." *American Sociological Review* 79(3): 467–84.

Cockx, Bart, and Matteo Picchio. 2012. "Are Short-Lived Jobs Stepping Stones to Long-Lasting Jobs?" *Oxford Bulletin of Economics and Statistics* 74(5): 646–75.

Connolly, Helen, Peter Gottschalk, and Katherine Newman. 2003. "Wage Trajectories of Workers in Poor Households." *Boston College Working Papers in Economics* no. 555. Revised July 25, 2005. Boston, Mass.: Boston College Department of Economics.

Dwyer, Rachel E., and Erik Olin Wright. 2019. "Low-Wage Job Growth, Polarization, and the Limits and Opportunities of the Service Economy." *RSF: The Russell Sage Foundation Journal of the Social Sciences* 5(4): 56–76. DOI: 10.7758/RSF.2019.5.4.02.

England, Paula. 2010. "The Gender Revolution: Uneven and Stalled." *Gender & Society* 22(2): 149–66.

Farber, Henry S. 2010. "Job Loss and the Decline of Job Security in the United States." In *Labor in the New Economy*, edited by Katharine G. Abraham, James R. Spletzer, and Michael Harper. Chicago: University of Chicago Press.

Flood, Sarah, Miriam King, Renae Rodgers, Steven Ruggles, and J. Robert Warren. 2018. Integrated Public Use Microdata Series, Current Population Survey: Version 6.0 [data set]. Minneapolis, Minn.: IPUMS.

Frank, Robert. 1985. *Choosing the Right Pond: Human Behavior and the Quest for Status.* New York: Oxford University Press.

Freeman, Richard B., and James L. Medoff. 1984. *What Do Unions Do?* New York: Basic Books.

French, Eric, Bhashkar Mazumder, and Christopher

Taber. 2005. "The Changing Pattern of Wage Growth for Low Skilled Workers." Working paper no. 2005-24. Revised May 3, 2006. Chicago: Federal Reserve Bank.

Gangl, Markus. 2006. "Scar Effects of Unemployment: An Assessment of Institutional Complementarities." *American Sociological Review* 71(6): 986–1013.

Gash, Vanesa. 2008. "Bridge or Trap? Temporary Workers' Transitions to Unemployment and to the Standard Employment Contract." *European Sociological Review* 24(5): 651–68.

Gathmann, Christina, and Uta Schönberg. 2010. "How General Is Human Capital? A Task-Based Approach." *Journal of Labor Economics* 28(1): 1–49.

Gautié, Jérôme, and John Schmitt, eds. 2010. *Low-Wage Work in the Wealthy World*. New York: Russell Sage Foundation.

Goldin, Claudia, and Lawrence F. Katz. 2008. *The Race Between Education and Technology*. Cambridge, Mass.: Harvard University Press.

Goos, Maarten, Alan Manning, and Anna Salomons. 2009. "Job Polarization in Europe." *American Economic Review* 99(2): 58–63.

Grieger, Lloyd, Sheldon H. Danziger, and Robert F. Schoeni. 2009. "Accurately Measuring the Trend in Poverty in the United States Using the Panel Study of Income Dynamics." *Journal of Economic and Social Measurement* 34(2-3): 105–17.

Hacker, Jacob. 2006. *The Great Risk Shift*. New York: Oxford University Press.

Handwerker, Elizabeth W. 2018. "Increased Concentration of Occupations, Outsourcing, and Growing Wage Inequality in the United States." Paper presented at the NBER Summer Institute, Cambridge, Mass. (July 24, 2018).

Handwerker, Elizabeth W., and James R. Spletzer. 2015. "The Role of Establishments and the Concentration of Occupations in Wage Inequality." *IZA* discussion paper no. 9294. Bonn: Institute of Labor Economics.

Heathcote, Jonathan, Fabrizio Perri, and Giovanni L. Violante. 2010. "Unequal We Stand: An Empirical Analysis of Economic Inequality in the United States, 1967–2006." *Review of Economic Dynamics* 13(1): 15–51.

Heckman, James, and Burton Singer. 1984. "A Method for Minimizing the Impact of Distributional Assumptions in Econometric Models for Duration Data." *Econometrica* 52(2): 271–320.

Heinze, Anja, and Nicole Gürtzgen. 2010. "Escaping Low-Earnings in Germany: Do Employer Characteristics Make a Difference?" Beiträge zur Jahrestagung des Vereins für Socialpolitik 2010: Ökonomie der Familie—Session: Dynamics of the Labor Market: Empirical Studies, no. F11-V1, Frankfurt-am-Main: Verein für Socialpolitik.

Holmes, Craig, and Gerbrand Tholen. 2013. "Occupational Mobility and Career Paths in the 'Hourglass' Labour Market." Working paper no. 113. Oxford: University of Oxford.

Horowitz, Jonathan. 2018. "Relative Education and the Advantage of a College Degree." *American Sociological Review* 83(4): 771–801.

Howell, David R., and Arne L. Kalleberg. 2019. "Declining Job Quality in the United States: Explanations and Evidence." *RSF: The Russell Sage Foundation Journal of the Social Sciences* 5(4): 1–53. DOI: 10.7758/RSF.2019.5.4.01.

Hunt, Jennifer, and Ryan Nunn. 2019. "Is Employment Polarization Informative About Wage Inequality and Is Employment Really Polarizing?" Paper presented at the 2019 ASSA Annual Meeting "Occupations and Job Polarization." Atlanta, Ga. (January 5, 2019).

Jarvis, Benjamin F., and Xi Song. 2017. "Rising Intragenerational Occupational Mobility in the United States, 1969 to 2011." *American Sociological Review* 82(3): 568–99.

Kalleberg, Arne L. 2000. "Nonstandard Employment Relations: Part-Time, Temporary, and Contract Work." *Annual Review of Sociology* 26: 341–65.

———. 2003. "Flexible Firms and Labor Market Segmentation: Effects of Workplace Restructuring on Jobs and Workers." *Work and Occupations* 30 (May): 154–75.

———. 2007. *The Mismatched Worker*. New York: W. W. Norton.

———. 2011. *Good Jobs, Bad Jobs: The Rise of Polarized and Precarious Employment Systems in the United States, 1970s to 2000s*. New York: Russell Sage Foundation.

Kalleberg, Arne L., and Ivar Berg. 1987. *Work and Industry: Structures, Markets and Processes*. New York: Plenum.

Kalleberg, Arne L., and Ted Mouw. 2018. "Occupations, Organizations, and Intragenerational Career Mobility." *Annual Review of Sociology* 44: 283–303.

Kalleberg, Arne L., Barbara F. Reskin, and Ken Hudson. 2000. "Bad Jobs in America: Standard and

Nonstandard Employment Relations and Job Quality in the United States." *American Sociological Review* 65(2): 256–78.

Kalleberg, Arne L., Jeremy Reynolds, and Peter V. Marsden. 2003. "Externalizing Employment: Flexible Staffing Arrangements in U.S. Organizations." *Social Science Research* 32(4): 525–52.

Kambourov, Gueorgui, and Iourii Manovskii. 2009. "Occupational Specificity of Human Capital." *International Economic Review* 50(1): 63–115.

Knabe, Andreas, and Alexander Plum. 2010. "Low-Wage Jobs: Stepping Stone or Poverty Trap?" *SOEP Papers on Multidisciplinary Panel Data Research* no. 337. Berlin: Free University Berlin.

Kronberg, Anne-Kathrin. 2013. "Stay or Leave? Externalization of Job Mobility and the Effect on the U.S. Gender Earnings Gap, 1979–2009." *Social Forces* 91(4): 1117–46.

Lambert, Susan J., Julia R. Henly, and Jaeseung Kim. 2019. "Precarious Work Schedules as a Source of Economic Insecurity and Institutional Distrust." *RSF: The Russell Sage Foundation Journal of the Social Sciences* 5(4): 218–57. DOI: 10.7758/RSF.2019.5.4.08.

Latner, Jonathan P. 2018. "Income Volatility and Mobility: A Conceptual Exploration of Two Frameworks." *Research in Social Stratification and Mobility* 53 (February): 50–63.

Long, J. Scott, and Sarah A. Mustillo. 2018. "Using Predictions to Compare Groups in Regression Models for Binary Outcomes." *Sociological Methods & Research*. Published online October 21, 2018. DOI: 10.1177/0049124118799374.

Mason, Geoff, and Wiemer Salverda. 2010. "Low Pay, Working Conditions, and Living Standards." In *Low-Wage Work in the Wealthy World*, edited by Jérôme Gautié and John Schmitt. New York: Russell Sage Foundation.

Massey, Douglas S., and Deborah S. Hirst. 1998. "From Escalator to Hourglass: Changes in the U.S. Occupational Wage Structure 1949–1989." *Social Science Research* 27(1): 51–71.

Maume, David J., and George Wilson. 2015. "Determinants of Declining Wage Mobility in the New Economy." *Work and Occupations* 42(1): 35–72.

McKnight, Abigail, Kitty Stewart, Sam Mohun Himmelweit, and Marco Palillo. 2016. "Low Pay and in-Work Poverty: Preventative Measures and Preventative Approaches." Evidence Review prepared for Employment, Social Affairs and Inclu-

sion, European Commission. Brussels: European Commission.

Mills, Melinda. 2011. *Introducing Survival and Event History Analysis*. Menlo Park, Calif.: Sage Publications.

Mishel, Lawrence, Heidi Shierholz, and John Schmitt. 2013. "Don't Blame the Robots: Accessing the Job Polarization Explanation of Growing Wage Inequality." *EPI* working paper. Washington, D.C.: Economic Policy Institute. Accessed March 19, 2019. https://www.epi.org/publication/technology-inequality-dont-blame-the-robots/.

Mood, Carina. 2010. "Logistic Regression: Why We Can't Do What We Think We Can Do, and What We Can Do About It." *European Sociological Review* 26(1): 67–82.

Mosthaf, Alexander, Claus Shnabel, and Jess Stephani. 2011. "Low-Wage Careers: Are There Dead-End Firms and Dead-End Jobs?" *Zeitschrift für ArbeitsmarktForschung* 43(3): 231–49.

Mouw, Ted, and Arne L. Kalleberg. 2010. "Occupations and the Structure of Wage Inequality in the United States, 1980s–2000." *American Sociological Review* 75(3): 402–31.

———. 2018. "Stepping Stone versus Dead End Jobs: Occupational Pathways out of Working Poverty in the United States, 1996–2012." Working paper. Chapel Hill: University of North Carolina.

Newman, Katharine. 2008. *Chutes and Ladders: Navigating the Low-Wage Labor Market*. Boston, Mass.: Harvard University Press.

Organization for Economic Cooperation and Development (OECD). 2018. *OECD Employment Outlook 2018*. Paris: OECD Publishing.

Pager, Devah. 2007. *Marked: Race, Crime, and Finding Work in an Era of Mass Incarceration*. Chicago: University of Chicago Press.

Panel Study of Income Dynamics (PSID), public use data set. 2018. Ann Arbor: Survey Research Center, Institute for Social Research, University of Michigan.

Pavlopoulos, Dimitris, and Didier Fouarge. 2010. "Escaping Low-Pay: Do Male Labour Market Entrants Stand a Chance?" *International Journal of Manpower* 31(8): 908–27.

Pavlopoulos, Dimitris, Didier Fouarge, Ruud Muffels, and Jeroen K. Vermunt. 2014. "Who Benefits from a Job Change." *European Societies* 16(2): 299–319.

Pedulla, David S. 2013. "The Hidden Costs of Contingency: Employers' Use of Contingent Workers and Standard Employee's Outcomes." *Social Forces* 92(2): 691–722.

Ren, Chunhui. 2019. "Fluctuating Courses and Constant Challenges: The Two Trajectories of Black-White Earnings Inequality, 1968–2015." *Social Science Research* 77(1): 30–44.

Salverda, Wiemer, and Ken Mayhew. 2009. "Capitalist Economies and Wage Inequality." *Oxford Review of Economic Policy* 25(1): 126–54.

Sanders, Carl. 2014. "Skill Uncertainty, Skill Accumulation, and Occupational Choice." Working paper. St. Louis: Washington University/Federal Reserve Bank of St. Louis. Accessed April 3, 2019. https://economics.wustl.edu/files /economics/imce/sandersjobmarketpaper 2010.pdf.

Sandoval, Daniel A., Mark R. Rank, and Thomas A. Hirschl. 2009. "The Increasing Risk of Poverty Across the American Life Course." *Demography* 46(4): 717–37.

Semyonov, Moshe, and Noah Lewin-Epstein. 2009. "The Declining Racial Earnings' Gap in United States: Multi-Level Analysis of Males' Earnings, 1960–2000." *Social Science Research* 38(2): 296–311.

Smith, Chelsea, Robert Crosnoe, and Shih-Yi Chao. 2016. "Family Background and Contemporary Changes in Young Adults' School-Work Transitions and Family Formation in the United States." *Research in Social Stratification and Mobility* 46(1): 3–10.

Sørensen, J. B. 1983. "Processes of Allocation to Open and Closed Positions in Social Structure." *Zeitschrift für Soziologie* 12(3): 203–24.

Stewart, Mark B., and Joanna K. Swaffield. 1999. "Low Pay Dynamics and Transition Probabilities." *Economica* 66(261): 23–42.

VanHeuvelen, Tom. 2018. "Moral Economies or Hidden Talents? A Longitudinal Analysis of Union Decline and Wage Inequality, 1973–2015." *Social Forces* 97(2): 495–530.

Weil, David. 2014. *The Fissured Workplace*. Cambridge, Mass.: Harvard University Press.

Western, Bruce, Deirdre Bloome, Benjamin Sosnaud, and Laura Tach. 2012. "Economic Insecurity and Social Stratification." *Annual Review of Sociology* 38: 341–59.

———. 2016. "Trends in Income Insecurity Among U.S. Children, 1984–2010." *Demography* 53(2): 419–47.

Williams, Richard. 2012. "Using the Margins Command to Estimate and Interpret Adjusted Predictions and Marginal Effects." *Stata Journal* 12(2): 308–33.

Wilson, George, and Vincent J. Roscigno. 2016. "Public Sector Reform and Racial Occupational Mobility." *Work and Occupations* 41(3): 259–93.

Wren, Anne, ed. 2013. *The Political Economy of the Service Transition*. Oxford: Oxford University Press.

Yamaguchi, Shintaro. 2012. "Tasks and Heterogeneous Human Capital." *Journal of Labor Economics* 30(1): 1–53.

Solidarity Within and Across Workplaces: How Cross-Workplace Coordination Affects Earnings Inequality

NATHAN WILMERS

The post–World War II period of wage compression provides a strong contrast to the last forty years of rising inequality. In this article, I argue that inequality was previously constrained by pay coordination that spanned multiple workplaces. Cross-workplace coordination practices range from multi-employer bargaining agreements to informal employer collusion. To quantify the influence of these practices on inequality, I draw on previously unstudied establishment-level Bureau of Labor Statistics microdata from 1968 to 1977. Inequality between workplaces did not increase during the 1970s and inequality was lower among workers likely to be covered by cross-workplace coordination. Unionization, large establishments, and pension provision reduced inequality across workplaces, not only among coworkers within workplaces. These findings indicate that cross-workplace coordination mitigated inequality during the postwar period of egalitarian economic growth.

Keywords: inequality, labor market institutions, wages, organizations, economic sociology

Since the 1970s, real earnings growth for most U.S. workers has sputtered and nearly stalled. At the same time, those at the top of the earnings distribution have enjoyed rapid gains (Song et al. 2018). Together, these trends mean rising earnings inequality amidst an erosion of job quality for the bulk of U.S. workers (Kalleberg 2009). As a result of these divergent earnings trajectories, average income in the bottom half of the income distribution has stagnated at around $16,000 per year since 1980, while overall income has grown 60 per-

cent during the same period (Piketty, Saez, and Zucman 2018).

This upward redistribution of the gains from economic growth stands in contrast to the post–World War II economic boom, during which earnings growth was broadly shared (Bernstein 2016; Kopczuk, Saez, and Song 2010). Part of the rise in inequality is attributable to technological change increasing demand for skills without a sufficient offsetting increase in the supply of educated workers (Goldin and Katz 2008). However, since at least 2000, the col-

Nathan Wilmers is assistant professor of work and organizational studies at the MIT Sloan School of Management.

© 2019 Russell Sage Foundation. Wilmers, Nathan. 2019. "Solidarity Within and Across Workplaces: How Cross-Workplace Coordination Affects Earnings Inequality." *RSF: The Russell Sage Foundation Journal of the Social Sciences* 5(4): 190–215. DOI: 10.7758/RSF.2019.5.4.07. Thank you to Tom Kochan, Tom VanHeuvelen, David Howell, Arne Kalleberg, and participants at the RSF job quality workshop for very helpful comments. Direct correspondence to: Nathan Wilmers at wilmers@mit.edu, Massachusetts Institute of Technology, Sloan School of Management, 100 Main St., Cambridge, MA 02142.

lege wage premium has stabilized while inequality has continued rising (Autor 2017). Moreover, the growth in earnings inequality since 1980 has largely been due to growing earnings differences in pay between firms, as highly paid workers increasingly work together and increasingly work at high-paying paying firms (Song et al. 2018). These patterns lend renewed urgency to research about organizational practices, like increased use of pay for performance compensation, and labor market institutions, like declining labor unions, that could exacerbate inequality (Western and Rosenfeld 2011; Cobb and Stevens 2017; Lemieux 2008). The key to returning to egalitarian growth may lie in reformed organizational and institutional arrangements, rather than in skill supply per se.

Prior research investigating institutional and organizational effects on earnings has emphasized two mechanisms. First, groups of similar workers impose fairness norms among themselves and instigate power struggles inside workplaces that chasten managers and executives—highly paid employees who might otherwise seek yet higher pay for themselves. When these workplace pay norms deteriorate, through a decline in collective bargaining (Western and Rosenfeld 2011; Farber et al. 2018), or due to outsourcing and occupational segregation across workplaces (Handwerker 2018), earnings inequality can increase. Second, direct government regulation of compensation has ebbed since the 1970s. Specifically, early research suggested that minimum wages—which rose little during the 1970s and declined steadily in real terms through the 1980s—played a role in heightening inequality in the 1980s (Lee 1999; Autor, Manning, and Smith 2016). Together, within-workplace fairness norms and government regulation are two mechanisms through which organizational practices and labor market institutions affect earnings and inequality, above and beyond changes in the competitive labor market's fundamental supply and demand for skill.

This vision of institutional earnings effects is bifocal: it sees politics and coordination bubbling up inside the workplace or imposed from above as policy constraint. Lost between micro- and macropolitics is the meso-level of interaction among networks of firms, which could also function to standardize earnings across different workplaces. Research in economic sociology emphasizes the importance of various interactions and connections between firms for a variety of outcomes—in the networked economy (Powell 1990), across noncompeting peer firms (Zuckerman and Sgourev 2006) and among buyers and suppliers (Whitford 2005; Wilmers 2018). Case studies in labor history emphasize how labor market institutions spanning multiple workplaces can yoke together compensation for workers employed at different employers. Indeed, cross-workplace coordination is particularly prominent in studies of wage determination in the kinds of low- and middle-skill jobs that have seen their quality degrade since the 1970s. For example, multiemployer collective bargaining agreements improved working standards in fragmented industries, from longshore and construction trades to garment workers, janitors, truckers, and actors (Hartman 1969; Carpenter 1972; Cobble 1991). Beyond formal multi-employer agreements, qualitative research on local labor markets during postwar wage compression found that tacit pay coordination among manufacturing companies standardized local area wage rates (Reynolds 1951). Among large industrial corporations, the spread of personnel departments focused on wage standardization abetted coordination and standardization across workplaces and companies (Jacoby 2004; Baron, Dobbin, and Jennings 1986). This theoretical and historical warrant justifies renewed attention to the ways that institutions and interactions spanning different workplaces affect earnings inequality.

In this article, I argue that understanding institutional and organizational wage effects—and by extension, understanding rising inequality and declining job quality—require attention to dynamics between workplaces (not just within them or imposed from above by direct government regulation). I draw on economic sociology and institutional labor economics to outline two ways that institutions and norms can affect earnings across different workplaces: through direct formal commitments (such as multi-employer collective bargaining agreements) and through informal pay coordination across workplaces. Rather than government fiat or workgroup solidarity, these cross-workplace processes involve multiparty commitments, workplace-spanning norms and tacit coordination.

To test these ideas about job quality and cross-workplace coordination, I use novel establishment-level survey data from the 1970s to assess the effects of unionization, workplace size, and compensation techniques on between-workplace earnings inequality. This empirical approach allows analysis of labor market institutions during a historical period in which prior research suggests they were particularly important (Goldin and Katz 2008; Kochan and Kimball, forthcoming). This period thus provides a strategic site at which to distinguish different channels through which norms and coordination contributed to pay compression during the post–World War II period. Moreover, these data provide the first series on between-workplace earnings inequality from prior to the 1980s. I contextualize these new data by presenting longer trends in inequality within- and between-employers and discussing implications for research on changes in labor market institutions and employer coordination since the 1970s.

By filling in the cross-workplace meso-level of processes of wage compression, this article contributes to debates around rising inequality and job quality in several ways. First, I use insights from economic sociology and industrial relations about norms and interactions across workplaces to broaden research on institutional and organizational wage effects. Second, I introduce new data from prior to the rise in inequality that allows workplace-level measurement of institutional and organizational sources of pay compression. Unlike studies using more recent data, which infer the effects of institutions and organizational practices through the consequences of their uneven deterioration, this analysis studies the institutional foundations of a relatively egalitarian earnings distribution during a period when these institutions were intact and influential. I can thus distinguish the precise channels through which institutional earnings effects operated.

Future research on the preconditions and risks involved in cross-workplace earnings co-ordination would provide insight about an understudied, but historically important, area for policymakers seeking to revive egalitarian growth. Beyond increasing educational attainment, bolstering single-company unionism or limiting outsourcing and beyond adjustments in the minimum wage, this article shows how cross-workplace coordination mechanisms can shape the earnings distribution.

SOLIDARITY AND REGULATION AS SOURCES OF EQUALITY

Research on institutional and organizational sources of pay compression focuses on two sources: workgroup solidarity and government regulation. In the former channel, social norms and solidarity within firms and within workplaces reduce inequality. In the latter channel, direct government regulation imposes minimum wages and standards on firms. I first outline theory and research on these two sources. Later, I specify the third, understudied, class of pay compression channels, which hinge on agreements and norms between workplaces.

A long tradition in organizational sociology and institutional labor economics attributes deviations from market wages to power struggles inside workplaces and companies. In Alvin Gouldner's study of bureaucratization, the informal solidarity of underground gypsum miners undermines managerial attempts at disciplining workers (1954). The solidaristic work group also grounded Hugh Clegg's theory of labor union power, according to which groups of similar workers use collective action to improve their working conditions (1972). A recent programmatic restatement describes the distinctive view of institutional labor economics as "organizations are characterized by groups with competing objectives and perspectives" (Osterman 2011, 640). Informal norms and processes of group conflict within a workplace ground institutional wage determination in intuitive ideas about small group cohesion and power.

Building on this research tradition, an influential explanation for recent increases in earnings inequality emphasizes the decline of group bargaining power dynamics and solidaristic processes within workplaces and companies. This argument proceeds from two directions.

First, pay-setting processes within organizations appear increasingly responsive to labor market prices. The spread of variable compensation links worker pay to individual performance (Lemieux, MacLeod, and Parent 2009). Norms that previously constrained executive pay have eroded (Piketty and Saez 2003). The decline of labor unions is associated with increased within-firm inequality between workers and executives (Rosenfeld 2006; Freeman 1984). For lower-paid workers, the pay premium associated with working at a large firm has been steadily declining since at least the late 1980s (Cobb and Lin 2017). The messy conflicts and loyalties of work group wage determination appear to be melting into a competitive labor market that sets wages according to skill.

Second, organizations appear increasingly homogenous with respect to their workers' skills, occupation, and education level (Weil 2014). When companies outsource low-wage work, earnings decline for affected workers (Goldschmidt and Schmieder 2017; Dube and Kaplan 2010). As workplace fissuring separates workers in different occupations and with different skill levels across employers, fairness norms and rent sharing have less influence over wages. When pay differences align with firm boundaries, within-firm compression effects are avoided. The work group, with its attendant politics, fairness norms, and comparison groups, is thus receding in importance as a force mitigating wage inequality. This is due to both increased penetration of market-driven wage determination and an increasingly fragmented employment structure.

Beyond intra-organizational fairness norms, researchers have also considered the effects of changing government policy on inequality. Most prominently, the declining real value of the federal minimum wage contributed to stagnating wages and inequality in the bottom of the earnings distribution (Lee 1999; Autor, Manning, and Smith 2016). Declining minimum wages are a direct reduction in regulatory intervention in the wage distribution. Indirect government policies have also been important. Increased international trade penetration, deregulation, increased low-wage immigration, and lowered top income taxes have all contributed to rising earnings inequality (Alderson and Nielsen 2002; Autor, Dorn, and Hanson 2013; Fortin and Lemieux 1997; Card 2009; Piketty and Saez 2003).

These pathways of workplace fairness norms and government policy intervention, coupled with changing supply and demand for skill (discussed later) provide powerful explanations for inequality dynamics. But they leave open several puzzles. First, if outsourcing is a way to successfully avoid costly internal fairness norms, why would companies wait until the 1980s to begin outsourcing? A possible explanation is that cross-workplace agreements lowered incentives to outsource prior to the 1980s (but see also Autor 2003). Second, if norms exist within workplaces, why would they not exist across workplaces? Given findings in economic sociology about the importance of firm identity and interactions with peers and competitors (White 1981; Zuckerman and Sgourev 2006), wage norms, comparisons and coordination are likely to exist across as well as within workplaces. Third, if establishment-level collective bargaining agreements compress earnings within a workplace, multi-employer collective bargaining agreements should compress earnings across multiple workplaces. Addressing these dilemmas in the current institutional-organizational account of earnings inequality requires more careful consideration of the third channel of organizational and institutional earnings effects: cross-workplace coordination.

EARNINGS COORDINATION ACROSS WORKPLACES

Cross-workplace wage coordination practices fall along a spectrum of more and less formal commitments across workplaces and employers. The most formal are multi-employer collective bargaining agreements. Unions also spur more tacit coordination processes, such as pattern bargaining and coercive comparison. Beyond unions, informal coordination among large establishments can stem from the social order of product markets and embeddedness emphasized by economic sociologists, or via professionalized compensation practices from human resources and personnel departments. Through all of these processes, earnings differences across workplaces are muted due to in-

stitutional constraints and organizational practices. In the following section, I outline these
coordination processes and formulate predictions about the effects of organizational practices and labor market institutions on inequality both within and between workplaces.

As noted earlier, collective bargaining
heightens and reflects within-firm workgroup
solidarity. But unions can also compress pay
between different workplaces (Western and
Rosenfeld 2011). Comparative research finds
that coordinated, industry-wide collective bargaining restricts inequality (Wallerstein 1999).
In the U.S. context, multi-employer bargaining
was widespread up to the 1980s in industries
ranging from construction and trucking to retail and hotels. Multi-employer bargaining is
particularly important in industries with many
fragmented employers who join together in employer associations to bargain with a union (Slichter, Healey, and Livernash 1960). In project-
based industries like construction or media
production, multi-employer contracts allow
standardized wage and benefit schedules even
as union members experience frequent moves
across employers. Unions representing these
workers sought to implement contracts that
would cover all members in a local labor market in a given occupation, such as building
trades or waitress unions (Cobble 1991), or industry, such as garment and other needle
trades (Carpenter 1972). In trucking and entertainment unions, these multi-employer agreements were national in scope.

In manufacturing, practices of pattern bargaining involved provisions bargained in a lead
contract setting a pattern of wage and benefits
standards for subsequent agreements in peer
employers represented by the same union or
operating in the same sector (Budd 1992). More
broadly, Arthur Ross identifies various levels of
"orbits of coercive comparison" ranging from
competitor firms within national product markets to rivalries between officials in different
unions, each of which originate pressures to
coordinate wage setting across groups of workers (1948). By activating equity concerns beyond
individual workplaces, these orbits of comparison serve to compress average wages among
unionized workplaces.

In both the formal multi-employer agreements and the less formal processes of pattern
bargaining and coercive comparison, unionization is expected to reduce cross-workplace inequality. Consistent with a union wage premium, these agreements will also tend to
increase wages among unionized workplaces
(however, even given higher average pay, some
of the most productive or profitable covered
workplaces could still receive lower pay than if
their wages were set independently). In this
way, collective bargaining can also heighten inequality between union and non-union firms.
In some cases union threat effects can lead
non-union companies to adopt union-level pay
scales (Farber 2005). But, in general, if pay compression in the union sector comes in part from
increased wages, then the growing gap between
union and non-union firms can heighten inequality (Rees 1962). This is particularly true
when comparing unionized companies to companies in other industries and geographical regions: some non-union companies face little
union threat.

Another informal source of cross-workplace
earnings coordination is normative pressures
exercised among employers directly. For example, in Lloyd Reynolds's classic study of the
1950s New Haven labor market, he finds employers who believe it is "not ethical to pay too
high a wage. . . . If you do, you will end up in
the same position as the gasoline stations who
indulge in excessive price cutting" (1951, 160).
Very small workplaces are more likely to fly under the radar of these normative pressures than
large workplaces are. Another 1950s labor market study, in Trenton, New Jersey, finds that
"gentlemen's" hiring codes against "labor pirat-
ing" were particularly strong in larger workplaces (Lester 1954, 63–64). There are two reasons for this. First, large workplaces are more
prominent and their wage-setting decisions are
more likely to be visible to peer workplaces. Research in economic sociology emphasizes the
ways that large and visible establishments set
patterns for their peers and competitors (White
1981; Podolny 2010). Second, assuming some
critical mass and tipping point dynamics of employee coordination are needed to maintain a
wage norm, it is easier for a small number of

Table 1. Predicted Inequality Effects of Labor-Market Institutions and Organizational Practices

	Within Firm	Among Similar Firms	Premium
Union	−	−	+
Large workplace	−	−	?
Pension	−	−	+
Performance pay	+	+	+

Source: Author's.

large workplaces to collude and coordinate earnings than for the many small workplaces that would be needed for the norm to cover enough workers. Normative pay coordination among employers at large workplaces is thus stronger than among small workplaces.

The stable, visible position of large workplaces leads them to transmit less variability in earnings for employees across workplaces. Unlike collective bargaining-driven coordination, however, these normative processes need not be associated with higher earnings for workers. As the Reynolds statement indicates, employers can use cross-workplace coordination to restrain earnings growth. Although these practices tend to be informal, some companies sign nonpoaching and noncompete agreements that can facilitate collusive reductions in worker earnings (Starr, Prescott, and Bishara 2018). Of course, research finds that large companies pay a premium (Cobb and Lin 2017). Less research, however, has considered the workplace-size effect. Thus the prediction of the effect of working at a large workplace on earnings is ambiguous.

Finally, beyond unionization and size, organizations' choices among compensation practices can also affect inequality. Variable compensation and bonuses can increase inequality (Lemieux, MacLeod, and Parent 2009). Variable compensation could increase inequality within establishments (if bonuses are tied to individual or team performance) or across establishments (if bonuses are tied to workplace-wide performance), or both. On the other hand, other compensation practices could decrease inequality. Specifically, workplaces that offer defined benefit pensions are required to offer pension coverage widely and pay benefits relatively equally, due to Internal Revenue Service

regulations designed to prevent employers from skewing pensions only to highly paid executives (Clark, Mulvey, and Schieber 2004). Beyond these within-workplace equality effects, pension provision can serve as a coordination mechanism: pension provision (particularly in the 1970s, when defined benefit pensions were at their zenith) is a large, observable portion of compensation, signaling workplaces with formalized personnel and human resources practices. In this way, the rise of nonwage compensation could actually diminish cross-workplace inequality (Dobbin 1992).

Table 1 summarizes these predicted effects of labor market institutions and organizational practices on different axes of inequality. Several labor market institutions are predicted to compress pay within workplaces and among similar workplaces, while also providing pay premiums that can heighten inequality between groups of workplaces.

CONTROLLING FOR COMPETITIVE LABOR MARKET FORCES

Alongside these various channels of institutional and organizational effects on pay, supply, and demand in the labor market are key determinants of workers' pay. In this article, I focus on clarifying how labor market institutions affect earnings, rather than on decomposing changing inequality into components due to institutions and skill supply (Western and Rosenfeld 2011; Lemieux 2008). Nonetheless, it is critical to control as much as possible for the effect of market forces on earnings in order to identify institutional and organizational features that affect earnings inequality. I address this issue with several strategies.

First, I focus on a period in which rising demand for skill did not translate into an increasing college-wage premium or rising inequality.[1] Most research on inequality focuses on the period after 1980, in which labor market institutions deteriorated, skill demand outpaced supply, and inequality grew—all simultaneously. The 1970s, by contrast, presents a case in which even proponents of skill supply explanations acknowledge that although demand for skill had already outpaced the supply of college graduates, inequality did not rise (Goldin and Katz 2008). This choice of period does not lend itself to quantifying the general importance of institutional compared to skill supply and demand determinants of inequality. It does, however, offer a strategic setting for understanding how institutional and organizational constraints affect the earnings distribution during a period of strong apparent institutional influence.

However, even if skill supply and demand were not shaping the overall national trend in earnings inequality during this period, it is likely that subnational variation in skill supply influenced pay: some regions could be undersupplied with educated workers and some industries could be particularly rapid adopters of skill-biased technology. To address this concern, I condition on the industry and region in which workplaces operate. This strategy addresses concerns about subnational variation insofar as market-driven inequality is common within regions or within industries.

Nonetheless, in some cases, significant within-region or within-industry variation in labor demand can exist. To address this possibility, I proxy for microlevel skill supply and demand by controlling for the share of managerial compared to production employment within each workplace. Insofar as the share of managerial workers tracks the implementation of skill-biased technology, this approach corrects for firm-specific labor demand.

This comparison of production to nonpro-

duction workers is similar to prior work using historical labor market data, which compares clerk earnings to unskilled laborers (Goldin and Margo 1992, see table VII for a summary of sources). Still, it hinges on the assumption that rough categories of managerial and production workers capture key differences in skill. In a supplementary analysis, I merge industry-level measures of organizational and institutional pay determinants into individual-level worker data. This allows a direct test of whether heterogeneity in skill, measured by educational attainment, explains institutional pay compression.

Taken together, these multiple strategies for holding constant skill supply and demand allow a research design that focuses on how institutional and organizational, rather than market-driven, inequality functions. But, despite this research design, it is likely that sorting on unobserved worker characteristics drives some of the variation in inequality modeled in the following section. I consider the implications of this sorting more thoroughly in the discussion.

DATA

I draw on workplace-level microdata from the Employer Expenditure for Employee Compensation (EEEC) surveys from 1968, 1970, 1972, 1974, 1976, and 1977.[2] These microdata have not previously been used to study inequality. As far as I know, they are the only U.S., nationally representative, workplace-level wage or earnings data series available from before the 1980s. They were acquired from the National Archives and had to be recoded from a combined Packed BCD (binary-coded decimal) and EBCDIC (extended binary coded decimal interchange code) format into a usable text format.

The EEEC data are based on workplace-level surveys of nonfarm employers that ask about employee compensation costs the respondent

1. As Claudia Goldin and Lawrence Katz put it in their canonical study of wage inequality and the supply and demand for skill: "But where supply-demand forces fall a bit flat, institutional factors can reconcile patterns in the skill premium. In that sense we combine the usual supply and demand framework with institutional rigidities and alterations. The broader framework is most important in understanding wage structure changes during the 1940s and in contrasting changes from the mid- to late 1970s to those of the early 1980s" (2008, 293).

2. The first survey covering the full nonfarm economy was fielded in 1968. After 1977, the survey was redesigned. The only years available from the National Archives are 1968 through 1977.

employers face. The sample frames were drawn from state unemployment insurance records and sampling was stratified by employment, industry, and geographical location (BLS 1971, 1974). The Bureau of Labor Statistics calculates survey weights based on sampling probability and correcting for nonresponse. However, these weights aim to be representative for employers rather than for workers. Because the latter is the relevant population for studying earnings inequality, I adjust the BLS weights by multiplying by the total hours compensated by each employer.

The survey asks about compensation separately by office and non-office employees. Office employees include all managerial, professional or clerical workers; non-office employees include all other workers, from production to janitorial to retail sales. Proprietors and unpaid family workers are excluded from the survey (BLS 1971, 1974). This distinction between office and non-office employees allows the rough control for workplace-specific skill composition introduced above.

Using these data, it is also possible to compare earnings and other compensation costs within workplaces between office and production employees. It is also possible to compare earnings levels among workplaces that participate in a given institutional or organizational condition that could affect average earnings at the workplace (such as the union earnings premium or the workplace-size premium). Finally, the data can be used to compare the degree of residual between-workplace inequality among workplaces covered by an institutional condition or organizational practice and those not covered. This final comparison provides the core test of the idea that cross-workplace earnings coordination reduces inequality. I specify more precisely the models needed to capture these various facets of inequality below.

Table 2 shows variable means from across waves of the EEEC. The weighted data are disproportionately composed of manufacturing firms (42 percent to 37 percent in these data, versus 27 percent to 22 percent from the Current Employment Statistics data). It is unclear from the historical BLS codebooks whether this manufacturing oversample was by design or whether it reflects problems in sampling strategy. During the 1960s, the EEEC was steadily broadened from a focus on manufacturing to include more and more service-sector establishments. This manufacturing oversample may be a holdover from this sampling strategy. Regardless, the data also include substantial portions of construction, transportation and utilities, retail and service workplaces. Over time, consistent with changes in the industry composition of the economy overall, FIRE and services become more prominent in the data. In a robustness test, I present results with weights adjusted for industry representativeness.

The EEEC can be used to construct several measures of worker pay, including average annual earnings, hourly wages, and overall compensation. I focus on logged overall annual compensation, defined as annual worker pay in the form of direct wage earnings, employer pension contributions, paid leave, and bonuses. Recent research shows that including nonwage forms of payment affects patterns in inequality (Piketty, Saez, and Zucman 2018). Because the EEEC is an employer-directed survey, asking about all costs incurred by employers to compensate workers, it is well suited to capture these nonwage payments that are neglected in worker-directed labor market surveys. I deflate average annual compensation with the consumer price index for all urban consumers; table 2 shows that after some earnings growth from 1968 to 1974, earnings slowed from 1974 to 1977, consistent with the onset of an overall pay slowdown beginning during this period.

The EEEC includes several measures that correspond to the organizational and institutional concepts discussed previously. First, the survey asks whether there is collective bargaining at a given workplace. Table 2 shows that between 38 and 45 percent of employment is at workplaces with some collective bargaining agreement. This percentage is rightly higher than estimates from household-based surveys, as workplaces all include employees that are not covered by a collective bargaining agreement.

Second, workplaces are categorized according to their size: fewer than twenty employees, twenty to ninety-nine, one hundred to 499, and

Table 2. Descriptive Statistics

	1968		1970		1972		1974		1976		1977	
	Mean	SD	Mean	SD	Mean	SD	Mean	SD	Mean	SD	Mean	SD
log(average annual compensation)	10.20	0.48	10.26	0.44	10.28	0.44	10.41	0.45	10.43	0.40	10.41	0.43
Union	0.44	0.50	0.45	0.50	0.37	0.48	0.40	0.49	0.45	0.50	0.38	0.49
Establishment size: < 20	0.21	0.41	0.18	0.39	0.22	0.42	0.08	0.28	0.01	0.11	0.06	0.24
Establishment size: 20–99	0.25	0.43	0.24	0.43	0.27	0.44	0.32	0.47	0.28	0.45	0.33	0.47
Establishment size: 100–499	0.23	0.42	0.22	0.42	0.23	0.42	0.27	0.44	0.27	0.44	0.30	0.46
Establishment size: 500+	0.31	0.46	0.35	0.48	0.28	0.45	0.32	0.47	0.44	0.50	0.31	0.46
Pension	0.05	0.21	0.71	0.45	0.67	0.47	0.75	0.43	0.80	0.40	0.76	0.43
Bonuses	0.40	0.49	0.37	0.48	0.33	0.47	0.39	0.49	0.37	0.48	0.35	0.48
Share office workers	0.30	0.30	0.34	0.32	0.35	0.32	0.33	0.35	0.34	0.35	0.35	0.37
Weekly hours	38	8	39	8	38	7	40	12	39	10	39	10
Metro area	0.06	0.23	0.55	0.50	0.51	0.50	0.78	0.42	0.76	0.43	0.73	0.44
Employees	1,597	4,664	1,964	5,369	877	2,173	94	221	1,973	6,084	135	429
Northeast	0.28	0.45	0.28	0.45	0.26	0.44	0.27	0.44	0.22	0.41	0.26	0.44
South	0.27	0.44	0.26	0.44	0.29	0.45	0.27	0.44	0.26	0.44	0.27	0.44
Midwest	0.29	0.45	0.31	0.46	0.31	0.46	0.32	0.47	0.35	0.48	0.32	0.47
West	0.16	0.37	0.15	0.36	0.14	0.35	0.15	0.36	0.16	0.37	0.16	0.36
Mining	0.01	0.12	0.02	0.12	0.02	0.12	0.02	0.12	0.01	0.11	0.02	0.14
Construction	0.06	0.24	0.07	0.25	0.06	0.23	0.06	0.23	0.03	0.16	0.04	0.20
Manufacturing	0.42	0.49	0.42	0.49	0.37	0.48	0.41	0.49	0.43	0.50	0.37	0.48
Transportation and utilities	0.09	0.29	0.10	0.30	0.08	0.27	0.08	0.27	0.13	0.34	0.09	0.29
Wholesale	0.05	0.23	0.06	0.24	0.06	0.25	0.08	0.27	0.05	0.22	0.06	0.24
Retail	0.14	0.34	0.12	0.33	0.16	0.37	0.13	0.33	0.12	0.32	0.14	0.35
FIRE	0.06	0.24	0.08	0.27	0.07	0.26	0.08	0.27	0.08	0.28	0.09	0.28
Services	0.16	0.37	0.14	0.35	0.18	0.38	0.15	0.36	0.15	0.35	0.19	0.39
N	4,258		3,752		5,015		3,747		1,813		2,681	

Source: Author's analysis based on the EEEC.

more than five hundred. Table 2 shows that though much of the size distribution remains constant over time, a drop-off is evident for the smallest workplaces (fewer than twenty employees) after 1972. The BLS methods books do not indicate any change in sampling approach at this time, but it is likely that this reduction in small workplaces is attributable to sampling strategy.

Much previous research on employer-size wage effects has focused on the size of the parent company rather than the size of the immediate workplace. But, insofar as wage determination happens within local labor markets, workplace size could also be important. A subset of survey years include information on affiliation with a larger parent company. In a robustness check, which follows, I test whether workplace size remains important, conditional on connection to a larger company.

Finally, workplaces are asked how much of total compensation is paid in the form of retirement and bonus payments. Using this compensation information, I construct a binary indicator showing whether a workplace pays pension or bonus payments.[3] Consistent with the discussion, I expect that bonus payments, as a form of variable compensation, will be associated with increased inequality, while pension payments will be associated with pay compression.

In addition to these main variables of interest, I construct controls for the share of office workers out of total employment, average weekly hours, metropolitan-nonmetropolitan location, Standard Industrial Classification (SIC) two-digit industry, year, and census region. These controls aim to adjust for the influence on earnings and inequality of different production technologies and local labor market settings and allow comparison across similar workplaces with different organizational practices and varying exposure to labor market institutions. However, a limitation of the EEEC data is that few other controls (particularly for worker composition) are available.

INEQUALITY IN THE 1970S
During the 1970s inflation and productivity stagnation marked a strong break from the rapid economic growth of the 1960s (Stein 2011). However, the Current Population Survey (CPS) indicates that earnings inequality actually held fairly steady, as the costs of economic recession and turmoil were shared across the earnings distribution (Western and Rosenfeld 2011). Data from the March CPS in figure 1 show that earnings variance increases steadily from the late 1970s, but was stable from 1968 to 1977. Household surveys like the CPS, however, do not distinguish earnings inequality between and within workplaces, which is important for testing the proposed theory.

The longest linked employer-employee data for the United States, the Social Security Administration (SSA) data, begins in 1978. Figure 1 shows that since 1980 both within- and between-firm earnings inequality have increased. This increase is particularly rapid between firms, which accounts for two thirds of increased inequality during this period. However, figure 1 also shows that the SSA data document declines in between- and within-firm inequality during its brief, pre-1980 coverage, from 1978 to 1980.

In figure 1, I also present the first between-workplace (or establishment) earnings inequality series available for the 1970s, based on the EEEC. Figure 1 shows that between-workplace annual earnings inequality declined steadily during the 1970s. The variance of logged earnings was around 0.23 in 1968 and declined around 20 percent to 0.18 by 1977. This level is slightly lower than the 0.25 with which the SSA series begins. This difference could be due to sample adjustments made to the SSA series (such as keeping only full-time workers). Other trends from the EEEC, not pictured here, show that hourly wage and hourly compensation measures of inequality also held steady during the 1970s (but did not decrease). The within-workplace ratio between office and non-office workers also held steady during the period.

3. Another approach here would be to use a continuous variable indicating the amount of compensation received as a bonus or as retirement payments. However, bonus and retirement payments are included as part of the overall compensation predicted as the dependent variable.

Figure 1. Earnings Inequality Between Workplaces Declined in the 1970s, Increased Since 1980

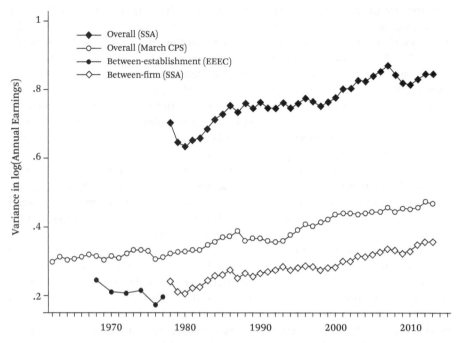

Source: Author's analysis based on the Social Security Administration earnings series (Song et al. 2018) and CPS data (Autor, Katz, and Kearney 2008).
Note: The SSA data include firms in private-sector-dominant industries and those making about a certain minimum threshold ($3,770 in 2013). March CPS data are restricted to private-sector, full-time, full-year workers, defined as working thirty-five hours and higher per week and at least forty weeks in the last year. For comparability with the SSA data, workers making less than $3,770 per year are excluded. EEEC data include private-sector establishments and are discussed in text.

These trends show, consistent with prior research, that earnings inequality overall did not increase until the 1980s. They also show, for the first time, that this pattern holds not only overall but also between workplaces. In the analysis that follows I ask which organizational and institutional pathways constrained inequality during this period. To do so, I delve deeper into the EEEC data to focus on variation in inequality and earnings across more and less institutionally and organizationally constrained workplaces.

METHODS

To study institutional and organizational effects on earnings inequality in more detail, I use two approaches: an ordinary least squares model of within-workplace pay ratios and a variance function regression model of between-workplace variance. The model of within-

workplace pay ratios allows institutional and organizational inequality effects to be measured where prior research most expects to find them: on the division of economic surplus between managerial and nonmanagerial employees within the same workplace. The variance function regression model, in contrast, is well suited to testing, first, differences in average pay among workplaces covered and not covered by labor market institutions and, second, between-workplace variance among workplaces participating in institutional and organizational coordination conditions relative to those that are not participating.

For the within-workplace model, I predict the ratio of logged pay for office relative to non-office production employees, similar to prior research on the CEO-to-worker pay ratio (Shin 2014). Because office workers tend to be managers, executives, and clerks, this approach captures an important dimension of within-workplace inequality. I first calculate the pay ratio as $log(w_{oi}/w_{pi})$, for office o to production p workers in each establishment i. I then model this ratio as a function of a vector, x_i', of labor market institutions and organizational characteristics predicted to affect within-workplace earnings inequality: union presence, workplace size, and pension and bonus compensation. I also include a vector of controls, z_i', for the share of office workers out of total employment, average weekly hours, metropolitan-nonmetropolitan location and SIC two-digit industry, year, and census region dummies:

$$log(w_{oi}/w_{pi}) = \pi_1 x_i' + \pi_1 z_i' + e_i. \qquad (1)$$

Ideally the controls in z_i' would adjust for any confounding influences that could influence both inequality and coverage by labor market institutions. Unfortunately, the EEEC data include limited information on each workplace. Most important, the EEEC does not include information on the composition of individual workers aside from the rough share of office workers out of total employment. Estimated π_1 effects should therefore be interpreted as a total effect of differences in pay for similar workers (such as through rent sharing) along with the degree of sorting of different workers across workplaces and job type categories. These two dimensions are likely intertwined: if a union forces an employer to pay managers less and unionized production workers more, it is likely that, over time, the employer will be able to hire only relatively lower-quality managers and perhaps higher-quality production workers. Prior work that includes worker fixed effects in analysis of firm size and union wage premiums finds that effects of institutional and organizational pay premiums persist even conditional on unobserved, time-invariant worker selection (Cobb and Lin 2017; Freeman 1984; Gittleman and Kleiner 2016). Nonetheless, unobserved worker sorting should be considered part of these estimates (as well as in the models that follow).

Second, I fit a variance function regression used in prior research on earnings inequality (Western and Rosenfeld 2011; Wilmers 2017; VanHeuvelen 2018). These models allow both the between-group and within-group components of between-workplace inequality to vary as a function of covariates. For example, as noted, collective bargaining agreements are associated with a union wage premium for union relative to non-union companies. But, consistent with the predictions about cross-workplace earnings coordination and multi-employer collective bargaining, inequality could be lower among union companies than among non-union companies. The variance function regression allows both of these effects to be modeled.

First, I predict logged earnings w_i, for all workers in workplace i:

$$w_i = \beta_1 x_i' + \beta_2 z_i' + e_i, \qquad (2)$$

where x_i' is the vector of labor market institutions and organizational practices; w_i' includes the controls noted. The estimates in β_1 indicate pay gaps between workplaces with different exposure to labor market institutions. For example, the workplace-wide wage premium associated with unionization is captured in these models. Likewise, larger workplaces and workplaces with retirement benefits are expected to offer higher compensation than small workplaces and those without retirement benefits. This equation of mean earnings at the workplace level thus captures differences in compensation between workplaces participating in these organizational and institutional categories relative to workplaces not covered by those categories. By controlling for z_i', this model also removes any variability in earnings attributable to a workplace's share of office workers out of total employment, average weekly hours, metropolitan-nonmetropolitan location and industry, year, and census region. As in other models of mean earnings, this means that x_i' coefficients are estimated conditional on these workplace characteristics. But it also means that the variation remaining in the residuals e_i has been stripped of inequality arising from differences in average pay across characteristics like industries, regions, and office–non-office workplace composition.

The next equation models the residuals from equation (2) to predict conditional variances:

$$log(\sigma_i^2) = \lambda_1 x_i' + \lambda_2 z_i', \qquad (3)$$

where σ_i is the residual from the mean earnings equation. I model this within-group variance using participation in labor market institutions and organizational characteristics, x_i' and the controls just introduced, w_i'. The estimates in λ_1 indicate the degree to which organizations participating in similar organizational practices and labor market institutions have more similar earnings relative to workplaces that do not participate in those institutions. This between-workplace dimension of inequality is the type expected to be governed by cross-workplace coordination processes. Workplaces covered by labor market institutions or with organizational features that make coordination likely should have lower inequality among them than workplaces outside those coordination circuits. For example, there should be less pay inequality among workplaces in a given region and industry that are unionized than among workplaces that are not unionized.

Taken together, these models capture the effects of labor market institutions and organizational characteristics on each of the three types of inequality discussed—inequality between types of employees within the same workplace, pay differences between different workplaces, and varying levels of inequality across peer workplaces.

FINDINGS

Table 3 presents the models of the ratio of office to production worker earnings. These models provide evidence on the influence of institutions and organizational practices on within-workplace inequality, which is the main axis of inequality considered in research on fairness norms and pay compression. Coefficients are sensitive to including EEEC survey weights in the model, so both weighted and unweighted models are presented in table 3.

Table 3 shows that collective bargaining is consistently associated with a lower office to production worker pay gap across both weighted and unweighted models. Conditional on controls, including industry, region, and office worker share, the office to production worker gap is around 10 percent to 15 percent smaller in union relative to non-union work-

places. Consistent with prior research and with theories of workgroup solidarity and fairness norms, unions are associated with a smaller gap between production and office employees in the same workplace.

Workplace size patterns are more ambiguous. The smallest workplaces (fewer than twenty employees) have the narrowest office to production worker pay ratios. However, relative to midsize workplaces (twenty to 499 employees), the largest workplaces have a smaller gap. This nonlinearity is consistent with work that emphasizes the pay-compressing effect of the largest, most bureaucratized organizations. It could also indicate more salient fairness norms imposed across workers and managers in smaller workplaces. Of course, apparent effects of workplace size can also involve a fixed level of inequality shifting within and between workplaces: if small workplaces achieve low inequality by outsourcing low-pay occupations, and larger workplaces concentrate more variety of occupations, then similar variability in pay across tasks can result from shifting tasks across organizational boundaries.

Finally, pay practices have mixed influences on within-workplace inequality. The relationship between a higher share of compensation costs in pension payments and pay gaps appears negative, as predicted, but is not robust to controls. Performance pay or bonus compensation, by contrast, is generally associated with a small increase in pay gaps.

Overall, these models of within-workplace pay inequality support prior research showing the importance of labor market institutions and organizational practices on pay compression within workplaces. These associations between labor market institutions and within-workplace pay compression, usually studied in more recent data, did indeed hold in the 1970s.

Next, I turn to the variance function regression results, which estimate the effects of labor market institutions and organizational characteristics on pay differences between groups of workplaces and on varying levels of inequality within groups of workplaces.

Table 4 presents results of the variance function regression models predicting average hourly compensation across all employees within each workplace. The β coefficients show

Table 3. Institutional and Organizational Effects on Within-Workplace Inequality

	Weighted		Unweighted	
	(1)	(2)	(3)	(4)
Union	-0.173***	-0.103***	-0.205***	-0.133***
	(0.009)	(0.010)	(0.010)	(0.010)
Establishment size: 20–99	0.258***	0.259***	0.323***	0.305***
	(0.014)	(0.014)	(0.016)	(0.015)
Establishment size: 100–499	0.248***	0.235***	0.374***	0.297***
	(0.015)	(0.015)	(0.017)	(0.016)
Establishment size: 500+	0.143***	0.164***	0.242***	0.190***
	(0.015)	(0.015)	(0.018)	(0.017)
Pension	-0.047***	-0.016	-0.052***	-0.018
	(0.012)	(0.012)	(0.014)	(0.013)
Bonuses	0.025**	0.030***	0.007	0.039***
	(0.009)	(0.008)	(0.009)	(0.009)
Share office workers		-0.290***		-0.437***
		(0.021)		(0.023)
Weekly hours		-0.018***		-0.020***
		(0.001)		(0.001)
Metro		0.042***		0.077***
		(0.010)		(0.009)
Constant	0.257***	0.911***	0.371***	1.006***
	(0.014)	(0.041)	(0.017)	(0.043)
R-squared	0.059	0.165	0.087	0.235
Year effects	Yes	Yes	Yes	Yes
Industry effects		Yes		Yes
Region effects		Yes		Yes
Observations	14,325	14,325	14,325	14,325

Source: Author's analysis based on the EEEC.
Note: Outcome is the office to production worker compensation ratio. Standard errors in parentheses. Workplaces with only office or only production employees are excluded from the models.
*p < .05; **p < .01; ***p < .001 (two-tailed tests)

that all measures of labor market institutions and organizational practices are associated with workplace-level wage premiums: workers in unionized workplaces, large workplaces, and workplaces with pensions and bonuses all earn a compensation premium relative to workers in other workplaces. However, consistent with the ambiguous prediction on workplace size, earnings do not increase linearly for larger workplaces. Although workplaces with more than twenty employees have consistently higher earnings, the differences between medium-sized workplaces (between twenty to ninety-nine and one hundred to 499 employees) and large workplaces (five hundred or more em-

ployees) are small and sensitive to controls. Nonetheless, these results overall suggest that the kinds of organizational practices and labor market institutions associated with lower within-workplace inequality are also associated with higher average earnings at the workplace level.

Table 4 also includes estimates of the conditional residual variances: these estimates indicate how levels of between-workplace inequality vary among workplaces covered by labor market institutions relative to those not covered. These λ coefficients show that unions, large workplaces, and pension provision are associated with lower residual inequality. In-

Table 4. Institutional and Organizational Effects on Workplace Earnings and Between-Workplace Inequality

	(1)		(2)	
	β	λ	β	λ
Union	0.210***	−0.505***	0.132***	−0.087**
	(0.006)	(0.030)	(0.004)	(0.032)
Establishment size: 20–99	0.058***	−0.012	0.033***	−0.127***
	(0.010)	(0.041)	(0.007)	(0.038)
Establishment size: 100–499	0.019	−0.139**	−0.002	−0.294***
	(0.010)	(0.044)	(0.007)	(0.043)
Establishment size: 500+	0.087***	−0.624***	0.042***	−0.714***
	(0.009)	(0.043)	(0.007)	(0.044)
Pension	0.233***	−0.369***	0.115***	−0.124***
	(0.008)	(0.039)	(0.005)	(0.030)
Bonuses	0.064***	−0.130***	0.017***	0.010
	(0.005)	(0.028)	(0.004)	(0.027)
Share office workers			0.591***	0.227***
			(0.008)	(0.048)
Weekly hours			0.027***	−0.010***
			(0.000)	(0.001)
Metro			0.045***	0.066*
			(0.004)	(0.028)
Constant	9.984***	−1.228***	9.075***	−1.929***
	(0.008)	(0.038)	(0.018)	(0.117)
R-squared	0.197		0.625	
Year effects	Yes	Yes	Yes	Yes
Industry effects			Yes	Yes
Region effects			Yes	Yes
Observations	21,266	21,266	21,266	21,266

Source: Author's analysis based on the EEEC.
Note: All estimates are β and λ coefficients from the variance function regression, predicting mean and variances of logged annual compensation. Standard errors are in parentheses and were calculated using the iterated weighting procedure described in the text.
*p < .05; **p < .01; ***p < .001 (two-tailed tests)

equality in average compensation is less among unionized workplaces and larger workplaces than among non-union workplaces and smaller workplaces. These variance patterns refer to residual or within-group inequality, after earnings differences across regions, industries, and other attributes are controlled out. Similarly, these patterns persist even with controls for conditional variances: if unionization tends to occur in industries or regions that have less earnings inequality, controls for industry and region in the variance equation correct for it. The λ coefficients should thus be interpreted

as conditional, within-group, or residual earnings variances between workplaces. The union pay compression coefficient shrinks when controls are included, but remains negative and statistically significant. Unlike the mean estimates for establishment-size earnings effects, which do not increase linearly, the between-establishment earnings variances associated with larger establishments are progressively more negative. This pattern is consistent with greater informal, cross-workplace earnings coordination among larger workplaces.

Contrary to predictions, the organizational

practice expected to increase between-workplace inequality—variable compensation—is not associated with higher variance. In the results presented later, variable compensation does increase between-workplace inequality for office employees. This difference in effects between office and production workers could reflect the quite different character of bonuses for each group.

Overall, the results of the conditional variance analysis demonstrate that labor market institutions and organizational practices affect inequality between workplaces in addition to within workplaces. This between-workplace pay compression is the type predicted by the presence of cross-workplace pay coordination practices.

ROBUSTNESS CHECKS AND ALTERNATIVE EXPLANATIONS

As noted, a key limitation of this analysis is that the EEEC is a workplace-level survey and the most disaggregated earnings information is available at the broad workgroup level. As a result, unobserved worker heterogeneity could drive some of the patterns in earnings identified. For example, unionized workplaces have more similar earnings to each other than to non-union workplaces, even in the same industry and region. This similarity could result from multi-employer collective bargaining or pattern bargaining in the union-sector workplaces, by which earnings levels across workplaces and employers are formally tied together. But, the same pattern could result from more similar workers, perhaps by education level, sorting into the union workplaces, whereas non-union workplaces receive workers with more heterogeneity in educational attainment. Indeed, relative homogeneity in skill among workers in the union workplaces might have motivated unions to organize those workplaces in the first place.

These models discussed previously control for this kind of worker heterogeneity only insofar as it is correlated with the office–production worker distinction. To further assess the role of individual worker characteristics in driving apparently institutional and organizational patterns in earnings inequality, I linked the EEEC to the March CPS. To do so, I calculated industry-region-year level versions of the institutional and organizational measures available in the EEEC and merged these into the individual-level March CPS data.[4]

Model 1 in table 5 shows that industry-level results of the variance function regression, and predicting individual-level CPS annual earnings rather than EEEC workplace-level annual compensation, are similar to the presented workplace-level results. Workers in industries with more unionization and larger workplaces have higher earnings and lower inequality. The exception to this consistency across data sets is pension presence: at the industry level, pension presence is not associated with lower inequality. The March CPS data also allow controls for workers' education level, age, gender, and race. Model 2 in table 5 shows that controlling for these worker characteristics reduces the size of the institutional and organizational coefficients, but they generally remain consistent with the EEEC workplace-level results.

This analysis of the linked CPS-EEEC data is reassuring, particularly for establishing the stability of the union and workplace-size inequality patterns. However, by moving to the individual worker-level CPS data, between- and within-workplace inequality can no longer be distinguished. Moreover, even with these controls for *observable* individual characteristics however, it is still possible that *unobservable* worker characteristics are driving apparently lower between-workplace inequality among unionized and large workplaces (I discuss this possibility further).

Assuming that the uneven distribution of human capital is not driving the results, another limitation of the main analysis is that not all institutional and organizational determinants of earnings are accounted for in these models. As noted, the main additional explanation for inequality levels is government regulation via the minimum wage. As the minimum wage is not a workplace-level institutional feature, it is difficult to control for here. During the period studied in this analysis, the real

---

4. Industry was used at the two-digit SIC code. Geographical region is four census regions.

Table 5. Institutional and Organizational Effects on Workplace Earnings and Between-Workplace Inequality (Industry-Region-Year-Level Measures Matched to Worker-Level March CPS)

	(1)		(2)	
	β	λ	β	λ
Union	0.132***	−0.253***	0.067***	−0.307***
	(0.009)	(0.042)	(0.007)	(0.057)
Establishment size: 20–99	0.143***	−0.313***	0.098***	−0.352***
	(0.016)	(0.081)	(0.013)	(0.107)
Establishment size: 100–499	0.023	−0.159*	0.067***	−0.347***
	(0.014)	(0.073)	(0.012)	(0.095)
Establishment size: 500+	0.133***	−0.323***	0.107***	−0.413***
	(0.014)	(0.072)	(0.012)	(0.094)
Bonuses	0.007	−0.121*	−0.023**	−0.052
	(0.010)	(0.049)	(0.008)	(0.065)
Pension	−0.081***	0.022	−0.061***	0.073
	(0.011)	(0.057)	(0.009)	(0.075)
LTHS			−0.219***	0.260***
			(0.005)	(0.043)
Some college			0.105***	0.263***
			(0.006)	(0.053)
College graduate			0.329***	0.426***
			(0.008)	(0.067)
Post-college			0.463***	0.589***
			(0.012)	(0.101)
Female			−0.550***	0.012
			(0.005)	(0.040)
Constant	10.194***	−0.663***	9.923***	−0.647***
	(0.012)	(0.061)	(0.018)	(0.148)
R-squared	0.011		0.364	
Year effects	Yes	Yes	Yes	Yes
Age effects			Yes	Yes
Race effects			Yes	Yes
Observations	50,765	50,765	50,765	50,765

Source: Author's analysis based on the EEEC for industry-level market institutions and the March CPS for individual earnings and controls.

Note: All estimates are β and λ coefficients from the variance function regression, predicting mean and variances of logged annual labor earnings. Age categories are less than twenty-one, twenty-one to twenty-nine, thirty to thirty-nine, forty to forty-nine, fifty to fifty-nine, and sixty or older. Race is white, black, and other.

*p < .05; **p < .01; ***p < .001 (two-tailed tests)

value of the federal minimum wage remained fairly constant before falling steadily through the 1980s.[5] Year fixed effects included in the models should absorb any year-to-year varia-tion in the value of the minimum wage. However, the minimum wage binds for only some workers and not others. It is possible that for some workplaces, say large workplaces, the min-

5. In 2015 dollars, after slipping slightly due to inflation from $10.86 in 1968 to $9.04 in 1972, small increases kept the real value of the minimum wage steady around $10 until a decade of decline began in 1980.

Table 6. Institutional and Organizational Effects on Workplace Earnings and Between-Workplace Inequality (Office Only)

	(1)		(2)	
	β	λ	β	λ
Union	0.064***	−0.605***	0.018*	−0.211***
	(0.008)	(0.051)	(0.007)	(0.056)
Establishment size: 20–99	0.128***	−0.177***	0.074***	−0.224***
	(0.011)	(0.040)	(0.010)	(0.043)
Establishment size: 100–499	0.119***	−0.538***	0.038***	−0.585***
	(0.011)	(0.042)	(0.010)	(0.046)
Establishment size: 500+	0.148***	−0.897***	0.056***	−1.212***
	(0.010)	(0.040)	(0.009)	(0.044)
Pension	0.088***	−0.264***	0.074***	−0.188***
	(0.010)	(0.038)	(0.008)	(0.032)
Bonuses	0.041***	−0.051	0.010*	0.067*
	(0.006)	(0.027)	(0.004)	(0.029)
Weekly hours			0.024***	0.008***
			(0.000)	(0.001)
Metro			0.050***	0.000
			(0.005)	(0.031)
Constant	10.302***	−1.288***	9.567***	−2.065***
	(0.010)	(0.038)	(0.026)	(0.144)
R-squared	0.039		0.400	
Year effects	Yes	Yes	Yes	Yes
Industry effects			Yes	Yes
Region effects			Yes	Yes
Observations	17,223	17,223	17,223	17,223

Source: Author's analysis based on the EEEC.

Note: All estimates are β and λ coefficients from the variance function regression, predicting mean and variances of logged annual compensation. Standard errors are in parentheses and were calculated using the iterated weighting procedure described in the text.

*p < .05; **p < .01; ***p < .001 (two-tailed tests)

imum wage is more likely to affect a larger number of workers. If this is the case, then apparently low inequality among large workplaces may by due, not to workplace size, but to increased exposure to the minimum wage.

To remove the potential influence of the minimum wage, I re-run the models focusing only on office workers. These managerial, professional, and clerical workers tend to be more highly paid than production workers and should be less likely to be directly affected by the minimum wage. Results in table 6 show that between-workplace inequality effects of institutional and organizational constraints are similar, and if anything more pronounced, for

this subset of employees. Based on this test drawing on more highly paid office employees, it is unlikely that varying minimum wage exposure is driving the overall results. Of course, this is not to say that the minimum wage does not have important distributional effects, only that it seems unlikely to drive the cross-workplace inequality effects associated with workplace-level institutional and organizational characteristics.

Another limitation of the main analysis is that I focus on workplace size rather than company size. As discussed, workplace size is likely to be important in local labor market settings where much wage determination occurs. How-

Table 7. Institutional and Organizational Effects on Workplace Earnings and Between-Workplace Inequality (1974–1977)

	(1)		(2)	
	β	λ	β	λ
Union	0.225***	−0.281***	0.159***	0.074
	(0.009)	(0.039)	(0.007)	(0.044)
Establishment size: 20–99	−0.200***	−0.061	−0.065***	−0.194*
	(0.027)	(0.083)	(0.017)	(0.083)
Establishment size: 100–499	−0.410***	−0.435***	−0.098***	−0.439***
	(0.027)	(0.086)	(0.018)	(0.088)
Establishment size: 500+	−0.332***	−0.840***	−0.020	−0.788***
	(0.027)	(0.087)	(0.018)	(0.091)
Large company	−0.053***	−0.048	−0.031***	−0.000
	(0.009)	(0.038)	(0.006)	(0.039)
Pension	0.207***	−0.214***	0.102***	−0.061
	(0.013)	(0.047)	(0.008)	(0.048)
Bonuses	0.070***	−0.183***	0.030***	−0.015
	(0.008)	(0.037)	(0.006)	(0.037)
Share office workers			0.466***	0.267***
			(0.012)	(0.065)
Weekly hours			0.022***	0.004**
			(0.000)	(0.001)
Metro			0.098***	0.095*
			(0.007)	(0.044)
Constant	10.457***	−1.114***	9.535***	−2.968***
	(0.026)	(0.080)	(0.032)	(0.181)
R-squared	0.157		0.621	
Year effects	Yes	Yes	Yes	Yes
Industry effects			Yes	Yes
Region effects			Yes	Yes
Observations	7,776	7,776	7,776	7,776

Source: Author's analysis based on the EEEC.
Note: All estimates are β and λ coefficients from the variance function regression, predicting mean and variances of logged annual compensation. Standard errors are in parentheses and were calculated using the iterated weighting procedure described in the text.
*$p < .05$; **$p < .01$; ***$p < .001$ (two-tailed tests)

ever, parent company size could also have important effects via company-wide pay-setting policies. In the later years of the survey (1974 to 1977), respondents were asked whether their workplace was connected to a larger parent company. To check whether workplace size effects persist conditional on this connection to a larger company, I re-run the analyses using the subsample of workplaces that responded to the parent company question. Results in table 7 show that the workplace-size effects hold

up and that parent company affiliation has little association with between-workplace earnings inequality.

Finally, as noted, the weighted EEEC data overrepresents establishments in the manufacturing industry. To test whether this sampling issue affects results, I adjust the EEEC weights to mirror employment composition at the broad industry level in the Current Employment Statistics. Table 8 displays the results of the re-weighted models. All estimates are qual-

Table 8. Institutional and Organizational Effects on Workplace Earnings and Between-Workplace Inequality (Industry Re-weighting)

	(1)		(2)	
	β	λ	β	λ
Union	0.210***	−0.412***	0.133***	0.062
	(0.006)	(0.030)	(0.004)	(0.034)
Establishment size: 20–99	0.057***	0.035	0.032***	−0.081*
	(0.009)	(0.035)	(0.007)	(0.034)
Establishment size: 100–499	0.018	−0.025	−0.003	−0.259***
	(0.010)	(0.041)	(0.007)	(0.041)
Establishment size: 500+	0.085***	−0.568***	0.039***	−0.733***
	(0.009)	(0.041)	(0.007)	(0.043)
Pension	0.238***	−0.323***	0.115***	−0.106***
	(0.008)	(0.035)	(0.005)	(0.030)
Bonuses	0.067***	−0.143***	0.018***	−0.001
	(0.005)	(0.028)	(0.004)	(0.028)
Share office workers			0.589***	0.308***
			(0.008)	(0.045)
Weekly hours			0.027***	−0.009***
			(0.000)	(0.001)
Metro			0.044***	0.015
			(0.004)	(0.027)
Constant	9.981***	−1.162***	9.067***	−2.025***
	(0.008)	(0.035)	(0.018)	(0.101)
R-squared	0.203		0.629	
Year effects	Yes	Yes	Yes	Yes
Industry effects			Yes	Yes
Region effects			Yes	Yes
Observations	21,266	21,266	21,266	21,266

Source: Author's analysis based on the EEEC.

Note: All estimates are β and λ coefficients from the variance function regression, predicting mean and variances of logged annual compensation. Standard errors are in parentheses and were calculated using the iterated weighting procedure described in the text.

*p < .05; **p < .01; ***p < .001 (two-tailed tests)

itatively similar to the main results and changing the weights does not affect the interpretation of most of the hypotheses. The key exception is that the association between unionization and between-workplace inequality shrinks slightly in the model with full controls (from −0.087 in the table 4 model to −0.062 in the re-weighted model) and loses statistical significance. This shift in the union coefficient suggests industry heterogeneity in the between-workplace wage compression influence of unions: collective bargaining was particularly successful at compressing wages in the manufacturing industry. However, the actual shift in the point estimate is small and not itself statistically significant.

Together, these checks provide evidence for the robustness of the main results presented earlier. Although the EEEC data have limitations, they show the importance of labor market institutions and organizational practices to limiting between-workplace inequality prior to 1980. But what happened to cross-workplace coordination after the 1970s? In the following section, I describe some key developments beyond the historical scope of the EEEC data.

Table 9. Inequality Effects of Labor-Market Institutions and Organizational Practices

	Within Firm	Among Similar Firms	Premium
Union	–	–	+
Large workplace	–	–	U
Pension	U	–	+
Performance pay	+	U	+

Source: Author's.

DEVELOPMENTS SINCE THE 1970S

In this article, I extend theories of the wage equalizing effects of labor market institutions and organizational practices to show that they affect inequality between workplaces in addition to inequality within workplaces. I do so by focusing on a period—the 1970s—in which strong labor market institutions compressed wages between workplaces. Understanding these patterns requires moving beyond theories that emphasize work group solidarity within workplaces and government regulation from above them, to considering patterns of coordination between workplaces. Table 9 summarizes the findings. The analysis clarifies the channels through which labor market institutions and organizational practices ensured good jobs prior to the take-off in inequality after 1980. Since the 1970s, many of these institutions and practices have deteriorated or transformed.

Most prominently, labor unions have declined in both membership and power. Moreover, this decline has been accompanied by an apparent disintegration of coordinated bargaining (Moody 1988; Kochan, Katz, and McKersie 1994). After the 1970s, multi-employer collective bargaining agreements shrank and sometimes disappeared. In the wake of trucking deregulation, the number of members covered by the Teamsters' National Master Freight Agreement dwindled from 450,000 members in the 1960s to fewer than seventy-five thousand by the mid-2000s, a process that transformed the jobs of long-haul truckers (Viscelli 2016). At the same time, unions in manufacturing industries such as auto and steel that previously set industry-wide wage standards faced increased foreign and non-union domestic competition (Stein 2011). For example, in the auto industry, pattern bargaining was in decline by the late

1980s (Budd 1992). Even in settings where coordinated bargaining survived, the wage advantage associated with it seemed to diminish in the 1980s (Kochan and Riordan 2016). Cross-workplace wage comparisons appear to have become substantially less coercive.

However, despite this general decline in union power and coordination, some service-sector unions have bucked the trend. For example, in the mid-2000s, the hotel workers union lined up the expiration of hotel contracts covering sixty thousand workers in six heavily unionized cities in order to impose more bargaining pressure on national hotel brands (Abowd 2009). Likewise, the service employees union sought to reinvigorate city-wide janitorial contracts through the Justice for Janitors campaign (Erickson et al. 2002). Several cities, including New York and Seattle, have adopted more formally corporatist industry-specific labor boards to set standards in low-wage industries like restaurants and domestic service. These different approaches to coordination could both increase union bargaining leverage and achieve the kind of cross-workplace pay coordination and compression that characterized union bargaining prior to the 1980s.

Just as the influence of unions has waned, the earnings benefits of working at a large workplace or a large firm seem to be eroding for lower-wage workers (Cobb and Lin 2017). As a result, inequality has increased in large companies. However, inequality between large companies has grown at a similar rate to that among smaller companies (Song et al. 2018). Moreover, an apparent fracturing of corporate board interlocks and other pathways of cross-company interaction may have left large companies less capable of coordinating (Mizruchi 2013). On the other hand, one concerning possibility is that cross-employer informal pay coordination remains, but, absent the normative constraints and commitments of the pre-1980s period, employers cooperate only by restraining wages. Consistent with this possibility, recent research finds that increased monopsony power by employers in local labor markets is associated with lower wages (Benmelech, Bergman, and Kim 2018; Azar, Marinescu, and Steinbaum 2017).

Finally, research has documented an increase in variable compensation since the 1970s (Lemieux, MacLeod, and Parent 2009). The results from the present analysis suggest that in the 1970s, the use of performance pay increased inequality among office workers rather than among production workers. The decline of defined-benefit pensions, by contrast, has affected workers across the occupation spectrum, but has rarely been considered as a source of rising earnings inequality (Cobb 2015). These shifts in compensation practices have continued since the 1980s. Their distributional implications show the importance of organization-level decisions in shaping societal earnings inequality.

FUTURE RESEARCH
The EEEC surveys provide novel nationally representative workplace-level data on wages and compensation from prior to the period of rising earnings inequality. They offer a unique opportunity to assess the effects of various institutional features that are usually studied only in their decline. However, a key limitation of these data is that they do not include individual worker characteristics. The apparent equalizing effects of labor market institutions could therefore be driven in part by increased sorting of similar workers across workplaces. However, these sorting processes themselves are of interest. Between-workplace inequality declining due to sorting indicates more heterogeneity in skill among coworkers. Industry-wide bargaining agreements can dampen incentives faced by employers and by workers for sorting within the industry: for better or worse, more productive companies would not be able to lure better employees. Future research should use linked worker-workplace data to investigate the relationship between increased worker sorting across workplaces and the decline of cross-workplace pay coordination institutions and organizational practices.

Another limitation of these data is that the specific mechanisms of cross-workplace earnings compression—multi-employer bargaining agreements, pattern bargaining, and employer networks or interaction—are not directly observable. Future research should explore measures of these between-workplace connections (Wilmers 2018; Kochan and Riordan 2016). Although such measures are difficult to obtain in nationally representative data, they are critical for understanding the processes through which cross-workplace coordination occurs.

Beyond these outstanding empirical questions, the results presented here raise the question of the conditions under which cross-workplace pay coordination is possible (Dunlop 1958). Further research on this issue would shed light on the prospects for a reinvigoration of between-workplace institutional wage compression.

For example, when coordinated workplaces face strong low-wage competition, coordination at a high wage will be difficult to sustain. As noted, the pattern bargaining practiced by core industrial unions was challenged by non-union and foreign competitors. Indeed, even in the heyday of pattern bargaining in Detroit manufacturing, smaller and less financially stable companies often deviated from the key bargaining agreement (Levinson 1960). Yet in other industries, dynamics were different: declining multi-employer collective bargaining coverage in the building trades was not driven by wage gaps with non-union contractors (Belman and Voos 2006). Outside the union context, informal wage norms will likely be difficult to maintain in the face of external competition. Relatedly, substantial productivity and profitability differences across employers could make coordination on wage levels more difficult.

Beyond these objective competition and performance considerations, important subjective aspects are central to understanding how solidarity among workers across workplaces is achieved. Much sociology of labor unions emphasizes the solidarity gleaned from worker interaction and mobilization on the job, in a particular workplace (Fantasia 1989). Comparative research on Scandinavian and other European countries with centralized bargaining suggests that solidarity and common worker interests can also stem from other sources (Katz 1993). This issue raises questions of worker identity and class consciousness. In some settings, like construction and restaurant unions in the United States, occupation-wide craft identities are crucial (Cobble 1991). In others, as with Sweden's blue-collar peak labor organization, broader identities of class and union member hold together centralized bargaining (Hibbs 1991).

Another area for future research concerns potential negative effects of cross-workplace coordination for workers. As noted throughout, cross-workplace pay coordination per se does not necessarily benefit workers. Future research should build on older studies of employer collusion (Reynolds 1951) in light of recent research on the monopsonistic effects of employer concentration in local labor markets (Benmelech, Bergman, and Kim 2018). If employers coordinate and set wages absent countervailing pressure from union organizations, workers are unlikely to benefit.

Second, even when coordination limits earnings inequality among peer workplaces (say, those represented by the same labor union), it can increase inequality between workplaces covered by favorable labor market institutions or organizational practices, relative to workplaces not so covered. The union–non-union gap is one source of what a past generation of structural sociologists called "industrial segmentation" (Tolbert, Horan, and Beck 1980; Kalleberg, Wallace, and Althauser 1981). Segmentation is a form of between-workplace inequality that exists between groups of workplaces (grouped by union status, size, and generosity of benefits provision). Moreover, just as with unions, insofar as large workplaces pay a premium to their workers, they can increase segmentation inequality between large and small workplaces. Here again, a labor market institution that fosters equality among its own workers could spur inequality between different groups of workplaces. Indeed, even pension provision can be a vector of increased segmentation between generous workplaces, like paternalistic companies that provide their employees excess pay and benefits (Jacoby 1997),

and outsider companies with poor pay and benefits. Future research should return to these themes and ask about the conditions under which these insider-outsider distinctions can be muted and overcome.

CONCLUSION

By bringing new data on the period of postwar wage compression, this analysis deepens our understanding of the institutional and organizational mechanisms that contributed to that unprecedented period of egalitarian economic growth. Unions and large workplaces did not just reduce inequality among managers and workers inside workplaces. They were also associated with lower inequality between workplaces, supporting wage norms and pay standardization across workplaces. These mechanisms of cross-workplace earnings coordination have been little studied as sources of the great compression in U.S. earnings. Alongside skill supply, workgroup solidarity, and government regulations, between-workplace coordination, commitments, and norms can affect earnings inequality.

Research on low-wage work and job quality would benefit from increased attention to these meso-level processes that affect wage determination. On the one hand, cross-workplace earnings coordination via multi-employer and pattern collective bargaining brought higher earnings to industries such as trucking, building services, and hotels, which have experienced low-wage job growth since the 1970s. Recent attempts by unions in hotels and other services to reinvigorate cross-workplace bargaining strategies could hold promise for spurring wage growth in low-wage jobs.

On the other hand, cross-workplace earnings coordination poses risks of segmentation, or exclusion of some workplaces and industries from the ambit of higher coordinated earnings. Moreover, employer collusion, absent countervailing union and worker pressure, could contribute to lower wages. The results here show that lower between-workplace inequality among larger workplaces was not accompanied by consistently higher earnings for larger workplaces. Understanding how these dynamics of monopsony and employer power can undermine earnings increases for low-wage jobs will become increasingly important if trends in corporate consolidation continue (Benmelech, Bergman, and Kim 2018; Wilmers 2018).

REFERENCES

Abowd, Paul. 2009. "UNITE HERE Won't Concede to Big Hotels." *Labornotes* 368 (October 28).

Alderson, Arthur S., and François Nielsen. 2002. "Globalization and the Great U-Turn: Income Inequality Trends in 16 OECD Countries." *American Journal of Sociology* 107(1): 244–99.

Autor, David H. 2003. "Outsourcing at Will: The Contribution of Unjust Dismissal Doctrine to the Growth of Employment Outsourcing." *Journal of Labor Economics* 21(1): 1–42.

———. 2017. "A Discussion of 'Recent Flattening in the Higher Education Wage Premium: Polarization, Skill Downgrading, or Both?' by Robert G. Valletta." In *Education, Skills, and Technical Change: Implications for Future U.S. GDP Growth*, edited by Charles R. Hulten and Valerie A. Ramey. Chicago: University of Chicago Press.

Autor, David H., David Dorn, and Gordon H. Hanson. 2013. "The China Syndrome: Local Labor Market Effects of Import Competition in the United States." *American Economic Review* 103(6): 2121–68.

Autor, David H., Lawrence F. Katz, and Melissa S. Kearney. 2008. "Trends in U.S. Wage Inequality: Revising the Revisionists." *Review of Economics and Statistics* 90(2): 300–323.

Autor, David H., Alan Manning, and Christopher L. Smith. 2016. "The Contribution of the Minimum Wage to US Wage Inequality over Three Decades: A Reassessment." *American Economic Journal: Applied Economics* 8(1): 58–99.

Azar, José, Ioana Marinescu, and Marshall I Steinbaum. 2017. "Labor Market Concentration." *NBER* working paper no. 24147. Cambridge, Mass.: National Bureau of Economic Research.

Baron, James N., Frank R. Dobbin, and P. Devereaux Jennings. 1986. "War and Peace: The Evolution of Modern Personnel Administration in U.S. Industry." *American Journal of Sociology* 92(2): 350–83.

Belman, Dale, and Paula B. Voos. 2006. "Union Wages and Union Decline: Evidence from the Construction Industry." *ILR Review* 60(1): 67–87.

Benmelech, Efraim, Nittai Bergman, and Hyunseob Kim. 2018. "Strong Employers and Weak Employees: How Does Employer Concentration Affect Wages?" *NBER* working paper no. 24307.

Cambridge, Mass.: National Bureau of Economic Research.

Bernstein, Jared. 2016. "Wages in the United States: Trends, Explanations, and Solutions." In *The Dynamics of Opportunity in America*, edited by Irwin Kirsch and Henry Braun. New York: Springer.

Budd, John W. 1992. "The Determinants and Extent of UAW Pattern Bargaining." *ILR Review* 45(3): 523–39.

Bureau of Labor Statistics (BLS). 1971. *BLS Handbook of Methods for Surveys and Studies*. Washington: U.S. Department of Labor.

———. 1974. *BLS Handbook of Methods for Surveys and Studies*. Washington: U.S. Department of Labor.

Card, David. 2009. "Immigration and Inequality." *American Economic Review* 99(1): 1–21.

Carpenter, Jesse T. 1972. *Competition and Collective Bargaining in the Needle Trades, 1910-1967*. Ithaca: New York State School of Industrial and Labor Relations, Cornell University.

Clark, Robert L., Janemarie Mulvey, and Sylvester J. Schieber. 2004. "Effects of Nondiscrimination Rules on Pension Participation." In *Private Pensions and Public Policies*, edited by William G. Gale, John B. Shoven, and Mark J. Warshawsky. Washington, D.C.: Brookings Institution Press.

Clegg, Hugh A. 1972. *The System of Industrial Relations in Great Britain*, 2nd ed. Lanham, Md.: Rowman and Littlefield.

Cobb, J. Adam. 2015. "Risky Business: The Decline of Defined Benefit Pensions and Firms' Shifting of Risk." *Organization Science* 26(5): 1332–50.

Cobb, J. Adam, and Ken-Hou Lin. 2017. "Growing Apart: The Changing Firm-Size Wage Premium and Its Inequality Consequences." *Organization Science* 28(3): 429–46.

Cobb, J. Adam, and Flannery G. Stevens. 2017. "These Unequal States: Corporate Organization and Income Inequality in the United States." *Administrative Science Quarterly* 62(2): 304–40.

Cobble, Dorothy Sue. 1991. *Dishing It Out: Waitresses and Their Unions in the Twentieth Century*. Working Class in American History. Urbana: University of Illinois Press.

Dobbin, Frank. 1992. "The Origins of Private Social Insurance: Public Policy and Fringe Benefits in America, 1920–1950." *American Journal of Sociology* 97(5): 1416–50.

Dube, Arindrajit, and Ethan Kaplan. 2010. "Does Outsourcing Reduce Wages in the Low-Wage

Service Occupations? Evidence from Janitors and Guards." *ILR Review* 63:287–306.

Dunlop, John T. 1958. *Industrial Relations Systems.* Carbondale: Southern Illinois University Press.

Erickson, Christopher L., Catherine L. Fisk, Ruth Milkman, Daniel J. B. Mitchell, and Kent Wong. 2002. "Justice for Janitors in Los Angeles: Lessons from Three Rounds of Negotiations." *British Journal of Industrial Relations* 40(3): 543–67.

Fantasia, Rick. 1989. *Cultures of Solidarity: Consciousness, Action, and Contemporary American Workers.* Los Angeles: University of California Press.

Farber, Henry. 2005. "Nonunion Wage Rates and the Threat of Unionization." *ILR Review* 58(3): 335–52.

Farber, Henry, Daniel Herbst, Ilyana Kuziemko, and Suresh Naidu. 2018. "Unions and Inequality Over the Twentieth Century: New Evidence from Survey Data." *NBER* working paper no. 24587. Cambridge, Mass.: National Bureau of Economic Research.

Fortin, Nicole M., and Thomas Lemieux. 1997. "Institutional Changes and Rising Wage Inequality: Is There a Linkage?" *Journal of Economic Perspectives* 11(1): 75–96.

Freeman, Richard B. 1984. "Longitudinal Analyses of the Effects of Trade Unions." *Journal of Labor Economics* 2(1): 1–26.

Gittleman, Maury, and Morris M. Kleiner. 2016. "Wage Effects of Unionization and Occupational Licensing Coverage in the United States." *ILR Review* 69(1): 142–72.

Goldin, Claudia, and Lawrence F. Katz. 2008. *The Race Between Education and Technology.* Cambridge, Mass.: Harvard University Press.

Goldin, Claudia, and Robert A. Margo. 1992. "The Great Compression: The Wage Structure in the United States at Mid-Century." *Quarterly Journal of Economics* 107(1): 1–34.

Goldschmidt, Deborah, and Johannes F. Schmieder. 2017. "The Rise of Domestic Outsourcing and the Evolution of the German Wage Structure." *Quarterly Journal of Economics* 132(3): 1165–217.

Gouldner, Alvin W. 1954. *Patterns of Industrial Bureaucracy.* New York: The Free Press.

Handwerker, Elizabeth Weber. 2018. "Increased Concentration of Occupations, Outsourcing, and Growing Wage Inequality in the United States." Paper presented at the NBER Summer Institute, Cambridge, Mass. (July 24, 2018).

Hartman, Paul T. 1969. *Collective Bargaining and Productivity: The Longshore Mechanization Agreement.* Berkeley: University of California Press.

Hibbs, Douglas A. 1991. "Market Forces, Trade Union Ideology and Trends in Swedish Wage Dispersion." *Acta Sociologica* 34(2): 89–102.

Jacoby, Sanford M. 1997. *Modern Manors: Welfare Capitalism Since the New Deal.* Princeton, N.J.: Princeton University Press.

———. 2004. *Employing Bureaucracy: Managers, Unions, and the Transformation of Work in the 20th Century,* revised ed. Series in Organization and Management. New York: Taylor & Francis.

Kalleberg, Arne L. 2009. "Precarious Work, Insecure Workers: Employment Relations in Transition." *American Sociological Review* 74(1): 1–22.

Kalleberg, Arne L., Michael Wallace, and Robert P. Althauser. 1981. "Economic Segmentation, Worker Power, and Income Inequality." *American Journal of Sociology* 87(3): 651–83.

Katz, Harry C. 1993. "The Decentralization of Collective Bargaining: A Literature Review and Comparative Analysis." *ILR Review* 47(1): 3–22.

Kochan, Thomas A., Harry C. Katz, and Robert B. McKersie. 1994. *The Transformation of American Industrial Relations.* Ithaca, N.Y.: ILR Press.

Kochan, Thomas A., and William Kimball. Forthcoming. "Unions, Worker Voice, and Management Practices: Implications for a High Productivity." *RSF: Russell Sage Foundation Journal of the Social Sciences* 5(5).

Kochan, Thomas A., and Christine A Riordan. 2016. "Employment Relations and Growing Income Inequality: Causes and Potential Options for Its Reversal." *Journal of Industrial Relations* 58(3): 419–40.

Kopczuk, Wojciech, Emmanuel Saez, and Jae Song. 2010. "Earnings Inequality and Mobility in the United States: Evidence from Social Security Data Since 1937." *Quarterly Journal of Economics* 125(1): 91–128.

Lee, David S. 1999. "Wage Inequality in the United States During the 1980s: Rising Dispersion or Falling Minimum Wage?" *Quarterly Journal of Economics* 114(3): 977–1023.

Lemieux, Thomas. 2008. "The Changing Nature of Wage Inequality." *Journal of Population Economics* 21(1): 21–48.

Lemieux, Thomas, W. Bentley MacLeod, and Daniel Parent. 2009. "Performance Pay and Wage Inequality." *Quarterly Journal of Economics* 124(1): 1–49.

Lester, Richard A. 1954. *Hiring Practices and Labor Competition*. Princeton, N.J.: Princeton University Press.

Levinson, Harold M. 1960. "Pattern Bargaining: A Case Study of the Automobile Workers." *Quarterly Journal of Economics* 74(2): 296–317.

Mizruchi, Mark S. 2013. *The Fracturing of the American Corporate Elite*. Cambridge, Mass.: Harvard University Press.

Moody, Kim. 1988. *An Injury to All: The Decline of American Unionism*. New York: Verso.

Osterman, Paul. 2011. "Institutional Labor Economics, the New Personnel Economics, and Internal Labor Markets: A Reconsideration." *ILR Review* 64(4): 637–53.

Piketty, Thomas, and Emmanuel Saez. 2003. "Income Inequality in the United States, 1913–1998." *Quarterly Journal of Economics* 118(1): 1–41.

Piketty, Thomas, Emmanuel Saez, and Gabriel Zucman. 2018. "Distributional National Accounts: Methods and Estimates for the United States." *Quarterly Journal of Economics* 133(2): 553–609.

Podolny, J. M. 2010. *Status Signals: A Sociological Study of Market Competition*. Princeton, N.J.: Princeton University Press.

Powell, Walter. 1990. "Neither Market Nor Hierarchy: Network Forms of Organization." *Research in Organization Behavior* 12: 295–336.

Rees, Albert. 1962. *The Economics of Trade Unions*. Chicago: University of Chicago Press.

Reynolds, Lloyd G. 1951. *The Structure of Labor Markets: Wages and Labor Mobility in Theory and Practice*. Westport, Conn.: Greenwood Press.

Rosenfeld, Jake. 2006. "Widening the Gap: The Effect of Declining Unionization on Managerial and Worker Pay, 1983–2000." *Research in Social Stratification and Mobility* 24(3): 223–38.

Ross, Arthur. 1948. *Trade Union Wage Policy*. Berkeley: University of California Press.

Shin, Taekjin. 2014. "Explaining Pay Disparities between Top Executives and Nonexecutive Employees: A Relative Bargaining Power Approach." *Social Forces* 92(4): 1339–72.

Slichter, Sumner H., James J. Healy, and E. Robert Livernash. 1960. *The Impact of Collective Bargaining on Management*. Washington, D.C.: Brookings Institution.

Song, Jae, David J. Price, Fatih Guvenen, Nicholas Bloom, and Till von Wachter. 2018. "Firming Up Inequality." *Quarterly Journal of Economics* 134(1): 1–50.

Starr, Evan, J. J. Prescott, and Norman Bishara. 2018. "Noncompetes in the U.S. Labor Force." *University of Michigan Law & Economics* research paper no. 18-013. Ann Arbor: University of Michigan.

Stein, Judith. 2011. *Pivotal Decade: How the United States Traded Factories for Finance in the Seventies*. New Haven, Conn.: Yale University Press.

Tolbert, Charles, Patrick M. Horan, and E. M. Beck. 1980. "The Structure of Economic Segmentation: A Dual Economy Approach." *American Journal of Sociology* 85(5): 1095–16.

VanHeuvelen, Tom. 2018. "Recovering the Missing Middle: A Mesocomparative Analysis of Within-Group Inequality, 1970–2011." *American Journal of Sociology* 123(4): 1064–116.

Viscelli, Steve. 2016. *The Big Rig: Trucking and the Decline of the American Dream*. Berkeley: University of California Press.

Wallerstein, Michael. 1999. "Wage-Setting Institutions and Pay Inequality in Advanced Industrial Societies." *American Journal of Political Science* 43(3): 649–80.

Weil, David. 2014. *The Fissured Workplace*. Cambridge, Mass.: Harvard University Press.

Western, Bruce, and Jake Rosenfeld. 2011. "Unions, Norms, and the Rise in U.S. Wage Inequality." *American Sociological Review* 76(4): 513–37.

White, Harrison C. 1981. "Where Do Markets Come From?" *American Journal of Sociology* 87(3): 517–47.

Whitford, Josh. 2005. *The New Old Economy: Networks, Institutions, and the Organizational Transformation of American Manufacturing*. Oxford: Oxford University Press.

Wilmers, Nathan. 2017. "Does Consumer Demand Reproduce Inequality? High-Income Consumers, Vertical Differentiation, and the Wage Structure." *American Journal of Sociology* 123: 178–231.

———. 2018. "Wage Stagnation and Buyer Power: How Buyer-Supplier Relations Affect U.S. Workers' Wages, 1978 to 2014." *American Sociological Review* 83: 213–242.

Zuckerman, Ezra W., and Stoyan V. Sgourev. 2006. "Peer Capitalism: Parallel Relationships in the U.S. Economy." *American Journal of Sociology* 111(5): 1327–66.

PART III

Consequences for Health and Well-Being

Precarious Work Schedules as a Source of Economic Insecurity and Institutional Distrust

SUSAN J. LAMBERT, JULIA R. HENLY, AND JAESEUNG KIM

Work schedules may fuel precariousness among U.S. workers by undermining perceptions of security, both economic and societal. Volatile hours, limited schedule input, and short advance notice are all dimensions of precarious work schedules. Our analyses suggest that scheduling practices that introduce instability and unpredictability into workers' lives undermine perceptions of security in unique ways for hourly and salaried workers. Although the data suggest that precarious scheduling practices are widespread in the labor market, workers who are black, young, and without a college degree appear to be at highest risk. The findings highlight the importance of examining constellations of scheduling practices and considering the direction of work-hour fluctuations when investigating the ramifications of today's scheduling practices for quality of employment and quality of life.

Keywords: work schedules, job quality, economic insecurity, institutional trust

Employer scheduling practices are part of broader societal transformations in which a growing proportion of social and economic risk is being shouldered by individuals and families rather than firms and government (Appelbaum and Batt 2014; Hacker 2006; Kalleberg 2011; Kalleberg and Vallas 2017; Lambert 2008; Standing 2011; Weil 2014). Across industries, frontline managers have adopted scheduling practices designed to keep labor flexible, facilitating their ability to meet their firm's accountability requirements that restrict outlays for labor. These practices—varying the number and timing of employees' work hours, providing little advance notice of work hours, and offering employees limited input into their work schedule—can undermine job quality by structuring instability and unpredictability into employees' work and personal lives, and if paid by the hour, earnings as well. In this article, we examine the prevalence of a broad set of scheduling practices in the U.S. labor market and consider their ramifications for workers' experiences of insecurity, both economic and societal.

Susan J. Lambert is associate professor in the School of Social Service Administration at the University of Chicago. **Julia R. Henly** is professor in the School of Social Service Administration at the University of Chicago. **Jaeseung Kim** is assistant professor in the College of Social Work at the University of South Carolina.

© 2019 Russell Sage Foundation. Lambert, Susan J., Julia R. Henly, and Jaeseung Kim. 2019. "Precarious Work Schedules as a Source of Economic Insecurity and Institutional Distrust." *RSF: The Russell Sage Foundation Journal of the Social Sciences* 5(4): 218–57. DOI: 10.7758/RSF.2019.5.4.08. The authors are grateful to the Russell Sage Foundation for supporting this research and to David Howe, Arne Kalleberg, and reviewers for helpful suggestions. Direct correspondence to: Susan Lambert at slambert@uchicago.edu, University of Chicago, School of Social Service Administration, 969 E. 60th St., Chicago, IL 60637.

Work schedules are a defining feature of the quality of employment. As John Robinson and his colleagues note, "Variations in the number of hours that individuals spend working provide important evidence in comparisons of the quality of employment across occupations, countries, and time" (2002, 44). Scholars lament that the decline of collective bargaining in the United States, coupled with increasing inequality in returns to human capital, is exacerbating stratification within the workforce, with spoils concentrated among the few (Kalleberg 2011; Standing 2011). The spoils of labor are wages and hours, and some workers are rich with both but others face a scarcity of hours at poverty wages (Jacobs and Gerson 2004; Schor 1993; Golden 2016; McCrate 2017). In addition to the sheer number of hours, other aspects of work schedules differentiate jobs in terms of their quality. For example, nonstandard timing jobs, which require work outside conventional nine-to-five weekday hours, are widespread and interfere with family roles and worker well-being (Presser 2003; Staines and Pleck 1983). In addition, short advance notice of work hours, regardless of timing or number, makes it difficult for workers to predict when they will need to work, complicating their ability to manage both work and nonwork responsibilities (Clawson and Gerstel 2014; Henly and Lambert 2014; Schneider and Harknett 2016).

Particularly relevant to the current focus is recent research suggesting that fluctuations in weekly hours—within the same job—may be a key source of increasing income volatility among U.S. households and thus a source of economic insecurity. Since 2013, "lack of money/low wages" has competed with "health care costs" as Americans' top response to the question "What is the most important financial problem facing your family today?," surpassing concerns about unemployment or job loss by a 2:1 ratio (Gallup 2018a). Many households are strapped for cash. According to the 2016 Survey of Household Economics and Decisionmaking, fewer than half (48 percent) of adults in the United States have the cash on hand to cover an emergency requiring $400, and 30 percent report that they are either finding it difficult to get by or are just getting by (Board of Governors of the Federal Reserve System 2017).

Instability of work hours may help explain why some households face difficulty paying bills. Recent research demonstrates that hour variations are an important contributor to growing household income volatility in the United States (Farrell and Greig 2016; Finnigan 2018; Gottschalk and Moffitt 2009; Morduch and Schneider 2017). Researchers reason that unstable work hours are thus also a likely source of insecurity both objectively, in terms of spurring financial crises, and subjectively, in terms of fostering uncertainty. Although compelling evidence of these ramification is provided by targeted and qualitative research (Edin and Shaefer 2016; Morduch and Schneider 2017), only recently have representative surveys provided data on the magnitude of work-hour fluctuations and the prevalence of other scheduling practices that may make household finances, and family life, not only unstable but also unpredictable. Notably, new items in recent rounds of the 1997 National Longitudinal Survey of Youth (NLSY97) suggest that hour volatility, short advance notice, and employer-driven schedule control are common among U.S. workers (Lambert et al. 2019). The NLSY97 only surveys young adults (in their mid-twenties to early thirties), however, and does not include measures of perceived economic or societal insecurity. It thus remains unknown how widespread work-hour volatility and other precarious scheduling practices are in the broader U.S. workforce and whether they can help explain workers' experiences of insecurity.

In this article, we capitalize on new and existing questions in the General Social Survey (GSS), a nationally representative survey of U.S. residents, to advance understanding of the prevalence, distribution, and ramifications for insecurity of several dimensions of work schedules that contribute to or detract from job quality. Drawing on new questions in the 2016 GSS that gauge the magnitude of weekly hour fluctuations, length of advance notice, and worker input into weekly hours, we first examine whether problematic aspects of work schedules are differentially experienced by vulnerable subgroups of workers and address the possibility that workers may "age out" of precarious work schedules. We then pool multiple survey years, from 2002 to 2014, to examine the relationship between fundamental aspects of work schedules and perceived insecurity. These analyses set the stage to consider how the more detailed aspects of work schedules captured in the 2016 GSS contribute new insight into the relationships between scheduling practices and insecurity. Throughout, we differentiate workers paid by the hour versus a salary given that earnings are a direct function of hours for the former but not the latter. Although our primary focus is on economic insecurity, we also explore the possibility that precarious work schedules fuel distrust in major institutions, which we conceptualize as a marker of societal insecurity.

WORK SCHEDULES AND PERCEIVED INSECURITY

How work hours are related to perceptions of insecurity may depend on the extent to which time and money are linked in workers' minds. Jeffrey Pfeffer and Sanford DeVoe explain that "Time and money are particularly well-connected in people's minds when they are paid by the hour because their income is then a direct function of the number of hours they work multiplied by their rate of pay" (Pfeffer and DeVoe 2012, 56). Time and money may be more loosely connected among those paid by a salary. By definition, a salary provides financial stability by smoothing income when demand or effort dips. Using data from both the 2002 GSS and the 1988 National Survey of Families and Households, DeVoe and Pfeffer find that income and hourly status interact in explaining perceived happiness, with a significantly larger relationship among workers paid by the hour as compared to those paid in other ways (2009). It seems reasonable to conclude that because the fortunes of hourly workers are more directly tied to number of hours worked, so might be their perceptions of insecurity, both financial and societal.

Even so, fluctuating hours may not always undermine security, even among hourly workers. The ramifications of work-hour fluctuations likely depend on their direction and magnitude; hours can surge up as well as plummet down (Lambert et al. 2019). Ramifications may also depend on whether work-hour fluctuations are by choice, and whether they are predictable. Moreover, as explained in the following section,

in some circumstances, fluctuating hours may actually enhance job security, for both workers paid by salary and by the hour (Lehndorff and Voss-Dahm 2005; Perlow 2012), and scheduling practices may unsettle more than family economics. We take these complexities into account in considering how the scheduling practices of key focus here—fluctuating weekly hours, advance notice, schedule input, and irregular timing—may help explain workers' perceptions of economic and societal insecurity.

Fluctuating Hours and Economic Insecurity

Recent research provides evidence that instability in work hours may help account for the growing volatility in U.S. household income. For example, using records of financial transactions recorded by JPMorgan Chase between 2012 and 2015, Diane Farrell and Fiona Greig decompose month-to-month variation in total credits to personal bank accounts into within-job volatility (for example, the amount deposited by an employer), between-job volatility (for example, lapses in paychecks, moves to new employers), and volatility in other sources of income (for example, public programs, retirement plans, additional job) (2016). Variation in earnings within the same job, as opposed to variation accompanying job loss or mobility, accounted for the overwhelming majority of month-to-month variation in labor income. Although their data do not reveal how workers are paid (by hour, salary, or other), Farrell and Greig reason that "volatility in paycheck amounts among weekly paid jobs could therefore be driven by variation in hours worked" (2016, 28). Jonathan Morduch and Rachel Schneider's analysis of data from the U.S. Financial Diaries study, which recorded the financial transactions of 235 low-income and middle-income families across a one-year period (2012 to 2013), offers additional evidence that variation in earners' take-home pay is a central driver of household income volatility; approximately half (47 percent) of month-to-month household income volatility was traced to fluctuations in earnings from the same job (2017). Most recently, Ryan Finnigan shows that working variable hours has become more prevalent since the Great Recession; the cumulative probability of hourly workers responding that their "hours vary" increased from 37 to 47 percent when comparing the four years before, 2004 to 2007, to the four years after, 2008 to 2012, the Great Recession (2018). Finnigan also finds that this increase in variable work hours largely accounts for the significant increase in earnings instability observed between the same time periods.

Volatility in work hours may not, however, dictate perceived financial insecurity. The meaning of fluctuating hours depends on the nature of the volatility. Small week-to-week fluctuations may do little to inform workers' perceived financial security, and whether work hours surge above or fall below usual or full-time hours makes a difference for household finances. Morduch and Schneider find that, on average, the families in their sample experienced 2.5 months with income at least 25 percent above and 2.5 months with income at least 25 percent below their annual monthly average (2017). Using data from the NLSY97 (2012 to 2013), Susan Lambert and her colleagues find that the majority of variation in weekly hour fluctuations during a one-month period was due to surges above usual hours (2019). Thus, the extent to which fluctuating work hours exacerbate or reduce workers' assessments of financial insecurity may depend on their magnitude and direction, especially among hourly workers whose earnings are most closely tied to the number of hours they work.

The relationship between fluctuating hours and job insecurity is also complex. Workers who incur fluctuations in work hours may do so as a means of demonstrating their commitment to an employer. In many hourly jobs, open availability—the willingness and ability to incur fluctuations in work hours, such as surges and shortfalls—has become a valued form of human capital as managers strive to implement labor flexibility to control outlays for labor (Carré and Tilly 2017; Haley-Lock and Ewert 2011; Lambert 2008; Lehndorff and Voss-Dahm 2005). For example, a study of a national U.S. retailer indicates that hourly sales associates who put constraints on their availability received fewer hours than their more available counterparts, controlling for work-hour preferences (Lambert, Haley-Lock, and Henly 2012). Several studies document that being willing and able to incur fluctuations in work hours is also highly valued in many salaried jobs. For example, Leslie Perlow's research demonstrates how organizations create norms among software engineers and consultants that foster a culture of working through deadlines and answering off-hour calls from bosses and clients (1997, 2012). *Face time* is used as a marker of employee performance, with career penalties incurred for those unable or unwilling to work on demand and at short notice. Whether penalties and payoffs are real or imagined, perceived job insecurity is typically conceptualized as a subjective uncertainty (see, for example, De Witte and Näswall 2003; Lee, Bobko, and Chen 2006) that has both cognitive and affective components (Huang et al. 2012). In today's workplaces, then, incurring fluctuating hours may be experienced as protection against job insecurity rather than a marker of it, by both hourly and salaried workers.

Schedule Input and Economic Insecurity

Whether fluctuations in the number of work hours exacerbate or mitigate economic insecurity may depend on who determines them. Work hours that are the result of workers' preferences are likely to be experienced as flexibility by workers (Jones 2017; Matos and Galinsky 2011). But when variation is employer driven, workers are more likely to experience it as uncertainty, and we posit, as a source of insecurity (Clawson and Gerstel 2014; Fugiel and Lambert 2019; Henly, Shaefer, and Waxman 2006; Lambert et al. 2019; McCrate 2012). Recent vignette studies—both a controlled experiment of applicants for jobs in a call center and a web-based representative panel—suggest that workers place a great deal of value on avoiding employer control over the timing of work shifts (Mas and Pallais 2016). To our knowledge, the 2016 GSS is the first nationally representative survey in the United States to include items about the extent of employee input into the number and timing of work hours.

In this article, we examine how input into both the number and timing of hours varies by worker characteristics, including age, gender, race, education, and occupation; we then explore how both types of schedule input may help explain perceived economic insecurity alone and in combination with work-hour volatility. It seems reasonable to expect that lack of input would contribute to financial insecurity, especially when work hours are highly volatile. Whether lack of employee input is related to job insecurity is less clear. On the one hand, employer-driven scheduling may lead workers to feel that they are fulfilling necessary business functions; on the other hand, having no input into their hours may make them feel undervalued and expendable. We do not anticipate that relationships between economic insecurity and schedule input into number or timing of hours will vary for hourly and salaried workers because we do not have a theoretical reason to expect that control is more or less important to insecurity based on how a worker is paid, net of other differences.

Advance Notice and Economic Insecurity

Schedule unpredictability concerns the difficulty workers have anticipating when they will and will not work. Research demonstrates that unpredictability is associated with elevated levels of work stress and work-to-life conflict, and for workers paid by the hour, unpredictable hours mean unpredictable earnings (Clawson and Gerstel 2014; Henly and Lambert 2014). The further in advance workers know when they will need to work, the more certain they can be of hours and earnings. Thus, lengthy advance notice may foster a sense of financial security and short notice may undermine it. Lengthy advance notice may also foster job security by enabling workers to manage personal responsibilities in ways that do not interfere with work responsibilities (Henly and Lambert 2014). The Quality of Work Life supplement to the 2014 GSS and recent rounds of the NLSY97 have included comparable questions on advance schedule notice. In the 2014 GSS, fully 40 percent of hourly workers reported that they know when they will need to work a week or less in advance, the shortest length of notice included as a response category. The percentage of workers reporting a week or less notice is somewhat lower in the NLSY97 (Round 16), with hourly workers (30.3 percent) more likely to receive a week or less notice than nonhourly workers (22.5 percent). The 2016 GSS includes refined response categories that allows us to unpack a

week or less advance notice into a day or less, two to three days, or four to seven days. We examine how length of advance notice varies by worker and occupational characteristics and then explore how short advance notice may help explain perceived economic insecurity alone and in combination with hour volatility and schedule input. We anticipate that short notice will increase the probability of financial and job insecurity, especially in the context of hour volatility and low input, and that the relationship to financial insecurity will be especially strong for workers in hourly jobs—because of the additional ramifications of short notice for financial budgeting.

Work Schedules and Societal Insecurity

Precarious scheduling practices also have potential ramifications for noneconomic forms of insecurity. As Richard Sennett observes, "What's peculiar about uncertainty today is that it exists without any looming historical disaster; instead it is woven into the everyday practices of a vigorous capitalism" (1998, 31). Nothing is more everyday in capitalism than work hours and schedules. We posit that the uncertainty introduced into daily life through precarious scheduling practices may fatigue workers' trust broadly. We explore this possibility by examining the relationship between precarious scheduling practices and workers' distrust of societal institutions.

Confidence in many major institutions— from Congress to the clergy—has declined since the 1970s (Gallup 2018b; Pew Research Center 2017). For example, when asked how much confidence "you, yourself have" in Congress, in 1973 (following the Watergate crisis), 42 percent of those polled responded "a great deal" or "quite a lot," but only 11 percent responded similarly in 2018 (Gallup 2018b). Similarly, although 65 percent of poll participants reported confidence in organized religion in 1973, only 38 percent did so in 2018.

Explanations for the increase in institutional distrust are varied. Some authors point to uncertainties introduced through increasing globalization, others stress the dismantling of local community power (for a review, see Abramson and Inglehart 1995); others emphasize increasing income inequality and a belief in meritocracy (Hayes 2012) or processes of social modernization (Dalton 2005). Building on Sennett (1998), we explore the possibility that distrust in institutions may also spring from more mundane uncertainties. Regardless of how paid, unstable, unpredictable work hours over which workers have little control may introduce uncertainty into the core of work and family life, shaking confidence that societal institutions act in the best interests of people like them.

RESEARCH QUESTIONS

1. What is the prevalence of precarious work schedules in the U.S. labor market? How are distinct features of work schedules distributed across population subgroups by personal and job characteristics? Do workers age out of precarious work schedules?

2. How are fundamental features of work schedules related to financial insecurity, job insecurity, and institutional distrust?

3. How are more nuanced features of work schedules related to economic (financial and job) and societal (distrust in institutions) insecurity? Specifically, does the magnitude and direction of work-hour fluctuations, short advance notice and lack of schedule input—alone and in combination—explain perceived insecurity? Do relationships vary for workers paid by the hour and a salary?

METHODS

The General Social Survey, begun in 1972, is a cross-sectional, nationally representative personal-interview survey of adults age eighteen years or older living in the United States. It uses an equal probability, multistage cluster sample design for selecting housing units in the entire United States.

Data and Sample

We conduct two sets of analyses. First, we combine GSS surveys from 2002, 2006, 2010, and 2014 to examine the relationships between fundamental aspects of work schedules and finan-

cial insecurity, job insecurity, and distrust in institutions; the sample includes respondents who were currently in the wage and salary workforce in those years (N = 3,564). Second, we use the 2016 GSS, which incorporated the Fluctuating Work Hours Module (developed by authors Susan Lambert and Julia Henly) in the 3rd ballot of the core survey. This sample is composed of respondents in the wage and salary workforce who responded to the 2016 Module (N = 525). The 2016 data are not included in the combined multiyear data set because questions asking about type of schedule and input into timing are different in 2016, as detailed in our section on measures. We weight variables to improve population representation.

Analytic Approach

To address the first research question, we present descriptive statistics on fundamental aspects of scheduling available in the GSS prior to 2016 using the multiyear pooled data set and on more nuanced scheduling features using data from the 2016 Fluctuating Work Hour Module. With 2016 data, we present personal (gender, race, age, education) and occupational (part time or full time, occupation, union status, level of earnings) subgroup differences. To address the remaining research questions, we estimate a series of linear (indices of financial insecurity and institutional distrust) and logistic (dichotomous variable indicating job insecurity) regressions that sequentially introduce different aspects of work schedules, alone and then in combination. It is not our goal to estimate the relative contribution of each dimension but rather to examine how distinct dimensions and constellations may be differentially related to different types of insecurity, as discussed in the literature review. These models include a block of control variables that capture worker characteristics shown to be associated with labor market opportunities and outcomes, including age (age^2), race, gender, education, household income, number of children, spouse and whether spouse works, and whether respondent works more than one job.[1] We estimate models separately for hourly and salaried

1. Definitions of control variables are included in the online appendix (https://www.rsfjournal.org/content/5/4/218/tab-supplemental).

workers.[2] The data are cross-sectional, and our findings can only offer associational knowledge.

We also conduct sensitivity analyses that add occupation, industry, union status, and relative earnings into the main models. To avoid model misspecification, we do not enter these variables in our primary models; conceptually, one path through which occupation, industry, and union membership may affect economic insecurity is through scheduling practices. Sensitivity analyses also include indices capturing workers' overall optimism and hopefulness for achieving life goals to take into account the possibility that workers' individual outlook may color their assessment of their work schedule and also their finances and confidence in institutions. The addition of these variables does little to change our results, and we thus summarize the findings from the sensitivity analyses in the online appendix.

Measures of Insecurity

We define the dependent and key independent variables we employ in the regressions.[3] Distributions on all variables are presented in table 1 and table 2, broken out for hourly and salary workers.

Financial insecurity is an index on which higher scores indicate greater insecurity. The index averages respondents' assessments of satisfaction with their current standard of living, their prospects of improving their standard of living, and how they think their standard of living compares to others in America and to their parents (items were standardized before averaging because questions used different response scales). Although this index has modest reliability (alpha = 0.51 in the multiyear and

0.54 in the 2016 GSS), each item added to reliability (that is, subtracting any item would have lowered estimated reliability). Moreover, the results of an exploratory factor analysis are consistent with a one-factor solution; each of these items met the convention of loading on a single factor at the level of 0.4 or higher. Perhaps most important, the overall pattern of results is substantively the same, showing only minor variations, when the individual items rather than the index are used (results available from the authors).

Job insecurity is a dichotomous variable that differentiates workers reporting job insecurity (coded 1) or not (coded 0). It is measured differently in the multiyear and 2016 data. In the multiyear data, it is measured by a single question that asks how true it is that "The job security is good." Workers are coded as job insecure if they respond "not too true" or "not at all true." In the 2016 data, job insecurity combines responses from two survey questions that ask about the extent to which workers worry about the possibility of losing their job and how difficult or easy it would be to find a job as good as their current one. Workers are coded as experiencing job insecurity if they say they worry at least a little about losing their job and they also think it will be fairly or very difficult to find another one.

Institutional distrust is an index, with higher scores indicating greater institutional distrust. The index averages responses to whether "you would say you have a great deal of confidence, only some confidence, or hardly any confidence" in each of a set of institutions. Our index averages together confidence in major companies, education, the executive branch of government, the U.S. Supreme Court, Con-

2. Little data were missing on the independent and control variables in the multiyear and 2016 GSS. The most data were missing on household income, which had 7.8 percent missing in the multiyear data (and 14 percent missing on respondents' earnings) and 5.5 percent missing (16 percent missing on respondents' earnings) in the 2016 GSS. Missing data on the remaining independent and control variables ranged from 1 to 2 percent. Because of the low proportion of missing responses on any one variable, we simply filled in missing data on the independent and control variables with the mean, normed separately for hourly and salaried subsamples as appropriate.

3. An online appendix presents the survey questions included in the Fluctuating Work Hours Module as well as the questions on economic insecurity and institutional distrust (https://www.rsfjournal.org/content/5/4/218/tab -supplemental). We constructed numerous alternative measures of both financial insecurity and fluctuating work hours to estimate sensitivity of findings to measurement decisions. The significant and statistically nonsignificant findings reported in this article largely hold regardless of measure or model.

gress, banks and financial institutions, organized labor, the press, and banks and financial institutions (alpha = 0.72 in both the multiyear and 2016 GSS).

Measures of Work Schedules in Multiyear GSS Data

Hours worked last week is the total number of hours workers reported working at all jobs in the past week; workers not working because of illness or vacation are asked to report typical hours. Note that this question asks about hours worked at all jobs; 18 percent of hourly workers and 14 percent of salaried workers reported they held more than one job.

Workers are asked whether they usually work a day, afternoon, night, split, irregular–on-call, or rotating shift. *Irregular shift* is coded 1 if working an irregular–on-call shift and 0 otherwise. *Nonregular timing* is coded 1 if working anything other than a day, afternoon, or night shift and 0 otherwise.

Little or no input into timing of hours is coded 1 if workers responded rarely or never to a question asking how often they are allowed to change their starting and quitting time on a daily basis.

Irregular with no input is coded 1 when irregular shift is equal to 1 and lack of input into timing is equal to 1, and 0 otherwise.

Nonregular with no input is coded 1 when nonregular timing is equal to 1 and lack of input into timing is also equal to 1, and 0 otherwise.

Measures of Work Schedules in 2016 GSS

Usual hours is the number of hours respondents reported they typically work each week at all jobs; 14 percent of hourly workers and 11 percent of salaried workers in the 2016 GSS reported holding more than one job.

Relative instability measures the magnitude of fluctuations in weekly work hours during the past month, conditioned on usual work hours. It is developed from three survey questions: usual work hours, the most hours worked a week in the past month (including overtime and work at home and other places), and the least hours worked a week in the past month (not including weeks with vacation or sick time). These questions refer to work at all jobs.

This measure of magnitude can be likened to a coefficient of variation as it norms the absolute difference of most and least hours by average or usual work hours: [most–least] ÷ usual. For example, an eight-hour difference between most and least weekly hours may have different consequences for workers who usually work forty-eight hours versus sixteen hours a week. In the first case, variation in hours is 17 percent of a worker's usual hours (relative instability ratio of 0.17) whereas in the second case, variation amounts to 50 percent of usual hours (relative instability ratio of 0.50).

Direction of work-hour volatility is assessed with three variables that calculate the proportion of the difference between greatest and fewest weekly hours that indicates an hour shortfall (below usual hours) or an hour surge (above usual and above full-time hours). For example, the proportion of variation due to a surge above full time (which we define as working more than forty-five hours a week) is calculated as [greatest hours–forty-five] ÷ [greatest-fewest]. To conserve space, significant findings related to the direction of volatility are reported in the text but not tables.

Little or no work-hour input is a dichotomous variable that differentiates workers who indicated that the total number of hours they work each week is "decided by my employer with little or no input from me" (coded 1), from workers who indicated more input (coded 0).

No input into work timing is a dichotomous variable that is coded 1 if workers chose the response "Starting and finishing times are decided by my employer and I cannot change them on my own" and 0 if they responded that they can decide the times they work within certain limits or completely on their own.

Nonregular timing is a dichotomous variable that is comparable, but not identical, to the *nonregular timing* variable constructed using the multiyear data. In the 2016 GSS, we coded workers 0 on nonregular timing if they chose "I have a regular schedule or shift (daytime, evening, or night)" when asked about their usual work schedule in their main job. They are coded 1 if they chose either of the other two alternatives of working a schedule or shift that regularly changes ("for example, from days to evenings or to nights") or one "where working times are decided at short notice" by their employer.

Week or less notice is a dichotomous variable that differentiates workers who indicated they know what days and hours they will need to work seven or fewer days in advance (coded 1) from workers who reported longer notice or that their schedule never changes (coded 0).

Volatility plus little input into number is coded 1 when relative instability is at least 0.25 and *little or no work-hour input* is coded 1; other workers are coded 0.

Volatility plus short notice is coded 1 when relative instability is at least 0.25 and *week or less notice* is coded 1; other workers are coded 0.

Volatility plus little input into timing is coded 1 when relative instability is at least 0.25 and *no input into work timing* is coded 1; other workers are coded 0.

Short notice plus little input into timing is coded 1 when *week or less notice* is coded 1 and *no input into timing* is coded 1; other workers are coded 0.

Short notice plus little input into number is coded 1 when *week or less notice* is coded 1 and *little or no work-hour input* is coded 1; other workers are coded 0.

RESULTS

In the following section, we present findings on the prevalence of precarious work schedules, first using the multiyear GSS data and then the more nuanced data on work schedules available in the 2016 GSS. We then present findings on the association of these work schedule variables with economic insecurity and distrust in institutions, using the multiyear and the 2016 data.

Prevalence and Distribution of Precarious Scheduling Practices

To address the first research question, we first present the prevalence of the fundamental features of work schedules for workers paid a salary and by the hour, using multiple years of the GSS. We then examine the full set of more nuanced features of work schedules available in the 2016 GSS. We discuss key differences in the distribution of each dimension of work schedules for workers paid a salary and by the hour,

and for the 2016 data, how they are distributed across workers with distinct personal and job characteristics. Overall, the data suggest that today's labor market is highly stratified in terms of how much input workers have into the timing and number of work hours, how widely weekly work hours fluctuate, and how far in advance workers know when they will need to work.

Fundamental Features of Work Schedules Using Multiyear GSS Data Set

Using data across multiple years of the GSS, we examine the number of work hours reported in the week prior to the survey, the extent of input into the starting and finishing times of work, and the percentage of respondents who report having a schedule with nonregular work timing (see table 1). Overall, respondents report working an average of 41.6 hours in the prior week, and hourly workers report statistically significantly fewer hours (38.9) than salaried workers (45.6). Hourly workers also report statistically significantly less input into their work schedule timing, with 60 percent of hourly and 37 percent of salaried workers reporting that their employer decides their starting and finishing times without their input. Work schedules that are mostly nonregular, meaning employees work primarily irregular, on-call, split, or rotating shifts, are not highly prevalent in the sample, but nevertheless, characterize an important minority of workers' schedules (9.8 percent of salaried workers and 15.3 percent of hourly workers). The hourly-salary difference is reduced to nonsignificance when the definition of nonregular timing is restricted to only those respondents who work irregular or on-call shifts.

Nonregular timing may be especially difficult for workers without input into work schedule timing. These data suggest, however, that only a small minority of workers have both limited input into the timing of their work schedule and an irregular or on-call shift, although experiencing both together is somewhat more common for hourly workers and when the definition of nonregular is expanded to include irregular, on-call, split, and rotating shifts. The multiyear data illustrate important subgroup differences beyond the hourly-salary distinc-

Table 1. Descriptive Statistics of Variables Included in Regressions with Multiyear Data

	Hourly (n=1,458)	Salary (n=2,141)	Total (n=3,599)
Dependent variables			
Financial insecurity	0.09 (0.63)	−0.18 (0.63)**	−0.01 (0.65)
Job insecurity	16.6	12.9*	15.1
Distrust in institutions	2.1 (0.4)	2.1 (0.4)	2.1 (0.4)
Independent variables			
Number of work hours last week	38.9 (13.5)	45.6 (13.0)**	41.6 (13.7)
Little or no input into timing	60.0	37.0*	50.8
Irregular or on-call shift	5.4	6.5	5.8
Nonregular timing (irregular, on-call, split, or rotating)	15.3	9.8**	13.1
Little or no input and irregular or on-call shift	2.7	1.2*	2.1
Little or no input and nonregular timing	9.6	3.2**	7.0
Control variables			
Age	40.5 (13.8)	44.1 (12.1)**	41.9 (13.3)
Race			
White, non-Hispanic	62.8	78.3**	69.0
Black	19.1	7.9**	14.6
Hispanic	15.2	8**	12.3
Other	3.0	5.7**	4.1
Female	55.3	50.6	53.4
High school or less	76.4	31.9**	58.6
Household income[a]			
1 (<$20,499)	26.9	5.9**	18.4
2 ($20,500~$36,399)	23.9	12.4**	19.2
3 ($36,400~$58,999)	22.4	22.6	22.5
4 ($59,000~$87,999)	15.4	23.6**	18.7
5 ($88,000<=)	11.4	35.5**	21.2
Low pay	33.7	33.4	33.6
No partner or spouse	52.6	36.7**	46.3
Spouse does not work	13.8	17.1^	15.1
Have children 18 or younger	35.2	32.4	34.1
Has more than one job	17.9	13.9*	16.3
Occupation			
Management, business, office, admin support	22.9	40.9**	30.1
Professional, related fields	15.4	34.6**	23.1
Service, sales, related fields	34.7	15.6**	27.1
Construction, production, transport, natural resources	26.9	8.9**	19.7
Union	12.6	13.8	13.3

Source: Authors' calculations based on combined waves of the General Social Survey (Smith et al. 2018), years 2002, 2006, 2010, and 2014.

Note: Percentages and means (standard deviations). Significance difference between hourly and salary workers.

[a]Income in constant dollars, inflation-adjusted to year 2000.

^$p < .1$; *$p < .05$; **$p < .01$

Table 2. Descriptive Statistics of Variables Included in Regressions, 2016 GSS

	Hourly (n=334)	Salary (n=191)	Total (n=525)
Dependent variables			
Financial insecurity	0.13 (0.65)	−0.28 (0.60)**	−0.01 (0.66)
Job insecurity	23.3	26.6	24.5
Distrust in institutions	2.1 (0.4)	2.1 (0.4)	2.1 (0.4)
Independent variables			
Usual hours	38.4 (11.7)	44.8 (12.5)**	40.7 (12.4)
Magnitude of volatility (relative instability ratio)	0.37 (0.54)	0.33 (0.40)**	0.35 (0.49)
Working hours decided by employer (no input into hours)	47.4	35.0*	42.9
Timing decided by employer (no input into timing)	64.5	33.6**	53.5
Nonregular timing	24.1	17.0	21.6
Week or less notice (short notice)	39.9	30.7	36.6
Volatility plus no input into the number of hours	18.2	12.7	16.2
Volatility plus short notice	27.4	21.1	25.1
Volatility plus no input into timing	27.8	12.7**	22.4
Short notice plus no input into timing	26.4	8.6	20.0
Short notice plus no input into number of hours hours	15.2	7.1*	12.3
Control variables			
Age	43.0 (14.1)	44.9 (12.5)	43.7 (13.6)
Race			
White, non-Hispanic	57.3	72.5**	62.8
Black	18.7	10.1**	15.6
Hispanic	19.6	10.6*	16.4
Other	4.4	6.8	5.2
Female	58.2	48.7*	54.8
High school or less	73.0	33.6**	58.8
Household income			
1 (<$29,999)	26.8	8.0**	19.9
2 ($30,000–$49,999)	19.6	10.7*	16.3
3 ($50,000–$89,999)	36.9	26.9^	33.2
4 ($90,000–$109,999)	6.6	11.9*	8.6
5 ($110,000<=)	10.2	42.5**	22.1
Low pay	34.9	28.7	32.6
No partner or spouse	51.4	34.5**	45.4
Spouse does not work	14.0	15.9	14.7
Have children 18 or younger	29.9	32.3	30.8
Has more than one job	14.1	11.2	13.1
Occupation			
Management, business, office, admin support	23.4	37.7**	28.5
Professional, related fields	18.1	35.4**	24.3
Service, sales, related fields	34.3	17.6**	28.3
Construction, production, transport, natural resources	24.2	9.3**	18.9
Union	9.6	10.2	10.1

Source: Authors' calculations based on the 2016 General Social Survey (Smith et al. 2018).
Note: Percentages and means (standard deviations). Significance difference between hourly and salary workers.
^*p* < .1; **p* < .05; ***p* < .01

tion in the distribution of these fundamental features of work schedules (see table A1). For brevity, we do not describe these differences here, and instead elaborate important subgroup trends in our discussion of the 2016 descriptive statistics.

Features of Work Schedules in the 2016 GSS

The 2016 data allow us to supplement the work schedule variables available in the multiyear data with items that assess work-hour fluctuations, employee input into the number of hours they work, and the advance notice workers receive about their work schedule. In addition to providing for the first time these more nuanced assessments of work schedule dimensions in a nationally representative sample of U.S. workers, the 2016 data include measures of the usual hours of work each week, work schedule timing, and nonregular hours. These measures are worded slightly differently than prior waves, but tap into the same constructs as those reported in table 1. The overall descriptive statistics of all work schedule variables in the 2016 data are presented in table 2.

Work-Hour Fluctuations

The 2016 data indicate salaried workers report usually working 44.8 hours per week, relative to 38.4 hours per week among workers paid by the hour, a statistically significant difference. As shown in table 3, the overwhelming majority of both hourly (79.2 percent) and salaried (81.6 percent) workers reported at least some fluctuations in weekly work hours during the one month queried in the 2016 GSS. The absolute difference between the most and least number of hours worked during a week of the month averaged more than a full day's work, at 13.2 hours. On average, hours fluctuated by 35 percent of what workers report as their usual hours, with hourly workers (0.37) reporting slightly more relative instability than salaried workers (0.33), though the difference is not statistically significant. The prevalence and magnitude of fluctuating hours observed in the 2016 GSS is comparable to that found in the NLSY97 (Round 16) data; more than 70 percent of the early-career employees in the NLSY97 report some fluctuations in weekly hours (Lambert et al. 2019). In both the GSS (0.35) and

NLSY07 (0.34), the relative instability ratios among hourly workers are enough to suggest that fluctuations in number of work hours may play a substantial role in helping account for the earnings volatility observed in recent research, such as the reported 20 percent month to month (Farrell and Greig 2016).

Subgroups vary on number of usual hours and the magnitude of fluctuations in work hours in ways that mostly align with socioeconomic status (for example, lower-status workers report fewer usual hours and more fluctuations) but not always. Differences between hourly and salaried workers are shown for each dimension of work schedules in table 3. Consistent with research (for a review, see Frazis and Stewart 2014), salaried workers report working more hours than hourly workers, and this difference is especially pronounced for whites, higher educated workers, and workers in professional, service, and sales occupations. The difference in usual hours worked is especially large between hourly and salaried workers not covered by a union contract. Workers twenty-six and younger, especially those in hourly jobs, report the largest absolute difference between the most and least number of weekly hours of any group; they are also among the highest in terms of relative instability. The magnitude of fluctuating hours among part-time hourly workers, whether measured in absolute or relative terms, is greater than among full-time hourly workers. Although relative instability varies significantly by race within both hourly and salary groups (significant levels not shown in table), it is white hourly workers who report the greatest relative instability.

Overall, the findings reported in table 3 suggest that a substantial proportion of workers across the U.S. workforce experience sizable fluctuations in weekly work hours, regardless of personal and job characteristics. But knowing the magnitude of the fluctuations may not be enough to understand the conditions under which fluctuations serve to mitigate or exacerbate financial insecurity.

Employee Input into Timing of Weekly Hours

Table 4 indicates that almost two-thirds (64.5 percent) of hourly workers and one-third (33.6 percent) of salaried workers report that the

Table 3. Descriptives of Usual Hours and Measures of Hour Fluctuations, 2016 GSS

	Usual Hours (Mean, SD)		Some Fluctuation (Most ≠ Least) (%)		Absolute Instability (Mean, SD)		Relative Instability Ratio (Mean, SD)	
	Hourly	Salary	Hourly	Salary	Hourly	Salary	Hourly	Salary
All employees	38.4 (11.7)	44.8 (12.5)**	81.6	79.2	12.7 (13.7)	14.0 (13.6)	0.37 (0.54)	0.33 (0.40)
Men	42.4 (11.8)	48.4 (11.7)**	82.1	83.8	14.6 (15.6)	15.3 (13.3)	0.37 (0.44)	0.30 (0.25)
Women	35.6 (10.8)	40.9 (12.3)**	79.4	74.3	11.4 (11.9)	12.7 (13.8)	0.38 (0.62)	0.35 (0.52)
Race								
White	36.8 (10.9)	46.1 (12.3)**	83.1	83.9	12.9 (14.3)	15.6 (14.1)	0.41 (0.65)	0.37 (0.44)
Black	40.9 (12.4)	41.9 (11.5)	77.1	67.3	11.2 (9.5)	8.2 (8.4)	0.28 (0.25)	0.18 (0.19)
Hispanic	41.3 (12.5)	42.4 (16.2)	77.5	73.7	12.4 (13.6)	14.9 (13.9)	0.32 (0.39)	0.32 (0.33)
Age								
26 and younger	37.7 (9.8)	47.0 (22.7)	93.1	85.2	15.8 (16.1)	12.8 (11.9)	0.42 (0.43)	0.34 (0.32)
27–35	41.5 (9.6)	46.9 (10.4)*	80.3	87.6	12.6 (13.7)	14.9 (13.4)	0.30 (0.30)	0.33 (0.34)
36–45	40.7 (10.8)	44.1 (14.8)^	74.6	79.6	13.6 (13.0)	14.8 (14.1)	0.37 (0.41)	0.32 (0.30)
46–54	41.1 (13.1)	44.7 (14.9)	88.1	78.5	13.1 (11.4)	15.8 (14.8)	0.39 (0.41)	0.43 (0.62)
55–64	35.1 (10.5)	44.8 (9.7)**	72.5	73.7	9.4 (13.3)	11.6 (12.3)	0.28 (0.36)	0.24 (0.24)
65 and older	26.2 (13.2)	38.6 (12.3)^	75.8	62.3	12.3 (15.8)	7.9 (9.4)	0.72 (1.52)	0.18 (0.20)
Work hours								
Full time	43.0 (8.7)	47.6 (9.6)**	79.0	81.2	12.3 (13.2)	14.6 (13.6)^	0.28 (0.30)	0.30 (0.27)
Part time	24.0 (7.3)	21.6 (9.5)	84.5	63.0^	14.2 (14.9)	9.7 (12.9)	0.66 (0.92)	0.58 (0.94)
Education								
High school or less	39.2 (11.7)	42.8 (13.5)^	80.0	70.0	13.1 (14.6)	9.7 (10.2)	0.38 (0.60)	0.23 (0.25)
More than high school, less than four-year college	39.6 (9.8)	50.7 (12.3)*	77.8	94.0^	10.6 (10.6)	19.1 (16.9)	0.26 (0.26)	0.36 (0.32)
College degree or more	35.0 (11.9)	45.1 (11.8)**	83.5	82.4	12.1 (10.9)	15.8 (14.2)^	0.39 (0.37)	0.38 (0.47)

Earnings								
Low pay	31.8 (11.4)	39.5 (11.1)**	81.6	68.6	13.6 (14.1)	9.8 (11.1)^	0.52 (0.84)	0.23 (0.26)**
Higher pay	42.5 (10.1)	48.1 (12.1)**	76.4	81.9	12.0 (13.7)	15.7 (14.8)*	0.29 (0.33)	0.35 (0.46)
Occupation								
Management, business, office, admin support	37.5 (10.7)	42.0 (13.3)^	78.5	74.1	11.5 (12.7)	12.8 (13.7)	0.42 (0.87)	0.36 (0.56)
Professional, related fields	39.3 (9.9)	47.0 (10.4)**	80.4	88.6	14.5 (15.7)	17.0 (14.5)	0.38 (0.44)	0.35 (0.29)
Service, sales, related fields	34.9 (12.4)	42.4 (11.0)**	84.2	69^	11.4 (10.8)	10.8 (12.1)	0.34 (0.32)	0.24 (0.25)
Construction, production, transport, natural resources	43.2 (11.2)	51.3 (16.7)	79.3	83.6	14.9 (16.4)	13.9 (11.7)	0.37 (0.43)	0.27 (0.23)
Union								
Non-union	37.7 (11.6)	44.5*(12.6)	79.6	79.1	12.2 (13.3)	13.9 (13.5)	0.36 (0.56)	0.33 (0.41)
Union	44.1 (11.5)	47.0 (11.8)	88.1	80.7	17.3 (15.8)	15.1 (14.6)	0.41 (0.42)	0.32 (0.30)
Total	40.7 (12.4)		80.0		13.2 (13.6)		0.35 (0.50)	

Source: Authors' calculations based on the 2016 General Social Survey (Smith et al. 2018).

Note. Percentages and means (standard deviations). All percentages are weighted. Total sample size is 525,334 for hourly workers and 191 for salaried workers.

^p < .1; *p < .05; **p < .01

starting and finishing times of their work shifts are decided by their employer. Only 3.5 percent of hourly workers report that they are entirely free to decide their starting and finishing times, versus almost one-fifth (18.1 percent) of salaried workers. Despite these statistically significant differences in schedule input between hourly and salaried workers in the sample overall, several subgroups of workers, even when paid by salary, nevertheless report little to no input into their work schedules. For example, as with their hourly counterparts, large shares of salaried African Americans (64.1 percent), workers twenty-six and younger (49.9 percent), and workers with a high school education or less (49.6 percent) report that starting and finishing times are decided by their employer. Service, sales, and related fields also provide salaried workers limited input into their schedule (60.5 percent). In addition, more than 70 percent of workers in jobs covered by a union contract also report that their start and end times are controlled by their employer whether salaried or paid by the hour. It may be that the timing of shifts in union jobs has been a matter of collective bargaining, but workers see it as solely employer driven because employers are the ones who construct the work schedule.

Employee Input into Number of Weekly Hours
Table 5 shows that almost half of hourly workers and more than one-third of salaried workers report that the total number of hours they work each week is decided by their employer with little or no input from them (see table 5, figures 1 and 2). Salaried workers are more than twice as likely as hourly workers (36.6 versus 16.7 percent) to report controlling the number of hours they work each week either freely or within limits set by their employer. White workers paid by salary are significantly less likely than workers of other races or ethnicities, regardless of how paid, to report little or no input into the number of hours they work (significance levels for comparisons across race not reported on table). At almost 60 percent, black hourly workers are particularly likely to report not having a say into the number of hours they work. The lack of work-hour control that black hourly workers report suggests that the lower relative instability in weekly work hours they incur relative to

white workers (see table 3) may be more a matter of employer practice than employee choice.

Input into the number of weekly hours varies in important ways for hourly and salaried workers across occupations and by union status. Workers with the least input into their hours are in hourly administrative support jobs (52 percent) and service and sales jobs (47.2 percent), and construction, production, and transportation jobs whether paid by the hour (53.2 percent) or by salary (50.3 percent). Regarding union status, it is non-unionized hourly workers (48.2 percent) and unionized salaried workers (57.9 percent) who report the least input into the number of hours they work. Again, the unionized salaried workers may have input through collective bargaining that is not reflected in their subjective reports of their input into work hours.

Overall, like fluctuations in work hours, the distribution of work-hour input both for timing and number of hours across subgroups suggests that although a substantial proportion of today's workers may not control the starting and finishing times of their workday and may have limited input into the number of hours they work each week, some groups are clearly at higher risk than others, in ways that mostly mirror broader stratification in the labor market and society.

Advance Schedule Notice
The descriptive trends regarding the advance schedule notice that workers receive indicate marked bifurcation in the labor market. On the one hand, almost half of workers (48.2 percent overall) report either that they know their work schedule four weeks or more in advance or that their schedule never changes, but on the other hand, more than one-third (36 percent) report one week or less advance notice in their work schedule (see figures 3 and 4 and table 6). The relative consistency in workers' reports in the 2016 GSS, the 2014 GSS, and Round 16 of the NLSY97 offers some confidence in these estimates of advance schedule notice, and suggests that experiencing a week or less schedule notice is the norm for an important minority of workers in today's labor market.

The 2016 GSS further breaks down the "one week or less" category (see table 6). These data

(*Text continues on p. 236.*)

Table 4. Descriptives of Input into Starting and Finishing Times of Work, 2016 GSS

	Employer Decides		Employee Decides Within Limits		Employee Decides	
	Hourly	Salary	Hourly	Salary	Hourly	Salary
All employees	64.5	33.6**	32.0	48.3**	3.5	18.1**
Men	66.3	30.3**	31.1	50.3**	2.6	19.4*
Women	63.2	37.1**	32.6	46.1**	4.2	16.8*
Race						
White	62.2	30.7**	34.7	46.2**	3.1	23.2**
Black	77.2	64.1	16.8	28.4*	6.0	7.5
Hispanic	61.8	37.5	36.2	58.1	2.1	4.4
Age						
26 and younger	69.7	49.9	30.4	40.4	0.0	9.7
27–35	60.0	36.3**	33.3	43.9^	6.7	19.8*
36–45	53.6	33.3*	42.5	55.7*	3.9	11.0
46–54	70.0	23.6**	24.7	50.0**	5.3	26.5*
55–64	74.8	38.6**	23.8	47.1^	1.3	14.3*
65 and older	62.4	35.4	33.5	33.3	4.0	31.3
Work hours						
Full time	67.5	33.6**	29.4	49.4**	3.1	17.0**
Part time	54.7	33.9	40.4	38.2	4.9	27.9^
Education						
High school or less	68.3	49.6*	48.2	27.6	2.5	11.2*
More than high school, less than four-year college	48.2	27.6	50.3	40.9	1.5	31.4^
College degree or more	56.9	25.7**	34.7	54.2	8.3	20.1
Earnings						
Low pay	65.3	49.8^	29.7	34.4	5.0	15.7*
Higher pay	62.4	27.0**	35.0	54.8**	2.7	18.2**
Occupation						
Management, business, office, admin support	47.2	19.2**	45.7	50.8	7.1	30.0**
Professional, related fields	52.9	34.0^	40.8	52.9	6.3	13.1
Service, sales, related fields	74.4	60.5	23.3	31.7	2.3	7.8
Construction, production, transport, natural resources	74.5	45.0^	25.5	46.0	0.0	9.0
Union						
Non-union	63.4	29.5**	33.2	50.9**	3.3	19.5**
Union	73.9	70.9	20.8	23.7	5.3	5.3
Total (N)	51.3 (266)		40.2 (208)		8.5 (44)	

Source: Authors' calculations based on the 2016 General Social Survey (Smith et al. 2018).
Note: Percentages and means (standard deviations). All percentages are weighted. Total sample size is 525,334 for hourly workers and 191 for salaried workers.
^$p < .1$; *$p < .05$; **$p < .01$

Table 5. Desccriptives of Employee Input into Number of Weekly Work Hours, 2016 GSS

	Little or No Input		Some Input		Decides Within Limits		Decides Freely		Outside Control	
	Hourly	Salary	Hourly	Salary	Hourly	Salary	Hourly	Salary	Hourly	Salary
All employees	47.4	35.0*	30.6	22.3*	12.1	27.0**	4.6	9.6*	5.3	6.1
Men	49.2	35.3*	23.9	15.5	15.2	30.9*	4.4	11.6**	7.4	6.7
Women	45.6	34.6	33.8	29.5	9.9	22.9**	5.2	7.6	5.6	5.5
Race										
White	46.5	31.5^	29.2	19.2*	15.8	29.3*	3.4	12.2**	5.1	7.7
Black	59.5	47.7	22.2	42.8	8.9	9.5	2.5	0.0	6.9	0.0
Hispanic	43.4	47.3	37.4	23.8	4.6	17.3^	9.9	6.9	4.8	4.7
Age										
26 and younger	26.1	43.5	55.0	16.3^	11.3	31.4	0.0	8.9^	7.6	0.0
27–35	43.9	43.0	35.4	24.6	10.5	22.1	3.1	7.4	7.0	2.9
36–45	48.6	23.8*	31.2	36.6	8.7	28.3**	5.8	5.2	5.8	6.1
46–54	57.7	36.0*	14.4	19.7	13.4	19.4	10.8	13.4	3.7	11.6
55–64	56.4	45.8	25.7	1.4*	13.5	35.3**	0.0	15.3**	4.4	2.3
65 and older	51.5	10.7	14.0	30.5	20.4	42.2	11.5	4.4	2.5	12.2
Work hours										
Full time	49.9	34.4*	29.9	23.1^	9.8	28.3**	3.5	8.2*	6.9	6.1
Part time	38.5	36.0	33.2	17.1	19.6	18.5	8.1	22.1*	0.6	6.4

Education									
High school or less									
50.0	46.4	29.8	25.5	12.2	16.8	3.2	4.1	4.8	7.2
More than high school, less than four-year college									
52.6	17.4^	26.1	32.4	1.5	33.4**	8.4	16.8	11.4	0.0
College degree or more									
35.2	30.8	35.3	19.0^	16.1	32.0*	8.4	11.8	5.0	6.3
Earnings									
Low pay									
53.5	47.2	30.1	18.6	10.9	25.7*	3.9	3.0	1.6	5.4
Higher pay									
44.4	31.4^	28.0	21.2	15.5	29.9*	6.8	11.5	5.2	6.0
Occupation									
Management, business, office, admin support									
52.2	31.9*	18.5	23.1	17.5	23.8	8.0	13.7	3.8	7.4
Professional, related fields									
31.5	35.5	39.9	20.3*	13.1	31.2^	8.7	11.1	6.7	1.9
Service, sales, related fields									
47.2	33.1	40.7	31.6	7.8	23.8*	0.0	3.5	4.3	8.0
Construction, production, transport, natural resources									
53.2	50.3	21.8	11.2	12.8	24.6	5.0	0.0	7.2	14.0
Union									
Non-union									
48.2	32.5**	28.7	23.5	12.9	27.5**	5.2	9.7^	5.0	6.8
Union									
37.7	57.9	48.4	10.5*	5.9	22.8*	0.0	8.7*	8.0	0.0
Total (N)									
42.8 (225)		27.1 (142)		19.1 (100)		5.7 (30)		6.3 (28)	

Source: Authors' calculations based on the 2016 General Social Survey (Smith et al. 2018).

Note: Percentages and means (standard deviations). All percentages are weighted. Total sample size is 525,334 for hourly workers and 191 for salaried workers.

^p < .1; *p < .05; **p < .01

Figure 1. Hourly Employees: Input into Number of Hours

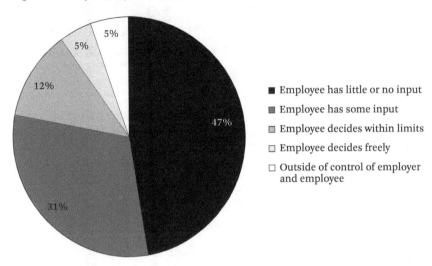

- Employee has little or no input
- Employee has some input
- Employee decides within limits
- Employee decides freely
- Outside of control of employer and employee

Source: Authors' calculations based on the General Social Survey (Smith et al. 2018).

Figure 2. Salaried Employees: Input into Number of Hours

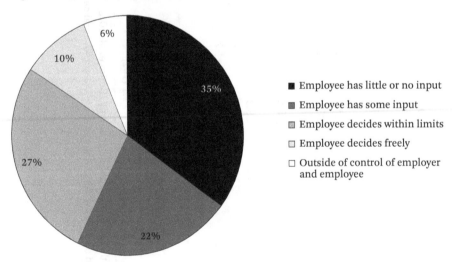

- Employee has little or no input
- Employee has some input
- Employee decides within limits
- Employee decides freely
- Outside of control of employer and employee

Source: Authors' calculations based on the 2016 General Social Survey (Smith et al. 2018).

show that subgroups of workers are subject to (or in some cases may choose) even less than one week's notice of their work hours. In fact, almost half of those with one week or less notice report that they know when they need to work only a day or less in advance. Hourly workers who are male (28.0 percent), Hispanic (29.7 percent), or have at most a high school degree (20.3 percent) are especially likely to have advance notice in their work schedule of a day or less. Hourly union workers are also subject to last-minute scheduling (25.6 percent). Despite the overall high rates of short notice among hourly workers, salaried workers are not immune to last-minute notice, particularly salaried workers of color; about a quarter of black

Figure 3. Hourly Employees: Advance Notice

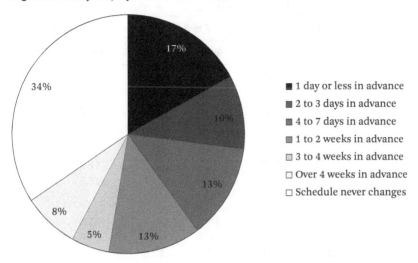

Source: Authors' calculations based on the 2016 General Social Survey (Smith et al. 2018).

Figure 4. Salaried Employees: Advance Notice

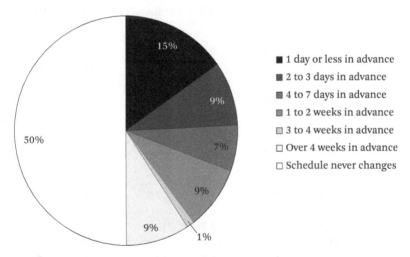

Source: Authors' calculations based on the 2016 General Social Survey (Smith et al. 2018).

(25.3 percent) and Hispanic (23.7 percent) workers paid by salary report knowing when they will need to work one day or less in advance. Moreover, an especially high percentage of both hourly (42.3 percent) and salaried (45.4 percent) workers in construction, production, and transportation jobs only know their schedules one day or less in advance.

Intersection of the Dimensions of Work Schedules
As reported earlier, the multiyear data indicate that only a small minority of workers experience the combination of limited input into the timing of their work and working a nonregular (irregular, on-call, rotating, or split shift) schedule. However, the 2016 data indicate that an important percentage of workers experience both

Table 6. Descripitves of Advance Schedule Notice, 2016 GSS

	1 Day or Less		2 to 3 Days		4 to 7 Days	
	Hourly	Salary	Hourly	Salary	Hourly	Salary
All employees	17.0	15.2	10.0	9.0	12.9	6.5*
Men	28.0	14.5**	6.8	10.2	15.4	7.8*
Women	9.1	16.0	12.3	7.7	11.2	5.1^
Race						
White	11.8	14	8.3	9.1	13.1	8.4
Black	14.9	25.3	11.1	5.3	12.8	0^
Hispanic	29.7	23.7	13.6	9.4	15.5	0^
Age						
26 and younger	10.5	19.4	18.9	15.3	18.5	0.0*
27–35	17.2	9.8	7.7	7.4	19.6	2.3**
36–45	21.3	6.8	7.5	10.0	9.3	6.9
46–54	22.5	19.3	17.2	9.7	2.6	5.6
55–64	14.7	24.7	2.2	7.1	16.5	13.8
65 and older	12.0	20.9	7.3	4.4	14.3	7.9
Work hours						
Full time	19.7	13.1^	6.9	9.4	10.1	6.1*
Part time	8.8	33.8	19.8	6.4	21.3	10.1
Education						
High school or less	20.3	21.7	9.2	10.4	15.3	4.8*
More than high school, less than four-year college	11.7	6.3	5.4	3.8	8.2	21.6
College degree or more	6.6	12.8	15.1	8.9	6.0	5.3
Earnings						
Low pay	14.3	25.9	19.7	10.7	20.6	1.8*
Higher pay	20.9	13.9	5.1	9.6	8.4	7.3
Occupation						
Management, business, office, admin support	6.2	14.4	7.4	7.2	10.6	9.0
Professional, related fields	8.1	7.8	7.7	10.3	6.0	6.3
Service, sales, related fields	11.5	16.8	16.5	5.3	21.0	5.3
Construction, production, transport, natural resources	42.3	45.4	5.5	19.3^	9.3	0.0
Union						
Non-union	16.1	15.9	10.0	9.3	12.9	7.2*
Union	25.6	9.0	6.1	6.6	14.0	0.0^
Total (N)	15.6 (82)		9.5 (50)		10.9 (57)	

Source: Authors' calculations based on the 2016 General Social Survey (Smith et al. 2018).
Note: Percentages and means (standard deviations). All percentages are weighted. Total sample size is 525,334 for hourly workers and 191 for salaried workers.
^$p < .1$; *$p < .05$; **$p < .01$

1 to 2 Weeks		3 to 4 Weeks		Over 4 Weeks		Schedule Static	
Hourly	Salary	Hourly	Salary	Hourly	Salary	Hourly	Salary
12.7	9.0	5.3	1.1*	7.7	9.1	34.3	50.0**
5.3	9.6^	6.0	2.2	3.2	10.9*	35.3	44.8
18.0	8.5*	4.8	0**	10.9	7.2	33.7	55.5**
16.1	10.6	5.6	1.2*	10.5	10.8	34.7	45.9*
14.4	13.5	2.0	0	6.6	0	38.2	55.9*
4.0	0	6.2	2.3	0	9**	31.0	55.7
8.2	0.0	6.5	5.7	9.0	0	28.4	59.6
7.6	5.5	5.7	0	9.9	7.8	32.4	67.2
12.6	12.6	3.9	1.8	9.1	8.4	36.4	53.5
20.1	9.6	5.7	0.0	3.2	9.7	28.8	46.0
14.1	5.5	1.9	0.0	8.8	15.5	41.8	33.4**
14.9	24.7	14.9	4.5	4.7	6.2	31.9	31.4
11.3	10.2	4.9	1.0*	7.7	9.0	39.4	51.2
17.4	0.0^	6.8	2.2	7.7	10.5	18.2	37.0
13.4	5.3	3.8	0.7	4.4	15.2**	33.7	41.9
9.2	20.0	10.5	0.0	11.0	11.4	44.0	36.8
11.6	9.6	9.0	1.5**	18.8	5.3**	33.0	56.5**
13.8	9.4	4.0	0.0	2.2	8.7^	25.4	43.5^
11.2	11.0	6.1	1.8*	10.2	10.5	38.1	45.8
13.9	3.8*	4.9	1.3	6.2	8.4	50.7	55.9
11.4	10.5	8.7	1.8^	18.0	7.2^	40.2	56.1
18.4	22.5	5.0	0.0	7.6	18.9	19.9	31.2
4.9	0.0	3.8	0.0	0.0	0.0	34.3	35.3
12.6	9.1	5.5	1.2*	8.2	8.6	34.7	48.7*
14.2	8.3	3.9	0.0	3.8	13.9	32.4	62.2
11.2 (59)		4.6 (24)		7.8 (41)		40.4 (212)	

limited input and either short notice or hour volatility. As reported in table 2, 16.2 percent of workers overall report little or no input into the number of hours they work while also working highly fluctuating hours, and more than one-fifth report having no input into the timing of their work in combination with either a volatile work schedule or a week or less notice. Notably, more than one-fourth (25.1 percent) of workers report the "double whammy" of both a volatile work schedule and one week or less of advance notice. In all cases, the likelihood of potentially problematic combinations is greater among hourly workers.

Unpacking further the intersection of very short notice and schedule input may help discern whether unpredictable schedules are employer driven or due to employee preference. Analyses, not reported on the tables, suggest the former is the case among a larger proportion of hourly workers than salaried workers. For example, among salaried workers reporting a day or less of advance notice, only 18.2 percent also report they have little or no say in the number of hours they work, whereas 38.1 percent of hourly workers who report a day or less of notice report they have little say in the number of weekly hours. Strikingly, among white workers who report a day or less of notice, 22.8 percent say that they have little or no input into the number of hours they work, but among black workers reporting a day or less, 69.2 percent say they have little or no input into the number of weekly hours. These patterns provide further evidence that examining the intersection of different dimensions of work schedules may be necessary to discern their meaning in the lives of workers and families and their contributions to inequality, as suggested in prior research (Lambert et al. 2019; McCrate 2012, 2017; Presser 2003).

Do Workers "Age Out" of
Precarious Work Schedules?
An examination of the descriptive data on schedule input and advance notice suggests that hourly workers may gain more predictability in their schedules as they age, whereas sala-

ried workers may gain more control over schedule timing and the number of hours they work. For example, the percentage of workers who report a day or less notice increases with age among salaried workers but decreases among hourly workers. The opposite is true of "my schedule never changes;" the proportion of hourly workers who choose this response increases with age and the proportion of salaried workers decreases. On the other hand, salaried workers but not hourly workers, gain control over their work hours as they age. By age fifty-five, more than half of salaried workers report that they can decide starting and finishing times within certain limits or entirely (61.4 percent) and more than one-third of salaried workers (35.3 percent) report that they control the number of hours they work "within limits." Hour fluctuations also dissipate somewhat with age, but less so for hourly workers. As shown in table 3, fluctuations in work hours, as measured by relative instability, drop over the age of fifty-four, except for hourly workers sixty-five or older. Even so, the trends by age also indicate that a substantial proportion of workers, even those fifty-five or older, do not age out of fluctuating work hours.

Fundamental Features of Work Schedules and Perceived Insecurity: Multiyear GSS Data

To address the second research question, we use the multiyear GSS data in regression models to estimate the extent to which fundamental aspects of work schedules can help explain workers' economic insecurity and distrust in institutions, providing a foundation for assessing the contribution the more nuanced measures in the 2016 GSS may make to understanding the relationship between precarious scheduling practices and perceived insecurity.[4]

The findings pertaining to financial insecurity support the contention that, per Pfeffer and DeVoe, how workers are paid matters (2012). As shown in table 7 (panel A), across all models employing the full sample, hourly workers report significantly greater financial insecurity than salaried workers, even after controlling for

---

4. Table A2, panel A, reports associations between the control variables and financial insecurity, job insecurity, and institutional distrust included in analyses of the multiyear data.

household income and composition. The sheer number of hours respondents report working in the prior week and whether respondents worked an irregular–on-call (or nonregular) schedule are not significantly related to financial insecurity for either hourly or salaried workers, suggesting that these basic work-hour conditions do not effectively differentiate the extent to which workers feel financially vulnerable overall.

Job insecurity shows a different pattern (table 7, panel B). As anticipated, hourly and salaried workers do not significantly differ in their overall assessments of job security, but they do vary in the aspects of work schedules that inform their perceptions of job insecurity. Among hourly workers, the more hours they work in the preceding week, the less insecure they feel in their job (table 7, panel B, models 2 through 7). Although working more hours may help protect hourly workers from a sense of job insecurity, it does not save them from the job insecurity that accompanies working an irregular schedule, especially when those hours are determined by the employer. An irregular or on-call schedule almost doubles the odds (OR = 1.89) of job insecurity among hourly workers, and triples the odds (OR = 3.23) when combined with a lack of input into start and end times, although caution is needed because only 5.4 percent of hourly workers report working an irregular or on-call schedule (see table 1). Working an irregular schedule is also positively associated with distrust in institutions alone (table 7, panel C, model 3) and especially when the irregularity of hours is determined by employer rather than the employee (table 7, panel C, model 6), but only among hourly workers. Working an irregular schedule or having nonregular hours does not appear to contribute to job insecurity or institutional distrust among salaried workers.

In sum, the pattern of relationships between these fundamental aspects of work schedules and economic and societal insecurity begin to flesh out themes we summarize in the literature review—the economic valuation of time, as marked by how workers are paid, seems to shape the meaning of work hours; working more hours may reduce feelings of job insecurity; and irregular or on-call hours, especially when under employer control, may have consequences beyond their economic ramifications.

Scheduling Practices, Economic Insecurity, and Institutional Distrust: 2016 GSS

In regard to the third research question, the new items in the 2016 GSS allow us to examine in greater detail the qualities of work schedules that may place workers at risk of economic insecurity and institutional distrust. All models control for the same set of personal characteristics included in the multiyear analyses.[5] In these models, however, we control for respondents' reports of usual work hours rather than hours worked last week. As detailed in table 3, weekly work hours vary a great deal during a one-month period and thus hours worked last week could be the exception rather than the rule.[6] We look at hourly and salaried workers separately to provide further insight into how the strength of the connection between work hours and earnings may shape the relationship between different dimensions of work schedules and perceptions of economic and societal insecurity.

Work Schedules and Financial Insecurity

The 2016 data provide additional information on the scheduling practices that contribute to greater financial insecurity among hourly workers, as observed in the multiyear data. Findings are consistent with our proposition that whether fluctuating hours contribute to or detract from job quality depends on the magnitude and direction of the volatility. As shown in table 8 (panel A, model 1), the magnitude of volatility in weekly work hours is negatively related to hourly workers' perceptions of finan-

---

5. Table A2, panel B, reports associations between control variables and financial insecurity, job insecurity, and institutional distrust in the 2016 data.

6. Analyses using "hours last week" rather than "usual hours" do not substantively change the parameter estimates of our key independent variables; the question on usual hours was not available in all of the years in the combined data set.

Table 7. Regressions for Fundamental Characteristics of Work Schedules, Multiyear GSS

	Model 1		Model 2					
	Full		Full		Hourly		Salary	
	B	(SE)	B	(SE)	B	(SE)	B	(SE)
Panel A. Financial insecurity (OLS)								
Hourly	0.083*	(0.032)	0.073*	(0.032)				
Hours last week			−0.002	(0.001)	−0.002	(0.002)	−0.001	(0.001)
Irregular schedule								
Nonregular timing								
Lack of input into timing								
Irregular with no input								
Nonregular with no input								
Panel B. Job insecurity (logits)								
Hourly	0.053	(0.164)	−0.002	(0.162)				
Hours last week			−0.011*	(0.005)	−0.017**	(0.007)	0.005	(0.008)
Irregular schedule								
Nonregular timing								
Lack of input into timing								
Irregular with no input								
Nonregular with no input								
Panel C. Distrust in institutions (OLS)								
Hourly	0.000	(0.021)	0.005	(0.021)				
Hours last week			0.001	(0.001)	0.001	(0.001)	0.000	(0.001)
Irregular schedule								
Nonregular timing								
Lack of input into timing								
Irregular with no input								
Nonregular with no input								

	Model 5					
	Full		Hourly		Salary	
	B	(SE)	B	(SE)	B	(SE)
Panel A. Financial insecurity (OLS)						
Hourly	0.060^	(0.031)				
Hours last week	−0.002^	(0.001)	−0.002	(0.002)	−0.002	(0.001)
Irregular schedule						
Nonregular timing						
Lack of input into timing	0.088**	(0.027)	0.053	(0.035)	0.122**	(0.040)
Irregular with no input						
Nonregular with no input						
Panel B. Job insecurity (logits)						
Hourly	−0.020	(0.159)				
Hours last week	−0.011*	(0.005)	−0.018**	(0.007)	0.005	(0.008)
Irregular schedule						
Nonregular timing						
Lack of input into timing	0.120	(0.138)	0.434*	(0.177)	−0.453^	(0.241)
Irregular with no input						
Nonregular with no input						
Panel C. Distrust in institutions (OLS)						
Hourly	0.007	(0.022)				
Hours last week	0.001	(0.001)	0.001	(0.001)	0.000	(0.001)
Irregular schedule						
Nonregular timing						
Lack of input into timing	−0.014	(0.017)	−0.001	(0.021)	−0.042	(0.027)
Irregular with no input						
Nonregular with no input						

Source: Authors' calculations based on multiyear General Social Survey data (Smith et al. 2018).

Note: N= Full = 3,564; salaried 2,121; hourly 1,443.

^p < .1; *p < .05; **p < .01

	Model 3						Model 4					
	Full		Hourly		Salary		Full		Hourly		Salary	
	B	(SE)	B	(SE)	B	(SE)	B	(SE)	B	(SE)	B	(SE)
	0.073*	(0.032)					0.072*	(0.032)				
	-0.002	(0.001)	-0.001	(0.002)	-0.001	(0.001)	-0.002	(0.001)	-0.002	(0.002)	-0.002	(0.002)
	0.051	(0.042)	0.087	(0.055)	-0.014	(0.068)						
							0.021	(0.033)	0.010	(0.042)	0.016	(0.061)
	0.006	(0.163)					-0.020	(0.159)				
	-0.011*	(0.005)	-0.017**	(0.006)	0.004	(0.008)	-0.011*	(0.005)	-0.017**	(0.007)	0.005	(0.008)
	0.571*	(0.262)	0.639^	(0.356)	0.486	(0.386)						
							0.267	(0.194)	0.342	(0.236)	0.005	(0.354)
	0.005	(0.021)					0.003	(0.021)				
	0.001	(0.001)	0.001	(0.001)	0.000	(0.001)	0.001	(0.001)	0.001	(0.001)	0.000	(0.001)
	0.097**	(0.037)	0.163**	(0.046)	0.018	(0.056)						
							0.031	(0.023)	0.040	(0.028)	0.032	(0.043)

	Model 6						Model 7					
	Full		Hourly		Salary		Full		Hourly		Salary	
	B	(SE)	B	(SE)	B	(SE)	B	(SE)	B	(SE)	B	(SE)
	0.072*	(0.032)					0.0170*	(0.032)				
	-0.002	(0.001)	-0.002	(0.002)	-0.001	(0.001)	-0.002	(0.001)	-0.002	(0.002)	-0.002	(0.001)
	0.106	(0.077)	0.120	(0.093)	0.017	(0.110)						
							0.047	(0.049)	0.031	(0.056)	0.077	(0.094)
	-0.023	(0.162)					-0.034	(0.163)				
	-0.011*	(0.005)	-0.017**	(0.006)	0.004	(0.008)	-0.012*	(0.005)	-0.018**	(0.007)	0.005	(0.008)
	1.166**	(0.374)	1.174**	(0.451)	0.937	(0.817)						
							0.591**	(0.255)	0.669*	(0.275)	-0.223	(0.693)
	0.003	(0.021)					0.005	(0.021)				
	0.001	(0.001)	0.001	(0.001)	0.000	(0.001)	0.001	(0.001)	0.001	(0.001)	0.000	(0.001)
	0.135*	(0.051)	0.179**	(0.061)	-0.013	(0.089)						
							0.011	(0.029)	0.012	(0.034)	0.013	(0.050)

Table 8. Regressions for New Dimensions of Work Schedules, 2016 GSS

	Model 1				Model 2			
	Hourly		Salary		Hourly		Salary	
	B	(SE)	B	(SE)	B	(SE)	B	(SE)
Panel A. Financial insecurity (OLS)								
Usual hours	−0.003	(0.004)	0.007*	(0.003)	−0.000	(0.003)	0.006*	(0.003)
Magnitude of fluctuations (relative instability)	−0.189**	(0.046)	0.038	(0.097)				
Week or less notice					−0.005	(0.095)	0.190^	(0.094)
Little or no input into number of hours								
Little or no input into timing of hours								
Nonregular timing								
Panel B. Job insecurity (logits)								
Usual hours	−0.006	(0.016)	0.004	(0.018)	−0.006	(0.016)	0.007	(0.016)
Magnitude of fluctuations (relative instability)	0.368	(0.235)	−0.300	(0.523)				
Week or less notice					0.706*	(0.319)	−0.232	(0.458)
Little or no input into number of hours								
Little or no input into timing of hours								
Nonregular timing								
Panel C. Distrust in institutions (OLS)								
Usual hours	0.003^	(0.002)	0.002	(0.004)	0.002	(0.002)	0.001	(0.004)
Magnitude of fluctuations (relative instability)	0.047	(0.038)	0.190**	(0.048)				
Week or less notice					0.013	(0.043)	0.009	(0.051)
Little or no input into number of hours								
Little or no input into timing of hours								
Nonregular timing								

Source: Authors' calculations based on the 2016 General Social Survey (Smith et al. 2018).
Note: Standard errors (SE). Total sample size is 525,334 for hourly workers and 191 for salaried workers.
^$p < .1$; *$p < .05$; **$p < .01$

cial insecurity. Further analyses of the direction of volatility (available from authors) indicates that surges above forty-five hours a week significantly lowers hourly workers' perceptions of financial insecurity; among the 81.6 percent of hourly workers incurring at least some fluctuations in hours, the larger the proportion of fluctuations above forty-five hours, the lower their financial insecurity ($b = -0.311$, $p < .05$). Among hourly workers, then, surging up into overtime seems to play a protective role when it comes to financial insecurity.

The opposite picture emerges for workers paid a salary. Although the number of hours worked was not significantly related to salaried workers' financial insecurity in the multiyear data, usual hours is positively associated with

financial insecurity among salaried workers in all of the models specified with the 2016 GSS data. The more hours salaried workers report that they usually work, the greater their financial insecurity. This finding is consistent with research indicating that some salaried workers may work long hours out of fear that not doing so will lower their chances for advancement (Perlow 2012).

In addition to the sheer number of work hours, lack of control over the timing (but not the number) of work hours is positively associated with financial insecurity among salaried workers, a relationship also found in the multiyear data. The findings also suggest that less than a week of advance notice plays a substantial role in heightening perceptions of financial

	Model 3				Model 4				Model 5			
	Hourly		Salary		Hourly		Salary		Hourly		Salary	
	B	(SE)	B	(SE)	B	(SE)	B	(SE)	B	(SE)	B	(SE)
	−0.000	(0.004)	0.007*	(0.003)	−0.001	(0.004)	0.006*	(0.003)	−0.001	(0.004)	0.008**	(0.003)
	0.069	(0.076)	−0.014	(0.068)								
					0.130	(0.095)	0.126^	(0.072)				
									−0.045	(0.099)	−0.132	(0.108)
	−0.011	(0.016)	0.011	(0.017)	−0.008	(0.017)	0.009	(0.017)	−0.001	(0.016)	0.009	(0.016)
	−0.348	(0.342)	0.368	(0.454)								
					−0.345	(0.334)	0.753^	(0.423)				
									1.349**	(0.333)	−1.702**	(0.576)
	0.002	(0.002)	0.000	(0.004)	0.002	(0.002)	0.001	(0.004)	0.002	(0.002)	0.001	(0.004)
	−0.042	(0.037)	−0.091	(0.067)								
					−0.022	(0.042)	−0.070	(0.073)				
									0.017	(0.060)	−0.067	(0.075)

insecurity among salaried workers, by itself (table 8, panel A, model 2) and in combination with volatile work hours (table 9, panel A, model 2), lack of input into start and end times (table 9, panel A, model 4), and lack of input into number of hours (table 9, panel A, model 5). Thus, although much research has focused on the importance of advance notice for hourly workers, these results suggest that short advance notice can undermine the financial security of workers paid a salary.

Work Schedules and Job Insecurity
In the multiyear data, the number of hours hourly workers report working in the last week is negatively associated with job insecurity across all models estimated. In the 2016 data,

usual weekly hours is not significantly associated with job insecurity for either hourly or salaried workers (table 8, panel B), and the non-significance holds when hours worked last week, rather than usual hours, is entered in models (not in table). Although the sheer number of hours does not help explain job insecurity in this smaller 2016 data set, other aspects of work schedules do. As in the multiyear data, working a nonregular schedule (that is, a schedule other than a "regular day, afternoon, evening schedule") is positively associated with hourly worker job insecurity (table 8, panel B, model 5). Short advance notice also heightens job insecurity among hourly workers, either alone (table 8, panel B, model 2) or in combination with work-hour volatility (table 9, panel B,

Table 9. Regressions for Combinations of Scheduling Practices, 2016 GSS

| | Model 1 | | | | Model 2 | | | |
| | Hourly | | Salary | | Hourly | | Salary | |
	B	(SE)	B	(SE)	B	(SE)	B	(SE)
Panel A. Financial insecurity (OLS)								
Volatility plus little input into number	0.115	(0.095)	0.098	(0.125)				
Volatility plus short notice					-0.038	(0.106)	0.269*	(0.111)
Volatility plus little input into timing								
Short notice plus little input into timing								
Short notice plus little input into number								
Panel B. Job insecurity (logits)								
Volatility plus little input into number	-0.256	(0.468)	0.558	(0.641)				
Volatility plus short notice					0.859**	(0.302)	0.320	(0.534)
Volatility plus little input into timing								
Short notice plus little input into timing								
Short notice plus little input into number								
Panel C. Distrust in institutions (OLS)								
Volatility plus little input into number	0.072	(0.068)	-0.108	(0.084)				
Volatility plus short notice					0.058	(0.051)	0.092	(0.066)
Volatility plus little input into timing								
Short notice plus little input into timing								
Short notice plus little input into number								

Source: Authors' calculations based on the 2016 General Social Survey (Smith et al. 2018).

Note: Standard errors (SE). Total sample size is 525,334 for hourly workers and 191 for salaries workers.

^$p < .1$; *$p < .05$; **$p < .01$

model 2). Together, these findings suggest that nonregular timing and lack of advance notice contribute to hourly workers' sense of job insecurity, especially when they work highly fluctuating hours.

Again, a different picture surfaces among salaried workers. Rather than contributing to job insecurity, working a nonregular schedule is negatively related to job insecurity among salaried workers (table 8, panel B, model 5). This relationship may reflect the value employers place on being willing and able to work outside standard hours, as discussed in the introduction. Were this the case, however, we would

also expect to see a significant negative relationship between the magnitude of work-hour fluctuations and job insecurity, and we do not; although the relationship between relative instability and job insecurity is negative, it is not statistically significant (table 8, panel B, model 1). The only other dimension of work schedules significantly associated with job insecurity among salaried workers is that lack of input into the timing (not the number) is positively associated with job insecurity, though only at the $p < .1$ level. These results provide further evidence that the nature of relationships between work scheduling practices and perceived

| Model 3 | | | | Model 4 | | | | Model 5 | | | |
| Hourly | | Salary | | Hourly | | Salary | | Hourly | | Salary | |
B	(SE)	B	(SE)	B	(SE)	B	(SE)	B	(SE)	B	(SE)
0.124	(0.084)	0.131	(0.119)								
				0.181^	(0.098)	0.264^	(0.137)				
								0.022	(0.093)	0.342^	(0.172)
-0.136	(0.335)	0.718	(0.680)								
				0.371	(0.396)	-1.755	(1.180)				
								-0.011	(0.465)	-0.480	(0.900)
0.062	(0.056)	-0.077	(0.101)								
				0.016	(0.050)	-0.150	(0.148)				
								0.065	(0.069)	-0.165	(0.178)

insecurity are likely different for workers paid by hour and salary. Although working a non-regular schedule may impede a sense of job security among hourly workers, it seems to play a protective role among salaried workers.

Work Schedules and Distrust of Institutions
Analyses of the multiyear survey data suggest that working irregular or on-call shifts, especially when they are employer controlled, is associated with distrust in institutions among hourly workers only. Supplemental analyses of the 2016 data help fill in this picture. Although the overall magnitude of fluctuations in weekly hours is not statistically significant in explaining hourly workers' distrust in institutions (table 8, panel C, model 1), those with highly volatile hours (relative instability is at least 0.25) report greater distrust in institutions than those with less volatility ($b = 0.106$, $p < .05$, not in table). The direction of the fluctuation matters, however. Workers who report shortfalls in weekly hours (at least 25 percent less than their usual hours) report significantly greater institutional distrust than workers who report smaller shortfalls in weekly hours (available from authors).

Although the multiyear data reveal no significant associations between work scheduling qualities and distrust in institutions among salaried workers, the 2016 GSS indicates that the more hours fluctuate, the greater salaried workers' distrust of institutions. But, like their hourly counterparts, it is salaried workers who experience shortfalls in hours (at least 25 percent less than their usual) who express the most distrust in societal institutions (available from the authors).

DISCUSSION

The sources of uncertainty are expanding in the U.S. labor market. This article considers employer scheduling practices as one determinant of uncertainty that is undermining the quality of jobs and quality of life in the United States. Recent research traces the relationship between fluctuations in weekly work hours to volatility in workers' earnings and household incomes and in turn, to financial insecurity and hardship. In this article, we look at these relationships from the workers' perspective by examining the ramifications of fluctuating work hours, alone and in combination with other scheduling practices, for perceived insecurity, both economic and societal. Our findings suggest that different dimensions of work schedules may serve to undermine, or bolster, hourly and salaried workers' perceptions of financial and job security and their trust in major institutions. Findings also suggest that workers who are black, young, and without a college degree are at highest risk of experiencing problematic combinations of scheduling practices.

The questions commonly used in national surveys to capture the nature of working time may underestimate the prevalence of problematic scheduling practices in today's U.S. labor market because they do not offer insight into several key dimensions—such as the magnitude and direction of work-hour fluctuations, length of advance notice, and amount of input into the number of weekly hours—that may be especially prevalent in today's workplaces. In particular, the new questions on the 2016 General Social Survey suggest that working fluctuating hours is significantly more common than captured by commonly used survey questions. For example, at most, one-fifth of workers would be identified as working fluctu-

ating hours if based on the common question of schedule type (for example, irregular, on-call, or split or rotating shift), whereas more than three-fourths of workers gave different responses when reporting the greatest versus fewest number of hours they worked a week in the past month. For most, these fluctuations were not inconsequential, averaging more than a full day of work and approximately one-third of their usual weekly hours—all within just a one-month period.

The new 2016 GSS questions enabled us to update and unpack the nature of work schedules in the U.S. labor market further by also examining the length of advance schedule notice and input into both timing and hours. Like fluctuating hours, these additional aspects of work schedules have the potential to undermine job quality. We find that two-fifths of hourly and one-third of salaried workers report one week or less advance schedule notice, almost two-thirds of hourly and one-third of salaried workers report that the starting and finishing times of their work shifts are decided by their employer, and almost one-half of hourly and one-third of salaried workers report that employers entirely decide the number of hours they work. Limited advance notice and input into work hours are especially commonplace among black and Hispanic workers in hourly jobs; in addition, although a substantial proportion of women report having precarious work schedules, the data suggest that men are at even greater risk. The data provide evidence that some, but certainly not all, workers age out of precarious work schedules, with hourly workers gaining more predictability as they age and salaried workers gaining more control.

Our analyses reveal several themes worthy of future research. One key theme concerns the importance of taking into account how workers are paid when investigating the implications of work hours for economic insecurity. Findings lend support to Pfeffer and DeVoe's observation that the structure of compensation can prime the economic valuation of time (2012). In our multiyear survey analyses, we find that workers paid by the hour report greater financial insecurity than those paid a salary, after adjusting for covariates. The differing relationships we observe between number of weekly hours and perceptions of economic insecurity among hourly versus salaried workers further highlight how employer practices that structure the tie between hours and earnings may alter workers' experiences of their work hours. Among hourly workers, the greater the number of usual weekly hours, the lower their job insecurity (multiyear GSS) and notably, work-hour surges above forty-five hours a week seem to further protect hourly workers from experiencing job insecurity (2016 GSS, not in table). This makes sense, given that earnings are a function of hours worked, and, if employers are following the law, hourly workers receive a premium when weekly hours exceed forty. Salaried workers do not receive such a premium, and in the 2016 GSS the number of hours salaried workers worked last week was positively related to financial insecurity across several models. Together, these findings suggest that working long hours may reduce economic insecurity among hourly workers, but may foster, or be a response to, economic insecurity among salaried workers. These analyses are associational, not causal; notably, salaried workers may be working longer hours because they feel insecure, rather than vice versa.

Another theme that emerges from our findings is that fluctuating hours are not always a marker of a poor-quality job. The ramifications of work-hour fluctuations depend on their magnitude and direction. In the 2016 GSS, the greater the volatility in weekly hours, the lower hourly workers' financial insecurity—especially when the majority of hour fluctuations were due to surges above forty-five hours a week. Thus, questions in surveys that ask about hour variations as a yes or no job characteristic or as a particular schedule type provide limited insight into the conditions under which fluctuating hours matter for workers' lives. Future research is needed to examine how the magnitude and direction of fluctuating hours are related to nonfinancial aspects of life. We find that working fluctuating hours is positively associated with workers' distrust of societal institutions, among both hourly (multiyear GSS) and salaried (2016 GSS) workers. Further analyses revealed that the direction of the fluctuations mattered, with distrust being highest among workers who reported a substantial shortfall in

weekly hours. The magnitude and direction of work-hour fluctuations may matter for family life as well. For example, although surges in work hours may help protect workers from financial insecurity, they may complicate caregiving and create stress (Henly and Lambert 2014).

The findings of this study also highlight the usefulness of considering scheduling practices in combination with one another. In the multiyear data, the combination of working an irregular or on-call schedule plus little input into the timing of work increased the odds of job insecurity among hourly and salaried workers. In the 2016 data, although work-hour volatility is not significantly related to financial insecurity among salaried workers when examined alone, the combination of hour volatility plus either short advance notice or lack of input into schedule timing are both positively associated with these workers' perceptions of financial insecurity. These findings add to evidence that fluctuations in work hours can be experienced as flexibility or as instability, depending on whether they are employee versus employer driven (Fugiel and Lambert 2019; Henly, Shaefer, and Waxman 2006).

The results suggest that advance notice is a salient aspect of job quality not only among hourly workers, but among salaried workers as well. The budding literature on advance notice has focused on the implications of schedule unpredictability mostly among low-paid hourly workers (Henly and Lambert 2014; Schneider and Harknett 2016). Daniel Clawson and Naomi Gerstel's recent examination of predictability in health-care settings, however, reminds us that it is not that unpredictability is unimportant to higher-status workers but that they are better equipped to avoid it (2014). The results of this study confirm that the length of advance schedule notice is a marker of job quality in hourly jobs. Among hourly workers, less than a week's notice is positively related to financial insecurity, when accompanied by a lack of input into the timing of hours, and job insecurity, when accompanied by volatile hours. Our findings also suggest that length of advance notice is a marker of the quality of salaried positions as well. Among salaried workers, a week or less of notice is positively associated with financial insecurity when examined alone and in combination with work-hour volatility and lack of input into both the number and timing of work hours.

The scheduling practices that undermine job quality can have consequences for communities and society. In this article, we explore the possibility that work schedules may be unsettling beyond their economic ramifications by undermining confidence in societal institutions. Our findings suggest that experiencing shortfalls in weekly hours may help cement the growing distrust in key societal institutions observed in the United States over several decades. This finding raises the possibility that growing rates of involuntary part-time employment may exacerbate American's distrust in institutions, and perhaps in one another. Such possibilities seem worthy of further investigation.

We remind readers that the observed associations, and the lack thereof, come from exploratory analyses. Although in some analyses we are able to capitalize on the larger sample afforded by pooling multiple years of the GSS, these years included only a handful of questions on work schedules. The 2016 GSS provided data on a richer set of work scheduling practices, however the one-year sample limited statistical power. Moreover, the very nature of our dependent variables set the bar high in terms of identifying the ramifications of scheduling practices. The questions making up our index of financial insecurity capture workers' assessment of overall economic well-being and standard of living, rather than the more tangible aspects of financial hardship that research suggests can occur when workers' hours vary at the behest of their employer and with little time to adjust expenses or budgets (Morduch and Schneider 2017). Examining the relationship between everyday scheduling practices and what seems a fairly distal outcome—confidence in societal institutions—is similarly ambitious.

Even with these conceptually ambitious measures, the results provide evidence that scheduling practices that introduce instability and unpredictability into workers' lives—volatile work hours, little input into the timing and number of hours, and short advance notice—undermine the quality of many American jobs. From a research standpoint, the findings attest to the merits of examining how different dimensions of work schedules, both fundamental and more nuanced aspects, operate in tandem to affect workers' assessments of their lives and livelihoods. The widespread prevalence of work-hour volatility, short advance notice, and limited input into the number and timing of hours—and the concentration of these among marginalized subgroups—suggest the merits of further study of the conditions under which, and for whom, these scheduling practices heighten insecurity and distrust.

Table A1. Descriptives of Fundamental Scheduling Practices by Subgroups

	Percent Hourly	Weekly Hours (Mean, SD)		Little or No Input into Timing		Irregular or On-Call Shift		Nonregular Timing	
		Hourly	Salary	Hourly	Salary	Hourly	Salary	Hourly	Salary
All employees	60.0	38.9 (13.5)	45.6 (13.0)**	60.0	37.0**	5.4	6.5	15.3	9.8**
Men	57.6	41.7 (13.6)	48.4 (13.5)**	62.6	28.7**	6.9	7.9	15.7	12.9
Women	62.1	36.5 (12.9)	42.9 (11.9)**	57.9	45.1**	4.2	5.1	14.9	6.8**
Race									
White	54.6	38.6 (14.1)	46.1 (12.9)**	56.5	33.9**	4.9	6.4	14.2	9.6*
Black	78.2	39.4 (13.1)	41.8 (12.7)	66.2	61.4	6.8	2.9	18.2	7.4*
Hispanic	74.1	39.8 (11.9)	45.2 (14.9)*	66.8	39.5**	5.6	9.1	16.3	13.3
Age									
26 and younger	78.6	36.2 (12.4)	46.9 (16.1)**	62.9	54.9	7.9	7.3	25.7	15
27–35	62.3	40.9 (12.5)	45.4 (13.0)**	59.0	42.0	5.3	6.7	13.9	11.5
36–45	54.8	39.8 (13.4)	45.5 (12.1)**	58.2	32.2**	4.0	6.2	12.9	8.8
46–54	54.7	41.4 (13.2)	47.4 (11.6)**	61.0	36.2**	3.7	4.4	12.2	7.0^
55–64	54.0	38.1 (14.0)	45.1 (11.9)**	58.4	31.7**	5.9	7.9	10	8.9
65 and older	59.5	26.7 (14.7)	38.1 (19.6)**	61.2	36.7**	7.1	9.4	17	14.8
Work hours									
Full time	54.8	44.8 (9.7)	48.1 (10.7)**	62.5	37.0**	4.8	6.3	13.6	9.9*
Part time	81.2	22.7 (7.9)	21.3 (8.4)	53.2	37.1*	6.8	8.5	20.0	9.1*

(continued)

Table A1. (*continued*)

	Percent Hourly	Weekly Hours (Mean, SD)		Little or No Input into Timing		Irregular or On-Call Shift		Nonregular Timing	
		Hourly	Salary	Hourly	Salary	Hourly	Salary	Hourly	Salary
Education									
High school or less	78.2	39.2 (13.1)	45.1 (13.3)	62.7	45.1**	5.1	7.8	14.6	12.5
More than high school, less than four-year college	63.0	39.5 (12.9)	46.7 (14.4)^	54.6	32.9**	4.5	11.4*	18.4	14.9
College degree or more	26.2	36.8 (15.7)	45.8 (12.7)	49.0	33.2**	7.3	5.1	17.1	7.6**
Earnings									
Low pay	58.5	42.6 (12.1)	47.9 (12.5**)	58.2	31.9**	5.1	5.8	14.3	9.5*
Higher pay	58.9	32.7 (13.6)	41.9 (12.8)**	63.1	50.9**	4.7	6.7	16.5	10.0*
Occupation									
Management, business, office, admin support	45.6	39.0 (11.7)	46.4 (11.5)**	53.5	26.5**	4.2	6.6	11.5	7.7
Professional, related fields	40.0	37.6 (14.8)	43.1 (12.5)**	52.5	47.0	4.5	4.3	12.8	5.8**
Service, sales, related fields	76.8	36.5 (13.8)	46.7 (15.1)**	63.0	40.1**	6.2	9.3	21.8	20.1
Construction, production, transport, natural resources	82.0	42.4 (12.9)	50.3 (15.9)**	65.3	43.7**	4.0	9.7*	10.1	17.2^
Non-union	59.7	38.3 (13.4)	45.9 (12.8)**	58.0	32.3**	5.4	7.1	15.3	9.4**
Union	62.2	41.9 (13.5)	44.2 (14.1)	72.7	70.8	5.1	2.6	14.8	12.6

Source: Authors' calculations based on multiyear General Social Survey data (Smith et al. 2018).

Note: All percentages are weighted. N = 3,564; salaried 2,121; hourly 1,443.

^p < .1; *p < .05; **p < .01

Table A2. Relationship Between Control Variables and Dependent Measures

Panel A. Multiyear GSS	Financial Insecurity				Job Insecurity				Institutional Distrust			
	Hourly		Salary		Hourly		Salary		Hourly		Salary	
	B	(SE)	B	(SE)	B	(SE)	B	(SE)	B	(SE)	B	(SE)
Last week hours	-0.002	(0.002)	-0.001	(0.001)	-0.017**	(0.007)	0.005	(0.008)	0.001	(0.001)	0.001	(0.001)
Age	0.004**	(0.001)	0.004^	(0.002)	0.007	(0.006)	-0.003	(0.011)	0.004**	(0.001)	0.004**	(0.001)
Age^2	-0.001**	(0.000)	-0.000*	(0.000)	-0.001^	(0.000)	-0.003**	(0.001)	-0.000**	(0.000)	-0.000**	(0.000)
Race												
White, non-Hispanic (ref)												
Black	-0.123**	(0.043)	0.058	(0.061)	-0.097	(0.178)	0.211	(0.328)	-0.026	(0.036)	0.007	(0.053)
Hispanic	-0.184**	(0.053)	-0.164*	(0.075)	0.016	(0.257)	0.334	(0.463)	-0.056^	(0.030)	-0.048	(0.049)
Other	-0.097	(0.088)	-0.159^	(0.087)	0.211	(0.421)	0.665	(0.538)	-0.150*	(0.060)	-0.086	(0.059)
Female	-0.067*	(0.034)	0.032	(0.044)	-0.140	(0.155)	-0.173	(0.237)	-0.025	(0.024)	0.016	(0.028)
High school or less	-0.001	(0.040)	0.168**	(0.046)	0.355^	(0.192)	-0.043	(0.295)	0.060*	(0.025)	0.022	(0.033)
Household income												
1 (<$20,499)	0.287**	(0.055)	0.327^	(0.168)	0.509*	(0.213)	1.784**	(0.507)	-0.077*	(0.037)	-0.051	(0.080)
2 ($20,500-$36,399)	0.120*	(0.051)	0.169*	(0.072)	0.441^	(0.230)	0.919*	(0.390)	-0.074*	(0.033)	-0.016	(0.050)
3 ($36,400-$58,999) (ref)												
4 ($59,000-$87,999)	-0.247**	(0.048)	-0.213**	(0.051)	-0.489	(0.309)	0.679*	(0.328)	-0.075*	(0.035)	0.067^	(0.036)
5 ($88,000<=)	-0.518**	(0.059)	-0.477**	(0.053)	-0.366	(0.360)	0.248	(0.361)	-0.099*	(0.048)	0.040	(0.035)
No partner or spouse	0.109**	(0.041)	0.012	(0.049)	0.012	(0.206)	-0.358	(0.283)	0.002	(0.025)	0.042	(0.029)
Spouse does not work	0.040	(0.058)	0.019	(0.063)	-0.256	(0.278)	-0.084	(0.324)	0.033	(0.034)	-0.030	(0.037)
Have children 18 or younger	0.028	(0.034)	0.079^	(0.045)	-0.076	(0.172)	-0.219	(0.236)	-0.056*	(0.023)	-0.029	(0.026)
Multiple jobs (1=yes)	-0.006	(0.047)	0.105^	(0.054)	0.199	(0.196)	0.757**	(0.275)	0.017	(0.027)	0.005	(0.035)
Year												
2002 (ref)												
2006	0.079	(0.049)	0.067	(0.045)	-0.103	(0.203)	0.035	(0.293)	0.064*	(0.029)	0.074*	(0.033)
2010	0.147**	(0.049)	0.301**	(0.054)	-0.205	(0.201)	0.500	(0.303)	0.093**	(0.030)	0.186**	(0.037)
2014	0.107*	(0.046)	0.159**	(0.054)	-0.574*	(0.230)	-0.142	(0.348)	0.120**	(0.029)	0.214**	(0.035)
N	2,141		1,454		2,121		1,443		2,140		1,452	

(continued)

Table A2. (continued)

Panel B. 2016 GSS	Financial Insecurity				Job Insecurity				Institutional Distrust			
	Hourly		Salary		Hourly		Salary		Hourly		Salary	
	B	(SE)	B	(SE)	B	(SE)	B	(SE)	B	(SE)	B	(SE)
Usual hours	-0.000	(0.004)	0.007*	(0.003)	-0.012	(0.016)	0.007	(0.016)	0.002	(0.002)	0.001	(0.004)
Age	0.002	(0.003)	0.005	(0.004)	0.035*	(0.013)	0.058**	(0.017)	0.001	(0.002)	0.004	(0.002)
Age²	-0.001**	(0.000)	-0.001**	(0.000)	-0.001^	(0.001)	-0.006**	(0.002)	0.000	(0.000)	0.000	(0.000)
Race												
White, non-Hispanic (ref)												
Nonwhite	-0.128	(0.102)	-0.150*	(0.073)	0.738^	(0.407)	-0.816	(0.528)	-0.156**	(0.051)	-0.051	(0.063)
Female	0.151	(0.090)	0.187*	(0.073)	-0.615	(0.375)	-0.299	(0.411)	-0.049	(0.051)	-0.012	(0.054)
High school or less	-0.003	(0.091)	-0.004	(0.076)	-0.842*	(0.340)	0.231	(0.595)	-0.017	(0.048)	0.002	(0.076)
Household income												
1 (<$20,499)	-0.379	(1.231)	-1.180^	(0.602)	1.985	(4.048)	0.781	(2.802)	0.033	(0.570)	0.448	(0.354)
2 ($20,500–$36,399)	0.229^	(0.123)	0.161	(0.123)	0.366	(0.440)	-0.080	(0.576)	-0.049	(0.051)	0.043	(0.076)
3 ($36,400–$58,999) (ref)												
4 ($59,000–$87,999)	0.706	(1.240)	1.672**	(0.571)	-1.342	(4.097)	-0.927	(2.775)	-0.049	(0.572)	-0.515	(0.332)
No partner or spouse	0.169	(0.112)	0.436**	(0.073)	0.527	(0.378)	1.026^	(0.525)	0.081	(0.062)	0.047	(0.062)
Spouse does not work	0.261*	(0.126)	0.122	(0.112)	1.056*	(0.505)	-1.070	(1.082)	0.109^	(0.060)	0.150^	(0.081)
Have children 18 or younger	-0.031	(0.107)	-0.027	(0.110)	0.556	(0.389)	-1.009*	(0.468)	0.041	(0.054)	0.110^	(0.054)
Multiple jobs (1=yes)	-0.124	(0.141)	0.043	(0.149)	0.322	(0.469)	0.077	(0.676)	0.009	(0.067)	0.043	(0.099)
N	334		191		330		188		334		191	

Source: Authors' calculations based on the General Social Survey (Smith et al. 2018).

^p < .1; *p < .05; **p < .01

REFERENCES

Abramson, Paul, and Ronald Inglehart.1995. *Value Change in Global Perspective*. Ann Arbor: University of Michigan Press.

Appelbaum, Eileen, and Rosemary Batt. 2014. *Private Equity at Work: When Wall Street Manages Main Street*. New York: Russell Sage Foundation.

Board of Governors of the Federal Reserve System. 2017. "Report on the Economic Well-Being of U.S. Households in 2016." Accessed April 5, 2018. https://www.federalreserve.gov/publications/files/2016-report-economic-well-being-us-households-201705.pdf.

Carré, Francoise, and Chris Tilly. 2017. *Where Bad Jobs Are Better: Why Retail Jobs Differ across Countries and Companies*. New York: Russell Sage Foundation.

Clawson, Dan, and Naomi Gerstel. 2014. *Unequal Time: Gender, Class, and Family in Employment Schedules*. New York: Russell Sage Foundation.

Dalton, Russell J. 2005. "The Social Transformation of Trust in Government." *International Review of Sociology* 15(1): 133–54.

DeVoe, Sanford E., and Jeffrey Pfeffer. 2009. "When Is Happiness About How Much You Earn? The Effect of Hourly Payment on the Money–Happiness Connection." *Personality and Social Psychology Bulletin* 35(12): 1602–18.

De Witte, Hans, and Katharina Näswall. 2003. "'Objective' versus 'Subjective' Job Insecurity: Consequences of Temporary Work for Job Satisfaction and Organizational Commitment in Four European Countries." *Economic and Industrial Democracy* 24(2): 149–88.

Edin, Kathryn J., and H. Luke Shaefer. 2016. *$2.00 a Day: Living on Almost Nothing in America*. New York: First Mariner Books.

Farrell, Diane, and Fiona Greig. 2016. "Paychecks, Paydays, and the Online Platform Economy: Big Data on Income Volatility." New York: J. P. Morgan Chase. Accessed March 15, 2018. https://www.jpmorganchase.com/corporate/institute/document/jpmc-institute-volatility-2-report.pdf.

Finnigan, Ryan. 2018. "Varying Weekly Work Hours and Earnings Instability in the Great Recession." *Social Science Research* 74 (August): 96–107.

Frazis, Harley, and Jay Stewart. 2014. "Is the Workweek Really Overestimated?" *Monthly Labor Review* 6 (June): 1–15.

Fugiel, Peter J., and Susan J. Lambert. 2019. "On-Demand and On-Call Work in the United States." In *Zero Hours and On-Call Work in Anglo-Saxon Countries*, edited by Michelle O'Sullivan, Jonathan Lavelle, Juliette McMahon, Lorraine Ryan, Caroline Murphy, Thomas Turner, and Patroc Gunnigle. New York: Springer Publishing.

Gallup Organization. 2018a. "Economy." Polls Between 2013 and 2018. Accessed April 13, 2018. http://news.gallup.com/poll/1609/Consumer-Views-Economy.aspx.

———. 2018b. "Confidence in Institutions." Polls Between 1937 and 2018. Accessed July 5, 2018. https://news.gallup.com/poll/1597/confidence-institutions.aspx.

Golden, Lonnie. 2016. "Still Falling Short on Hours and Pay: Part-time Work Becoming New Normal." Washington, D.C.: Economic Policy Institute. Accessed February 27, 2019. https://www.epi.org/publication/still-falling-short-on-hours-and-pay-part-time-work-becoming-new-normal.

Gottschalk, Peter, and Robert Moffitt. 2009. "The Rising Instability of U.S. Earnings." *Journal of Economic Perspectives* 23(4): 3–24.

Hacker, Jacob. 2006. *The Great Risk Shift: The Assault on American Jobs, Families, Health Care, and Retirement and How You Can Fight Back*. New York: Oxford University Press.

Haley-Lock, Anna. and Stephanie Ewert. 2011. "Serving Men and Mothers: Workplace Practices and Workforce Composition in Two U.S. Restaurant Chains and States." *Community, Work & Family* 14(4): 387–404.

Hayes, Christopher. 2012. *Twilight of the Elites: America after Meritocracy*. New York: Random House.

Henly, Julia R., and Susan J. Lambert. 2014. "Unpredictable Work Timing in Retail Jobs: Implications for Employee Work-life Outcomes." *Industrial and Labor Relations Review* 67(3): 986–1016.

Henly, Julia R., H. Luke Shaefer, and R. Elaine Waxman. 2006. "Nonstandard Work Schedules: Employer- and Employee-Driven Flexibility in Retail Jobs." *Social Service Review* 80(4): 609–34.

Huang, Guo-hua, Xiongyinig Niu, Cynthia Lee, and Susan J. Ashford. 2012. "Differentiating Cognitive and Affective Job Insecurity: Antecedents and Outcomes." *Journal of Organizational Behavior* 33(6): 752–69.

Jacobs, Jerry A., and Kathleen Gerson. 2004. *The Time Divide: Work, Family and Gender Inequality*. Cambridge, Mass.: Harvard University Press.

Jones, Kerry. 2017. "The Most Desirable Employee Benefits." *Harvard Business Review*, February 15, 2017. Accessed February 27, 2019. https://hbr .org/2017/02/the-most-desirable-employee-benefits.

Kalleberg, Arne L. 2011. *Good Jobs, Bad Jobs: The Rise of Polarized and Precarious Employment Systems in the United States, 1970s to 2000s*. New York: Russell Sage Foundation.

Kalleberg, Arne L., and Steven P. Vallas. 2017. *Precarious Work*. Bingley, UK: Emerald Publishing.

Lambert, Susan J. 2008. "Passing the Buck: Labor Flexibility Practices that Transfer Risk onto Hourly Workers." *Human Relations* 61(9): 1203–27.

Lambert, Susan J., Anna Haley-Lock, and Julia R. Henly. 2012. "Schedule Flexibility in Hourly Jobs: Unanticipated Consequences and Promising Directions." *Community, Work & Family* 15(3): 293–315.

Lambert, Susan J., Julia R. Henly, Peter Fugiel, and Joshua Choper. 2019. "The Magnitude and Meaning of Work Hour Volatility among Early-Career Employees in the US." Unpublished manuscript, University of Chicago.

Lee, Cynthia, Philip Bobko, and Zhen Xiong Chen. 2006. "Investigation of the Multidimensional Model of Job Insecurity in Two Countries." *Applied Psychology: An International Review* 55(4): 167–95.

Lehndorff, Steffen, and Dorothea Voss-Dahm. 2005. "The Delegation of Uncertainty: Flexibility and the Role of the Market in Service Work," In *Working in the Service Sector: A Tale from Different Worlds*, edited by Gerhard Bosh and Steffen Lehndorff. New York: Routledge.

Mas, Alexandre, and Amanda Pallais. 2016. "Valuing Alternative Work Arrangements." *NBER* working paper no. 22708. Cambridge, Mass.: National Bureau of Economic Research. Accessed February 27, 2019. http://www.nber.org/papers /w22708.

Matos, Kenneth, and Ellen Galinsky. 2011. "Workplace Flexibility in the United States: A Status Report." New York: Families and Work Institute.

McCrate, Elaine. 2012. "Flexibility for Whom? Control Over Work Schedule Variability in the U.S." *Feminist Economics* 18(1): 39–72.

———. 2017. "Unstable and On-Call Work Schedules in the United States and Canada." *Conditions of Work and Employment Series* no. 99. Geneva: International Labour Office. Accessed February 27, 2019. https://www.ilo.org/wcmsp5/groups /public/---ed_protect/---protrav/---travail /documents/publication/wcms_619044.pdf.

Morduch, Jonathan, and Rachel Schneider. 2017. *The Financial Diaries: How American Families Cope in a World of Uncertainty*. Princeton, N.J.: Princeton University Press.

Perlow, Leslie A. 1997. *Finding Time: How Corporations, Individuals, and Families Can Benefit from New Work Practices*. Ithaca, N.Y.: Cornell University Press.

———. 2012. *Sleeping with Your Smartphone*. Cambridge, Mass.: Harvard Business School Publishing.

Pew Research Center. 2017. "Sharp Partisan Divisions in View of National Institutions." Washington, D.C.: Pew Research Center, U.S. Politics & Policy. Accessed February 27, 2019. http:// www.people-press.org/2017/07/10/sharp -partisan-divisions-in-views-of-national -institutions.

Pfeffer, Jeffrey, and Sanford E. DeVoe. 2012. "The Economic Evaluation of Time: Organizational Causes and Individual Consequences." *Research in Organizational Behavior* 32(1): 47–62.

Presser, Harriet B. 2003. *Working in a 24/7 Economy: Challenges for American Families*. New York: Russell Sage Foundation.

Robinson, John P., Alain Chenu, and Anthony S. Alvarez. 2002. "Measuring the Complexity of Hours at Work: The Weekly Work Grid." *Monthly Labor Review* 125(4): 44–54.

Schneider, Daniel, and Kristen Harknett. 2016. "Schedule Instability and Unpredictability and Worker Health and Wellbeing." Working paper. Washington, D.C.: Washington Center for Equitable Growth. Accessed February 27, 2019. http:// cdn.equitablegrowth.org/wp-content/uploads /2016/09/12135618/091216-WP-Schedule -instability-and-unpredictability.pdf.

Schor, Juliet. 1993. *The Overworked American: The Unexpected Decline of Leisure*. New York: Basic Books.

Sennett, Richard. 1998. *The Corrosion of Character: The Personal Consequences of Work in the New Capitalism*. New York: W. W. Norton.

Smith, Tom W., Michael Davern, Jeremy Freese, and Michael Hout. 2018. General Social Surveys,

1972–2016 [machine-readable data file]. Chicago: NORC, University of Chicago. Data available from the GSS Data Explorer website at http://gssdataexplorer.norc.org (accessed April 8, 2019).

Staines, Graham L., and Joseph H. Pleck. 1983. *The Impact of Work Schedules on the Family*. Ann Arbor, Mich.: Institute for Social Research.

Standing, Guy. 2011. *The Precariat: The New Dangerous Class*. London: Bloomsbury Academic.

Weil, David. 2014. *The Fissured Workplace: Why Work Became So Bad for So Many and What Can Be Done to Improve It*. Cambridge, Mass.: Harvard University Press.

Evaluating Employment Quality as a Determinant of Health in a Changing Labor Market

TREVOR PECKHAM, KAORI FUJISHIRO, ANJUM HAJAT,
BRIAN P. FLAHERTY, AND NOAH SEIXAS

The shifting nature of employment in recent decades has not been adequately examined from a public health perspective. To that end, traditional models of work and health research need to be expanded to include the relational and contractual aspects of employment that also affect health. We examine the association of three health outcomes with different types of employment in the contemporary U.S. labor market, as measured by a multidimensional construct of employment quality (EQ) derived from latent class analysis. We find that EQ is associated with self-rated health, mental health, and occupational injury. Further, we explore three proposed mediating mechanisms of the EQ-health relationship (material deprivation, employment-related stressors, and occupational risk factors), and find each to be supported by these data.

Keywords: employment quality, occupational health, latent class analysis, mental health, work-related injury

Rapid technological innovation, globalization processes, economic recessions, and demographic changes over the past several decades have caused a number of adaptive changes in the labor market, including the fundamental transformation of the nature and organization of work (Bosch 2004; Kalleberg 2009). Most notable is the shift away from maintaining a stable workforce toward more flexible and economically competitive employment practices (Benach et al. 2014; Bosch 2004; Kalleberg 2009; Weil 2014). Consequently, the number of workers in permanent, full-time, regularly scheduled work with secure wages and benefits has declined; and concurrently, nonstandard arrangements have increased (Howard 2016;

Trevor Peckham is a doctoral student in environmental and occupational health sciences and clinical instructor in health services at the University of Washington. **Kaori Fujishiro** is senior epidemiologist at the National Institute for Occupational Safety and Health. **Anjum Hajat** is assistant professor of epidemiology at the University of Washington. **Brian P. Flaherty** is associate professor of psychology at the University of Washington. **Noah Seixas** is professor of environmental and occupational health sciences at the University of Washington.

© 2019 Russell Sage Foundation. Peckham, Trevor, Kaori Fujishiro, Anjum Hajat, Brian P. Flaherty, and Noah Seixas. 2019. "Evaluating Employment Quality as a Determinant of Health in a Changing Labor Market." *RSF: The Russell Sage Foundation Journal of the Social Sciences* 5(4): 258–81. DOI: 10.7758/RSF.2019.5.4.09. Trevor Peckham was supported by the National Institute on Minority Health and Health Disparities of the National Institutes of Health under award number F31MD013357. The findings and conclusions in this article are those of the authors and do not necessarily represent the official position of the National Institutes of Health or the National Institute for Occupational Safety and Health, Centers for Disease Control and Prevention. Direct correspondence to: Trevor Peckham at tpeckham@uw.edu; 4225 Roosevelt Way NE, Suite 100, Box 354695, Seattle, WA 98195.

Kalleberg 2000). In addition to the growth of atypical forms of employment, other dimensions of work also became destandardized, including working hours, opportunities for advancement, and worker-employer relations (Scott-Marshall and Tompa 2011). These changes have far-reaching consequences for the labor market experiences of millions of Americans; however, they have not been adequately examined from a public health perspective and compel the need for a new understanding of the elements of jobs that contribute to poor health (Peckham et al. 2017; Scott-Marshall and Tompa 2011; Tompa et al. 2007). This paucity of research reflects the typical exclusion of occupation as a primary social determinant of health (Ahonen et al. 2018), as well as lack of measures that adequately capture employment conditions. This study offers an initial exploration of health consequences of different types of employment in the contemporary U.S. labor market as measured by a multidimensional construct of employment quality. Further, we explore potential mechanisms by which EQ affects health.

We begin by clarifying important terms for interdisciplinary audiences. Although often used interchangeably, *job*, *work*, and *employment* have specific and distinct meanings in this article. Employment refers to the contractual relationship between the employer and employee, and this is our central focus. Work refers to what the worker does, and *work quality* concerns the nature of tasks and the physical and social environment in which the work occurs. Jobs are a broader term capturing the combination of work and employment.

JOBS AND HEALTH: SHIFTING FOCUS FROM WORK QUALITY TO EMPLOYMENT QUALITY

The shifting nature of employment arrangements and labor experiences has challenged the adequacy of traditional approaches to investigating the relationship between work and health. The vast majority of occupational health studies have focused on work quality. Traditional occupational health research has focused on physical hazards, such as exposure to chemical agents or dangerous and physically demanding tasks or environments. This line of research has made tremendous contributions to general public health; for example, the International Agency for Research on Cancer, an agency within the World Health Organization, routinely evaluates occupational exposure as a basis for their human carcinogen designation. As economic activity in developed economies has moved away from industrial production and into service occupations, more attention has been directed at the psychological and social environment in the workplace. Since the early 1980s, job stress research has flourished, built on the fundamental premise that if the resources available to the worker are adequate for the demands in the workplace, then the health of the worker will be protected and enhanced; however, if the workplace demands overwhelm the worker's resources, his or her health will be compromised (Karasek 1979). A significant body of literature has provided convincing evidence that support this premise (Daniels, Tregaskis, and Seaton 2007; Siegrist et al. 2007). Both lines of occupational health research—one focusing on physical, chemical, and biological hazards and the other on psychological and social work environment—assume that health risks arise from *work* tasks and environments, and thus have paid little attention to *employment* conditions.

In the EU over the last several decades, policy interest in improving the quality of jobs has been significant (Lisbon European Council 2000). This has driven empirical and theoretical research to identify high- versus low-quality jobs. Although no ultimate consensus has been established as to how to measure job quality, researchers agree on the reality of a conceptual distinction between work quality (the nature of tasks and work environment) and employment quality (the relational and contractual aspects of the employer-employee relationship) (Holman and McClelland 2011; Muñoz de Bustillo et al. 2009). Although workers experience both work quality and employment quality at the same time, by distinguishing the two, researchers can build on the large body of literature on work quality and health while clarifying the relationship between work quality and employment quality that may influence health. The distinction will help identify policy directions for protecting the health of working people.

EMPLOYMENT QUALITY AS A MULTIDIMENSIONAL CONSTRUCT

To better understand health consequences of employment quality (EQ), we first need to recognize that the quality of employment is a multidimensional construct characterized by various conditions of the employer-employee relations. Several scholars have proposed ways to conceptualize EQ as a multidimensional construct (Holman and McClelland 2011; Muñoz de Bustillo et al. 2009). In this study, we build on a number of recent EU studies that have conceptualized EQ with the following seven dimensions: employment stability, material rewards, workers' rights and social protections, standardized working time arrangements, training and employability opportunities, collective organization, and interpersonal power relations (Julià et al. 2017; Van Aerden et al. 2014). These dimensions were drawn from a critical review of the employment quality literature with a specific focus on implications for worker well-being (Van Aerden et al. 2014), and thus together they capture various contractual arrangements and employment practices that employees experience.

A second important consideration is that jobs represent packages or configurations of different work and employment features, and that health implications stem from particular patterns in these features. One way to operationalize this is a typological approach, which identifies patterns of employment characteristics that holistically represent worker's experience. Using the Standard Employment Relationship (SER)—permanent, full-time, regularly scheduled work with secure wages and benefits—as a reference point, we can characterize the experience of EQ with differences in the pattern of employment conditions across the seven EQ dimensions. For example, some jobs may offer a short-term contract, low pay, and too few hours; others may have too many work hours, high pay, and good benefits (Van Aerden et al. 2014). Although this is still a new approach, two European studies have reported significant association between EQ types and some general health indicators (Van Aerden, Gadeyne, and Vanroelen 2017; Van Aerden et al. 2016).

The typological approach complements the more traditional variable-based approach, which focuses on individual aspects of EQ (such as employment stability, work schedule, pay) separately and identifies their independent associations with health while assuming other aspects to be constant. Studies using the variable-based approach have linked nonstandard employment—usually measured as perceived job insecurity or nonpermanent contract—to a variety of health outcomes, including increased injury rates and injury severity, musculoskeletal symptoms, and poor physical and mental health (Benach et al. 2014; Kim et al. 2012; Quinlan, Mayhew, and Bohle 2001; Silverstein et al. 1998). Poor health has been also associated with long working hours (O'Reilly and Rosato 2013; Virtanen et al. 2012), irregular and asocial work schedules (Jamal 2004; Martens et al. 1999), and mismatched preferences regarding working times (Wooden, Warren, and Drago 2009). Although they all suggest that components of EQ have potential health implications, being in disparate literatures and addressing only single aspects of EQ at a time, these findings have not formed a coherent approach for investigating health implications of the broader concept of EQ. Further, because poor employment conditions (for example, instability, irregular shift, low pay) tend to cluster in the same job, the variable-based approach is limited in its ability to illuminate health implications of poor EQ for workers, who experience jobs as a package.

EMPLOYMENT QUALITY AND HEALTH

A theoretical underpinning for EQ's health consequences is the fundamental cause theory of health (Link and Phelan 1995). It posits that money, knowledge, power, prestige, and social connections are personal resources that enable individuals to accumulate health advantages over time; hence the unequal access and distribution of these personal resources are fundamental causes of health inequalities. Most studies that apply this theory have used education as the proxy for the personal resources (see, for example, Masters, Link, and Phelan 2015). Recently, Emily Ahonen and her colleagues argued that jobs, with their complexity in providing both health-enhancing and damaging contexts throughout the adult life, influence the access and distribution of personal resources and thus are a crucial component in the application of fundamental cause theory (2018). According to this theory, EQ may affect health by influencing individuals' access to money, knowledge, power, prestige, and social connections, which in turn shape their ability to accumulate health advantages over time. In the context of EQ, we operationalize these personal resources with three specific pathways that lead from EQ to health: material deprivation, stressors related to employment conditions, and occupational risk factors (Julià et al. 2017; Tompa et al. 2007).

The first pathway, material deprivation, involves whether the employment condition provides a worker sufficient income as well as nonwage material benefits (for example, health insurance, paid sick leave) to acquire necessities and health-enhancing goods. The association between income and health is well documented (Fritzell, Nermo, and Lundberg 2004). The mechanism is not only through access to necessities and goods, but also though psychosocial distress associated with deprivation such as low self-esteem (Gardner, Dyne, and Pierce 2004); poor satisfaction with jobs (Faragher, Cass, and Cooper 2005; Leigh and De Vogli 2016) and life in general (Cheung and Lucas 2015); and difficulties in long-term life planning (Bosmans et al. 2016; Julià et al. 2017; Tompa et al. 2007).

The second pathway is through employment-related stressors such as job insecurity and earning unfairness. If the employment contract is short term or hours fluctuate unexpectedly, workers will experience anxiety about keeping the job (job insecurity) and less control over their professional and personal lives, which may hinder career development, create powerlessness, and negatively affect family and other personal relationships. These effects are all associated with poor health (Clarke et al. 2007; Lewchuk, Clarke, and de Wolff 2008). Moreover, if two workers perform the same work tasks side by side but are paid differently because of their different employment conditions (for example, a SER secretary and a clerical worker sent from a temp agency), the sense of unfairness arises, which is also associated with poor health (Elovainio et al. 2010).

Finally, EQ may affect health through differential exposures to occupational risk factors. Even though work tasks are similar, workers under different employment conditions may be exposed to occupational hazards differently. SER workers, to whom the employer is committed long term, may receive thorough training, have opportunities to develop skills to perform tasks safely, and be able to change work processes so that they are safe. The employers are likely to be motivated to keep SER jobs safer because SER employee turnover is expensive. For non-SER workers (for example, short-term, substitute, subcontractors), employers may not invest many resources in their safety. Because of the power relations represented in employment conditions, some non-SER workers may be reluctant to refuse hazardous tasks (Aronsson 1999; Foley 2017; Quinlan, Mayhew, and Bohle 2001; Tompa et al. 2007). Besides occupational safety, job strain—a combination of high job demands and little control (Karasek 1979)—and workplace social support are robust predictors of health (de Lange et al. 2003; Thoits 2011). Employment conditions may influence the workers' experience of both. Non-SER workers who are paid by the amount produced may have higher job demands than SER workers receiving hourly wages or salaries. Short-term contracts may not allow non-SER workers to form supportive connections in the workplace. All three mechanisms are conceptually plausible, but to date little systematic investigation has been done as to their importance in the relationship between EQ and health.

THE CURRENT STUDY

Using data from the General Social Survey (2002–2014), we examine the association of EQ and three health indicators (self-rated health, mental health, and occupational injury) and explore three proposed mediating mechanisms (material deprivation, employment-related stressors, and occupational risk factors). Self-rated health is an indicator of broad health status (Idler and Benyamini 1997) and its significant association with EQ was reported previously in EU data (Van Aerden, Gadeyne, and Vanroelen 2017; Van Aerden et al. 2016). Mental health—also associated with EQ (Van Aerden, Gadeyne, and Vanroelen 2017; Van

Aerden et al. 2016)—and occupational injury are more specific and contrasting health indicators. For mental health, material deprivation and employment-related stressors would be more salient mediating mechanisms, whereas traditional occupational risk factors would be more salient for occupational injury. Because our data are self-reported and cross-sectional, it is important to have contrasting health indicators so as not to capture completely spurious associations. Further, although the proposed mediating mechanisms are not competing hypotheses—rather, most likely all mechanisms are in effect simultaneously—the most salient mechanism may differ by the type of health consequence (for example, acute versus chronic) and by specific EQ features that distinguish a given employment condition from SER (for example, material rewards, employment stability, power relations). In this study, we investigate the linkages between EQ and health, as well as explore plausible mechanisms deserving of future investigation in this emerging field.

DATA AND METHODS

This study uses data from the General Social Survey (GSS). The GSS is a nationally representative, repeated cross-sectional survey of non-institutionalized American adults conducted in face-to-face personal interviews by the National Opinion Research Center (Smith et al. 2013). In 2002, 2006, 2010, and 2014, the GSS included a module on the Quality of Work Life (QWL), which assessed an assortment of employment conditions among employed GSS respondents. This module was developed in collaboration with the National Institute for Occupational Safety and Health and with advice from a panel of experts in organizational behavior, occupational safety and health, and human resource management. A total of 5,961 respondents, pooled across the four survey years, completed the QWL module and indicated that they were currently employed (either in full- or part-time work, or temporarily not working due to strike, vacation, or temporary illness). From this sam-

ple, exclusion criteria were applied at two stages of our analysis: first, prior to latent class analysis to determine EQ categories, and, second, prior to regression analyses with health outcomes. All analyses are adjusted for survey sampling probabilities that account for number of adults in the household and nonresponse. Year-specific response rates for the GSS were between 70.1 percent and 71.4 percent.

Construction of an Employment Quality Typology

The primary independent variable, a typology of EQ, was constructed by latent class analysis (LCA), which identifies mutually exclusive and exhaustive EQ types based on patterns of EQ indicator responses. In the GSS, we identified eleven indicators of EQ conditions that represent the seven dimensions of EQ described earlier (see table A1).[1] The conceptualization and choice of EQ indicators is based on an established framework (Julià et al. 2017), and indicators we used from the GSS are similar to prior studies of EQ in Europe (Van Aerden, Gadeyne, and Vanroelen 2017; Van Aerden et al. 2014, 2015, 2016). LCA modeling in this study was conducted using the mixture modeling function with maximum likelihood (ML) estimation, including sample weights provided by the GSS, in Mplus version 8 (Muthén and Muthén 2010). Missing values were modeled with ML estimation assuming missing at random (Little and Rubin 2014).

In constructing EQ categories, we evaluate wage earning and self-employed worker populations separately: these employment arrangements are fundamentally different such that we expect the meaning of some EQ indicators to be dissimilar across the two groups (for example, mandatory overtime could be self-imposed for self-employed workers). Self-employment status was determined using the item "Are you self-employed or do you work for someone else?" Respondents with no information on self-employment were excluded (n = 5). We further excluded respondents without information for at least two EQ indicators (n = 23), re-

1. See the online appendix (https://www.rsfjournal.org/content/5/4/258/tab-supplemental) for tables A1 through A8.

taining as many respondents as possible that contributed EQ items for the LCA. The final sample included in LCA modeling was 5,933 workers (n = 5,125 for wage earners, n = 808 for the self-employed).

Analyzing the wage earning and self-employed groups separately, we increased the number of classes stepwise and then selected the best LCA models through a two-step procedure that includes assessment of formal fit indices and a substantive interpretation of EQ types. Three model-fit indices, Bayesian Information Criteria, Akaike Information Criteria, and Vuong-Lo-Mendell-Rubin likelihood ratio test, indicate that the optimal solution within the wage earner sample was between four and seven EQ categories (see table A2). After taking into account the conceptual meaning of each measurement model by examining conditional response probabilities—that is, the within-class distributions of each response category—we chose a six-class model as the most meaningful (see table A3). In the self-employed sample, both fit indices and substantive interpretation indicated the two-category solution was best (see tables A2 and A4). Therefore, based on a combination of model fit and interpretation, eight EQ categories are identified as the most stable and meaningful solutions, six employment types within wage earners and two within self-employed workers. Further, an evaluation of LCA output show a clear pattern of nonrandom distribution of category-specific item response probabilities. This suggests that each of the included indicators possess predictive power for determining membership into the EQ types (Flaherty 2002)

We labeled the eight EQ types based on the probability of endorsing particular responses that distinguish one EQ type from another (see tables A3 and A4). These labels are meant to reflect the characteristic employment conditions that together create the workers' experience of employment in each of the EQ types (see table 1). In addition to the SER-like type, the portfolio and precarious job types identified in the GSS are similar to those seen in prior studies of the EU labor market, and thus these labels are adopted in this article (Van Aerden, Gadeyne, and Vanroelen 2017).

Health Indicators

Given the multitude of potential manifestations of poor health associated with low-quality employment (Benach et al. 2014; Kim et al. 2012), and our expectation that the health consequences and mechanisms of EQ may vary depending on the patterns of employment conditions one is exposed to, we explore the relationship between EQ and three broad indicators of health. First, we examine self-rated health (SRH), measured by the standard question: "In general, would you say your health is excellent, very good, good, fair or poor? (fair/poor = 1, good/very good/excellent = 0)." The SRH measure has strong predictive validity of mortality and morbidity (DeSalvo et al. 2006; Idler and Benyamini 1997; Singh-Manoux et al. 2007). Second, we assess frequent mental distress (FMD), measured using the general mental health item from the Centers for Disease Control and Prevention (CDC) four-item health-related quality of life index (HRQOL-4): "Now, thinking about your mental health, which includes stress, depression, and problems with emotions, for how many days during the past thirty was your mental health not good?" FMD is defined as fourteen or more mentally unhealthy days and is commonly used as a proxy for poor mental health in population health surveillance (Brown et al. 2003; CDC 1998, 2000, 2004). Last, we examine work-related injury. The number of injuries a respondent has experienced at work are assessed with the following question: "In the past twelve months, how many times have you been injured on the job?" The injury measure includes a count of injuries from zero to six and seven or more.

Measures of Sociodemographic Characteristics

We adjust health outcomes models for five sociodemographic characteristics. Demographic variables included are sex (male, female), race-ethnicity (non-Hispanic white, non-Hispanic African American, Hispanic, other), nativity (born in the United States, born outside the United States), and age. Age is trichotomized into three groups corresponding with three meaningful periods in a working career: lift-off (younger than thirty), a mid-career period

Table 1. Characteristics of Employment Quality Types Identified in the United States

Wage-Earner Types		Proportion of Overall Workforce
SER-like	Most similar to the Standard Employment Relationship (SER). These jobs have a very high probability of permanent, regular arrangement, full-time hours, adequate wages, working during the day shift, and have adequate information or equipment to complete work. Further, they have low probability of negative EQ conditions, such as excessive work hours, workplace harassment, or a lack of opportunity to develop.	22.2
Portfolio	Very high stability, pay, schedule control, opportunity, and strong power relations, but with long hours. Relative to all other types, these jobs have the highest probability of a permanent arrangement, high income, schedule control, employee involvement, and development opportunity, and low probabilities of experiencing harassment. These jobs also have a high probability of long work hours.	14.9
Inflexible skilled	Highly paid and involved class of workers, but with long and excessive work hours and little control over schedule. These jobs have high probability of high wages, opportunity to develop, union representation, and involvement in decision-making, but also high probability of irregular shifts, low schedule control, workplace harassment, long and mandatory extra working hours.	15.3
Dead-end	Stable, standard, full-time working arrangements with adequate wages, but with low opportunity and poor interpersonal and collective power relations. These jobs are mostly permanent, regular arrangements with middle-to-high wages, but with long and excessive work hours. However, these jobs are distinguished by having very low levels of development opportunity, schedule control, and employee involvement. They lack adequate information or equipment to perform job, and experience high workplace harassment. Counterintuitively, these jobs also have the highest union representation.	12.0
Precarious	Nonstandard working arrangements, low wages, lack of opportunity, and poor interpersonal and collective power relations. Compared to other wage-earner job types, these jobs have a high probability of nonpermanent working arrangements, low wages, part-time hours, and irregular shifts. Further, these jobs have low development opportunity, schedule control, union representation, and employee involvement, and experience high workplace harassment.	11.5
Optimistic precarious	Non-standard arrangements with low wages, but opportunity to develop and strong interpersonal power relations. These jobs are mostly similar to precarious job type, but distinguishing features are low probability of full-time hours and high levels of schedule control, employee involvement, and development opportunity. They also have lower experience of harassment at work.	10.5

Table 1. (*continued*)

Self-Employed Types		Proportion of Overall Workforce
Skilled contractor	High wages, opportunity to develop, and strong interpersonal power relations, but with nonstandard working arrangements and long and excessive hours. These jobs are mostly nonpermanent arrangements with long and excessive hours, and relatively high probability of irregular work times. These jobs also have high levels of schedule control, decision-making involvement, and development opportunity, accompanied by low levels of workplace harassment.	5.3
Job-to-job	Highly nonstandardized working arrangements with low income, but with opportunity to develop and strong interpersonal power relations. These jobs are predominately nonpermanent arrangements, with low income, few hours, and low union representation. The jobs also have high schedule control and opportunity to develop, and low harassment experience.	8.3

Source: Authors' compilation based on General Social Survey (Smith et al. 2013).
Note: For additional information on EQ types, see tables A3 and A4.

(thirty to fifty), and the end-of-career period (fifty-one and older) (Vanroelen et al. 2010). Educational attainment is included as less than high school, high school, associate degree, bachelor's degree, and graduate degree. In this study, these variables are hypothesized to confound the EQ-health association: each predict labor market position and are associated with physical and mental health status.

Measures of Potential Mediating Factors
We use the rich information on employment conditions available within the QWL to examine potential mediating mechanisms in the EQ-health association. To examine the first pathway, *material deprivation*, we use inadequate income, "Do you feel that the income from your job alone is enough to meet your family's usual monthly expenses and bills" (no = 1, yes = 0) and inadequate fringe benefits, "My fringe benefits are good" (not too or not at all true = 1, very or somewhat true = 0). Second, we assess two indicators of an *employment-related stressors* pathway: job insecurity and earnings unfairness. Perceived job security is measured as degree of agreement with the statement "The job security is good" (not too or not at all true = 1, very or somewhat true = 0). Unfairness of earn-

ings is measured with the question "How fair is what you earn on your job in comparison to others doing the same type of work you do" (much less than deserved = 1, somewhat less, about as much, somewhat more, or much more = 0). This is a distinct construct from inadequate income, though the two may be correlated, because the earning fairness is asked as social comparison whereas inadequate income was asked as a comparison with one's needs. The third pathway, *traditional occupational risk factors*, is represented with three variables: job strain, high physical exposure, and low social support. Job strain was constructed from three items on job control (learn new things, variety, allows own decisions) and three items on job demands (work fast, enough time, no excessive work) all from the Job Content Questionnaire, specifically designed for job strain (Karasek et al. 1998). Each set of items were summed, split at the sample median score, and made into a quadrant: low-strain jobs (low demand and high control), high-strain jobs (high demand and low control), active jobs (high demand and high control), and passive jobs (low demand and low control) (Karasek et al. 1998). A dichotomized measure of high physical exposures combines two items asking whether a respondent's job regularly requires forceful hand movements or awkward positions and repeated lifting, pushing, pulling, or bending (both present = 1, one or neither present = 0). The third occupational risk factor mediator is low levels of social support, which is commonly studied alongside job strain as a factor that moderates negative impacts of job strain (de Lange et al. 2003). This measure is constructed by combining four items: two measures of coworker support (such as "The people I work with take a personal interest in me") and two measures of supervisor support (such as "My supervisor is helpful to me in getting the job done"). The social support variable is dichotomized such that high support is coded as a minimum average response of somewhat true or better, and is otherwise coded as low support.

Statistical Analysis

In the GSS sample of wage earners and self-employed workers, relatively little data are missing in each variable included in regression analyses: only earnings unfairness (3.1 percent) and workplace social support (5.6 percent) variables had more than 2 percent missing. Because we did not have a theoretical basis for imputing these values from available GSS data, respondents who did not provide information on earnings fairness or social support were excluded from the analysis. Those who had missing data on other variables—that is, in order of most to least missing data (all less than 2 percent): job strain, benefits adequacy, job security, income adequacy, FMD, physical hazards exposure, occupational injury, SRH, and age—were also excluded. Due to the large number of variables and a high degree of non-overlapping missingness, the exclusion steps reduced the total weighted sample by 9.5 percent (n = 5,480). The final sample characteristics are presented in table 2. Respondents removed from the analysis were older, more likely to be born outside the United States, and reported less FMD than the analysis sample (see table A5). The proportion of removed respondents also varied by survey year; in addition to general concerns of secular trends, this provided further rationale for adjusting all regression models for year to account for potential survey effects.

To examine the relationship between EQ and health, as well as potential mediators of this relationship, we use Poisson regression with a robust error variance. The robust Poisson approach provides efficient and reliable estimates of a ratio measure of effect when the outcome measure is common and odds ratios overestimate risk (Coutinho, Scazufca, and Menezes 2008; Zou 2004). Model parameters are exponentiated to the ratio scale for presentation. For binary outcomes (SRH and FMD), the results of the robust Poisson are interpreted as prevalence ratios; for count data (injuries in last year), coefficients represent rate ratios. We conducted all regression analyses in r (Version 1.1.423) using the glm2 package (Marschner 2011); all data are included in the models with GSS survey sample weights, and robust 95 percent confidence intervals are calculated from Huber-White standard error estimates determined by the sandwich r package (Zeileis 2004).

The EQ typology is introduced into the analyses as each respondent's estimated probability of membership into the eight job types. Estimates from the wage earner and self-employed LCA models are combined so that each respondent is assigned eight scores between 0 and 1, which add to 1 (self-employed workers have zero probability of membership in the six EQ types identified in wage earners, and vice versa). This approach reduces classification errors relative to modal assignment (classification into a single, most likely class), as the latent class probabilities inherently include information regarding the uncertainty of classifying individuals to a specific category (Hagenaars and McCutcheon 2002).

Evaluating each health indicator separately, we build a sequence of regression models: a basic model with EQ and survey year only, a model additionally controlled for demographics (age, sex, race-ethnicity, and nativity), and a model that additionally controls for education. The SER-like job type is used as the reference category for all analyses. Thus, the effect estimates describe the ratio of outcome occurrence with 100 percent probability of belonging to a particular EQ type compared with the outcome occurrence with 100 percent probability of belonging to the SER-like job type (Van

Table 2. Characteristics of Sample Used in Regression Analysis (Weighted)

Characteristic	Level	Frequency (Percent)	
n		5,480	
Survey year	2002	1,659	(30)
	2006	1,579	(29)
	2010	1,075	(20)
	2014	1,166	(21)
Sociodemographic characteristics			
Age	Thirty or younger	1,342	(24)
	Thirty-one to fifty	2,621	(48)
	Fifty-one and older	1,518	(28)
Sex	Male	2,695	(49)
	Female	2,785	(51)
Race-ethnicity	White	3,889	(71)
	Black	728	(13)
	Other	233	(4)
	Hispanic	630	(11)
Nativity	U.S. born	4,811	(88)
	Not U.S. born	669	(12)
Highest degree	Less than high school	491	(9)
	High school	2,824	(52)
	Junior college	516	(9)
	Bachelor	1,083	(20)
	Graduate	566	(10)
Health indicators			
Self-reported health (SRH)	Good	4,755	(87)
	Poor	725	(13)
Frequent mental distress (FMD)	Absent	4,924	(90)
	Present	556	(10)
Work-related injuries in past year	0	4,882	(89)
	1	382	(7)
	2	99	(2)
	3 or more	116	(2)

Source: Authors' compilation based on General Social Survey (Smith et al. 2013).

Aerden, Gadeyne, and Vanroelen 2017; Van Aerden et al. 2016).

To examine the three mediating mechanisms, we followed the mediation test principles recommended by Reuben Baron and David Kenny (1986). That is, we first establish the association between EQ and all of the mediating variables (having examined the EQ-health association in our primary analysis), and then continue our nested regression analyses: a model with each of the three sets of mediating variables, and a model with all mediation variables. Log-likelihood ratio tests are conducted to assess the overall significance of EQ as well as model improvements as we include additional variables. Evidence for mediation is identified when EQ coefficients have a smaller magnitude or less statistically significant relationship with the health outcomes when mediator variables were introduced relative to the regression equation in which mediator variables were not introduced.

RESULTS

In summarizing our findings, we first detail the relationship between EQ and our three health outcomes, including self-reported health, frequent mental distress, and work injury. Next, we describe associations between EQ and indicators of material deprivation, employment-related stressors, and occupational risk factors, operationalized here as potential mediating mechanisms of the EQ-health relationship. Finally, we report on exploratory analyses examining if the associations between EQ and health outcomes are explained by the proposed mediators.

Association Between EQ and Three Health Indicators

EQ and the three health indicators were significantly associated in the basic model (that is, adjusted for survey year only), and additional adjustments for age, sex, race-ethnicity, nativity, and education did not substantively affect the associations (see tables A6 through A8). The associations of EQ with SRH, FMD, and work injury, adjusted for these demographic characteristics, are presented as model 1 in tables 3, 4, and 5, respectively. Compared with SER-like jobs, portfolio job holders were less likely to report poor SRH. Inflexible skilled job holders reported worse FMD and more work injuries. Dead-end and precarious job holders were more likely to report poor SRH, poor FMD, and more injuries. In contrast, optimistic precarious job holders were not different from SER in any of the health indicators. The two types of self-employed jobs did not differ from SER-like in SRH, but respondents in both skilled contractor and job-to-job types reported more injuries, and those from the job-to-job type also reported worse mental health.

Association Between EQ and Proposed Mediating Variables

Before presenting mediation results, we first examine the associations of EQ types and proposed mediating variables (see table 6). All these variables are coded in the direction of health compromising. Portfolio job holders had lower levels of material deprivation and traditional occupational hazards than SER-like job holders, and did not differ significantly on employment-related stressors. Self-employed skilled contractors had a similar profile to portfolio job holders but were more similar to SER-like job holders in fringe benefits and social support. One difference is the higher exposure to physical hazards among skilled contractors than the SER-like type. Inflexible skilled job holders are similar to skilled contractors but are more likely to perceive unfairness in earnings compared with SER. Dead-end, precarious, and job-to-job types are similar in that they have higher levels of material deprivation, employment-related stressors, and occupational risk factors relative to SER-like jobs. Optimistic precarious jobs are distinct from any other EQ types in that despite high levels of material deprivation and job insecurity, they are similar to SER-like jobs in terms of fair earning and occupational risk factors. Taken together, the different patterns of associations between EQ types and mediating variables generally suggest health-protecting features in portfolio and skilled contractor jobs; health-damaging features in dead-end, precarious, job-to-job, and optimistic precarious jobs; and a complex combination of each for inflexible skilled jobs.

Exploration of Potential Mediating Mechanisms

The results of regression models that include the mediating variables are presented in tables 3 through 5. When included in the EQ-SRH models, the material deprivation variables are associated with higher likelihood of reporting poor SRH, inadequate fringe benefits having a more robust association (see table 3, model 2). Inclusion of material deprivation variables resulted in slightly attenuated associations in some EQ types. In particular, our results suggest that dead-end and precarious jobs' higher likelihood of reporting poor SRH, as well as portfolio jobs' lower likelihood, may be explained by different levels of material deprivation experienced by those job holders. Employment-related stressors were strongly associated with poor SRH (model 3). When these mediators were included, associations for dead-end and precarious jobs were attenuated. Traditional occupational risk factors were also strongly associated with poor SRH (model 4),

(*Text continues on p. 273.*)

Table 3. Regression Analysis of Association of EQ and Self-Rated Health (SRH), and Inclusion of Potential Mediators

Independent Variable	Model 1 Estimate (95% CI)	Model 2 Estimate (95% CI)	Model 3 Estimate (95% CI)	Model 4 Estimate (95% CI)	Model 5 Estimate (95% CI)
EQ typology (ref = SER-like)	<0.001[a]	<0.001[a]	<0.001[a]	0.001[a]	0.049[a]
Portfolio	0.62 (0.39–0.97) *	0.67 (0.43–1.05)	0.60 (0.38–0.95) *	0.64 (0.41–1.02)	0.66 (0.41–1.04)
Inflexible skilled	0.75 (0.50–1.12)	0.76 (0.51–1.13)	0.72 (0.49–1.07)	0.67 (0.45–1.01)	0.66 (0.45–0.99) *
Dead-end	1.84 (1.31–2.57) ***	1.63 (1.16–2.29) **	1.45 (1.02–2.06) *	1.20 (0.84–1.72)	1.07 (0.74–1.55)
Precarious	1.65 (1.15–2.37) **	1.34 (0.92–1.93)	1.37 (0.95–1.97)	1.27 (0.87–1.85)	1.04 (0.71–1.53)
Optimistic precarious	1.31 (0.90–1.89)	1.12 (0.77–1.63)	1.25 (0.86–1.80)	1.35 (0.94–1.95)	1.17 (0.81–1.70)
Skilled contractor	1.13 (0.64–1.98)	1.17 (0.67–2.03)	1.12 (0.64–1.96)	1.09 (0.62–1.90)	1.09 (0.63–1.89)
Job-to-job	1.03 (0.69–1.54)	0.90 (0.60–1.35)	0.92 (0.63–1.36)	0.99 (0.66–1.47)	0.85 (0.57–1.26)
Material deprivation					
Inadequate income		1.14 (0.96–1.35)			1.07 (0.90–1.26)
Inadequate fringe benefits		1.51 (1.28–1.78) ***			1.33 (1.12–1.59) ***
Employment-related stressors					
Unfair earning			1.32 (1.10–1.60) ***		1.17 (0.97–1.42)
Job insecurity			1.64 (1.37–1.97) ***		1.43 (1.18–1.73) **
Traditional occupational risk factors					
Job strain (ref = low strain)				<0.001[a]	0.002[a]
Active jobs				1.39 (1.11–1.75) **	1.35 (1.07–1.69) **
Passive jobs				1.19 (0.97–1.47)	1.18 (0.96–1.45)
High strain jobs				1.65 (1.29–2.11) ***	1.56 (1.22–1.99) ***
High physical exposures				1.35 (1.14–1.59) ***	1.31 (1.11–1.55) **
Lack of workplace social support				1.25 (1.05–1.49) *	1.06 (0.88–1.28)
AIC[b]	4252	4225	4216.5	4215.1	4185.8
Log likelihood ratio test comparing each model with model 1, χ^2(df), p-value		χ^2=31.04, df=2, p<.001	χ^2=39.47, df=2, p<.001	χ^2=46.94, df=5, p<.001	χ^2=84.18, df=9, p<.001

Source: Authors' compilation based on General Social Survey (Smith et al. 2013).

Note: Prevalence ratios and 95 percent confidence intervals are shown. All models are adjusted for age, gender, race, nativity, education, and survey year.

[a] *p*-value for the log likelihood ratio test.

[b] Akaike Information Criteria.

* $p < .05$; ** $p < .01$; *** $p < .001$

Table 4. Regression Analysis of Association of EQ and Frequent Mental Distress (FMD), and Inclusion of Potential Mediators

Independent Variable	Model 1 Estimate (95% CI)		Model 2 Estimate (95% CI)		Model 3 Estimate (95% CI)		Model 4 Estimate (95% CI)		Model 5 Estimate (95% CI)	
EQ typology (ref = SER-like)	<0.001[a]		<0.001[a]		0.003[a]		0.022[a]		0.285[a]	
Portfolio	1.03 (0.60–1.75)		1.12 (0.66–1.91)		0.98 (0.57–1.66)		0.94 (0.55–1.60)		0.94 (0.55–1.61)	
Inflexible skilled	1.87 (1.20–2.91)	**	1.90 (1.22–2.94)	**	1.73 (1.12–2.67)	*	1.44 (0.92–2.26)		1.41 (0.91–2.20)	
Dead-end	2.76 (1.78–4.28)	***	2.45 (1.57–3.81)	***	1.95 (1.26–3.03)	**	1.46 (0.92–2.32)		1.28 (0.80–2.02)	
Precarious	2.59 (1.66–4.03)	***	2.06 (1.30–3.27)	**	1.91 (1.23–2.98)	**	1.83 (1.18–2.86)	**	1.45 (0.92–2.29)	
Optimistic precarious	1.58 (0.97–2.58)		1.35 (0.82–2.24)		1.48 (0.90–2.42)		1.68 (1.03–2.74)	*	1.49 (0.91–2.46)	
Skilled contractor	1.60 (0.79–3.25)		1.75 (0.86–3.56)		1.57 (0.78–3.17)		1.37 (0.70–2.68)		1.46 (0.75–2.87)	
Job-to-job	1.87 (1.16–3.03)	*	1.65 (1.01–2.68)	*	1.61 (1.03–2.53)	*	1.65 (1.04–2.64)	*	1.44 (0.91–2.27)	
Material deprivation										
Inadequate income			1.39 (1.13–1.7)	**					1.26 (1.03–1.55)	*
Inadequate fringe benefits			1.35 (1.1–1.65)	**					1.09 (0.88–1.35)	
Employment-related stressors										
Unfair earning					1.70 (1.38–2.10)	***			1.42 (1.15–1.76)	**
Job insecurity					1.74 (1.42–2.15)	***			1.44 (1.16–1.80)	**
Traditional occupational risk factors										
Job strain (ref = low strain)							<0.001[a]		<0.001[a]	
Active jobs							1.95 (1.50–2.52)	***	1.82 (1.41–2.36)	***
Passive jobs							1.11 (0.85–1.45)		1.09 (0.84–1.42)	
High strain jobs							1.63 (1.20–2.22)	**	1.53 (1.13–2.08)	**
High physical exposures							1.26 (1.04–1.53)	*	1.22 (1.00–1.47)	*
Lack of workplace social support							1.68 (1.37–2.06)	***	1.42 (1.14–1.78)	**
AIC[b]	3531.5		3510.5		3476.2		3457.5		3429.2	
Log likelihood ratio test comparing each model with model 1, x^2(df), p-value			x^2=25.05, df=2, p<.001		x^2=59.31, df=2, p<.001		x^2=84.05, df=5, p<.001		x^2=120.3, df=9, p<.001	

Source: Authors' compilation based on General Social Survey (Smith et al. 2013).

Note: Prevalence ratios and 95 percent confidence intervals are shown. All models are adjusted for age, gender, race, nativity, education, and survey year.

[a] p-value for the log likelihood ratio test.

[b] Akaike Information Criteria.

*p < .05; **p < .01; ***p < .001

Table 5. Regression Analysis of Association of EQ and Workplace Injuries, and Inclusion of Potential Mediators

Independent Variable	Model 1 Estimate (95% CI)		Model 2 Estimate (95% CI)		Model 3 Estimate (95% CI)		Model 4 Estimate (95% CI)		Model 5 Estimate (95% CI)	
EQ typology (ref = SER-like)	<0.001[a]		<0.001[a]		<0.001[a]		<0.001[a]		<0.001[a]	
Portfolio	0.85 (0.42–1.71)		0.90 (0.45–1.81)		0.82 (0.41–1.66)		0.95 (0.47–1.90)		0.97 (0.48–1.94)	
Inflexible skilled	3.61 (2.04–6.39)	***	3.66 (2.07–6.48)	***	3.41 (1.92–6.05)	***	2.64 (1.46–4.79)	**	2.61 (1.43–4.79)	**
Dead-end	3.93 (2.21–7.00)	***	3.58 (2.02–6.34)	***	3.29 (1.77–6.11)	***	2.34 (1.31–4.18)	**	2.19 (1.20–3.99)	*
Precarious	2.30 (1.25–4.25)	**	1.91 (1.02–3.57)	*	1.95 (1.06–3.57)	*	1.55 (0.85–2.83)		1.34 (0.73–2.46)	
Optimistic precarious	0.97 (0.46–2.05)		0.87 (0.40–1.86)		0.95 (0.45–2.00)		1.06 (0.51–2.19)		0.99 (0.47–2.09)	
Skilled contractor	2.26 (1.03–4.96)	*	2.41 (1.11–5.24)	*	2.22 (1.02–4.83)	*	1.79 (0.82–3.91)		1.87 (0.86–4.04)	
Job-to-Job	2.12 (1.05–4.25)	*	1.93 (0.96–3.88)		1.98 (1.00–3.90)	*	1.70 (0.86–3.38)		1.60 (0.82–3.16)	
Material deprivation										
Inadequate income			1.28 (0.97–1.68)						1.17 (0.89–1.55)	
Inadequate fringe benefits			1.29 (1.00–1.66)	*					1.10 (0.83–1.45)	
Employment-related stressors										
Unfair earning					1.70 (1.28–2.25)	***			1.36 (1.01–1.81)	*
Job insecurity					1.12 (0.8–1.56)				0.96 (0.67–1.39)	
Traditional occupational risk factors										
Job strain (ref = low strain)							<0.001[a]		<0.001[a]	
Active jobs							1.28 (0.90–1.83)		1.23 (0.87–1.75)	
Passive jobs							0.87 (0.64–1.18)		0.87 (0.64–1.18)	
High strain jobs							1.25 (0.85–1.84)		1.23 (0.84–1.82)	
High physical exposures							3.23 (2.35–4.43)	***	3.14 (2.29–4.30)	***
Lack of workplace social support							1.43 (1.10–1.86)	**	1.35 (1.02–1.79)	*
AIC[b]	6,663.4		6,633.1		6,614		6,290.9		6,269.7	
Log likelihood ratio test comparing each model with model 1, χ^2(df), p-value			χ^2=34.34, df=2, p<.001		χ^2=53.46, df=2, p<.001		χ^2=382.5, df=5, p<.001		χ^2=411.7, df=9, p<.001	

Source: Authors' compilation based on General Social Survey (Smith et al. 2013).

Note: Prevalence ratios and 95 percent confidence intervals are shown. All models are adjusted for age, gender, race, nativity, education, and survey year.

[a] *p*-value for the log likelihood ratio test.

[b] Akaike Information Criteria.

*p < .05; **p < .01; ***p < .001

Table 6. Relative Comparison of Prevalence of EQ-Health Mediators Within Each Employment Category Relative to SER-Like Jobs

	Material Deprivation		Employment-Related Stressors		Occupational Risk Factors		
	Inadequate Fringe Benefits	Inadequate Income	Job Insecurity	Unfairness of Earnings	High Strain Jobs[a]	High Physical Exposures	Low Social Support
EQ typology (ref = SER-like)							
Portfolio	Lower	Lower	n.s.	n.s.	Lower	Lower	Lower
Inflexible skilled	n.s.	Lower	n.s.	Higher	n.s.	Higher	n.s.
Dead-end	Higher	n.s.	Higher	Higher	Higher	Higher	Higher
Precarious	Higher	Higher	Higher	Higher	Higher	Higher	Higher
Optimistic precarious	Higher	Higher	Higher	n.s.	n.s.	n.s.	n.s.
Skilled contractor	n.s.	Lower	n.s.	n.s.	Lower	Higher	n.s.
Job-to-job	Higher	Higher	Higher	Higher	n.s.	Higher	Higher

Source: Authors' compilation based on General Social Survey (Smith et al. 2013).

Note: Lower/Higher: statistically significant difference (*p*-value < 0.05) compared to *SER-like* jobs in Poisson regression with mediator as dependent variable (adjusted for survey year). n.s.: not statistically different from *SER-like* jobs.

[a] While the job strain measure contains four categories, only a dichotomous measure of high strain or not is tested for association with EQ in this analysis.

and when these were included, associations for dead-end and precarious jobs were again attenuated. This suggests that both employment-related stressors and occupational risk factors may also explain the significant associations of EQ with SRH in dead-end and precarious job types. Finally, model 5, in which all mediating variables are included, shows large attenuation of all EQ associations. The association between EQ as a whole and SRH is also slightly diminished (that is, the *p*-value for the log-likelihood ratio test for EQ changed from <.001 to .049). Some mediators also show diminished associations with poor SRH, which indicates they are likely correlated with each other. Models with mediator variables are all significantly better at explaining the outcome variance than model 1.

Results for poor mental health (FMD) are shown in table 4, models 2 through 5. The material deprivation model (model 2) shows some attenuation in EQ coefficients from model 1 and the most pronounced attenuation in the precarious type. In the employment-related stressor model (model 3) and particularly the occupational risk factor model (model 4), we see attenuation of EQ coefficients for inflexible skilled, dead-end, and precarious types. Notably, precarious and job-to-job types consistently show higher likelihood of reporting poor mental health when individual sets of mediators are included. However, when all mediators are included in the model (model 5), all coefficients for EQ types reduced their magnitude from model 1, and EQ as a whole is no longer significantly associated with FMD ($p = 0.285$). Together with the observation that the mediators had strong and significant associations with FMD in expected directions in all models, model 5 finding suggests that these mediating variables may play an important role in the EQ-mental health association.

Table 5, models 2 through 5 present potential mediation in the EQ association with occupational injuries. In general, EQ's association with occupational injuries did not change as much as it did with other outcomes when mediator variables were included in the model. Also the mediator variables are not as strongly associated with this outcome, aside from physical hazards exposure and low social support (components of occupational risk factors). The most striking difference from model 1 can be seen in model 4, in which traditional occupational risk factors were included as mediators. The coefficients for inflexible skilled, dead-end, and precarious jobs—the highest likelihoods of reporting occupational injuries in model 1—diminished drastically in model 4, and more modest attenuation was seen for skilled contractors and job-to-job. When all mediators were included (model 5), EQ's association with occupational injury was similar to what we saw in model 4. Inflexible skilled jobs and dead-end jobs constantly had significantly higher likelihoods of reporting injuries compared with SER-like jobs, suggesting some other mechanisms are in effect.

DISCUSSION

In this study, we examine the association between EQ and three indicators of health: general health, mental health, and occupational injury. Overall, we find significant associations between some EQ types and each of the three health indicators when compared with SER-like jobs after adjusting for sociodemographic characteristics. This study is part of a growing trend within occupational health research to expand its framework to consider the relational and contractual aspects of employment that affect health. A primary strength of this analysis is that EQ is measured using a multidimensional, typological approach, such that the EQ-health associations we find reflect health implications of employment as a package, rather than each aspect of employment. Another contribution of this study is an initial exploration of three possible mediating mechanisms between EQ and health, with these data generally supporting their plausibility.

EQ Types and Health

The eight EQ types in our study had distinct associations with health. As expected, dead-end and precarious job holders had consistently higher likelihoods of reporting poor general and mental health as well as occupational injury. These EQ types are characterized by an accumulation of several unfavorable employment conditions, including high workplace harassment and low opportunity to develop, control over schedule, and employee involvement (see table A3). Also, dead-end and precarious job holders were similar in their experience of three mediating mechanisms: high levels of material deprivation, employment-related stressors, and occupational risk factors. Yet these two job types differed across several dimensions of EQ, including indicators of stability, material rewards, working time arrangements, and collective organization. To protect the health of workers in these EQ types, we need to investigate more purposefully the specific combination of employment conditions and work quality they experience as a package.

Likewise, inflexible skilled job holders and job-to-job workers also had worse mental health and injury experience than SER-like job holders. The two, however, represent clearly distinct combinations of EQ conditions: inflexible skilled jobs resemble stable, relatively well-paid employment but with excessive and inflexible hours; job-to-job workers experience a highly nonstandard employment arrangement with low pay and relatively low hours. They also starkly differ in their experience of the mediating mechanisms: inflexible skilled workers reported similar profile with SER-like workers except for higher physical hazards and unfair earnings; job-to-job workers reported all unfavorable experiences except for job strain. These differences, both in EQ characteristics and proposed mediating mechanisms, suggest that their poor health is a manifestation of distinct combinations of employment and working conditions that may warrant different approaches for intervention.

Unlike Karen Van Aerden and her colleagues (2016), who report high health risks for portfolio jobs from EU data, in our data portfolio jobs were generally not different from SER in terms of health. The U.S. portfolio jobs we identified are similar to European—characterized by generally the most favorable employment conditions—with one exception: the U.S. portfolio job holders did not suffer from mandatory extra days of work, whereas a defining feature of the EU portfolio jobs was uncompensated exceptional working times (Van Aerden et al. 2016). Portfolio job holders in our study reported a higher sense of material resource adequacy, fairness in their earnings and security in their jobs, and lower levels of occupational hazard exposures than SER-like. In European contexts, these relationships may be different.

Somewhat unexpectedly, optimistic precarious job holders did not differ from SER-like job holders on any of the three health indicators. This EQ type is characterized as very destandardized: that is, having the lowest hours, very low income, and highest probabilities of both irregular hours and nonpermanent arrangements within wage earners. Likewise, these job holders report higher levels of material resource inadequacy and job insecurity. Yet, these jobs also have an overall profile that includes several favorable EQ conditions, including relatively high schedule control, development opportunity, and employee involvement in decision making, suggesting the possibility that these workers are opting in to these types of jobs. Indeed, despite low pay and feelings of inadequate income, their sense of earnings unfairness is not different from SER-like job holders. This would generally comport with a recent study of Italian workers that found workers in nonstandard employment arrangements are a heterogeneous group and that voluntariness into these jobs was relevant to health status (Pirani 2017). Our finding of similar health to SER-like jobs suggests these workers may have other sources of health-protecting resources.

The two classes identified among the self-employed are quite different from each other. Skilled contractors resemble a highly paid, independent workforce, similar to portfolio job holders but engaged in jobs with time-specific contracts. Job-to-job workers have low pay and hours, with little involvement, and generally seem to have the weakest attachment to the labor market—although the extent to which this is by choice is uncertain, as they also possess flexibility and development opportunities. In occupational safety and health studies, self-employment has been understudied (Stephan and Roesler 2010), and if it is addressed, the heterogeneity among the self-employed has been neglected. Our findings indicate that there may be important differences among working people who self-identify as self-employed. Our study finds job-to-job workers to report poor mental health and yet the proposed mediators do not seem to explain the relationship. Because our sample sizes for the self-employed workers were limited (n ~800), these intriguing results need additional exploration with specific focus on self-employment.

The Value of a Multidimensional, Typological Approach and Policy Implications

In conceptualizing EQ as a multidimensional construct, we believe that we are better able to capture key dimensions of workers' employment experience that affect health and well-being. This approach also has potential to inform policymakers to enhance worker health through improved job quality. It is important to highlight that researchers in sociology, economics, and public health have struggled to conceptualize and measure EQ. Some researchers have focused too narrowly, especially on single dimensions such as employment arrangement or wages; others have attempted to include more nuance in their conception of poor- or low-quality jobs, only to find these conceptions quickly become too difficult to use in empirical analysis of actual working populations. A widely studied such concept is precarious employment, which can be defined generally as an accumulation of many unfavorable employment features (Julià et al. 2017). Deeply rooted in the tradition of sociological and labor relations literatures (Arnold and Bongiovi 2013; Kalleberg and Hewison 2013), the concept of precarious employment has been applied across analytical levels (for example, precarious employment, precarious work, precarious workers as a social class) and tends to have different meanings in different contexts (Burchell et al. 2014; Campbell and Price 2016). The development of specific scales to measure precarity is an active area of research (Lewchuk et al. 2014; Vives et al. 2015); however, even these approaches assess employment conditions using an aggregate scale ranging from low to high rather than something more dynamic. The LCA approach we used allows for conceiving of jobs as packages of employment features, and thus facilitates the conceptualization that health consequences of EQ will depend on specific patterns of features to which one is exposed.

The advantage of a typological approach, relative to dimensional approaches (that is, focusing on aspects of EQ separately), is its emphasis on the structure and distribution of simultaneously occurring employment conditions (Bergman and Magnusson 1997). In other words, a typological approach can identify profiles of risks for various segments of the labor force, which can be useful for policymakers to develop comprehensive interventions (Vanroelen et al. 2010). Dimensional approaches investigate specific features of employment conditions while assuming that all other aspects are constant. Thus, although potentially useful in identifying risk factors, resulting findings would suggest that policymakers effect narrowly focused interventions. Such interventions may improve job quality for some but may have no impact on others—or possibly even produce worse conditions for others. For example, based on research showing correlation between long work hours and poor health, one might propose limiting working hours to improve health. However, to cover the excess hours previously worked by permanent full-time employees, employers may create part-time jobs with unpredictable and inadequate hours. A typological approach would encourage policymakers to address unpredictable and inadequate hours, as well as inadequate pay, as a package. We believe that our approach is meaningful because it addresses a general picture of current U.S. labor market practice and the holistic experiences of American workers engaged in different types of employment.

The quality of one's employment is modifiable through both policy levers and employer-driven workplace modifications. Overall, our findings suggest that if EQ conditions could be modified to resemble more closely the standard model of employment, many workers might experience better health. One example of an ambitious policy agenda can be found in the EU's attempt to secure "more and better jobs" (Lisbon European Council 2000). As our exploration of mediating mechanisms suggests, the health-enhancing process may be through adequate material resources, fair earnings and job security, and lower exposures to occupational risk factors. If they are indeed mediating the EQ-health relationship, then changing these conditions may also help protect the health of working people. More generally, workplace policies can effectively redistribute resources to reduce inequality (for example, secure scheduling redistributes power from employers to workers) and can benefit all workers regardless of their personal resources or behaviors. Although employment conditions have received less attention than other aspects of socioeconomic position, such as education and income, the modifiable nature of employment makes it a critical determinant of health deserving of further consideration in both research and policy realms. Further, by specifically delineating between concepts of employment quality versus work quality, the EQ concept can be used to supplement and complement policy efforts to improve job quality as a whole.

Limitations of This Study and Future Research Directions

A major limitation of this study is its reliance on self-reported cross-sectional data. The cross-sectional nature of the GSS data means that reverse causation—that is, poor health contributes to selection into jobs with poor employment conditions—cannot be ruled out as a possible explanation. In terms of self-reported measures, it would be ideal to obtain EQ indicators directly from employment records to overcome some of the inherent bias in self-reported data. Additionally, better (that is, more objective) measures of health outcomes would eliminate some of the bias found in these metrics. In particular, we found stronger mediation in associations between EQ and poor mental health, which may be inflated because these are especially sensitive to the person's mental state at the time of data collection; for example, a worker in a poor mental health state may be more likely to perceive their EQ conditions as negative or poor than another worker in a better state of mental health (Conway and Lance 2010). Another limitation in this study is unmeasured confounding. For instance, unobserved factors such as early-life health, social support outside of the job, or local economic and policy contexts may confound the EQ-health association, potentially biasing effect estimates. However, the patterns of associations across health indicators give us some confidence that the observed associations are not artificial.

Another data-related limitation is the exclusion of a sizable portion (9.5 percent) of the

overall GSS QWL sample in our regression analyses due to missing information. The majority of missingness occurred in covariates associated with our hypothesized mediation mechanisms; therefore, it is possible (but not likely) that if missing information on these variables is associated with other confounding characteristics, it could bias our results. As a crude sensitivity analysis, we repeated all regression models excluding only those with missing data required for the specific model; these exclusions showed no effect on our findings.

As for measure of EQ typology, EQ indicators included here are limited to those available within GSS data; in particular, detailed information on nonwage benefits, workers' rights, and employability opportunities are lacking. Yet the GSS QWL module is among the richest individual-level data pertinent to EQ characteristics and health, and allows for an initial exploration of this construct in the United States. Further, we do not believe that having more indicators related to certain EQ dimensions is a problem for our LCA-based approach. This is primarily because each indicator represents a distinct aspect of the EQ construct. For instance, number of hours worked, when one works, and how much schedule flexibility one has each represent different facets of working time arrangements and power dynamics. Indeed, we find little evidence that EQ indicators are strongly correlated with each other, based on several statistical tests we conducted for association of categorical variables. In other words, rather than risking "overweighting" certain EQ dimensions, our LCA approach is able to identify heterogeneity within the diverse range of employment configurations seen among U.S. workers. Nevertheless, surveys need to better characterize both EQ and the health consequences of different occupational settings. The National Academy of Sciences recently called for improved surveillance of work-related exposures and health, including methods to include workers in nonstandard employment arrangements and other under-represented working groups (2018).

The mediation analysis we present is exploratory. Here we attempt to lay out our conceptual understanding of how EQ affects health, which has been rarely explored in the public health literature. In our study, EQ was associated with all of the variables representing proposed mediating mechanisms. When the mediators were included in the models, most had significant associations with the outcome variable in expected directions, and most EQ-health associations were attenuated. This supports that the hypothesized mediating processes linking EQ and health are plausible, and each mediation mechanism suggests a potential avenue for intervention. However, before concrete recommendations can be formed, more rigorous investigation with stronger study design must be pursued. Although we posit a strong conceptual rationale that EQ is antecedent to the evaluated mediators (for example, job insecurity, workplace social support, and the like would arise from one's current job rather than contributing to selection into that job), the GSS data do not provide definitive empirical support. Thus, these results should be seen as suggestive evidence that the mechanisms proposed are useful. As this area of research continues to develop, we anticipate more suitable longitudinal data will become available for investigating the mediation questions of interest.

Despite these limitations, to our knowledge, this is the first study to rigorously evaluate a multidimensional construct of EQ to examine associations with employee health in the U.S. context. Although some studies have started to report multidimensional EQ and health relationships, they have been mostly restricted to Europe. The generalizability of European research to the U.S. context may be limited because of vast differences between the respective labor laws and regulation as well as social safety nets. These differences are reflected in the common finding that social class-based health disparities in Europe are less severe relative to those in the United States (Avendano et al. 2009; Avendano and Kawachi 2014). Fundamental causes theory suggests that the process of accumulating health advantages based on personal resources (that is, money, knowledge, power, prestige, and social ties) is firmly embedded in the dynamics of a given society (Masters, Link, and Phelan 2015). Because employment quality is likely to be an important part

of this process, for EQ research to be useful in making changes, it needs to be embedded in the national context.

CONCLUSION

The changing labor market has created new forms of employment that health researchers are not yet well equipped to investigate. Yet a long history of occupational health research makes us suspect certain combinations of employment features may contribute both to poor health of workers and to widening health inequalities in the society. It is therefore important to develop a conceptual framework and effective tools for investigating EQ from a public health perspective. This study is part of the emerging effort in this direction. Being exploratory in nature, this study generates many future research questions, some of which have been discussed above. Additional directions include replicating the EQ typology using different sources of U.S. data; exploring antecedents (especially socially determined characteristics) for workers to go into certain EQ types; and investigating at a macrolevel changes in EQ over time especially in relation to economic tides and population health in general. We argue that EQ should be recognized as a social determinant of health because of its complex and wide-reaching impacts on personal resources and chances for accumulating health advantages. We also argue that because of its complexity, EQ is better captured with a typological approach, as in this study, rather than in a variable-based approach of investigating single aspects separately. This approach can illuminate the clustering of disadvantages on the same segment of population, and potentially leads to policy-level solutions.

REFERENCES

Ahonen, Emily Q., Kaori Fujishiro, Thomas Cunningham, and Michael Flynn. 2018. "Work as an Inclusive Part of Population Health Inequities Research and Prevention." *American Journal of Public Health* 108(3): 306–11.

Arnold, Dennis, and Joseph. R. Bongiovi. 2013. "Precarious, Informalizing, and Flexible Work: Transforming Concepts and Understandings." *American Behavioral Scientist* 57(3): 289–308.

Aronsson, Gunnar. 1999. "Contingent Workers and

Health and Safety." *Work, Employment and Society* 13(3): 439–59.

Avendano, Mauricio, M. Maria Glymour, James Banks, and P. Johan Mackenbach. 2009. "Health Disadvantage in US Adults Aged 50 to 74 Years: A Comparison of the Health of Rich and Poor Americans with That of Europeans." *American Journal of Public Health* 99(3): 540–48.

Avendano, Mauricio, and Ichiro Kawachi. 2014. "Why Do Americans Have Shorter Life Expectancy and Worse Health Than Do People in Other High-Income Countries?" *Annual Review of Public Health* 35(1): 307–25.

Baron, Reuben M., and David A. Kenny. 1986. "The Moderator-Mediator Variable Distinction in Social The Moderator-Mediator Variable Distinction in Social Psychological Research: Conceptual, Strategic, and Statistical Considerations." *Journal of Personality and Social Psychology* 51(6): 1173–82.

Benach, Joan, Alejandra Vives, Marcelo Amable, Christophe Vanroelen, Gemma Tarafa, and Carles J. M. Muntaner. 2014. "Precarious Employment: Understanding an Emerging Social Determinant of Health." *Annual Review of Public Health* 35: 229–53.

Bergman, Lars R., and David Magnusson. 1997. "A Person-Oriented Approach in Research on Developmental Psychopathology." *Development and Psychopathology* 9(2): 291–319.

Bosch, Gerhard. 2004. "Towards a New Standard Employment Relationship in Western Europe." *British Journal of Industrial Relations* 42(4): 617–36.

Bosmans, Kim, Stefan Hardonk, Nele De Cuyper, and Christophe Vanroelen. 2016. "Explaining the Relation Between Precarious Employment and Mental Well-Being. A Qualitative Study Among Temporary Agency Workers." *Work* 53(2): 249–64.

Brown, David W., Lina Balluz, Earl S. Ford, Wayne H. Giles, Tara Strine, David G. Moriarty, Janet B. Croft, and Ali Mokdad. 2003. "Associations Between Short- and Long-Term Unemployment and Frequent Mental Distress Among a National Sample of Men and Women." *Journal of Occupational and Environmental Medicine* 45(11): 1159–66.

Burchell, Brendan, Kirsten Sehnbruch, Agnieszka Piasna, and Nurjk Agloni. 2014. "The Quality of Employment and Decent Work: Definitions,

Methodologies, and Ongoing Debates." *Cambridge Journal of Economics* 38(2): 459–77.

Campbell, Iain, and Robin Price. 2016. "Precarious Work and Precarious Workers: Towards an Improved Conceptualisation." *Economic and Labour Relations Review* 27(3): 314–32.

Centers for Disease Control and Prevention (CDC). 1998. "Self-Reported Frequent Mental Distress Among Adults—United States, 1993–1996. *MMWR. Morbidity and Mortality Weekly Report* 47(16): 326.

———. 2000. "Measuring Healthy Days: Population Assessment of Health-Related Quality of Life." Atlanta, Ga.: CDC.

———. 2004. "Self-Reported Frequent Mental Distress Among Adults—United States, 1993–2001. *MMWR. Morbidity and Mortality Weekly Report* 53(41): 963.

Cheung, Felix, and Richard Lucas. 2015. "When Does Money Matter Most? Examining the Association Between Income and Life Satisfaction Over the Life Course." *Psychology and Aging* 30(1): 120–35.

Clarke, Marlea, W. Kurt Lewchuk, Alice de Wolff, and Andy King. 2007. "'This Just Isn't Sustainable': Precarious Employment, Stress and Workers' Health." *International Journal of Law and Psychiatry* 30(4–5): 311–26.

Conway, James M., and Charles E. Lance. 2010. "What Reviewers Should Expect from Authors Regarding Common Method Bias in Organizational Research." *Journal of Business and Psychology* 25(3): 325–34.

Coutinho, Leticia M. S., Marcia Scazufca, and Paulo R. Menezes. 2008. "Methods for Estimating Prevalence Ratios in Cross-Sectional Studies." *Revista de Saúde Pública* 42(6): 992–98.

Daniels, Kevin, Olga Tregaskis, and Jonathan S. Seaton. 2007. "Job Control and Occupational Health: The Moderating Role of National R&D Activity." *Journal of Organizational Behavior* 28(1): 1–19.

de Lange, Annet H., Toon W. Taris, Michiel A. J. Kompier, I. L. D. Houtman, and Pauline M. Bongers. 2003. "'The Very Best of the Millennium': Longitudinal Research and the Demand-Control-(Support) Model." *Journal of Occupational Health Psychology* 8(4): 282–305.

DeSalvo, Karen B., Nicole Bloser, Kristi Reynolds, Jiang He, and Paul Muntner. 2006. "Mortality Prediction with a Single General Self-Rated Health

Question. A Meta-Analysis." *Journal of General Internal Medicine* 21(3): 267–75.

Elovainio, Marko, Tarjo Heponiemi, Timp Sinervo, and Nicola Magnavita. 2010. "Organizational Justice and Health; Review of Evidence." *Giornale Italiano Di Medicina Del Lavoro Ed Ergonomia* 32(3 Suppl B) (July): B5–9.

Faragher, E. Brian, M. Cass, and Cary L. Cooper. 2005. "The Relationship Between Job Satisfaction and Health: A Meta-Analysis." *Occupational and Environmental Medicine* 62(2): 105–12.

Flaherty, Brian P. 2002. "Assessing Reliability of Categorical Substance Use Measures with Latent Class Analysis." *Drug and Alcohol Dependence* 68 (Suppl 1): S7–20.

Foley, Michael P. 2017. "Factors Underlying Observed Injury Rate Differences Between Temporary Workers and Permanent Peers." *American Journal of Industrial Medicine* 60(10): 841–51.

Fritzell, Johan, Magnus Nermo, and Olle Lundberg. 2004. "The Impact of Income: Assessing the Relationship Between Income and Health in Sweden." *Scandinavian Journal of Public Health* 32(1): 6–16.

Gardner, Donald G., Linn Van Dyne, and Jon L. Pierce. 2004. "The Effects of Pay Level on Organization-Based Self-Esteem and Performance: A Field Study." *Journal of Occupational and Organizational Psychology* 77(3): 307–22.

Hagenaars, Jacques A., and Allan L. McCutcheon. 2002. *Applied Latent Class Analysis*. Cambridge: Cambridge University Press.

Holman, David, and Charlotte McClelland. 2011. "Job Quality in Growing and Declining Economic Sectors of the EU. Work and Life Quality in New and Growing Jobs." *Walqing* working paper 2011.3. Manchester, UK: University of Manchester.

Howard, John. 2016. "Nonstandard Work Arrangements and Worker Health and Safety." *American Journal of Industrial Medicine* 60(1): 1–10.

Idler, Ellen L., and Yael Benyamini. 1997. "Self-Rated Health and Mortality: A Review of Twenty-Seven Community Studies." *Journal of Health and Social Behavior* 38(1): 21.

Jamal, Muhammed. 2004. "Burnout, Stress and Health of Employees on Non-Standard Work Schedules: a Study of Canadian Workers." *Stress and Health* 20(3): 113–19.

Julià, Mireia, Christophe Vanroelen, Kim Bosmans, Karen Van Aerden, and Joan Benach. 2017. "Precarious Employment and Quality of Employment in Relation to Health and Well-Being in Europe." *International Journal of Health Services* 47(3): 389–409.

Kalleberg, Arne L. 2000. "Nonstandard Employment Relations: Part-Time, Temporary and Contract Work." *Annual Review of Sociology* 26(1): 341–65.

———. 2009. "Precarious Work, Insecure Workers: Employment Relations in Transition." *American Sociological Review* 74(1): 1–22.

Kalleberg, Arne L., and Kevin Hewison. 2013. "Precarious Work and the Challenge for Asia." *American Behavioral Scientist* 57(3): 271–88.

Karasek, Robert A., Jr. 1979. "Job Demands, Job Decision Latitude, and Mental Strain: Implications for Job Redesign." *Administrative Science Quarterly* 24(2): 285.

Karasek, Robert, Chantal Brisson, Norito Kawakami, Irene Houtman, Paulien Bongers, and Benjamin Amick. 1998. "The Job Content Questionnaire (JCQ): An Instrument for Internationally Comparative Assessments of Psychosocial Job Characteristics." *Journal of Occupational Health Psychology* 3(4): 322–55.

Kim, Il-Ho, Carles. Muntaner, Faraz Vahid Shahidi, Alejandra Vives, Christophe Vanroelen, and Joan Benach. 2012. "Welfare States, Flexible Employment, and Health: A Critical Review." *Health Policy* 104(2): 99–127.

Leigh, J. Paul, and Roberto de Vogli. 2016. "Low Wages as Occupational Health Hazards." *Journal of Occupational and Environmental Medicine* 58(5): 444–47.

Lewchuk, Wayne, Marlea Clarke, and Alice de Wolff. 2008. "Working Without Commitments: Precarious Employment and Health." *Work, Employment and Society* 22(3): 387–406.

Lewchuk, Wayne, Stephanie Procyk, Michelynn Lafleche, Dan Rosen, Diane Dyson, John Shields, Luin Goldring, Peter Viducis, Alan Meisner, and S. Vrankulj. 2014. "Is Precarious Employment Low Income Employment? The Changing Labour Market in Southern Ontario." *Just Labour* 22 (Autumn): 51–73. Accessed February 28, 2019. https://justlabour.journals.yorku.ca/index.php/justlabour/article/view/5/5.

Link, Bruce G., and Jo Phelan. 1995. "Social Conditions as Fundamental Causes of Disease." *Journal of Health and Social Behavior* 35: 80–94.

Lisbon European Council. 2000. "Presidency Conclusions." Accessed February 28, 2019. http://www.europarl.europa.eu/summits/lis1_en.htm.

Little, Roderick J. A., and Donald B. Rubin. 2014. *Statistical Analysis with Missing Data*. Hoboken, N.J.: John Wiley & Sons.

Marschner, Ian C. 2011. "glm2: Fitting Generalized Linear Models with Convergence Problems." *R Journal* 3(2): 12.

Martens, M. F. J., Frans J. N. Nijhuis, Martin P. J. Van Boxtel, and André J. Knottnerus. 1999. "Flexible Work Schedules and Mental and Physical Health: A Study of a Working Population with Non-Traditional Working Hours." *Journal of Organizational Behavior* 20(1): 35–46.

Masters, Ryan K., Bruce G. Link, and Jo C. Phelan. 2015. "Trends in Education Gradients of 'Preventable' Mortality: A Test of Fundamental Cause Theory." *Social Science and Medicine* 127: 19–28.

Muñoz de Bustillo, Rafaelk, Enrique Fernández-Macías, José I. Antón, and Fernando Esteve. 2009. *Indicators of Job Quality in the European Union*. Brussels: European Parliament Committee on Employment and Social Affairs.

Muthén, Linda K., and Bengt O. Muthén. 2010. *Mplus User's Guide*, 6th ed. Los Angeles, Calif.: Muthén and Muthén.

National Academies of Sciences. 2018. *A Smarter National Surveillance System for Occupational Safety and Health in the 21st Century*. Washington, D.C.: National Academies Press.

O'Reilly, Dermot, and Michael Rosato. 2013. "Worked to Death? A Census-Based Longitudinal Study of the Relationship Between the Numbers of Hours Spent Working and Mortality Risk." *International Journal of Epidemiology* 42(6): 1820–30.

Peckham, Trevor K., Marissa G. Baker, Janice E. Camp, Joel D. Kaufman, and Noah S. Seixas. 2017. "Creating a Future for Occupational Health." *Annals of Occupational Hygiene* 41(1): 24–32.

Pirani, Elena. 2017. "On the Relationship Between Atypical Work(s) and Mental Health: New Insights from the Italian Case." *Social Indicators Research* 130(1): 233–52.

Quinlan, Michael, Claire Mayhew, and Philip Bohle. 2001. "The Global Expansion of Precarious Employment, Work Disorganization, and Consequences for Occupational Health: A Review of Recent Research." *International Journal of Health Services* 31(2): 335–414.

Scott-Marshall, Heather, and Emile Tompa. 2011. "The Health Consequences of Precarious Employment Experiences." *Work* 38(4): 369–82.

Siegrist, Johannes, Morten Wahrendorf, Olaf von dem Knesebeck, Hendrik Jurges, and Axel Borsch-Supan. 2007. "Quality of Work, Well-Being, and Intended Early Retirement of Older Employees—Baseline Results from the SHARE Study." *European Journal of Public Health* 17(1): 62–68.

Silverstein, Barbara, Esther Welp, Nancy Nelson, and John Kalat. 1998. "Claims Incidence of Work-Related Disorders of the Upper Extremities: Washington State, 1987 Through 1995." *American Journal of Public Health* 88(12): 1827–833.

Singh-Manoux, Archana, Alice Guéguen, Pekka Martikainen, Jane Ferrie, Michael Marmot, and Martin Shipley. 2007. "Self-Rated Health and Mortality: Short- and Long-Term Associations in the Whitehall II Study." *Psychosomatic Medicine* 69(2): 138–43.

Smith, Tom W., Peter V. Marsden, Michael Hout, and Jibum Kim. 2013. General Social Surveys, 1972–2012. [machine-readable data file]. Storrs, CT: The Roper Center for Public Opinion Research, University of Connecticut [distributor].

Stephan, Ute, and Ulrike Roesler. 2010. "Health of Entrepreneurs Versus Employees in a National Representative Sample." *Journal of Occupational and Organizational Psychology* 83(3): 717–38.

Thoits, Peggy A. 2011. "Mechanisms Linking Social Ties and Support to Physical and Mental Health." *Journal of Health and Social Behavior* 52(2): 145–61.

Tompa, Emile, Heather K. Scott-Marshall, Roman Dolinschi, Scott Trevithick, and Sudipa Bhattacharyya. 2007. "Precarious Employment Experiences and Their Health Consequences: Towards a Theoretical Framework." *Work (Reading, Mass.):* 28(3): 209–24.

Van Aerden, Karen, Sylvie Gadeyne, and Christophe Vanroelen. 2017. "Is Any Job Better Than No Job at All? Studying the Relations Between Employment Types, Unemployment and Subjective Health in Belgium." *Archives of Public Health* 75(1): 55.

Van Aerden, Karen, Guy Moors, Katia Levecque, and Christophe Vanroelen. 2014. "Measuring Employment Arrangements in the European Labour Force: A Typological Approach." *Social Indicators Research* 116(3): 771–91.

———. 2015. "The Relationship Between Employment Quality and Work-Related Well-Being in the European Labor Force." *Journal of Vocational Behavior* 86(1): 66–76.

Van Aerden, Karen, Vanessa Puig-Barrachina, Kim Bosmans, and Christophe Vanroelen. 2016. "How Does Employment Quality Relate to Health and Job Satisfaction in Europe? A Typological Approach." *Social Science and Medicine* 158: 132–40.

Vanroelen, Christophe, Fred Louckx, Guy Moors, and Katia Levecque. 2010. "The Clustering of Health-Related Occupational Stressors Among Contemporary Wage-Earners." *European Journal of Work and Organizational Psychology* 19(6): 654–74.

Virtanen, Marianna, Katriina Heikkilä, Markus Jokela, Jane E. Ferrie, G. David Batty, Jussi Vahtera, and Mika Kivimäki. 2012. "Long Working Hours and Coronary Heart Disease: A Systematic Review and Meta-Analysis." *American Journal of Epidemiology* 176(7): 586–96.

Vives, Alejandra, Francisca González, Salvador Moncada, Clara Llorens, and Joan Benach. 2015. "Measuring Precarious Employment in Times of Crisis: The Revised Employment Precariousness Scale (EPRES) in Spain." *Gaceta Sanitaria / S.E.S.P.A.S* 29(5): 379–82.

Weil, David 2014. *The Fissured Workplace: Why Work Became So Bad for So Many and What Can Be Done to Improve It*. Cambridge, Mass.: Harvard University Press.

Wooden, Mark, Diana Warren, and Robert Drago. 2009. "Working Time Mismatch and Subjective Well-Being." *British Journal of Industrial Relations* 47(1): 147–79.

Zeileis, Achim 2004. "Econometric Computing with HC and HAC Covariance Matrix Estimators." *Journal of Statistical Software* 11(10): 1–17.

Zou, Guangyong. 2004. "A Modified Poisson Regression Approach to Prospective Studies with Binary Data." *American Journal of Epidemiology* 159(7): 702–06.